The Rise and Fall of Comradeship

Hitler's Soldiers, Male Bonding and
Mass Violence in the Twentieth Century

This is an innovative account of how the concept of comradeship shaped the actions, emotions and ideas of ordinary German soldiers across the two world wars and during the Holocaust. Using individual soldiers' diaries, personal letters and memoirs, Kühne reveals the ways in which their longing for community, and the practice of male bonding and togetherness, sustained the Third Reich's pursuit of war and genocide. Comradeship fueled the soldiers' fighting morale. It also propelled these soldiers forward into war crimes and acts of mass murder. Yet, by practicing comradeship, the soldiers could feel morally sacrosanct. Post-1945, the notion of *Kameradschaft* as the epitome of humane and egalitarian solidarity allowed Hitler's soldiers to join the euphoria for peace and democracy in the Federal Republic, finally shaping popular memories of the war through the end of the twentieth century.

THOMAS KÜHNE is Strassler Chair in Holocaust History and Professor of History at Clark University, Massachusetts. His research, published in English, German, and other languages, focuses on modern Germany and explores the cultural history of war and genocide, and the construction of collective identity through mass violence. His awards include fellowships from the John Simon Guggenheim Memorial Foundation, the Institute for Advanced Study in Princeton, and the German Bundestag Research Prize.

The Rise and Fall of Comradeship

Hitler's Soldiers, Male Bonding and
Mass Violence in the Twentieth Century

Thomas Kühne

Clark University

CAMBRIDGE
UNIVERSITY PRESS

University Printing House, Cambridge CB2 8BS, United Kingdom

One Liberty Plaza, 20th Floor, New York, NY 10006, USA

477 Williamstown Road, Port Melbourne, VIC 3207, Australia

4843/24, 2nd Floor, Ansari Road, Daryaganj, Delhi - 110002, India

79 Anson Road, #06-04/06, Singapore 079906

Cambridge University Press is part of the University of Cambridge.

It furthers the University's mission by disseminating knowledge in the pursuit of
education, learning and research at the highest international levels of excellence.

www.cambridge.org
Information on this title: www.cambridge.org/9781107046368

© Thomas Kühne, 2017

This edition is a revised, expanded and updated translation of *Kameradschaft: Die
Soldaten des nationalsozialistischen Krieges und das 20. Jahrhundert*, published by
Vandenhoeck & Ruprecht in 2006 (9783525351543).

First published 2017

Printed in the United States of America by Sheridan Books, Inc.

A catalogue record for this publication is available from the British Library

ISBN 978-1-107-04636-8 Hardback
ISBN 978-1-107-65828-8 Paperback

Contents

Acknowledgements

To Omer Bartov, Christopher Browning, and Michael Geyer: their inquiries into Germany's ways of warfare and the men who carried out the Holocaust inspired my interest in the mindsets of Hitler's soldiers.

To Detlef Bald, Dagmar Ellerbrock, Ute Frevert, Dieter Langewiesche, Bernhard Mann, Cornelia Rauh, Hans-Ulrich Wehler†, Wolfram Wette, and Benjamin Ziemann: their comments, critiques, and insights enabled me to write and publish an initial German version of this book some ten years ago.

To Margaret Lavinia Anderson, Dan Bar-on†, Volker Berghahn, Donald Bloxham, Dirk Bonker, Kathleen Canning, Nicola Di Cosmo, Jennifer Evans, Karen Hagemann, Dagmar Herzog, Danny Kaplan, Thomas A. Kohut, Elissa Mailänder, Andrew I. Port, James Retallack, Mark Roseman, Helmut Walser Smith, Eric D. Weitz: conversations with them on German history, the Holocaust, and the study of masculinities prompted me to revise, expand, and rewrite in English and for an Anglophone audience my earlier German book.

To my colleagues at Clark University, the Strassler Center for Holocaust and Genocide Studies and the History Department: the stimulation and cooperation of Taner Akçam, Debórah Dwork, Nina Kushner, Mary Jane Rein and many others made working on this book a pleasure.

To David Strassler: his generosity laid the ground not only for this book.

To Sarah Patey for her thorough and sensitive copy editing of the entire manuscript, and to Michael Geheran for providing draft translations of the third part of this book.

To the staff of the archives and libraries and to the many individuals that provided me with books, articles, paperclips, documents, letters, diaries, and memoirs: the German Bundesarchiv and its branches in Berlin, Koblenz, Freiburg, and Ludwigsburg; the Bibliothek für Zeitgeschichte in Stuttgart; the Landeshauptarchiv in Koblenz; Clark University's Goddard Library; Fritz Farnbacher, Dirk Heinrichs, Walter Kempowski†,

Hans–Jörg Kimmich†, Elly Napp, Hermann Schneider, and Helmut Wißmann may be named in lieu of many others.

To Michael Watson and his team at Cambridge University Press: I am deeply grateful for their diligence and patience.

THOMAS KÜHNE
Worcester, Massachusetts
October 2016

Introduction
A Concept from a Different World

"Comradeship" – this is a "notion from a different world," said the German magazine *Der Stern* (The Star) in 1999, echoing the sentiments of a group of high school students at a meeting with German World War II veterans. The dialog proved to be a difficult one. The kids wanted to know why the soldiers had joined Hitler's army, the Wehrmacht, and why they had participated in Hitler's terrible war instead of just deserting or staying at home. The ex-servicemen – all of them of the generation of the students' grandparents – scarcely understood the question. "That would have meant betraying our comrades in arms," they argued, unable to put across to the young Germans the sacrilege they would have committed by deserting. The students had their own ideas about why the generation of their grandparents had gone to war. "There were clearly enough soldiers who just enjoyed bumping people off," said one of the students.[1]

Pacifist sentiment had grown in Germany since the end of the Second World War, but at the end of the twentieth century it mushroomed faster than ever before. Germans, just like most of their European fellow citizens, had not experienced war in half a century. Compulsory military service was formally suspended in Germany only in 2011. This break from an almost two hundred year old tradition was the long-delayed consequence of German society's increasing disdain for soldiers and soldiering. Antimilitarism had been known in Germany before but only in the last two decades of the twentieth century did it dominate the mind-set of Germans. "Soldiers are murderers," the German left-wing journalist Kurt Tucholsky had claimed in 1932. He was put on trial for it, and Germans in the 1980s still faced prosecution when repeating the Tucholsky quote in public. But in 1995, German judges changed their minds, in accordance with the shift in public opinion. Calling soldiers "murderers" was no longer illegal, and so Tucholsky's phrase was widely used to denounce soldiers in general, and to blur the difference between killing combatants and murdering civilians.

In fact, two spectacular events in 1995 seemed to support this equation of soldiers and murderers: the genocidal wars in former Yugoslavia, and the Wehrmacht exhibition of the Hamburg Institute for Social Research. Europeans were shocked by the violent breakup of Yugoslavia. It belied the illusion that the continent had overcome war permanently. The lesson Germans drew from the explosion of violence at their front doors was to condemn any kind of military action as evil. In summer 1995 the Srebrenica massacre showed how easily war descends into genocide. A few weeks before, the exhibition "War of Annihilation: Crimes of the Wehrmacht 1941 to 1944" had opened in Hamburg. For the first time, the entire German public recognized that their ancestors had been involved in an even more evil war – in war crimes and eventually in genocide, committed not only by a few SS men but by ordinary Germans. To be sure, public memory in Germany had never left any doubt of German responsibility for the Holocaust and other mass crimes in Europe, but this discourse on the Nazi past had limited the responsibility to certain core groups of perpetrators, the Nazi elite, the SS, the leadership of the Wehrmacht, or just pathological sadists, and thus distracted attention from ordinary Germans' complicity in the crimes. Attracting hundreds of thousands of visitors, the 1995 exhibition destroyed the myth of the innocence of ordinary Germans in the Third Reich. Amateur photos of the mass shootings of the Jews in the East documented that ordinary German soldiers had *witnessed* the Holocaust and that these soldiers had approved or even *enjoyed* what they saw – and what they did. High school and college students visited the exhibition, looked at the photos, and sometimes recognized their own beloved grandpas shaving the beards of Jews or applauding their public humiliation. Even those who did not recognize their own relatives were left wondering what their grandfathers, or fathers, had done during the war – whether they were "murderers among us."[2]

The former soldiers, all of them as old as the students' grandfathers, were embarrassed, upset, and shocked by such representations of what they considered honorable service to their country. It certainly was not lust for violence that had driven them but selfless duty, and there was no pleasure but only suffering and sacrifice, they pretended. And there was comradeship. Comradeship, as they remembered it, was the human side of the war, the counter to aggression, destruction, and inhumanity, the proof that they had not been the monsters depicted in the exhibition, and subsequently by German youth. "Comradeship and solidarity within the platoons and companies" as well as the "devotion to Volk and fatherland" – altruism, not sadism – gave the soldiers "the emotional strength and the morals to fight their fight," one Wehrmacht veteran explained in one of the many letters to the editors of German news-papers published during spring and summer 1995 in response to the accusations of the Wehrmacht exhibition. And this campaign went on for years. In the papers, not only the veterans themselves but also their widows and former comrades, occasionally even their children, took out advertisements urging the German public to honor the selfless attitude of the German World War II soldiers, who had, as the ads claimed, given or risked their lives in order to save those of their wounded comrades.[3]

In fact, the German World War II generation was much more divided over the meaning of comradeship than these voices suggest. On the one hand the members and leaders of the veterans' associations who enthused about it. One of them – a former officer of the Fallschirmpanzerdivision (Paratrooper Panzer Division) Hermann Göring, born 1915 – responded to my research project with a comment that it would "put finally on record for future generations what has really driven us, the generation that is about to pass away."[4] But there were less enthusiastic responses as well. A former war correspondent (*Propagandaberichterstatter*) and Waffen-SS officer, who after the war became one of the most popular German screenwriters and did not shy away from publishing a rather apologetic memoir of his war experiences, doubted that a historian such as I could ever understand the concept of comradeship. "Kameradschaft," he said, "is a concept that only continues to exist as an empty notion, it is detached from its meanings, hovers somewhere in the air, available for dissection on a desk." Members of the postwar generations could never grasp the meaning of comradeship, he claimed. Even former soldiers used the term "without knowing that they devaluate the term just by using it," he continued. And, he added, "You certainly wouldn't know either, unless you had an idea of what it means, how you feel, if you are in a landscape of death together with somebody else...this poor sod next to you." Born into such an "entirely unnatural mode of being," comradeship is a concept, he said, that shyly seeks to protect its "intimacy." A mystic or even holy concept, in other words, that cannot be analyzed but only experienced. German society in the 1990s, however, "no longer bore any understanding for the entire war thing," there was no chance for the concept of comradeship to be understood.[5]

A different type of indignantly critical feedback on my book project came from my father. Born in 1925 into a social democratic family, he was conscripted at the age of eighteen into an infantry division of the Wehrma-cht that went into Soviet captivity in May 1945 in the Courland Pocket. He was one of those ex-servicemen who always looked back disdainfully at his forced service. He had never joined any of the veterans' associations or meetings, had never tried to stay in touch with any of his comrades.

In his view, the sacred aura of comradeship as evoked by veteran activists was simply a lie. There was not much comradeship at all, he insisted, rather the opposite. When the Courland Army surrendered to the Soviets, the commanding officer of his battalion got into his car and escaped to Germany – letting his men face their fate; few of them survived; the CO, however, got home safely, as my father learned after returning from Soviet captivity.[6]

None of these assessments should be discarded out of hand. In fact, they correspond to academic disputes about the fighting morale, the emotions, ideologies, and behavior of the Wehrmacht soldiers and about the meaning of male bonding and male sociability more broadly. Scholars since the war have wondered why these soldiers kept fighting until the bitter end, instead of deserting or mutinying as their predecessors had done at the end of the First World War when they realized that there was no chance for victory – just as the Wehrmacht soldiers could have done as early as summer 1943. One answer was provided by American sociologists immediately after the war. After interviewing German POWs in American captivity, Edward Shils and Morris Janowitz concluded that the soldiers had been fighting for the same reason American and other soldiers had fought: not so much out of patriotism, nationalism, or hatred of the enemy, and not out of antisemitism as the American public at that time believed, but because they did not want to let down their comrades. Avoiding the loaded term comradeship, Shils and Janowitz presented their own theory of combat motivation. "Primary group" relations, i.e. solidarity and cohesion in the small, face-to-face units of an army, based fighting morale, not the soldiers' identification with anonymous, imagined "secondary" groups such as the entire army or their country.[7]

Shils's and Janowitz's theory paved the way for a humane depiction of the Wehrmacht soldiers that resonated well with the way these servicemen presented themselves to the German and the international audience over the following decades – until the 1995 exhibition shattered the image. Unlike the SS-Einsatzgruppen, and apart from a few exceptions, the Wehrmacht, so its former members claimed, had remained untainted and not been complicit in the Nazi mass crimes in the East.[8] Only in the 1980s did military historians – though not yet the public – start arguing about the reputation of the Wehrmacht and the guilt of the ordinary soldiers. Most powerfully, the historian Omer Bartov showed in two books, the first published in 1985, that ordinary German soldiers had by no means been free of antisemitism. On the contrary, Bartov wrote, antisemitism was at the core of a racist ideology of hatred that, together with the experience of enormous casualties, primitive living conditions at the Eastern front, and the Wehrmacht's draconian military justice, brutalized and barbarized these soldiers and enabled their complicity in the Holocaust. At the same time, primary group relations, Bartov pointed out, could not have survived under the conditions of the massive casualties sustained by the Wehrmacht from late 1941 on.[9]

Subsequent inquiries into the emotional and ideological world of the soldiers, based on their private letters and other ego-documents such as diaries and memoirs, have highlighted that the Wehrmacht was as diverse as the rest of German society, even under the Nazi regime, and yet widely supported the Nazi genocidal project in the East.[10] No consistent picture, however, has emerged of the meaning of comradeship and the role of primary group relations in the Wehrmacht. In part, this inconsistency is the result of conceptual uncertainties and empirical restrictions. The sociological concept of the primary group only partly overlaps with the ideologically loaded term comradeship, which may describe not only real face-to-face relations but also imagined groups of any size such as the entire army or the entire German nation.[11] Instead of essentializing primary groups and assuming that they worked alike in all armies and historical settings, students of military cultures have rightly proposed to "historicize" them by examining their specific fabric and stature; and instead of juxtaposing primary and secondary groups, one has to examine how both, in a given army or unit, or in the mind-sets of individual soldiers, intersected, mutually enforced, or contradicted each other. Soldiers, and groups of soldiers, have agency. They can work on strengthening or loosening their social ties; the solidarity in face-to-face units can be used to propel the army's fighting power or to launch a mutiny. Which option the soldiers choose depends not least on the secondary symbols they support – symbols of patriotism or rebellion, for instance.[12]

Unaffected by military sociology, the Holocaust historian Christopher Browning, in his 1992 book on the German Police Battalion 101, nevertheless illuminated how group pressure, a basic feature of comradeship, enabled the perpetration of the Holocaust. While not explicitly addressed in Browning's book, comradeship again does not appear as the epitome of altruistic solidarity but as the engine of evil per se, deeply ingrained in the machinery of Nazi terror.[13] Widely praised in Germany just as in America and other parts of the world, the book's argument thus yet raised concerns among readers who still appreciated comradeship as a core virtue of soldiers. An officer of the German Bundeswehr, for instance, warned about generalizing Browning's findings. The social psychology of Himmler's murder troops had nothing to do with the military virtue of comradeship, he clarified. Instead, he said, Himmler's men had "completely perverted this concept of dedicated commitment between soldiers."[14]

While historians and sociologists debated whether or not certain ideals of social cohesion were realized (and if so, how; how much; when; where; and in which parts of the army), the fabric of male solidarity in military and paramilitary formations more generally came under attack from different quarters. Feminist and antimilitarist inquiries and theories cast dark shadows on the moral quality of concepts such as comradeship. Most influentially, the German literary scholar Klaus Theweleit in the 1970s, studying memoirs of the post-1918 German Freikorps soldiers, denounced their misogynistic aggressiveness. In his theory, male solidarity – comradeship was the term used by contemporaries to idealize it – appears as the engine of the patriarchal order and, more specifically, of all-male groups embracing tough and "hard" manliness and despising women, femininity, domesticity, tenderness, and compassion.[15]

Theweleit himself understood his findings in a quasi-universal sense, not limited to Germany, the Nazis, or the Freikorps. And subsequently some strands of feminist thinking polemically denounced "male comradeship" as the hotbed of all kinds of misogynistic violence, as the German military sociologist Ruth Seiffert noted critically even before the mass rape of women in former Yugoslavia in the mid-1990s seemed to indeed confirm such critique from yet another different angle.[16] At the same time, inquiries into the workings of "the masculine bond," as represented by popular Hollywood Vietnam War movies, inspired and grounded more nuanced assessments but left no doubt that male sociality was tied to men's domination of women as well as other men.[17]

Male identity is defined by the "repudiation of femininity," pioneers in the field of masculinities have widely confirmed. Being a man means, first of all, "not being like a woman," states Michael Kimmel. Being a man means to be stronger than women (physically, mentally, or intellectually) and to rule over or control them, and by extension also over other men who are classified as weak and feminine, such as homosexuals, as R. W. Connell has argued in an influential theory on hegemonic masculinities.[18] And yet a broad range of inquiries into representations of male emotionality, their appropriation by different men and in different societies, and the fabric of male sociability and interaction have cautioned against overemphasizing the anti-feminine fabric of masculinity. Instead, we are asked to "explore the locus of expression of 'non-masculine' sentiments by men."[19] In other words, how far does the repudiation of femininity go, and what counts as femininity? The language of intimacy and the pathos of tenderness, care, empathy, and even love that permeate the evocation of comradeship in testimonies and recollections of former soldiers cloud the emotional and moral ambiguity of manliness.

In public and in academic debates the concept of comradeship vac-
illates between glorification and demonization; it is subject to mysti-
fications and controversies about its historical reality, or unreality, its
quality, and its meaning. At stake are the historical semantics of the word
comradeship as well as its social practice. Inquiring into both semantics
and practices, this book examines the place of comradeship within the
war experiences of Hitler's ordinary soldiers, that is, the bulk of German
men who joined the Wehrmacht voluntarily or were drafted into the army
from the entire social and ideological diversity of German society. How
did comradeship impact way they experienced, perceived, and acted in
the war? Was it merely a chimera, or was it "real" – and if so, in which
ways? In what ways did the soldiers understand and practice comradeship (if at all), and to what degree did the meanings they assigned to
the concept and the ways they appropriated it establish the cohesion and
unity it aims to reinforce?

A history of experience illuminates how individuals and groups perceived, interpreted, and constituted social reality. Amorphous as it is, the
concept of experience allows for an integrative view of sensory impressions, emotions, cognitive frameworks, social imaginaries, ideas, and the
knowledge that enables individuals to make choices. It tracks the ways
historical actors select, appropriate, and archive impressions in order
to act. These processes depend on situational circumstances as well as
dispositions – the "knowledge" people have acquired about the world
and themselves from childhood onward. As the sociologists Peter Berger
and Thomas Luckmann have explained, knowledge is a container of
socially constructed, and thus changeable, conceptions of reality including languages, traditions, mental representations, mythical truths, scien-
tific findings, vernacular wisdoms, and popular fantasies. Knowledge is a
complex set of "tutorials" – often framed as discourses – that affect and
determine which impressions individuals notice, how they appropriate
these impressions, whether they use them to confirm or to question previously acquired frameworks of meaning, and how they translate them
into action. The choices people make are informed by their past experiences; they are also affected by ideas and expectations about the future.[20]

Experiences are tied into a continuum of past, present, and future
actions, perceptions, and wisdoms. A history of war experiences of soldiers therefore has to analyze the sequence of three time-periods: first,
the cultural preconditions of the war, the "knowledge," imaginaries, and
attitudes that have shaped individual and collective expectations of the
war – the cultural "baggage" the draftees and volunteers carried with
them when they entered the army, became soldiers, and carried out their

duties as soldiers, whether on the battlefield or as occupational troops. Second, the actual experiences in war – from basic training to the front lines or rear areas, hospitals, retreats, defeat, death, or captivity. Third, the aftermath of the war, its remembrance and memorialization in private circles and public forums, the coping with traumas, and the production of glory in intimate conversations, by veterans' associations, through memorial sites and monuments, or in popular culture including movies, autobiographies, and novels.[21]

Diversity is operative at any of these stages of experience. The same event – a battle, for instance – is likely to be experienced in different ways by different people, according to their various roles, functions, assignments and social backgrounds. Although military organizations heavily invest in fostering the uniformity of their members – with the actual uniform as its most powerful symbol – and although the soldiers often behave uniformly, their war experiences vary. Their experiences are contingent upon their role within the army as well as upon their civilian identity – their cultural "baggage" – especially in a mass army. A private is likely to experience a battle in a different way than his battalion leader, and the battalion leader may experience it yet differently than the division general. Wehrmacht soldiers of a frontline unit in the East may have different experiences than soldiers deployed with the occupation army in France. A private with a socialist or Catholic or pacifist background coerced into the army is likely to experience the same unit, the same tasks, and the same battles differently than a devoted Nazi or the son of an aristocratic family of professional soldiers who volunteered for service. Different peoples, social classes, generations, regions, sexes establish their own containers for knowledge (although these containers may overlap). Experiences therefore depend on the individual's place and role in society, on his or her social identity – private or professional – or even multiple and possibly conflicting identities. This is true not only for diverse and liberal societies but also for "totalitarian" dictatorships, which have never reached their own goal of "totally" controlling and indoctrinating their citizens.[22]

And yet the issue of cohesion and unity is a crucial one for an inquiry into the social impact of a concept such as comradeship on soldiers fighting for a regime that valued cohesion and unity more than anything else. Creating a racially and ideologically purified society, a *Volksgemeinschaft* (people's community), was the ultimate goal of the Nazis. They never reached it, as a substantial amount of research since the 1980s into the mind-sets of Germans in the Third Reich has suggested. Social and cultural cleavages, such as the gap between working classes and middle classes, between Catholicism and Protestantism, between northern and southern regions of Germany, and not least between different generations, continued to shape German mind-sets under the Nazi regime.[23]

More recent studies have emphasized that Germans during the war and during the Holocaust may have been more affected by the regime's efforts to realize the idea of a *Volksgemeinschaft* than previously assumed. For the concept of the *Volksgemeinschaft* had two sides, an inclusive and exclusive one. On the one hand, Nazi propaganda envisioned and promised social harmony – class unity instead of class conflict – at home, within German society. While this inclusive side of the *Volksgemeinschaft* was never realized, its exclusive dynamic caught hold of Germans. The Holocaust and other parts of the Nazi genocidal project could be carried out only because Germans supported them, whether enthusiastically, or by looking the other way and then being haunted by pangs of conscience resulting from the knowledge that it was the German fatherland and the Germans at large who were and would be held responsible for the crimes. While the *Volksgemeinschaft* as the epitome of a harmonious nation may not have become a reality, yet a different kind of *Volksgemeinschaft*, united by racist ideologies and the shared knowledge of complicity in a mass crime of unforeseen dimensions, materialized during the war, not only in the minds of the tens of thousands of SS men, police officers, and NSDAP functionaries and state officials who managed the occupation and exploitation of the conquered territories and executed the Nazi genocidal project, but also within the army. For it was the army that kept the bulk of adult German men, 17 million in total, under control and had, by separating them physically and emotionally over years from their families and friends – from the foundations of their civilian identities – more effective means at hands to brainwash, or "re-educate," Germans than the Nazi rulers could ever have acquired at home.[24]

Following the tripartite progression of war experiences, this book examines the significance of comradeship for German World War II soldiers in three chronological steps. Part I explores the ideas about comradeship operative in the 1920s and 1930s – the discourse about comradeship that filled the cultural "baggage" of German men who joined the Wehrmacht and shaped these men's expectations of their service and the war they were to fight. While the available sources do not make it possible to track the content and workings of these expectations in individual biographies of soldiers, a well-documented public discourse on comradeship in the interwar period grants access to the various compartments of that cultural baggage. Germans talked about comradeship in a wide array of media, most importantly when they tried to cope with the legacy of the First World War. Ex-servicemen and their associations stressed how the experience of comradeship had helped them to survive physically, morally, and emotionally during the war – and even beyond. In fact, some of them, especially the militarist and nationalist veterans, suggested that the experience of comradeship in war should be taken as a model to heal the current civilian society from its social and political maladies, such as Germany's suffering from military defeat in 1918, from the humiliating peace treaty, and from ongoing class and ideological conflicts.

The political Left doubted these political appropriations of wartime comradeship and advocated an egalitarian concept of comradeship among the rank-and-file who defied their superiors, while in the rightist discourse the military leader represented the ideal comrade and obtained charisma from a comradely leadership style. Despite such disputes about the true meaning of comradeship, all major strands of the veterans' movement, echoed by many younger Germans and by numerous popular war novels and movies that reached out to Germans of all age cohorts, agreed on an almost holy core to the concept of comradeship. Comradeship was hailed as the model of altruistic male solidarity, of quasi-sacred community, of humanity, of moral goodness. He who performed good comradeship in war was morally sacrosanct and granted the ultimate experience of communal security. After 1933, the myth of comradeship, and its extension into propaganda, emphasized the flipside of this security more than before: its coercive implications. The benefits of comradeship were reserved for those who surrendered their Selves, their individual desires and their agency, to the group of comrades. The myth of comradeship leveled the ground for a conformist ethics that honored only what served group cohesion and denounced the concept of individual responsibility. The myth of comradeship made German soldiers ready to join in or look the other way when their army waged criminal and even genocidal war on Europe.

How did German soldiers deal with this concept when they conquered, occupied, and eventually were chased out of other countries? This is the basic question of Part II. Ideologically diverse as the army was, the soldiers did not appropriate the concept of comradeship uniformly. A core group of enthusiastic or "born" soldiers was fascinated with the myth of comradeship. They had internalized it before joining the army, and they entered it in order to experience comradeship. From basic training to the battlefields, from the initial victories to the retreats and defeats at the end of the war, they found what they were looking for by creating it: male bonding and male solidarity. Homoerotic desires and the longing for "homosocial," all-male togetherness, drove the type of comradeship they produced. Strategies of Othering were necessary as well. To come into being, comradeship needed both – inclusion and exclusion. The Other was exchangeable. During basic training, it could be the hated drill-sergeant, and at the front line it was the enemy soldier. In between, not only racist enemy fantasies but also the civilian world at home and women, real or imagined, assembled the Other and propelled a concept of comradeship that allowed for anything that strengthened group cohesion and condemned whatever jeopardized it. Embedded in the emotionally loaded symbolism of revenge and retribution, this social mechanism propelled the dynamic of military and genocidal violence from 1939 to 1945.

Not all soldiers prized comradeship. Numerous men, rooted in anti-Nazi or antimilitarist, socialist, Christian, or liberal social milieus, were forced into military service, pulled out of their civilian lives as individuals against their will, and never cottoned on to the attractions of male bonding. They remained at a distance from the apotheosis of group life that the concept of comradeship demanded. These outsiders had a hard time surviving physically and emotionally in a social culture that did not leave many choices for bonding, socializing, and communicating. The vast majority of Wehrmacht soldiers, however, maneuvered somewhere between these extremes. They tried to adjust to the service and occasionally accepted a defensive concept of comradeship – the depressed rather than euphoric amity of men who shared a deep sense of being used, exploited, and estranged from whatever their goals in life would have been had they had a choice. Other soldiers oscillated back and forth, often annoyed at the enforced community and mourning the loss of their civilian identities, and yet occasionally enjoying group pleasure or willing to sacrifice themselves for comrades or fatherland. More often than not, the soldiers' efforts to overcome the split between community and individuality led them into an emotional desert. Forlorn and disrupted, facing increasingly overpowering enemies, they knew that they were tied into a grand brotherhood of crime and resorted to a cynical couldn't-care-less attitude that absorbed the remnants of sublime comradeship among close buddies. Abandoning themselves to moral and emotional apathy, the Wehrmacht soldiers embodied, at the end of the war, a new type of *Volksgemeinschaft*, united by moral numbness and led by warriors resigned to a somber fate.

The denazification and demilitarization of Germany was a common goal of the Allied victors, and indeed German society overall from 1945 remained reluctant to revive the traditions of militarism and belligerence that had shaped their national identity for more than a hundred years. A veterans' culture soon resurfaced but it never attracted more than a small minority of the soldiers who had survived the war. And yet, thanks to the rearmament of Germany in the age of the Cold War and the retreat into privacy and silence of those soldiers who no longer wanted to be reminded of soldiering and soldierly virtues, the concept of comradeship emerged again, just as it had after the First World War, as a leitmotif of the public memorialization of the Second World War, as shall be shown in Part III. Understood as untainted by and in fact morally counter to criminal warfare, it helped whitewash the image of the Wehrmacht after the damage the involvement in criminal and genocidal warfare had caused. The tide turned in the 1980s and, most obviously, in the 1990s. The generational shift, the rise of pacifist attitudes, and increasingly critical views of the Nazi past coalesced into questioning the moral essence of comradeship. Once widely accepted as the epitome of altruistic solidarity and cooperation, of moral goodness, of humaneness per se, the concept came, by the end of the twentieth century, to be seen as a euphemism for criminal complicity and cover-ups – for collectively committed, clandestine evil.

NOTES

1 *Der Stern*, June 10, 1999, pp. 152–58 ("Der Erinnerung eine Zukunft geben"). Unless otherwise noted, the English word comradeship – not camaraderie or others – is used throughout this book as equivalent to the German word *Kameradschaft*.

2 Hamburger Institut für Sozialforschung (ed.), *Besucher einer Ausstellung: Die Ausstellung "Vernichtungskrieg: Verbrechen der Wehrmacht 1941–1944" in Interview und Gespräch* (Hamburger Edition, 1998); Thomas Kühne, "Die Viktimisierungsfalle: Wehrmachtverbrechen, Geschichtswissenschaft und symbolische Ordnung des Militärs," in Michael Th. Greven and Oliver von Wrochem (eds.), *Der Krieg in der Nachkriegszeit: Der Zweite Weltkrieg in Politik und Gesellschaft der Bundesrepublik* (Opladen: Leske + Budrich, 2000), pp. 183–96.

3 *Frankfurter Allgemeine Zeitung*, April 29, 1995, p. 10, letter of Hans Joachim Mischke; ibid., April 27, 1998, ad on behalf of Hans von der Bruch by his "comrade in war" Lothar Kappe.

4 Letter of Alfred Otte to author, Sept. 9, 1994; see Alfred Otte, *Die weißen Spiegel: Vom Regiment zum Fallschirmpanzerkorps* (Friedberg: Podzun-Pallas, 1982).

5 Letter of Herbert Reinecker to author, Sept. 14, 1994; see Herbert Reinecker, *Ein Zeitbericht unter Zuhilfenahme des eigenen Lebenslaufs* (Erlangen: Straube, 1990).

6 Author's interview with Carl-Lotar Kühne, 1995 and 1997; Carl-Lotar Kühne, *Die 14. Panzerdivision*, typescript, 1998. Cf. *Frankfurter Allgemeine Zeitung*, May 20, 1997, letter to the editor by Erwin Frank.

7 Edward Shils and Morris Janowitz, "Cohesion and Disintegration in the Wehrmacht in World War II," *Public Opinion Quarterly*, 12 (1948), 280–315.

8 Klaus Naumann, "The 'Unblemished' Wehrmacht: The Social History of a Myth," in Hannes Heer and Klaus Naumann (eds.), *War of Extermination: The German Military in World War II, 1941–1944* (New York: Berghahn, 2000), pp. 417–29.

9 Omer Bartov, *Hitler's Army: Soldiers, Nazis, and War in the Third Reich* (New York: Oxford University Press, 1991); Bartov, *The Eastern Front, 1941–45: German Troops and the Barbarisation of Warfare* (Basingstoke: Macmillan, 1985).

10 Literature reviews in Thomas Kühne, "Der nationalsozialistische Vernichtungskrieg und die 'ganz normalen' Deutschen: Forschungsprobleme und Forschungstendenzen der Gesellschaftsgeschichte des Zweiten Weltkriegs. Erster Teil," *Archiv für Sozialgeschichte*, 39 (1999), 580–662; and Jochen Böhler, "Die Wehrmacht im Vernichtungskrieg: Neue Erkenntnisse zum Denken und Handeln deutscher Soldaten," in Martin Cüppers, Jürgen Matthäus, and Andrej Angrick (eds.), *Nationalsozialistische Verbrechen: Taten und Bewältigungsversuche: Festschrift für Klaus-Michael Mallmann zum 65. Geburtstag* (Darmstadt: Wissenschaftliche Buchgesellschaft, 2013), pp. 89–102. An important contribution to the debate is Stephen G. Fritz, *Frontsoldaten: The German Soldier in World War II* (Lexington: University Press of Kentucky, 1995).

11 See Bartov, *Hitler's Army*, p. 6.

12 As a recent intervention in the lengthy debate, see Guy L. Siebold, "Key Questions and Challenges to the Standard Model of Military Group Cohesion," *Armed Forces & Society*, 37 (2011), 448–68.

13 Christopher Browning, *Ordinary Men: Reserve Police Battalion 101 and the Final Solution in Poland* (New York: HarperCollins, 1992).

14 K. Burg, Review of Browning, *Ordinary Men*, *Militärgeschichtliche Mitteilungen*, 52 (1993), 565.

15 Klaus Theweleit, *Male Fantasies*, 2 vols. (Minneapolis: University of Minnesota Press, 1989).

16 Ruth Seiffert, "Feministische Theorie und Militärsoziologie," *Das Argument*, 190 (1991), 861–73.

17 Susan Jeffords, *The Remasculinization of America: Gender and the Vietnam War* (Bloomington: Indiana University Press, 1989), p. xiii.

18 Michael Kimmel, "Masculinity as Homophobia: Fear, Shame, and Silence in the Construction of Gender Identity," in Harry Brod and Michael Kaufman (eds.), *Theorizing Masculinities* (Thousand Oaks, CA: Sage, 1994), pp. 119–41 (at 126–27, 130–31); R. W. Connell, *Masculinities* (Berkeley: University of California Press, 1995); cf. John Tosh, "Hegemonic Masculinity and the History of Gender," in Stefan Dudink, Karen Hagemann, and John Tosh (eds.), *Masculinities in Politics and War: Gendering Modern History* (Manchester University Press, 2004), pp. 41–58.

19 Miguel Vale de Almeida, *The Hegemonic Male: Masculinity in a Portuguese Town* (Providence, RI: Berghahn, 1996), p. 116; a classic study is: Eve Kosofsky Sedgwick, *Between Men: English Literature and Male Homosocial Desire* (New York: Columbia University Press, 1985). On the Israeli army: Danny Kaplan, *The Men We Loved: Male Friendship and Nationalism in Israeli Culture* (New York: Berghahn, 2006); Kaplan, *Brothers and Others in Arms: The Making of Love and War in Israeli Combat Units* (New York: Haworth, 2003). The historical research on Germany is surveyed in Jürgen Martschukat and Olaf Stieglitz, *Geschichte der Männlichkeiten* (Frankfurt: Campus, 2008), pp. 112–36.

20 Peter L. Berger and Thomas Luckmann, *The Social Construction of Reality: A Treatise in the Sociology of Knowledge* (Garden City, NY: Doubleday, 1966); Karl Mannheim, *Essays on the Sociology of Knowledge*, ed. Paul Kecskemiti (New York: Oxford University Press, 1952); Reinhard Koselleck, *Futures Past: On the Semantics of Historical Time* (New York: Columbia University Press, 2004), pp. 255–75. For a critical assessment, see Kathleen Canning, "Feminist History After the Linguistic Turn: Historicizing Discourse and Experience," *Signs*, 19 (1994), 364–404. An early model for utilizing the sociology of knowledge for writing war history is Lloyd B. Lewis, *The Tainted War: Culture and Identity in Vietnam War Narratives* (Westport, CT: Praeger, 1985).

21 Reinhard Koselleck, "Der Einfluß der beiden Weltkriege auf das soziale Bewußtsein," in Wolfram Wette (ed.), *Der Krieg des kleinen Mannes: Eine Militärgeschichte von unten* (Munich: Piper, 1992), pp. 324–43.

22 Michael Geyer and Sheila Fitzpatrick (eds.), *Beyond Totalitarianism: Stalinism and Nazism Compared* (New York: Cambridge University Press, 2009).

23 Richard Evans, "Coercion and Consent in Nazi Germany," *Proceedings of the British Academy*, 151 (2007), 53–81; Evans, *The Third Reich in Power, 1933–1939* (New York: Penguin, 2005); Evans, *The Third Reich at War* (New York: Penguin, 2009).

24 Critical assessments of these debates include Christopher Browning and Lewis H. Siegelbaum, "Frameworks for Social Engineering: Stalinist Schema of Identification and the Nazi *Volksgemeinschaft*," pp. 231–65, and Sheila Fitzpatrick and Alf Lüdtke, "Energizing the Everyday: On the Breaking and Making of Social Bonds in Nazism and Stalinism," pp. 266–301, both in in Geyer and Fitzpatrick (eds.), *Beyond Totalitarianism*. My view is detailed in Thomas Kühne, *Belonging and Genocide: Hitler's Community, 1918–1945* (New Haven, CT: Yale University Press, 2010).

Part I

The Myth of Comradeship, 1914–1939

1 Healing

Immediately after the Great War, Joseph Schneider, a Bavarian pastor, asked "hundreds" of homecoming soldiers about their war experiences. The result depicted the reality of that war: emotional, moral, and cognitive confusion, the experience of disaster, destruction, contingency, and helplessness, an abundance of traumas, and the inability of most servicemen to cope with them. About half of Schneider's interviewees denied recalling any significant war experience; they did not want to be reminded of it. A third of the soldiers were overwhelmed by memories of death, injuries, fighting, and suffering. Only one out of eight addressed aspects of their social experience, mostly in somber terms. Ten percent of all interviewees complained about "non-comradeship," "injustice," and "unfairness" in the army. By contrast, only one out of fifty soldiers – 2 percent – named "comradeship" as their decisive experience.[1]

When Schneider published the results of his time-consuming poll in 1926 he must have been unhappy with them. Confined to a short appendix to an ambitious moral breviary, they simply contradicted the lessons from the war Schneider wanted to spread. Meaning and consolation was needed, not a reminder of chaos, trauma, and disaster. Two million German soldiers were killed, one out of seven who served. Another 2.7 million were crippled, physically or mentally. Four out of ten males from the age of eighteen to fifty did not survive the war, or did so only with some kind of permanent disability. According to estimates of the German Labor Ministry in 1923, 533,000 war widows and 1,192,000 orphans survived the dead soldiers.[2] Innumerable people suffered and many died from famine and disease. The destruction of the war was felt in almost each kin, neighborhood, and community. As a consequence of the war, the country was haunted by immeasurable economic misery and a huge rate of inflation that destroyed the assets of the middle class. And Germany had been found guilty for the entire war by its former enemies, punished with territorial losses, and charged with reparation payments that were to burden the following two generations of Germans.

What did all that suffering, death, deprivation, humiliation add up to? And how could it be overcome? The empirical truth of trauma and frustration reflected in Schneider's polls did not provide an answer to these gnawing questions. Mythical truth did, however. Myths are simplifications and can be "debunked as falsifications of reality. But simplification is their strength," a student of war myths rightly says, "since only by ignoring the great mass of infinite data can we identify essential order." Myths "articulate salient patterns that we see in our past and hold as our present value and purpose."[3] This kind of mythical truth helped Germans too, by ordering the chaos of "infinite data" the Great War had left. It was the mythical truth of seemingly timeless experiences, wisdoms, and moralities as they had been established long before the war.[4] In the early nineteenth century, Ludwig Uhland wrote a poem, "The Good Comrade" ("Der gute Kamerad"), that was then set to music and sung by Germans whenever they mourned fallen soldiers. The poem is about two soldiers who fight side by side until one takes a bullet and dies. The other is filled with grief. He has lost a "part of myself." In the 1920s, every German knew the song and its meaningful message: In the midst of all the killing and suffering in which the two are inextricably bound – the surviving comrade reloads his gun right when his comrade dies – the soldier in war preserves and perpetuates the essence of humanity: brotherly love. And he knows that God is with him. He will enter heaven and meet his comrade again, as the song promises at its end: "My friend, I cannot ease your pain, / In life eternal we'll meet again / And walk once more as one."[5]

The Great War seemed to renew and even to expand the myth of comradeship. In 1916 the war volunteer Walter Flex published an autobiographical appropriation of the Uhland song, *The Wanderer Between Two Worlds*. It was a bestseller before the war ended. It told the story of Lieutenant Ernst Wurche, Flex's closest friend and comrade in war, who had died in 1915. In the novel, a sacral aura protects Wurche's moral identity. He carries the *New Testament* in his pocket. It was none of his choosing that the world was "fraught with murder." He was thrown into this world, just as the two comrades in Uhland's poem are drawn into war with no choices other than to march and to fight. As *miles Christi* Wurche knows how to accept war without abandoning Christian morals. Embodying humanity per se, he is ready to sacrifice himself on behalf of the men of his unit, his companions, his apostles, so to say, just as Jesus Christ had done on behalf of humankind.

Wurche's comradeship, however, is not only motivated by Christian values. It is also deeply embedded in the patriotic discourse that arose in the nineteenth century. It gives rise to a vision of how to overcome the antagonisms that economic and social change had entailed on the German fatherland. Although he had grown up in the educated middle class, a privilege that entitled him to aspire to the socially exclusive Wilhelmine officer corps, Wurche commits himself to soldierly comradeship. He aspires to overcome civilian class antagonisms. Already as a recruit Wurche had relished the social diversity of his comrades, according to Flex's novel. As an officer, he practices "good comradeship" with ordinary soldiers from all social classes, "with artisans, blue-collar workers, and Polish farmworkers."[6]

After the war, the gospel of comradeship as the epitome of altruism, charity, empathy, humanity, and social harmony was sung even more vocally, in war novels, in newspapers, and above all at veterans' meetings. One spectacular such occasion was the grand reunion of the Baden infantry regiment "Kaiser Friedrich III" No. 114 in Constance in August 1925. More than 10,000 people attended the "Day of the 114th." It included the solemn dedication of a chapel commemorating the fallen soldiers of the regiment. Set against a devastated landscape, a torched village, and barbed wire – the brutal reality of the Great War – the altarpiece showed the good of the war: comradeship. It was reminiscent of the very familiar scene from the Passion of Christ, the *Pietà* – the Virgin Mary cradling the dead body of Jesus, which epitomized the myth of Christian martyrdom. In the altarpiece, a youthful soldier mourns his fallen comrade, holding his head tenderly, thus creating an island of humanity in the midst of the deserts of inhumanity, of destruction and mutilation. In the background, a flame rises to the heaven, a flame of sacrifice, and a reminder of Christ's sacrifice, now re-enacted by the fallen soldier. As the Catholic priest Schaack explained during the ceremony, the surviving soldier kneels next to his fallen comrade as if he wanted to tell him, "you have fought the good fight, you have finished the race, you have kept the faith," just as Saint Paul at the end of his life wrote to Timothy, "I have fought the good fight, I have finished the race, I have kept the faith."[7] The "good fight" was the one that was fought on behalf of the Christian faith and the Christian values of mercy and charity. He who fought the "good fight" followed the model of Jesus Christ, as stated in Saint John's Gospel 15:13: "Greater love has no one than this: to lay down one's life for one's friends." He who does so is sacred, is promised "eternal life" (John 3:16).

A sacral aura surrounded the soldiers naturally, whether they had died in or survived the war, suggested the speakers on the Day of the 114th. As comrades, they embodied humanity per se. Comradeship was the epitome of selflessness, of mutual charity, of community. The soldier, "in the grip of the horror of all the mass deaths, despised, and degraded," was rescued from this hell only by "the supporting, compensating, alleviating counterweight of his comrade," the town's Protestant pastor said. "It was he who had loyally shared all the suffering and the meagre joys as well . . . The comrade was worth more than anything on earth. That was the comrade – that is comradeship." The "secret of comradeship," the Catholic priest added, lay in the "enduring awareness of what is human." Returning from the firing line, "in the company of dear comrades, soldiers were able to recover their sense of what it means to be a human being."[8]

Just like the Uhland song and the Flex novel, the Constance painting and the comments of the reunion's speakers also remained silent about the less altruistic, less empathic and less human sides of the soldiers' experiences, such as isolation, unfairness, selfishness, as addressed by Joseph Schneider's interviewees. Rather, the speakers apodictically claimed that the war had produced good comrades in quantities. They were not the only ones who did so. The more the war became history, the more evident this claim appeared and the more deliberately it was articulated all over Germany. "Not one of us," stated the journal of the Volksbund Deutsche Kriegsgräberfürsorge, or National Association for War Cemeteries, in a poem in 1931, "would not have shared his last piece of bread with his comrades, not one would not have taken care of an injured comrade, not one of us would not have felt: Brother–; not one of us would not have his heart lacerated by the death of his friend."[9]

This meaningful and comforting truth, not the one of chaos and disaster, was the one Joseph Schneider wanted to spread in order to help his readers cope with their traumatic memories. And so he too stated in his book: "Out there" – in the trenches – "was the world of the good comrade." That his polls told a different story Schneider could easily explain away. Only few "resentful" and unlucky fellows who had "unfortunately" been condemned to endure the war in the company of mean people had thus been burdened with negative experiences, he said. The experiences of these very few were outweighed by "thousands" of soldiers (he had queried only "hundreds"), and these "thousands" would commemorate those who gave their lives on behalf of their comrades silently, "in their hearts," rather than just verbally, "with their lips." Only these memories were worth preserving, as only they taught the "unifying" effect of the perils experienced during war. Soldierly brotherhood guaranteed security and emotional warmth in the midst of the cold bleakness of mass death. Comrades always took care of each other; they shared food and cigarettes, worries and happiness, risks and danger. The past war, suggested Schneider, had evoked the "forces of compassion" in the soldiers and raised them to apostles of "peace." In the present, they now accomplished "a mission," as one of Schneider's interviewees attested. The experience of comradeship in war, claimed this soldier, would "always prompt him to stand ready as a model of peacefulness to quarrelsome people."[10] Comradeship, in other words, not only had consoled the soldiers in war and death. It also led the present into a world of peace *yikes* and harmony. That was the good of the war.

Which was true? The statistical results of random interviews with *too bad* unknown soldiers, or the public assessments of vocal opinion leaders? *not* The answer is not as easy and clear as a critical view of the simplifications of the myth of comradeship might suggest. Drawing on a broad variety *true* of evidence including private letters, diaries, and memoirs, students of military cultures have shown that comradeship, and other types of male bond – friendship, brotherhood, buddy systems, primary groups, mateship, homoeroticism, even male love – feature in almost all kinds of war, probably around the world and throughout the history of humanity, but certainly in those fought by Western nations in the twentieth century. Often inspired by the inquiries of American sociologists and psychologists since World War II into soldiers' fighting morale, these accounts are less interested in the idealizing discourse on trench community observed by Joseph Schneider, Walter Flex or the speakers of the 1925 Constance meeting. Instead, they examine the concept of comradeship as one of those virtues and practices that make men fight – that make them overcome their reluctance to kill and their fear of being killed.

The military historian Richard Holmes, for instance, states in his authoritative 1985 account of the behavior of men in battle that

to the infantryman crouched behind a hummock of peat and heather while bullets snap over his head, or to the tank driver nudging through a hedge with the thrum of armour-piercing shot in his ears, neither ideology nor religion give much incentive for the one to get up and sprint to the next cover, or for the other to drive steadily across a field already scorched by his comrades' oily cremations. For the key to what makes men fight – not enlist, not cope, but fight – we must look hard at military groups and the bonds that link men within them.

Consequently Holmes draws a long line from the homosexual love of the Sacred Band of Thebes in the fourth century BC to the buddy systems in twentieth-century wars and armies, including the French Foreign Legion, the Chinese Red Army, and the US Army in Korea.[11] There is no shortage of anecdotal evidence supporting the idea that male solidarity, whether conceived as comradeship, friendship, brotherhood, or alike, has made soldiers fight, or helped them cope with the experience of mass death, since ancestral times. Exactly this universality and eternality of comradeship allowed the myth of comradeship to prosper.

bestie vibes only

Closer inquiries into social life in the trenches and rear areas, and into the emotional, moral, and ideological world of the World War I soldiers, if taken together, suggest an ambiguous picture, however. By and large, three different views prevail. A significant stream of social historians, dedicated to uncovering the misery and exploitation of the lower classes in history, and relying on the testimonies of ordinary soldiers, has denounced the idea of comradeship as a nationalist propaganda lie or a post-factum legend. Another group of historians points to the astonishing fighting morale of most World War I armies, including the Germans. It cannot be explained, they hold, without referring to the combat cohesion of smaller or larger fighting units, whether or not this is called comradeship. And yet other historians, interested in recovering forgotten ideas about masculinity and gender regimes, suggest that the war allowed numerous soldiers to enjoy a culture of homoerotic if not homosexual relationships, intense emotional bonds they would not have experienced in civilian society.

The latter view is best understood as a response to an enormously influential, extremely critical view on soldierly male bonding and ideas of masculinity at large – the literary critic Klaus Theweleit's interpretation of the memoirs of the German Freikorps soldiers.[12] These men sought to perpetuate war beyond the armistices in 1918, and so they fought a civil war against communists, Jews, and women in the German borderlands, and within Germany in the aftermath of the Great War. In Theweleit's view, the Freikorps men radicalized common Western and German ideas about cold, tough and "hard" masculinity, long since paradigmatically represented by the military, into a concept of male bonding as a sort of institutionalized war against women, femininity, domesticity, tenderness, and compassion. Freikorps masculinity not only prepared the way in Germany to a misogynist brutalization of politics and the rise of the Nazi state and eventually the Holocaust, Theweleit suggested. He also universalized the Freikorps's *Male Fantasies* (the title of the book) into a theory of masculinity as the anti-feminine, anti-family, anti-emotional paradigm per se.

Historians using different sources or following the same analysis as Theweleit in a more nuanced fashion have doubted the validity of his general theory of masculinity. They have drawn attention to the idea of comradeship and other types of male friendship as appropriated by less martial men, especially World War I soldiers. Most explicitly, Joanna Bourke questioned Theweleit's argument by scrutinizing a variety of sources, including private letters, of British World War I servicemen. For these "ordinary" men, she says, "home remained the touchstone for all their actions. Rather than fleeing domesticity and femininity, the

servicemen . . . pursued these two ideals." In war, Bourke says, men *BESTIE VIBES ONLY!*
indulged in a culture of homoeroticism that allowed and encouraged
tenderness, even "love," between men. "My *wife*" – said a soldier in a
letter about his mate – is already in bed and "wants me to keep her
warm," adding that "it is nice to have someone to keep each other
warm." In fact, male bonding in war revolved around symbolic acts
of femininity – mothering, nursing, even sleeping together – carried out
exclusively by men among men. Comradeship made war endurable and
"more human," claimed British servicemen. "You wouldn't believe the
Humanity between men out here," one British soldier told his wife in
1917. Comradeship, Bourke concludes, "is at the heart of most histories
of 'life at the front.'"[13]

Following Bourke's pioneering study, the historians Robert Nelson
and Jason Crouthamel have shown that German World War I soldiers too
fostered feminine masculinities, homoeroticism, and tender comradeship
during the war, just as British servicemen did.[14] The sources they use,
especially the soldiers' amateurish newspapers, allow solid insights into
ordinary soldiers' thinking, feeling, and acting. They show that the notion
of comradeship as a humane counter against the inhumanity of war, and
against the inhumane acts of the soldiers themselves, did not emerge only
after the war and was not limited to songs and tales. Rather, it was part
of the soldiers' reality, or at least of the way they understood this reality.
According to Nelson, even the idea of a national comradeship, uniting an
entire country by erasing domestic social and ideological antagonisms,
was already present in German soldiers' newspapers during the war.[15]

Bourke, Nelson, Crouthamel, and other historians assemble an impressive range of enthusiastic testimonies on different facets of comradeship
in war. But do these testimonies articulate mere desires and fantasies, or
actual daily practices? Do they reflect the normality of war, or exceptions *not*
from normality? Inquiries such as Bourke's caution against generalizing *universal*
individual voices: "While the war provided an intimate environment for
love between men, it at the same time exposed the fragility of brotherhood."[16] Class and other civilian distinctions, and not least the gaps
between different military ranks, challenged and often undermined the
experience of brotherhood in war. One way or another, most of the positive experiences reflect the world of privileged soldiers such as junior
officers, war volunteers, or NCOs. Only occasionally do they reflect the
moods of the mass of the soldiers who served at the bottom of the military
hierarchy.

By no means, however, did privileged soldiers paint only rosy pictures
of the social reality in platoons and battalions. Relying on selected memoirs of German war volunteers, most of them from the educated and

affluent middle class, the historian Eric Leed showed as early as in 1979 in his *No Man's Land* how their craving for heroic manliness and classless brotherhood was soon frustrated by anonymous mass death and social antagonisms between soldier-workers and soldier-players, rankers and officers, volunteers and draftees. The army at war, in other words, did not overcome but rather extended civilian antagonisms from the home front to the battlefront. Critically examining the most popular of those postwar writings, Leed found "that nothing was more problematic than that complex of cooperation, unity of will, and cessation of individual ego that was supposed to have characterized the *Frontgemeinschaft*." One of Leed's witnesses is Franz Schauwecker, a typical war volunteer, who would in the late 1920s become a prolific "spokesman of veterans' nationalism who attempted to redefine the war experience into a national experience." Very soon after the war, however, Schauwecker had published a rather disillusioned account of the experience of frontline community.

Inside my company my own comrades – for the most part dockworkers from Stettin – played tricks against me with genuine rapture whenever possible, even after the first big battle, because they, the men of action, saw in me the ill-developed, physically inferior, and further, the foolish war volunteer, the puerile player with life and death, and because they, the socialist workers, suspected in me the pampered, well-to-do privileged man of education . . . I was alone, which is to say, I was solitary, which signifies I was forsaken.

Yet Leed maintained that the volunteers found some sort of comradeship, although one that was "much less exalted, luminous, and altruistic than expected" (or claimed in later war memories), a product of the "material conditions of life in the trenches" and the experience of proletarianization and marginalization, or, as Carl Zuckmayer, another war volunteer, put it in his memoirs, a comradeship entrenched in "the monstrous boredom, the exhaustion, the unheroic, mechanical day-to-day of war in which terror, fear and death were inserted like the striking of a time-clock in an endless industrial process."[17]

While Leed relied on the literary memoirs of educated men, social historians such as Benjamin Ziemann in his 1997 book on the war experiences of German peasant soldiers have studied war letters, diaries, and reports from, or about, drafted lower-class men. They exposed, even more deliberately than the volunteers, the idea of common, widespread frontline comradeship as a lie.[18] "I have a special idea of what comradeship means," wrote a soldier in January 1918 in a private letter. "Worst of all are the rich farmers who stuff themselves full. If there was anything edible to be bought they are ready to snatch it away from the poor devils' mouths at a moment's notice."[19] Social antagonisms and

Social barriers to widespread comradeship 25

political and economic conflicts that had previously disrupted civilian society continued seamlessly in the military and belied the monarchy's propaganda about the *Burgfrieden*, a "peace within the fortress," and about a nation being united into a true grand community through "comradeship," "the most splendid emanation of the war," as the leader of the Conservative Party in Prussia, Ernst von Heydebrand, himself enthused in 1916.[20] Most severe was the division that separated the industrial proletariat from the middle and upper classes. As the officers were exclusively from the latter group, this class gap extended directly into the army, belying idealizations such as Ernst Wurche's. "Nobody needs to lecture me about comradeship between men and officers!" wrote a soldier in 1915 in a private letter, mocking at the officers "living the life of Riley" while the rank-and-file soldiers alone were burdened with misery and depravation.[21]

While tensions between rankers and officers may be considered as unavoidable in any mass army, German servicemen, most of them from the lower urban and rural classes, experienced a plethora of social injustices, all of them resulting from the social exclusiveness and the demonstrative privileges of the officer "caste," who enjoyed much better food, much higher wages, and much more generous leaves. On top of all this, officers habitually insulted, mistreated, humiliated, and abused ordinary soldiers. Consequently, rank-and-file soldiers were filled with "hatred of officers," as one critical observer noted as early as 1916.[22] To be sure, exceptions did exist, as even Ziemann in his critical analyses of a broad range of testimonies admits. But the few fair or approachable officers could "do little to change the deep sense of bitterness that ordinary soldiers felt toward officers." As one of the former, Victor Klemperer, himself coming from the educated middle class, noted after the war, "on the whole, for every hundred critical remarks about officers there was no more than one good one. This was inevitably followed by: 'He's not like the others.'"[23] Suspicions about businessmen at home, who seemed to profit from and thus be interested in prolonging the war, and disillusionment with a government unable or unwilling to intervene, only added to the widespread anger.

Social frictions, especially between officers and rank-and-file soldiers, and the resentments of frontline soldiers against rear units and the home front, did not constitute a German peculiarity but were a commonality of many World War I armies. Looking at France, the historian Stéphane Audoin-Rouzeau found that although "mutual aid between soldiers was universal" and "the soldiers felt themselves swept up on extraordinary surges of friendship" when faced with wounded or killed comrades, "the real brotherhood" remained an exceptional experience, limited to individuals. It was not one "all soldiers" experienced. The "fraternity of the trenches was largely illusory," he says, and especially the notion of an egalitarian comradeship crossing the class gap between, say, "an intellectual and an uneducated working man," was a middle-class legend that grew only after the war. The French front soldiers, the *poilu*, Audoin-Rouzeau holds, remained tied to their civilian origins and identities or abandoned themselves to indifference.[24]

But then, assessments such as these aim at a very emphatic, indeed not easily realized notion of comradeship, and they rely on anecdotal evidence just as do those that testify the opposite: the power of comradeship, or other types of male bond. While historians following the social history paradigm look at soldiers' experiences from a bottom-up perspective and establish a long record of discontent, discord, and disintegration, of suffering and abuse, numerous military historians, interested in "what makes men fight," challenge this kind of victimization. In an effort to bring soldiers' agency back into the picture, these historians want to explain why World War I armies such as the French, British, and German, in spite of extreme hardships, massive losses, increasing war weariness, and anger about social injustices, continued fighting, functioning, and obeying orders.[25]

To be sure, mutinies spread through the French army in 1917 and caused a serious crisis. And according to the argument of a former doyen of German military history, Wilhelm Deist, German soldiers in the second half of 1918 circumvented military discipline on a large scale, shirked, deserted, and escaped into a "covert strike."[26] But Deist's calculation of up to a million "covert strikers" relied on corrupted sources and thus overestimated the degree of dissolution.[27] The French mutinies, on the other hand, remained an episode. They did not overwhelm the military order. The mutineers did not question the republican state at war. They rather demanded to be respected as citizen-soldiers of a democratic republic instead of being wasted in useless military operations. In 1918, as Leonard V. Smith has shown, even the most mutinous French division regained its former elite reputation.[28]

Not only the British, also the French and even the German armies kept fighting. Why so? As any solid sample of sources reflecting the soldiers' motivations and perceptions reveals, neither patriotism nor hatred of the enemy provides the answer. Nor does coercion, although the fear of punishment and stigmatization for desertion and similar acts certainly mattered. But the soldiers did have the choice of deserting and shirking duties instead of sacrificing life and limb on the altar of their fatherland. However, only few took it – about 0.5 percent in the British as well as German armies.[29] The rest stayed on duty, in the trenches or elsewhere.

They may have moaned and hated their superiors but, as Alexander Watson states, "the disgruntlement and war-weariness felt by soldiers ... by no means automatically translated into rejection of the war" itself but was aimed "against those people" at the home front or in the rear units "who were perceived to be prolonging it unnecessarily or behaving inappropriately."[30] As Christoph Jahr rightly adds, "no social system runs without frictions." By articulating anger and frustration, the soldiers released pressure. Discontent and complaints, even the hatred of officers, did not break the system but actually stabilized it, just as relief valves do in a pressure vessel.[31]

According to inquiries into the sociology and psychology of the French, the British, and the German World War I armies, it seems as if the myth of comradeship as presented, for instance, at the Constance veterans' meeting, wasn't so wrong after all, although the myth's attempt to merge complex and contradictory experiences into one formula is exactly this: a myth. Yet the observations of three experts on World War I France seem to be true for other armies accordingly: The soldiers' tenacity "rested on myriad forms of consent," on a "war culture" that "proved so resilient precisely because its organization was primarily horizontal rather than vertical." The war culture "rooted itself in shared practices of representation, and in shared created experience." One of the keystones of this culture was "the basic solidarities of small groups" that "carried on their own war, often at the fringe of official authority," "lived together according to their own rules and hierarchies," and established a "very specific sociability, based on sharing" – sharing food, drink, and tobacco; duties, skills, and dangers; human warmth, homesickness, and the mourning of fallen comrades.[32]

The positive value of this horizontal, "basic" sociability may have been tenuous, and obviously it often belied the high expectations triggered by emphatic and holy notions of comradeship. What an American observer, James Hall, said of the British World War I army applies to other armies as well: "Hardship and dangers, shared in common, tend to break down artificial barriers. But even then, although there was goodwill and friendliness between officers and men, I saw nothing of genuine comradeship."[33] Note that Hall doubted "genuine comradeship," not less spectacular forms of solidarity, commonalities, or "friendliness." In fact, a plethora of testimonies, letters, and diaries indicates that the experience and the practice of comradeship was embedded in, and more and more pervaded by, fatigue, apathy, indifference, fatalism, and war-weariness, a mood of passivity that was often symbolically inflated as doing one's duty. The soldiers were in "a state of mind," as the historian Omer Bartov has put it, "that combined a good measure of self-pity with immense pride in their ability to endure inhumane conditions for the sake of a nation seemingly ignorant of and indifferent to their terrible sacrifice," a "camaraderie" that the combat troops on both sides of the line shared.[34]

Tearing the men out of the mood of passivity and self-pity, and enlivening their pride in enduring a terrible war, was the job of their immediate superiors, the junior officers, who led the small fighting units into battle. According to research by Leonard Smith, Gary Sheffield, Alexander Watson, and others on the French, British, and German armies, the junior officers were more successful in doing so than bottom-up history pretends. Yet the differences among the three armies were considerable. Most historians agree that the "peacetime industrial relations" of British society "hold the key to British military resilience in the First World War," even if at the beginning of the war the class gaps between officers and ranks – and the social elitism and exclusivity of the former – were as marked as in the German army. In 1914, only 2 or 3 percent of British officers had started their career as rankers, and the officers kept the ranks at a distance, symbolically and practically. But unlike in Germany, the British officer corps opened up as the army grew in numbers. By 1917–18, 40 percent of British officers came from the lower middle or working classes.

Even more social leveling resulted from the way civilian social relations extended into the British military. Admittedly, the idea of paternalistic responsibility for subordinates operated not only in the British officer corps. German military manuals even codified it to make discipline, hierarchy, and elitism bearable. In Britain much more than in Germany, however, paternalism was embedded in and enforced by civilian traditions of smoothing class antagonism. Paternalism from the top and deference at the bottom were tied into a concept of hierarchy that promoted cooperation instead of conflict. By contrast, the pre-1914 German Socialist movement, despite its reformist tendencies, never lost its revolutionary impulse. As Gary Sheffield has put it, British "ranks tended to judge officers largely in terms of deference, which can be defined as 'respect for, and obedience to, leaders of society.' Deference, not to be confused with subservience, was one of the principal bonds of the Edwardian society . . . inculcated through religion and education . . . Men in the ranks saw deference as 'the natural exchange' for paternalism. Officers who did not look after their men, who did not show leadership qualities in battle," undermined the basis of this sensitive balance. What is crucial, of course, is not the norm but the practice. As we have seen, the writings of German ranks featured very frequent condemnations of "bad" officers, i.e. of those who did not live up to the paternalistic norm, whereas in the

British army they were rare or "likely to be followed by a complimentary reference to another," i.e. a good officer.[35]

In the French army, a similar and yet different culture of deference smoothed officer–ranker relations as well. Tied into the political culture of a democratic republic, the French officer corps was much more permeable than the British or the German. By the beginning of the war, nearly 60 percent of the lieutenants had been promoted from the ranks. And during the war, even during the mutinies, the junior officers maintained trustful relations with the ranks by treating them "as fellow Frenchmen," as fellow citizen-soldiers, that is. This trust was "based in officers' sharing their privations and perils" and also in officers' gestures of sympathy, sometimes even toward mutineers. Throughout the war, sociability "created 'horizontal' links among men of varying ranks who shared common hardships and dangers," states Leonard Smith. "In the end," he says, "comradeship made deference possible."[36]

There was no strong tradition of deference in German society. As we have seen, bottom-up accounts suggest that this society extended its deeply politicized class antagonisms seamlessly into the military. Yet the "well-attested 'officer hate' that spread throughout the Kaiser's army" from 1916 on may have been overrated by the "current historiographical consensus," bemoans Watson. "Theoretically," he says, "the 'officer hate' should have drastically undermined the combat efficiency of the German army. That this did not happen" Watson explains by differentiating the target of that hate. It "was directed primarily against middle-ranking staff officers and rear-line commanders, not the junior combat officers who led the men at the front." And so he concludes: "The inter-rank *Frontgemeinschaft* survived." This apodictic assessment is based on letters and diaries praising individual officers' paternalistic care for their men's material and emotional needs, their dedication to the comradely culture of sharing, and, most important, to their role as models of leadership in battle; it is confirmed by casualty statistics indicating that German junior officers did not hesitate to storm into battle at the head of their units, rather than looking for a place in the rear. "In the British army, 11.7% of men and 13.6% of officers were killed. In the German army, despite the fact that it fielded a lower proportion of officers at the front, and in contrast to the 13.3% of NCOs and men killed, 15.7% of reserve officers and a frighteningly high 24.7% of active officers fell during the First World War."[37]

In a case study on a Bavarian infantry division, Christian Stachelbeck adds further insights and evidence to Watson's provocative argument. As Stachelbeck shows, it was not only the officers who managed to keep the close combat units together but also the experienced ranks and NCOs, the "veterans" of these units. These veterans, the "mainstays" (*Korsettstangen*) of their units took care of the newcomers and the replacements, shared with them the secrets of surviving trench warfare, and played a crucial role in motivating them to fight, carrying them along in battle, not least by exerting social pressure on those who would otherwise dodge away or shirk the fields of death. Stachelbeck confirms Watson's appraisal of the German frontline comradeship. Understood as a synonym for both solidarity and conformity in small units, it ensured fighting effectiveness during the war.[38] This way, comradeship was no longer the emphatic synonym for solemn male homoeroticism or sanctified mutual altruism. Rather, it gave identity to the social cohesion of a somber community of fate, of soldiers who knew about the senselessness of the war they fought and yet drew a modicum of agency from performing the fatalistic resilience of a *Frontschwein*, or doughboy.[39] Even when "burnt out by battle," slumped "over in exhaustion," states the historian Michael Geyer, they were not simply "transmogrified into a 'community' welded together by overwhelming, external force" but absorbed in small combat units that were driven by a mixture of fear and rage – "soldiers who were scared to death and therefore killed unconditionally."[40]

What is the result of these inquiries into the reality of comradeship in war? There is no clear answer other than this: It was all about ambiguity. Comradeship was a leitmotif in various armies during the Great War, not just a German peculiarity. Any attempts to precisely determine its proliferation are doomed to fail, however. The virtue of comradeship was invoked to fuel combat cohesion and fighting power – the aggressive side of soldiering. At the same time, it served as a synonym for male friendship, even male love, of homoeroticism and tenderness. The concept does not carry a clearly defined meaning. Instead, it is the name of an amorphous set of different, even contradictory attitudes, emotions, and actions. It radiates uncertainty – and contingency. As a cultural concept, it was polyvalent; as an individual experience, unreliable. In its core meaning as an emphatic ideal of solidarity, of sharing goods, emotions, danger, and death, soldiers experienced comradeship only occasionally, or at most much less than glorifying or sentimentalizing accounts during or after the war suggested. In a broader sense, understood as a synonym of sociability, cohesion, and conformity, it may have been more common than critical voices after the war and some historians have claimed. The concept emerged to address small or primary group relations and extended into the realm of larger, anonymous or secondary groups as well – the regiment, the entire army, even the nation, although these latter usages were rare until 1918. Different soldiers, observers, and opinion-makers could engage with, highlight, doubt, or ignore any of these different meanings of comradeship. In the experience of comradeship, horizontal and vertical social relations could compete, exclude, or reinforce each other. Comradeship could refer to both or to either: solidarity between equals, especially rankers, and the cooperation between non-equals, i.e. men and officers, especially junior officers. In the British and French armies vertical comradeship was embedded in strong paternalistic or democratic civilian traditions and facilitated combat morale. The German army, however, was penetrated by overheated civilian cleavages, and this impeded its fighting power.

The clash across civilian cleavages, or more precisely its political emanations, at the end of the war, the revolution of 1918, the abrupt change from monarchy to democracy, in conjunction with the consequences of military defeat, with the humiliating burdens imposed on Germany by the peace treaty of Versailles, determined the way Germans coped with, and remembered, the war. Germany was being held responsible for it, charged astronomical amounts of reparation, and robbed of its symbol of power, the conscripted army. The stigma of defeat and guilt nourished the legend of the "stab in the back" that allowed Germany's nationalist political milieu to to blame the Jews, the socialists, and even the women – those who had stayed at home – for defeat and subsequent misery. To them, a new war was the only way of resurrecting Germany's lost grandeur.[41]

Although much more than simply a vehicle of the legend of the stab in the back, the myth of comradeship as advocated at the Constance veterans' reunion in 1925 could be used as such. This myth seemed to prove the notion of the trenches as the only safe haven of an ideal world, sharply contrasting with the treacherous home front. In fact, this version of the myth of comradeship was the one the nationalist milieu eagerly adopted right after the war. As in other defeated nations, in Germany "the reality of the war experience came to be transformed into what one might call the Myth of the War, which looked back upon the war as a meaningful and even sacred event," as the historian George L. Mosse has said in his examination of the cult of the fallen soldier.[42]

At the center of this myth stood the experience of comradeship, the force that would heal the nation from its misery, its fractionalism, and its humiliation. As powerful as this myth would become, it was by no means undisputed. In the immediate wake of the war not even the nationalist and militarist camp in Germany was sure what to make of that experience. Rather, the immediate remembrance of the war reflected the contingency that had shaped the experience of comradeship during the war. Former war volunteers, many of them junior officers, had been closer to the realm of comradeship of ordinary soldiers, but in their early postwar accounts disillusionment prevailed, not enthusiasm. Franz Schauwecker was no exception. Siegfried Wegeleben, although proud of his career as war volunteer, was even franker than Schauwecker. He denounced the entire rhetoric about the blessings of comradeship as a mere tactic to obfuscate egoism among soldiers. In his view, the idea that the "holy war" had produced a "pure culture of altruism" and "contained an inexhaustible fountain of morality" was simply nonsense.[43]

For different reasons, another former junior officer, Lieutenant Ernst Jünger, marginalized the experience of comradeship in war. Of course, Jünger knew about comradeship as a synonym for male tenderness and mutual charity in war; his fictionalized war memoirs render homage to the ideal of a comradely officer who occasionally talked to an NCO "like a brother" or "circulated a bottle of 98% without distinctions of rank."[44] But this type of comradeship was not part of the lesson that Jünger wanted his readers to take from the war. Instead, his lesson was a deliberately elitist one, not one about social harmony. The "storm of steel" had brewed a new race of men, Jünger thought. As devastating as the war had been, it had cleared the way for a grand future that was void of weakness, of ambiguities, of doubts, and of suffering. Barbarity and barbarians, "new men," "conquerors, men of steel, primed in the cruelest kind of battle," would reign in the new world, a world without the moral restrictions that civilian society imposed on proper warfare. Looking for mythical models, Jünger's ultimate warrior discarded the Bible but enthused about Asian despots, who had lived up to a moral code that valued killing just as Christians valued charity. Jünger did not deny the moral and emotional challenges even a dedicated warrior faced in battle, or the need to cope with them. But his soldier gained his pride from "overcoming" scruples and pangs of conscience. "Humanity" was not part of his sentiments, desires, or duties, even less so domesticity. Killing was his passion, and to Jünger there was no doubt, "that we will kill: solidly, ruthlessly, and by every trick in the book." Jünger's model of a soldier was the lonely warrior, a cold figure who despised and fled the warmth and security of a comradely, family-like, or homoerotic community.[45]

As a writer, Jünger was not alone but echoed by a small but vocal group of war fanatics who craved a world without peace. "Finally to go beyond good and evil! Finally to be a man, an anti-man, a super-man!" exulted the elitist journal *Der Weisse Ritter*, or *The White Knight*, in 1923, alluding to Friedrich Nietzsche's quest for a "dangerous life." "Male freedom," the journal demanded, was free of women and of ideas of guilt and allowed full scope to make mankind "tremble."[46] While an abstract idea of male solidarity, not least against women, floated in all these fantasies, they were without the notion of comradeship. The born warrior did not

look him up

need it. He certainly felt an affinity to those like him and would recognize them at once. Based on this sense of sameness, the alpha-warrior may have felt himself to be part of a battle community. But this community was an abstract and also a deliberately exclusive one, admitting only men, who "came to see the world, and their role in it, through the prism of struggle, sacrifice, and destruction."[47]

Jünger contented himself with martial prose and left the task of fighting eternal wars to fellow-soldiers and would-be soldiers. Their units included the Freikorps, the Feme murderers, and the Nazi thugs. Even more deliberately than Jünger's warrior figure, these men basked in the glory of moral transgression. The tang of criminality encouraged rather than discouraged them. Ernst von Salomon's 1930 autobiographical novel on his adolescence as Freikorps warrior, *The Outlaws*, was one of the most popular paeans to an ethics of terror. Salomon described himself as a young man who grew into a valuable, tough, and merciless member of a criminal gang of assassins. The years he spent in prison for these crimes did not generate any regrets. Instead, Salomon praised "man's lust for destruction." He meant not only physical but also moral destruction, the destruction of whatever civilization praises as good – securing order, providing stability, saving life, protecting the weak, feeling pity. Terrorists like him promulgated a new ethic of collectivity. Good was what "animated the whole company," its cohesion and unity, that is.[48] Salomon's autobiography provided a mythical frame for the political violence practiced by the Storm Troopers of the Nazi Party against communists and socialists in the early 1930s. SA men did not hide murder; they staged it. When they marched in Charlottenburg, a Berlin suburb, they sang, "We are the Nazi guys from the murderer unit of Charlottenburg."[49] Unleashing brutality in bar brawls, fighting together furiously in the streets, and committing murder together served as social "cement," as Joseph Goebbels said.[50]

It was not by accident that neither Salomon nor Goebbels described their ideas of social unity as "comradeship" but rather imagined them as an abstract community or named them friendship – the friendship of outlaws, of terrorists, of barbarians. Comradeship, by contrast, was to them a notion reserved to a humane type of sociality. It was the code word of the civilian-soldier's "sentimentalized" and moralized virtue of humanity, as Albrecht Erich Günther, a friend of Ernst Jünger and intellectual precursor of the Nazis, contemptuously explained in 1934. Of no use for the eternal warrior, the outlaws, or the Nazi thugs, the humanity of comradeship suited the citizen, explained another insider. Comradeship, these warriors knew, only constrained the radicalization of violence they craved for.[51]

More traditional military experts still concurred in the 1930s. Wehrmacht psychologists like Max Simoneit and Erich Weniger shunned fantasies of perpetual war against civilians, yet were suspicious toward mass armies, which, in their views, had first clogged, and then deserted from, the battlefields of the past war and might do so again in a future war. Instead, these professionals enthused about "independent" fighter heroes who would be elevated above the sluggish mass of conscripted soldiers. The rank-and-files, explained Weniger in 1938, when looking back on the Great War, had put on uniforms only to hide their civilian identities, i.e. their fears of killing and being killed. Their fighting power, if there was any, depended on comradely "contiguousness." Comradeship, in other words, was the virtue of the "weak," the ordinary, the citizen-soldiers. The strong ones, the born fighters, did not need it. They formed a "battle community," something entirely different from languid comradeship.[52]

What these different assessments of born soldiers, hero fighters, and enthusiasts of barbarian brutality had in common was their distance from the notion of comradeship. Comradeship was seen as the social virtue and the emotional survival kit of the drafted – indeed unwilling – soldier, not of the born soldier. Yet it was precisely the figure of the drafted soldier that challenged the interwar discourse on war experiences and future wars, more than did any elitist ideas about autonomous warriors and bloodthirsty killers. Anyone in the interwar period planning for a future war in Europe knew that this war needed both the few born warrior heroes and the many drafted citizen-soldiers, that it would mobilize masses of people, if not all, as Erich Ludendorff, the distinguished World War I general, demanded in his influential 1935 pamphlet on *Total War*.[53] Total war could not separate the civilian from a warrior society, nor could it isolate the morality of mass death from the morality of bourgeois security. The two needed to be combined. A future army in war would have to accommodate a variety of attitudes, emotions, and identities, and it would need to rely on a variety of soldiers. Not all of them were equally fit for war, as the Great War's innumerable emotional cripples had clearly shown.[54] Eventually, in the revolution of 1918, the citizen had even defeated the soldier, Carl Schmitt stated disdainfully in 1934, articulating the trauma of all nationalist and belligerent Germans.[55] How to avoid its repeat?

The citizen and the soldier – this polarity caught on multiple overlapping antagonisms, such as those between different individuals, institutions, times, spaces, emotions, ideologies, between families and barracks, security and danger, freedom and compulsion, between the restraints on killing and the lust for killing. Not only did this antagonism separate different people, spaces, and ideologies, however, it also split individuals into two halves. Most of the ordinary soldiers had to cope with this split. In a militarized society, the citizen-soldier may have shown off his uniform, and yet he felt as if he were disguising himself. Thus, the interwar discourse on war experience worked continuously on this idea of a split personality. Walter Flex's *The Wanderer Between Two Worlds* offered the most popular formula to address what Werner Picht diagnosed in 1937, when the future war was within sight. Unlike the warrior, the simple "front soldier," Picht said, lived in "two worlds," a "world of peace," a "world of production and fulfilling happiness," and a world of "murder machines" and destruction. "A rift goes through the center of his mind and soul" and it deepens, Picht bemoaned, all the more his next of kin, his friends at home, or the society he belongs to are unable or unwilling to empathize with him.[56]

The murder machines jeopardized not only the soldiers' physical but also their moral integrity. Ubiquitous fear of getting killed was enmeshed in the horror of being forced into committing "mass murder," as soldiers, terrified of their own "brutalization," came to realize early in the war. Even at the front line, the ordinary soldier was stuck in his civilian identity, in the world of peace. "Thou shalt not kill," said its most basic law. The assignment to kill was "unnatural" to the soldier. It left him traumatized, a military pastor explained in 1922. To the ordinary soldier, killing in battle was murder even if ordered and sanctioned by military or civilian authorities.[57]

And it was not only the soldiers themselves who nurtured such ideas. The loved ones at home did so as well and could not always avoid mistrusting the homecoming soldiers. The soldiers had of course risked life and limb for their fatherland and their families, but at the same time they had lived through a world contrary to the one they were defending – a frightening world that had turned the values of the civilian world upside down. When returning from the moral no-man's-land, was the soldier still the same as the civilian had been before the war? Would he be able to return to civilian morality, to a world of peace and humanity? Or had he become a barbarian?

Radical bellicism, glorifying the lonely soldier or the outlawed warrior, was one way of resolving the dilemma of the citizen-soldier. The lonely soldier and the outlawed warrior were cleansed from civilian morality. They thus secured a place in popular war culture as well as in elitist military discourses, but they never stirred up a mass movement. The same is true for the opposite radical answer to that dilemma, the pacifist one. Pacifism encouraged swearing off war forever, overthrowing the concept of citizen-soldier by splitting off the soldierly part, but it did not gain significant popularity in interwar Germany either. Around 1920 a

Never-War-Again movement mobilized mass demonstrations of up to 500,000 marchers, and anti-war associations mushroomed all over the country.[58] Some prominent former officers became antimilitarists and denounced the armed forces as "criminal and inhumane."[59] But they remained rare exceptions, and pacifist mass demonstrations and platforms ebbed away in the early 1920s.

What became popular was the reconciliation of the extremes, moderate pacifism on the one hand, and moderate militarism on the other. The first accepted armed forces for defensive purposes and honored the sacrifice of the citizen-soldiers for their country. This viewpoint was represented in Weimar Germany especially by the Social Democrats and by social democratic war veterans and war disabled leagues. One such was the Reichsbund der Kriegsbeschädigten und ehemaligen Kriegsteilnehmer, or National Association of Disabled Soldiers and Veterans, founded in 1918; another was the Reichsbanner Schwarz Rot Gold (literally, "Imperial Banner Black Red Gold"), founded in 1924 in response to the increasingly anti-democratic and anti-republican attitude of the hitherto dominant, conservative, nationalist, militarist associations representing the other approach to reconciling the extremes. They included the Kriegervereine (Servicemen's Leagues), established locally as early as in the nineteenth century and then united nationwide as the Kyffhäuserbund, as well as post-1918 associations such as the Stahlhelm (Steel Helmet), and the Jungdeutscher Orden (Young German Order), or "Jungdo."[60]

Notwithstanding their deep ideological divisions, all these associations faced one common problem: They reached only a minority of former soldiers. Exact membership numbers are not available, yet even optimistic estimates suggest that the Kyffhäuserbund never gathered much more than 2 million men, the Stahlhelm 400,000, the Jungdo 200,000, the Reichsbanner about 1 million, and the Reichsbund a lower five-digit number, and all were subject to many fluctuations.[61] And these figures included many double or triple memberships. More than 10 million German soldiers had survived the war[62] – most of them, as Schneider's polls indicated, not interested in spending time and money supporting the organized perpetuation of war memories, but rather in fostering their civilian identities, their professional careers, their private fortunes. The veterans' associations found themselves in a defensive position. They could not afford to dedicate themselves only to elitist ideologies if they wanted to reach out to the bulk of former soldiers. These were the citizen-soldiers who were proud of their service for the fatherland and yet had no desire to engage in perpetual war. Consequently, the veterans'

movement worked on integrating and harmonizing different and contradictory experiences, emotions, and morals.

The myth of comradeship helped to build these bridges. It helped the
citizen-soldier to cope with his split personality, and it allowed society
at home to empathize with him, just as Picht suggested. Immediately
after the war, local Stahlhelm branches invited the families of their members to Christmas festivities so that the veterans could give proof to "our
wives and children that, even though we were 'brutalized' during the
war, we still harbor a true German sense of love for home and domesticity."[63] By trading war stories about comradeship, the soldiers showed
they had preserved their civilian identities. More than this, however, they
lent momentum to the myth of comradeship by re-enacting their frontline comradeship after returning home, just as one of the good comrades
interviewed by Joseph Schneider did by serving as "a model of peacefulness to quarrelsome people."[64]

This ameliorating conception of comradeship as moral and emotional
counter to the horrors of war was not limited to Germany. Comradeship in war mattered to the World War I armies in general, albeit with
variations due to national differences, and so the memorialization of
comradeship took similar yet not identical forms in different countries,
such as Germany and Britain. The one was defeated and the other
had emerged victorious from the war. But soldiers in both countries
struggled with physical, emotional, and moral traumas. The myth of
comradeship provided relief in both cases. "The good comradeship of
male society," asserted one British veteran, carried "men through the
most heavy trials of danger and physical exhaustion." In Britain, too, the
fallen soldiers, epitomizing the country's suffering from mass death and
destruction, were remembered for the "ethical triumph over evil" they
had achieved, rather than for the military victories their self-sacrifices
may have enabled.[65] The soldiers' comradeship, their service to their
country "as a band of brothers," as the inscription of a war memorial
in Cheltenham, England, proclaimed, substantiated that ethical triumph.
This inscription of course referred to William Shakespeare's famous Saint
Crispin Day speech, i.e. Henry V's invocation of the "band of brothers"
that had risen from the "blood" shed together in battle and that "shall
be remembered" until "the ending of the world."[66]

In Britain, the Saint Crispin Day speech served as the literary reference
for the myth of comradeship just as in Germany the Uhland song did.
And just as in Germany, the British imagery of remembrance elevated the
solidarity of the soldiers in war "into an ideal of brotherly love, modeled
on the Christian ideal" as spelled out in Saint John's gospel, 15:13.[67] As

in Germany, British World War I memoirists recalled comradeship as a general, not only exceptional, "feeling that existed throughout whatever unit they belonged to," as the historian Jessica Meyer has observed. As in Germany, the "spirit of equality" was a crucial part of the harmonizing fabric of comradeship. As one man wrote, "all the time I was in the army I never saw or heard chaps quarrelling," despite there being "so many fellows together from all walks of life, some rich, some poor." And so the experience of comradeship was invoked as a model to "heal" the social wounds of civilian society, from which the British postwar society suffered as well. One of the first British postwar movies, Maurice Elvey's *Comradeship* (1919), showed how the experience of comradeship effectually destroyed class and other social barriers between the soldiers in war, and how a new, harmonious society at home arose by appropriating and disseminating this experience; a veterans' club, actually called "Comrades Club," served to extend the soldiers' comradeship in war into nationwide postwar comradeship. In the 1920s the veterans' associations indeed propagated the idea of smoothing the social conflicts of civilian society by adopting the notion of comradeship in war, however romanticized.[68]

In Britain, however, the idea of appropriating the mythical model of the frontline community in the Great War for renewing the social and political condition of the entire nation remained a peripheral one. Instead, the cult of the Unknown Soldier, buried in Westminster Abbey in 1920 and soon in other countries such as France, the United States, and Italy as well, established a different path to symbolically overcoming class gaps through war memory. Representing the entire nation and all classes, the Unknown Soldier silenced class conflicts by shifting them into the anonymity of the war dead.[69] War memory in Britain as in other victorious countries was not faced with the burden of "explaining," or explaining away, the impact of class conflicts on military defeat. Nor was it tasked with giving meaning to the loss of national honor and power, and envisioning a future war to regain both. In countries such as Britain, war memory could focus on the past – on mourning. Germany, by contrast, became obsessed with drawing lessons for the future from the past.

NOTES

1 J[osef] Schneider, *Lebensweisheit für Deutsche, besonders Reichswehr und Polizei* (Berlin-Charlottenburg: Offene Worte, 1926), p. 130; Alan Kramer, *Dynamic of Destruction: Culture and Mass Killing in the First World War* (Oxford University Press, 2007), pp. 211–67; and Jay Winter, *The Experience of World War I* (New York: Oxford University Press, 1989). On the concept of war trauma,

see Jenny Edkins, *Trauma and the Memory of Politics* (Cambridge University Press, 2003), with further literature.

2 Rüdiger Overmans, "Kriegsverluste," in Gerhard Hirschfeld, Gerd Krumeich, and Irina Renz (eds.), *Enzyklopädie Erster Weltkrieg*, 2nd edn. (Paderborn: Schöningh, 2004), pp. 663–66; Robert Weldon Whalen, *Bitter Wounds: German Victims of the Great War, 1914–1930* (Ithaca, NY: Cornell University Press, 1984), pp. 95, 131.

3 John Hellmann, *American Myth and the Legacy of Vietnam* (New York: Columbia University Press, 1986), pp. ix–x.

4 More generally on the way resorting to "traditional modes of seeing the war" helped peoples to cope with the experience of collective trauma and disruption of continuities, see the now classic account by Jay Winter, *Sites of Memory, Sites of Mourning: The Great War in European Cultural History* (Cambridge University Press, 1995), p. 5.

5 Uli Otto and Eginhard König, *"Ich hatt' einen Kameraden...": Militär und Kriege in historisch-politischen Liedern in den Jahren von 1740 bis 1914* (Mainz: Conbrio, 1999). On the historical context, see George L. Mosse, *Fallen Soldiers: Shaping the Memory of the World Wars* (New York: Oxford University Press, 1990), pp. 15–50.

6 Walter Flex, *Der Wanderer zwischen beiden Welten*, new edn. (Kiel: Orion-Heimreiter, 1986), pp. 8–9, 13–15, 17.

7 *Deutsche Bodensee-Zeitung*, August 31, 1925. Cf. 2 Timothy 4:7.

8 Special pages in *Konstanzer Zeitung* and *Deutsche Bodensee-Zeitung* on "the Day of the 114th," both August 31, 1925.

9 *Kriegsgräberfürsorge*, April 1931, pp. 51–52.

10 Schneider, *Lebensweisheit für Deutsche*, pp. 31–32.

11 Richard Holmes, *Acts of War: The Behavior of Men in Battle* (New York: Free Press, 1986), pp. 270–73, 290–315 (quotation at p. 291).

12 Theweleit, *Male Fantasies*.

13 Joanna Bourke, *Dismembering the Male: Men's Bodies, Britain and the Great War* (London: Reaktion, 1996), pp. 22–25, 126–27, 131–32, 136. Cf. Jessica Meyer, *Men of War: Masculinity and the First World War in Britain* (Basingstoke: Palgrave Macmillan, 2009), pp. 74–79, 145–47, 155–60, 164; Michael Roper, *The Secret Battle: Emotional Survival in the Great War* (Manchester University Press, 2009), pp. 126–30, 206–07, 284, 303–04.

14 Robert L. Nelson, *German Soldier Newspapers of the First World War* (Cambridge University Press, 2011); Jason Crouthamel, *An Intimate History of the Front: Masculinity, Sexuality and Ordinary German Soldiers in the First World War* (Basingstoke: Palgrave Macmillan, 2014).

15 Nelson, *German Soldier Newspapers*, pp. 9, 92, 103–06, 240.

16 Bourke, *Dismembering the Male*, pp. 145 (quotation), 27, 144–53.

17 Eric J. Leed, *No Man's Land: Combat & Identity in World War I* (Cambridge University Press, 1979), pp. 86 (Schauwecker quotation), 90–91, 93–94; see Franz Schauwecker, *Im Todesrachen: Die deutsche Seele im Weltkrieg* (Halle: Diekmann, 1919), pp. 16, 18, 100–01, 246, 307. Carl Zuckmayer, *Als wärs ein Stück von mir* (Frankfurt: S. Fischer, 1966), p. 207, translation as in Leed, *No Man's Land*, pp. 86–87.

18 Benjamin Ziemann, *Front und Heimat: Ländliche Kriegserfahrungen im südlichen Bayern 1914–1923* (Essen: Klartext, 1997); abridged English version: Benjamin Ziemann, *War Experiences in Rural Germany, 1914–1923* (Oxford: Berg, 2007), pp. 29–154. Cf. Bernd Ulrich and Benjamin Ziemann (eds.), *German Soldiers in the Great War: Letters and Eyewitness Accounts* (Barnsley: Pen & Sword Military, 2010), pp. 101–30; Anne Lipp, *Meinungslenkung im Krieg: Kriegserfahrungen deutscher Soldaten und ihre Deutung 1914–1918* (Göttingen: Vandenhoeck & Ruprecht, 2003), pp. 106–28. Wolfgang Kruse, "Krieg und Klassenheer: Zu Revolutionierung der deutschen Armee im Ersten Weltkrieg," *Geschichte und Gesellschaft*, 22 (1996), 530–61, argued that the revolution of 1918 in Germany emerged from the experience of social injustices and class gaps within the army (rather than at the home front). Based on their more thorough research, both Ziemann and Lipp have challenged Kruse's thesis, however.

19 Ziemann, *War Experiences in Rural Germany*, p. 77.

20 Quoted in Martin Hobohm, "Soziale Heeresmißstände als Teilursache des deutschen Zusammenbruchs von 1918," in *Das Werk des Untersuchungsausschusses der Verfassunggebenden deutschen Nationalversammlung und des deutschen Reichstages 1919–1930*, Part 4: *Die Ursachen des Deutschen Zusammenbruchs im Jahre 1918*, vol. II-11/1 (Berlin: Deutsche Verlagsgesellschaft für Politik und Geschichte, 1929), p. 263. See Jeffrey Verhey, *The Spirit of 1914: Militarism, Myth and Mobilization in Germany* (New York: Cambridge University Press, 2000).

21 Quoted in Aribert Reimann, *Der große Krieg der Sprachen: Untersuchungen zur historischen Semantik in Deutschland und England zur Zeit des Ersten Weltkrieges* (Essen: Klartext, 2000), p. 123.

22 Hermann Kantorowicz, *Der Offiziershaß im deutschen Heer* (Freiburg: Bielefeld, 1919).

23 Ziemann, *War Experiences in Rural Germany*, p. 79, also for the translation from Victor Klemperer, *Curriculum Vitae: Jugend um 1900*, vol. II (Berlin: Aufbau, 1989), p. 372.

24 Stéphane Audoin-Rouzeau, *Men at War 1914–1918: National Sentiment and Trench Journalism in France During the First World War* (Providence: Berg, 1992; French orig. 1986), pp. 46–52.

25 On the German army, see Hew Strachan, "The Morale of the German Army," in Hugh Cecil and Peter H. Liddle (eds.), *Facing Armageddon: The First World War Experienced* (London: Leo Cooper, 1996), pp. 383–98; Michel Geyer, "Vom massenhaften Tötungshandeln, oder: Wie die Deutschen das Krieg-Machen lernten," in Peter Gleichmann and Thomas Kühne (eds.), *Massenhaftes Töten: Kriege und Genozide im 20. Jahrhundert* (Essen: Klartext, 2004), pp. 105–42; Geyer, "How the Germans Learned to Wage War: On the Question of Killing in the First and Second World Wars," in Alon Confino, Paul Betts, and Dirk Schumann (eds.), *Between Mass Death and Individual Loss: The Place of the Dead in Twentieth-Century Germany* (New York: Berghahn, 2008), pp. 25–50.

26 Wilhelm Deist, "The Military Collapse of the German Empire: The Reality Behind the Stab-in-the-Back Myth," *War in History*, 3/2 (1996), 186–207 (German orig. 1986).

27 Alexander Watson, *Enduring the Great War: Combat, Morale and Collapse in the German and British Armies, 1914–1918* (Cambridge University Press, 2008), pp. 206–08. For a more nuanced assessment, see Benjamin Ziemann, *Gewalt im Ersten Weltkrieg: Töten – Überleben – Verweigern* (Essen: Klartext, 2013), pp. 120–33.

28 Leonard V. Smith, *Between Mutiny and Obedience: The Case of the French Fifth Infantry Division During World War I* (Princeton University Press, 1994).

29 Watson, *Enduring the Great War*, pp. 42–43.

30 Ibid., p. 77.

31 Christoph Jahr, *Gewöhnliche Soldaten: Desertion und Deserteure im deutschen und britischen Heer 1914–1918* (Göttingen: Vandenhoeck & Ruprecht, 1998), p. 97.

32 Leonard V. Smith, Stéphane Audoin-Rouzeau, and Annette Becker, *France and the Great War, 1914–1918* (Cambridge University Press, 2003), pp. 97–100.

33 James Norman Hall, *Kitchener's Mob: The Adventures of an American in the British Army* (Boston, MA: Houghton Mifflin, 1916), p. 14.

34 Omer Bartov, *Mirrors of Destruction: War, Genocide, and Modern Identity* (Oxford University Press, 2000), p. 12. Cf. Ziemann, *War Experiences in Rural Germany*, pp. 29–154; Leed, *No Man's Land*, pp. 73–114; Nelson, *German Soldier Newspapers of the First World War*, pp. 94–96; Reimann, *Krieg der Sprachen*, p. 122.

35 Gary Sheffield, "Officer–Man Relations, Discipline and Morale in the British Army of the Great War," in Cecil and Little (eds.), *Facing Armageddon*, pp. 413–24 (at 416–19). See also John Bourne, "The British Working Man in Arms," pp. 336–52, and Peter Simkens, "The War Experience of a Typical Kitchener Division – the 18th Division," pp. 297–313, both in Cecil and Little (eds.), *Facing Armageddon*.

36 Smith, *Between Mutiny and Obedience*, pp. 37, 88–89, 183, 202, 225.

37 Watson, *Enduring the Great War*, pp. 234, 136, 108–39.

38 Christian Stachelbeck, *Militärische Effektivität im Ersten Weltkrieg: Die 11. Bayerische Infanterie 1915–1918* (Paderborn: Schöningh, 2010), pp. 334–45. See also Scott Stephenson, *The Final Battle: Soldiers on the Western Front and the German Revolution of 1918* (Cambridge University Press, 2009), pp. 17–66.

39 Watson, *Enduring the Great War*, pp. 210–11, 230–31.

40 Geyer, "How the Germans Learned to Wage War," p. 45.

41 Boris Barth, *Dolchstoßlegenden und politische Desintegration: Das Trauma der deutschen Niederlage im ersten Weltkrieg 1914–1933* (Düsseldorf: Droste, 2003); Wolfgang Schivelbusch, *The Culture of Defeat: On National Trauma, Mourning, and Recovery* (New York: Metropolitan, 2001), pp. 205–08.

42 Mosse, *Fallen Soldiers*, p. 7.

43 Siegfried Wegeleben, *Das Felderlebnis: Eine Untersuchung seiner Entwicklung, seines Wesens und seiner Bedeutung* (Berlin: Furche-Verlag, 1921), pp. 25–26, 35–36, 105–09.

44 Ernst Jünger, *The Storm of Steel: From the Diary of a German Storm-Troop Officer on the Western Front* (New York: Howard Fertig, 1975), pp. 39, 173.

45 Ernst Jünger, *Der Kampf als inneres Erlebnis* (Berlin: Mittler, 1922), pp. 21–22, 26; Jünger, *Das Wäldchen 125: Eine Chronik aus den Grabenkämpfen 1918*, 3rd edn. (Berlin: Mittler; 1928), p. 239; Jünger, *In Stahlgewittern: Aus dem Tagebuch eines Stosstruppführers* (Berlin: E. S. Mittler, 1922), p. 94. Contrary to many scholarly legends (e.g. Mosse, *Fallen Soldiers*, pp. 79–80), Jünger did not pioneer the myth of frontline community in the 1920s but instead mitigated the solipsistic nature of his warrior figure with the increasingly popular myth of comradeship only in the later revisions (and English translations) of his famous fictional memoir, as Eva Dempewolf has shown in *Blut und Tinte: Eine Interpretation der verschiedenen Fassungen von Ernst Jüngers Kriegstagebüchern vor dem politischen Hintergrund der Jahre 1920 bis 1980* (Würzburg: Königshausen & Neumann 1992), 64–77; see also Ernst Jünger, *In Stahlgewittern: Historisch-kritische Ausgabe*, 2 vols., ed. Helmut Kiesel (Stuttgart: Klett-Cotta, 2013).

46 *Der Weisse Ritter*, 5 (1923), as facsimiled in Benno Hafeneger and Michael Fritz (eds.), *Wehrerziehung und Kriegsgedanke in der Weimarer Republik: Eine Lesebuch zur Kriegsbegeisterung junger Männer*, vol. II (Frankfurt: Brandes & Apsel, 1992), pp. 48–49. On Nietzsche's morality, see Simon May, *Nietzsche's Ethic and his War on Morality* (New York: Oxford University Press, 1999).

47 Bartov, *Mirrors of Destruction*, p. 20.

48 Ernst von Salomon, *The Outlaws* (London: Jonathan Cape, 1931), pp. 141, 66, 138, 261ff., 62–64, 342–46, 358ff., 420ff. German orig: *Die Geächteten* (Berlin: Rowohlt, 1931).

49 Sven Reichardt, "Vergemeinschaftung durch Gewalt: Das Beispiel des SA-'Mördersturms 33' in Berlin-Charlottenburg zwischen 1928 und 1932," in *Beiträge zur Geschichte der nationalsozialistischen Verfolgung in Norddeutschland*, 7 (2002), 20–36 (at pp. 23, 30).

50 Joseph Goebbels, *Das erwachende Berlin* (Berlin: Zentralverlag der NSDAP, 1934), p. 126, as quoted in Sven Reichardt, "Fascist Marches in Italy and Germany: Squadre and SA before the Seizure of Power," in Matthias Reiss (ed.), *The Street as Stage: Protest Marches and Public Rallies Since the Nineteenth Century* (Oxford University Press, 2007), pp. 169–89 (at 185); Reichardt, *Fachistische Kampfbünde: Gewalt und Gemeinschaft im italienischen Squadrismus und in der deutschen SA* (Cologne: Böhlau, 2002), pp. 406–75, 589–93.

51 Albrecht Erich Günther, "Kameradschaftslehre," *Deutsches Volkstum*, 16 (1934), 14; Günther, *Geist der Jungmannschaft* (Hamburg: Hanseatische Verlagsanstalt, 1934); Werner Elert, *Zur Geschichte des kriegerischen Ethos* (Leipzig: Deichert, 1928).

52 Erich Weniger, *Wehrmachtserziehung und Kriegserfahrung* (Berlin: Mittler, 1938), pp. 132–37, 142–44; Max Simoneit, *Wehrpsychologie: Ein Abriß ihrer Probleme und praktischen Folgerungen* (Berlin: Mittler, 1933), p. 125; Simoneit, "Wehrpsychologische Gedanken über den Angriffsgeist der Infanterie," *Militärwissenschaftliche Rundschau*, 3 (1938), pp. 547–56 (at 552–53).

53 Erich Ludendorff, *Der Totale Krieg* (Munich: Ludendorffs Verlag, 1935).

54 Max Simoneit, "Die allgemeine Wehrpflicht als psychologisches Problem," *Soldatentum*, 3 (1936), 58–62 (at pp. 58–59).

55 Carl Schmitt, *The Concept of the Political* (New Brunswick, NJ: Rutgers University Press, 1976; German orig. 1934), pp. 46ff. and 27. Why this

assessment is true in a more complex way than Schmitt, alluding to the legend of the stab in the back, put it, is explained in Thomas Kühne, "Todesraum: War, Peace, and the Experience of Mass Death, 1914–1945," in Helmut Walser Smith (ed.), *The Oxford Handbook of Modern German History* (Oxford University Press, 2011), pp. 527–47.

56 Werner Picht, *Der Frontsoldat* (Berlin: Herbig, 1937), pp. 31–39.

57 Raymond Dreiling, *Das religiöse und sittliche Leben der Armee unter dem Einfluss des Weltkriege* (Paderborn: F. Schöningh, 1922), pp. 39, 43–44, 50; Philipp Witkop (ed.), *Kriegsbriefe gefallener Studenten* (Munich: G. Müller, 1928), pp. 109–10, 83, 123, 244; cf. Ziemann, *War Experiences in Rural Germany*, pp. 93–94; Leed, *No Man's Land*, pp. 194–95. For oft-quoted accounts of the split personality of citizen-soldiers, see S. L. A. Marshall, *Men Against Fire: The Problem of Battle Command in Future War* (New York: Morrow, 1947), p. 78; and J. Glenn Gray, *The Warriors: Reflections on Men in Battle* (New York: Harcourt, Brace, 1959), p. 8, both commenting on Americans in World War II.

58 Dieter Riesenberger, *Geschichte der Friedensbewegung in Deutschland: Von den Anfängen bis 1933* (Göttingen: Vandenhoeck & Ruprecht, 1985), p. 134.

59 Hermann Paasche, *Meine Mitschuld am Weltkriege* (Berlin: Neues Vaterland, 1919), pp. 4–5. Cf. Lothar Wieland, "Vom kaiserlichen Offizier zum deutschen Revolutionär – Stationen der Wandlung des Kapitänleutnants Hans Paasche (1881–1920)," in Wolfram Wette (ed.), *Pazifistische Offiziere in Deutschland 1871–1933* (Bremen: Donat, 1999), pp. 169–79 (at 176).

60 James M. Diehl, *Paramilitary Politics in Weimar Germany* (Bloomington: Indiana University Press, 1977); Christopher James Elliott, *Ex-Servicemen's Organisations and the Weimar Republic*, Ph.D. dissertation, University of London (1971); Volker R. Berghahn, *Der Stahlhelm: Bund der Frontsoldaten 1918–1935* (Düsseldorf: Droste, 1966); Whalen, *Bitter Wounds*; Benjamin Ziemann, *Contested Commemorations: Republican War Veterans and Weimar Political Culture* (Cambridge University Press, 2013); Karl Rohe, *Das Reichsbanner Schwarz Rot Gold: Ein Beitrag zur Geschichte und Struktur der politischen Kampfverbände zur Zeit der Weimarer Republik* (Düsseldorf: Droste, 1966).

61 Figures: *Kyffhäuser*, July 5, 1936, p. 726, and Dieter Fricke (ed.), *Lexikon zur Parteiengeschichte: Die bürgerlichen und die kleinbürgerlichen Parteien und Verbände in Deutschland*, vol. III (Cologne: Pahl-Rugenstein, 1985), p. 326; Diehl, *Paramilitary Politics in Weimar Germany*, p. 294; Ziemann, *Contested Commemorations*, pp. 64–68.

62 Overmans, "Kriegsverluste," pp. 664–65.

63 *Stahlhelm*, Dec. 15, 1921, p. 345.

64 Schneider, *Lebensweisheit für Deutsche*, pp. 31–32.

65 Alex King, *Memorials of the Great War in Britain: The Symbolism and Politics of Remembrance* (Oxford: Berg, 1998), p. 176. Cf. Gabriel Koureas, *Memory, Masculinity and National Identity in British Visual Culture, 1914–1930: A Study of "Unconquerable Manhood"* (Aldershot: Ashgate, 2007), p. 135.

66 William Shakespeare, *Henry V*, act IV, scene iii, line 60, in *The Annotated Shakespeare*, vol. II, ed. A. L. Rowse (New York: Potter, 1978), p. 580.

67 Jessica Meyer, *Men of War: Masculinity and the First World War in Britain* (Basingstoke: Palgrave Macmillan, 2009), pp. 85, 145–46.

68 Douglas Higbee, "Constructions of Comradeship: Ivor Gurney and the British First World War Veterans' Movement," *Literature and Culture 1914–1945*, 4 (2008), 39–61 (at pp. 44, 46, 49–51). See Bryony Dixon and Laraine Porter, "'How Shall We Look Again?' Revisiting the Archive in British Silent Film and the Great War," in Michael Hammond and Michael Williams (eds.), *British Silent Cinema and the Great War* (Basingstoke: Palgrave Macmillan, 2011), pp. 170–85 (at 177) on Elvey's *Comradeship*.

69 Koureas, *Memory, Masculinity and National Identity*, pp. 21, 33, 47, 79, 81; Neil Hanson, *Unknown Soldiers: The Story of the Missing of the First World War* (New York: Knopf, 2006), pp. 305–41; Benjamin Ziemann, "Die deutsche Nation und ihr zentraler Erinnerungsort: Das 'Nationaldenkmal für die Gefallenen im Weltkriege' und die Idee des 'Unbekannten Soldaten' 1914–1935," in Helmut Berding, Klaus Heller, und Winfried Speitkamp (eds.), *Krieg und Erinnerung: Fallstudien zum 19. und 20. Jahrhundert* (Göttingen: Vandenhoeck & Ruprecht, 2000), pp. 67–92.

2   Coalescence

As with all myths, the myth of comradeship needed to be implemented and re-enacted to become true, not just retold and reiterated. Myths revolve around eternal truths – values, virtues, and wisdoms that never change. They are not just history but live in the present also. Myths, explains the anthropologist Victor Turner, "have ontological efficacy. They re-create or transform those to whom they are shown or told and alter" their capacity so that they become "capable of performing the tasks" that await them. The myth is "felt to have something akin to a salvic power." It does not offer choices, it does not invite debate, it "does not describe what ought to be done; it expresses what must be."[1] So the former World War I soldiers set about making it real. Each of its hundreds of thousands of members, claimed the social democratic Reichsbund in December 1918, would never forget "the one comrade who had rescued him from the line of fire when he was lost there helpless, his limbs destroyed," and would seek to renew the altruistic spirit of comradeship in the present by helping those in need.[2] Consequently, the veterans' associations established private social security systems to support their needy members, those comrades who struggled with re-adjusting to civilian life; special care was taken of the families of these comrades. Fund-raising events for them also included an important symbolic message. "Practicing comradeship by providing social security," said the *Kyffhäuser* news magazine in 1929, "gives the lie to the 'thoughtlessly spread untruth according to which the past war had brutalized people, dismissing them as being something like robbers and murderers.'"[3]

But extending comradeship from the past war to the postwar present meant more than demonstrating charity. It encompassed a political and social utopia, the vision of a German fatherland that had overcome the misery of the present and realized what the war had not been able to conclude: social unity and harmony. The veterans were destined to spearhead this utopia. "Factionalism, disruption, and malevolence has soaked our fatherland," bemoaned the Catholic priest to the Constance veterans' meeting in 1925, and the left-liberal mayor too lamented the "selfishness" that had spread like a plague in Germany since the end of the war, alluding to the social, ideological, and political antagonisms that divided the country. "We need," demanded the priest, "to steep and cleanse our whole public life in the spirit of comradeship." The Day of the 114th, the proof of war comradeship's continuous vitality, would show "the whole fatherland" the path out of the "unspeakable hardship" into which it had descended, announced the Constance mayor in his address to the assembly.[4]

The vision of a truly united nation had been on the political agenda of German conservatives and liberals since the turn of the century. The anonymous and splintered society characteristic of modernity was to be rebuilt as a community of shared concerns – the nation as family, a *Volksgemeinschaft*, a "people's community" that would pour warmth and harmony into the cold and disrupted national society. When the war started in August 1914, the "spirit of 1914" seemed to sweep away the splintered atmosphere. The Social Democratic Party supported the Reichstag's request for war loans and abandoned its previous opposition to the monarchy's authoritarian nation-state. Thus, the *Burgfrieden* – the truce, a "peace within the fortress" – was established. But the grand national consensus proved to be a chimera. It could not overcome ineradicable social and economic conflicts but rather deepened them both in the army and in civilian society. In 1918 the frustration of the socialist working class and its party leaders about the unwillingness of the monarchy to yield to their reform program led to the revolution and even tougher class and party struggles.[5]

Yet the idea of creating a united nation through war did not die. Quite the opposite. The *Burgfrieden* may not have lasted at the home front but it did so in the frontline communities and in the army at large, claimed the soldiers. Contrary to the disillusionment experienced and admitted even by proud war volunteers and advocates of the nationalist agenda, such as Franz Schauwecker, vocal veterans claimed that the front army, united by a common enemy and unimaginable hardship, and not least by a sense of being abandoned by both the rear army and the home front, had bridged the cleavages and class gaps of civilian society in the spirit of comradeship. Remarkably, Schauwecker himself became one of the most vociferous advocates of this idea. "Ploughing through the flaming seas of war," the soldiers embodied "Germany in exile," he wrote.[6] Germany, in other words, no longer existed at home but only, in a spiritual way, in the trenches and on the battlefields. Schauwecker, in his influential book *Aufbruch der Nation* (1930), or "Advent of the Nation" (English title: *The Furnace*) wrote even more emphatically about the uniting experience of shellfire: "Now where it's life or death, where we squelch in filth and lie under fire and share mud, lice, bread and poverty – now at least we are really together . . . Here we have it, unity, whose sense we shall never lose, unique unity – the nation."[7]

In this fashion, as the epitome of a spiritual nation, frontline comradeship was invoked on the Day of the 114th. The long list of fallen soldiers of the 114th regiment, which named members of the aristocracy, the middle class, the working class, and rural society, seemed to prove that civilian antagonisms had not mattered in the soldiers' community.[8] The solidarity they had practiced on a daily basis, their comradeship, had ignored class antagonisms and military hierarchies, claimed the veterans.

The Day of the 114th was to demonstrate that this unity could indeed be renewed in the present, as the welcome note suggested: "Just as we ignore different origins, classes, and ranks today and treat all of them equally, so you shall do this in your everyday lives in the future: Ignore the differences, remain good comrades, never to be divided by whatever hardship or danger you might face, and value your fatherland, our German Reich and its people over anything else!" As its conveners and supporters saw it, the assembly was the veritable nucleus of a *future* grand *Volksgemeinschaft*, performing social harmony among men – former soldiers – whatever strata or sections of society they belonged to.

Indeed many observers, especially from local newspapers, enthusiastically confirmed that "weather-beaten peasants from the Black Forest, together with their wives and children," stood "next to city slickers and small-towners." In the same way, regional differences no longer mattered. "All kinds of accents, from north to south of Germany, could be heard, and all of these people got along well with each other – they all enjoyed hearty comradeship." Even the deepest political gulf dividing Germany – that between supporters and opponents of the Weimar Republic as a democratic state – seemed to be bridged. Other public gatherings often saw disputes over which flag to hoist – the black, red, and gold of the Weimar Republic, or the black, white, and red of the past *Kaiserreich*. While the former stood not only for democracy and parliamentary rule but also for a foreign policy that accepted the Versailles Treaty and embraced peace and reconciliation in Europe, the latter represented the rightists' and conservatives' hatred of exactly this agenda, and their desire to rebuild an authoritarian state, to overthrow the Versailles Treaty, and to arm for a future war to undo the defeat of 1918. But on the Day of the 114th both flags were flying "peacefully together."[9] And significantly, two soldiers were on sentry guard in front of the chapel: One wore the uniform of the old monarchical army, the other one the uniform of the new republican army.[10]

Paralleling antagonistic political ideologies and social identities is not the same as harmonizing them, however. The Day of the 114th did not introduce a common flag or uniform for both camps. What it did do was to stage some kind of truce between the rivals. It was a restricted truce. The official speakers represented only three of the four major political parties of the country and also the region: Mayor Moericke was a liberal, actually a left-liberal; the Reverend Schaack stood for the Catholic Center Party; and General Fölkersamb was a conservative. But no speaker from the Social Democratic Party had been invited, although a fifth of the Constance voters were faithful to it, nor one from the leftist veterans' association Reichsbanner Schwarz Rot Gold.

The people's community in miniature, which the Day of the 114th claimed to be, did not fully reflect the nation. Rather, it concealed the far-reaching antagonism between the social democratic working class and the liberal or conservative middle classes on the subject of the reality of comradeship in the past war. Mayor Moericke and General Fölkersamb believed that a relation of mutual trust had united officers and privates in the past and that this relationship was a cornerstone of any kind of comradeship. As one officer explained, "among real comrades," social status or military rank didn't count. But, he added, there was no comradeship and no joint action without "unconditional trust" between "leader and followers."[11] In this view, the future *Volksgemeinschaft* should have a strong paternalistic component as well.

Speaking on behalf of the rank-and-file soldiers, the Social Democrats begged to differ. As they saw it, the "fine title of 'comrade'" was only employed by the "so-called comrades" who as officers had found ways of tormenting their subordinates and treating them like "pigs" on the parade ground, and often "financially exploiting" them too. Hiding in the rear, these pseudo-comrades had made fortunes during the war and could easily remember it as a cheerful event.[12] What bothered the Social Democrats even more was the idea of using this kind of comradeship as a model for a German *Volksgemeinschaft*. They offered telling numbers to illustrate the present "reality" of comradeship. In 1924, they calculated, the German state had spent 848 million marks on pensions for former soldiers of the "old army." And although the number of these pensioners naturally decreased from year to year, the total amount spent on them was to rise in 1925 by another 286 million marks. This amount alone, just like the share of the retired officers alone (250 million marks), was more than the total amount granted to those disabled by the war (217 million marks). "On balance," the Social Democrats explained, "47,000 healthy and mostly wealthy officers get more in benefits than 766,000 invalids."[13] Consequently, they took a rather dim view of the comradely rhetoric and also of veterans' summits such as the one in 1925. For a long time, the Social Democrats had mocked at the "ballyhoo" of the regimental days and castigated it as cheap attempts to "polish up" militarist attitudes and crypto-absolutist ideas which had, in the view of the Social Democrats, governed imperial Germany and driven it into the disastrous war. In the eyes of the Social Democrats, the 1925 veterans' assembly was but a "demonstration against the republic."[14]

The Day of the 114th, however, was not designed to stage dissent but consent and harmony. The Catholic Center Party, which was located somewhere in the middle between rightists and leftists, therefore took an ambivalent position. On the one hand, it complained – although less sharply than the social democratic press – about "the superiors, who, unfortunately, in Germany's toughest time were no comrades of their underlings." Yet the Center press was taken by the idea of building a *Volksgemeinschaft* based on soldierly comradeship. "Some former officers," the Center press reported enthusiastically, "mingled with their previous rankers and talked to them just as if they were simple comrades. What could be seen here was in fact the long desired Volksgemeinschaft *en miniature*."[15]

In the 1930s, *Volksgemeinschaft* would become the code word for the Nazi utopia of an ideologically united and racially cleansed German nation, one without Jews. The Nazis, however, did not invent this loaded concept. It had appeared before 1914 and was then popularized during and after the war. Fusing two emotionally heavily loaded concepts, *Volk*, or people, and *Gemeinschaft*, or community, this code word exuded the warmth of the family and extended it into the realm of the nation. What that meant in terms of political constitution, class relations, foreign policy, and so on, was however not determined. Rather, the concept served different political camps to address a common desire somehow to overcome the misery of the present and its political, social, and ideological antagonisms. Amorphous as it was, it adhered even to the democratic parties. They tied it in to the existing pluralistic society and parliamentary constitution, relied especially on the welfare state to ease class conflicts, and sought to combine the vision of harmony within the nation with the idea of harmony between the nations. *Volksgemeinschaft*, people's community, and *Völkergemeinschaft*, peoples' community – the idea pursued by the League of the Nations – belonged together, the republicans said. The rightist political camps in Germany were driven by the opposite idea of *Volksgemeinschaft*. For them, its substance was not democracy but dictatorship (or monarchy), not welfare state but ideological uniformity, and not international reconciliation but preparing for war to undo the Versailles Treaty.[16]

In 1925, the *Volksgemeinschaft* did not yet figure prominently in the political agenda of the Nazis, and even less was it tethered to a genocidal program. Antisemitism was omnipresent in Weimar Germany anyway, especially in the rural areas and small towns, and wherever rightist and militarist groups dominated. During the war, the infamous *Judenzählung*, or Jews Count, had indicated the beginning of a new era of antisemitism, now officially sanctioned by the government. Although Jewish German soldiers often still enjoyed comradely relationships with their gentile fellows, and continued to do so as veterans in Weimar Germany, antisemitic policies and membership statutes found their way into the veterans' associations, most prominently the Stahlhelm. Local branches of the Kyffhäuserbund observed less consistent rules, reflecting the regional diversity of Germany's political landscape.[17] The veterans' associations of Constance in 1925 followed the antisemitic line of other groups. In a way, their *Volksgemeinschaft en miniature* strikingly anticipated the racist *Volksgemeinschaft* the Nazis established nationwide from 1933 on. Jews were not welcome at the Day of the 114th, at least not in prominent roles. While former army chaplains, both Protestant and Catholic, naturally gave commemorative addresses, the assembly committee rudely denied this honor to their Jewish counterpart, Rabbi Chrone, notwithstanding the fact that Jewish Germans had served in the Baden regiment, that almost half of the German Jewish soldiers had been decorated for bravery, that Jewish soldiers had died on the battlefield alongside their gentile comrades, and that Jewish veterans felt comradely just as non-Jews did.[18]

The fights about comradeship in the past war and the lessons to be drawn from it did not stop in 1925. In the following year, the Baden section of the Reichsbanner called for a Day of the Republicans in Constance that was to counter and to dwarf the Day of the 114th. Known for its long liberal tradition, Constance was the perfect place for such an event; in 1848 it had been a center of the democratic revolution in Germany. This tradition was to be revived at the Day of the Republicans. Its speakers presented the democratic "spirit of 1848" as an alternative to the nationalist "spirit of 1914" that had been conjured up at the veterans' meeting the year before. Remarkably, however, the Day of the Republicans did not renounce the symbolism of the past war. By holding a field service, a commemoration, and a banner dedication, the republicans demonstrated that they honored both the soldiers who had sacrificed their lives on behalf of the nation and the values of a nation in arms. The head of the Center party in Baden, Monsignor Schofer, reminded the audience in his ceremonial sermon of the *miles Christi*, the epitome of the virtuous fighter for a holy cause, which historically had been the Christian faith, and could now be understood as the *Volksgemeinschaft*, the domestic peace of the German nation. Free of any "egoism" – in the political language of interwar Germany this was a synonym for class consciousness and partisanship, the antonym to *Volksgemeinschaft* – the *miles Christi* bequeathed one thing more than anything else: "comradeship," which, as Schofer explained, was exactly "what the Holy Scripture calls charity." As a matter of course, the song of "The Good Comrade" concluded the ceremony. As the Reichsbanner explained, this song was misused if deployed for the glorification of nationalism and violence. Overall, the Day of Republicans also celebrated a unified fatherland filled with the spirit of comradeship: This was, however, not with a future war in view, but rather to foster international reconciliation.[19]

Despite its ambitious goals and splendid enactment, the demonstration on behalf of the republic was meek. Ten thousand participants had been expected; eleven thousand had attended the Day of the 114th. But the republican gathering attracted only three thousand. The local battalion of the Reichswehr, the overtly anti-democratic army of the democratic state, abstained from honoring this assembly. Even the liberal media took a reserved attitude and only noted that the Reichsbanner had done a good job in bridging internal social gaps but wasn't and wouldn't be able to reconcile the platforms of the three political parties that supported it. In other words: The Constance liberals were enthused by the militarist *Volksgemeinschaft* utopia but kept their own democratic version at a safe distance from it.[20]

War memories in Constance remained disputed until the downfall of the first German republic. Around Christmas 1927, the Reichsbanner produced a veritable scandal by enacting a show that bitterly ridiculed the officers' debaucheries during the war. As the 114th veterans' association complained in a memorandum to the mayor, "the former officers have been slurred in the most embarrassing way. For instance, one tableau vivant showed a storm attack. While the foreground was filled with dead or injured privates, the officers meanwhile enjoyed a revelry in a rear fortress, together with a bunch of sluts!" This provocation would not be forgotten years later when the city council tried to build at least a tiny bridge over the gaps between pro- and anti-republican war memories. For many years, the two camps had had been unable to agree on commemorating the fallen soldiers on All Saints' Day together at the local cemetery. Rather, the social democratic war victims' associations held their ceremony in the morning hours, whereas the afternoon was reserved for the conservative groups. When the city council tried changing at least this absurdity, both the conservatives and the leftists refused to compromise.[21]

Rightists and leftists, nationalists and socialists, bellicists and pacifists, militarists and antimilitarists clashed throughout the Weimar era and all over Germany over the proper way to commemorate the past war and to take the right lessons from it. Collective memory was deeply divided in Germany. In fact, Weimar politics was shaped by a multiplicity of competing parties, associations, and ideologies. The socialist working-class movement had fallen apart in the war. The communists, adhering to the Soviet dictatorship, and the Social Democrats (SPD), deeply rooted in the concept of parliamentary democracy, found barely any basis for collaboration. Despite deep differences in cultural, welfare, and economic politics, the mostly agnostic Social Democrats partnered with the mostly Protestant left liberals (DDP) and the Catholic Center Party in defending the democratic republic decisively against the Right as well as the extreme Left. At the more conservative end of the political spectrum, the rightist counterpart to the left liberals, the pro-republican German People's Party (DVP) and the anti-republican, mostly monarchist German National People's Party (DNVP) promoted big business and landed interest but disagreed on foreign politics.

Notwithstanding these and other complexities und nuances, the political and ideological landscape was shaped by dichotomies, and so was the collective memory of the Great War. Labels such as leftists, republicans, pacifists, and antimilitarists on the one hand refer to the SPD, the DDP, or the Center Party, although the latter was also the political home of rather conservative Germans. The leftists defended the democratic constitution, worked on reconciliation in Europe, especially with France, and considered only diplomatic but not military revisions of the Versailles Treaty. They included radical as well as moderate pacifists, the latter accepting defensive wars. Analyzing the causes of and responsibility for the Great War, they blamed the old political elites in imperial Germany and social militarism. Labels such as rightists, militarists, or nationalists on the other hand refer to the DVP, the DNVP, and also the Nazis; these parties and their voters disdained the democratic constitution and international reconciliation, craved the revival of a powerful, belligerent, united, and authoritarian, monarchist, or dictatorial Germany, and wanted to overthrow the Versailles Treaty militarily. The defeat in 1918 was considered a result of the alleged "stab in the back" of the otherwise victorious German army, executed by a conspiracy of socialists, Jews, and women at the home front.[22]

However, not even rightist war memory simply glorified the lost world of Wilhelmine authoritarianism. The monarchy had too obviously failed to honor the millions of ordinary soldiers who had to sacrifice life and limb just as much – in fact more than – the well-offs while being denied equal suffrage in many constituencies, most obviously in Prussia. Whatever they thought about Weimar's parliamentary democracy, nationalists could not ignore the democratic dynamic the battlefields of the Great War had unleashed. Franz Schauwecker even spoke of "democracy" as a "manifestation" of the war. This "sovereign democracy of front soldiers," however, was not one of voters, demagogues, and party officials but of loyal comrades and charismatic leaders. As Wilhelm Ritter von Schramm, a friend of Ernst Jünger, explained, this democracy was embedded in a "hierarchy based on feats and real merits," not based on birthright or on insignia. Just as equal societies of "free men" had done in ancient times, this "legislative" community selected its leaders autonomously, free of any formal or written procedures, driven only by the "mystery" of trust and loyalty, and it dismissed them if they were no good. The leader was the one "who embodied the essence and the spirit of comradeship best." Born out of comradeship, he also engendered comradeship.[23]

Obviously, this idea of a frontline community led by charismatic leaders reflected the ideological world of rising fascism rather than the reality of the past war, although some junior combat officers had indeed relied on mutual trust instead of formal discipline to fuel the fighting morale of their troops. The myth of comradeship, however, presented these leaders as the rule rather than the exception. A charismatic leader par excellence and the epitome of a comradely lieutenant, Walter Flex's Wurche transcended the frozen caste mentality of the Wilhelmine officer corps. He knew that "discipline was a matter of course" if "one owned the hearts of his men." And Wurche was only one of the many comradely leaders that populated war memory after 1918. Even when badly injured, the comradely officer stayed on the battlefield until the last of his men was carried to the casualty station. And vice versa. Soldiers never hesitated to sacrifice themselves for their superiors, according to the myth. Melting into their platoons, officers like Wurche did not need formal authority to secure obedience. They were sure of unconditional loyalty.[24]

As we have seen, Wurche transcended the class boundaries of civilian society and thus anticipated what would later become a key characteristic of the nationalist version of the myth of comradeship. Note that not even nationalist war memory simply denied Germany's social antagonisms before and during the war. Rather, it stressed the diversity of social backgrounds of the soldiers in order to narrate the social harmony in the frontline communities as the result of a learning process. The myth of comradeship showed how soldiers had healed, and been healed from, those civilian social conflicts. In the myth, civilian selves, mired in class conflicts, managed to overcome their individualities, egoisms, or class identities as soldiers and eventually merged into the entirety of the soldierly community, the nucleus of the ideal nation.[25]

One of these success stories, presented by a Stahlhelm veteran, and former NCO, was about the comradely purification of a working-class soldier named Mahlert. Mahlert, the NCO remembered, had always been a defiant "man of somber temper," a typical member of the socialist movement, in other words. Empathetic as the comradely veteran was, he knew that only "hard drudgery in a brick manufacture and painful worries about his family" had made Mahlert so stubborn. But he changed, thanks to the war and to comradeship. When Mahlert was heavily wounded in battle, his NCO risked his own life to bandage and to save the life of his man. The wages of this act of altruism would soon be paid. "When his lust for life revived, Mahlert's heart and lips overflowed with gratefulness to his saviour." The experience of a comradeship "that had saved him from death quickened his faith in humankind" and cured him from proletarian stubbornness and class egoism.[26]

Stories like this "proved" the myth of comradeship. They showed that the experience of comradeship in war healed civilian antagonism and leveled the way to a truly united German fatherland. Just as the Constance Day of the 114th did, nationalist veterans rehearsed the *Volksgemeinschaft*, even if only *en miniature*. In a sense, this claim was well based. When their local branches met – weekly, monthly, or whenever – for their internal meetings, at the pub (the *Stammtisch*), or for a public gathering, people of different or even antagonistic sections of society came together, craftsmen and clerks, peasants and businessmen, white- and blue-collar workers, businessmen and teachers, members of the old and the new middle classes, of the upper and the lower classes, of urban and rural society. People with different ideological, cultural, and political identities, conservatives and liberals, Catholics and Protestants (sometimes even Jews) met and established an egalitarian sociability. The boozy cosiness of the veterans' movement generated islands of social harmony – in the midst of a sea of political fights and class conflicts.[27]

One might argue, and in fact contemporary critics did argue, that this kind of social harmony was limited to those parts of German society that had already managed to get along with each other before 1914 – in essence, the middle classes. Hence, the touchstone of the veterans' claim to represent the entire German nation was the working class, especially the socialist majority of it. The Stahlhelm boasted that workers – a vague category, of course – made up as much as 50 percent or even more of its membership. More realistic estimates give about 10 percent. Stick and carrot helped to attract even Social Democrats. Employers threatened to fire workers if they didn't join the Stahlhelm, or offered jobs if they did, and the Stahlhelm's welfare and charity program promised to support families (of members) in need. In the view of the nationalist middle classes, this type of paternalism did not contradict the ideal of a harmonious *Volksgemeinschaft*, which would in any case rely on authoritarian elements – the charismatic leaders. Instead, each single blue-collar worker who joined the nationalist movement seemed to prove the harmonious potential of "comradeship in the present" and the prospect of overcoming social antagonisms.[28] And even leftist critics of the Stahlhelm understood what it meant for a turner or a farm laborer to be asked to take a seat next to his boss at the *Stammtisch*, or to march in the same line as him. Eventually, the *Volksgemeinschaft* envisioned would not foster individual political rights, including individual franchise, but would create unity through symbolic political participation in mass marches and mass gatherings. Hence, the veterans' "comradely" sociability was a foretaste of what was to come from 1933 on: the absorption of the individual into the community.[29]

It was not only the veterans' movement that anticipated the *Volksgemeinschaft*. Some entrepreneurs did so as well when they tried to translate the model of the comradely officer in war into a new leadership style in their factories. Karl Arnhold, for instance, the founder of the German Institute for Technical Worker Training (Deutsches Institut für technische Arbeitsschulung, or Dinta), asked that "the spirit of comradeship" be transferred "into the companies."[30] As junior officers, entrepreneurs like Hans Constantin Paullsen (a leading aluminum industrialist in the Third Reich) had learned to spur their troops before, during, and after the battle, and at the end of the war they may have even prevented them from deserting, mutinying, or revolting, by renouncing social arrogance, by demonstrating paternalism and care, by empathetic leadership.[31] Now, a comradely, harmonious, trustful "company community" was to replace strikes and unions, often both vilified as social "egoism," and to prevent workers from making "absurd demands" and from railing against the employer "just because the latter is more affluent."[32]

Similarly, various strands of Weimar's youth culture worked toward the *Volksgemeinschaft* utopia by appropriating the myth of comradeship. Elderly representatives of the prewar youth associations established the voluntary labor service and labor camp movement in order to bring together the youth of antagonistic social classes. Just like recruits in the military, boys would be separated from the rest of society to absorb the ideals of an alternative, more harmonious, allegedly egalitarian, comradely social organization. Working-class and middle-class youth came together in camps to work hard on communal projects, to relax in team activities, and to take part in reconciliatory round-table talks between former class "enemies," thus staging the envisioned *Volksgemeinschaft*. In fact, rival political parties collaborated to support the labor service program, suggesting that the idea of extending the past frontline comradeship into the present and thus preparing the ground for establishing a grand national *Volksgemeinschaft* was not just a chimera.[33]

Typically, pacifists, socialists, and left liberals took a different stance, mistrusting the nationalist idea of using past war experience, especially cross-class comradeship, as a model to reorganize present politics and society. Extending frontline unity into a *Volksgemeinschaft* was all too obviously meant to destroy the very idea of a democratic republic and pluralistic society that was the only positive result of the war, in the view of many leftists. Particularly embarrassing to them was the claim that there had been widespread comradeship between men and officers in war. Such comradeship had occurred only rarely, if at all, proclaimed Kurt Tucholsky, a prominent leftist journalist, in 1919, merely expressing what most worker-soldiers probably knew all too well.[34] One of them was Fritz Einert, a former private. After the war he worked as a clerk for a hardware factory in Thuringia and was a member of both the SPD and the Reichsbanner. Just like the simple worker before and after the war, he argued in a memoir, the enlisted man in wartime was an "object of exploitation." While an officer cadet, who had no clue about the war, wasted his generous salary in the officers' casino, the proletarian soldier risked life and limb in the mud of the trenches but would barely be compensated at all.[35] The historian Martin Hobohm relied on testimonies like this when he submitted to the Reichstag in 1929 a detailed account of the "army's social misery as a reason for the German breakdown in 1918." His assessment was designed to rebut the legend of the stab in the back, arguing that the breakdown was not the result of socialist agitation but of massive discrimination against ordinary soldiers.[36]

Leftist war memory, whether preserved in private recollections, deployed in political propaganda, or appropriated by popular culture, never stopped castigating the rightist claim of comradeship between officers and men in war. Most popularly, a broad range of antimilitarist war novels, including Heinrich Wandt's *Rear Area Gent* (*Etappe Gent*, 1921), Theodor Plivier's *The Kaiser's Coolies* (*Des Kaisers Kulis*, 1929), Erich Maria Remarque's *All Quiet on the Western Front* (*Im Westen nichts Neues*, 1929), Ernst Johannsen's *Four from the Infantry* (*Vier von der Infanterie*, 1929), and Adam Scharrer's *Unpatriotic Companions* (*Vaterlandslose Gesellen*, 1930), satirized the officers' aristocratic arrogance, their casino debauchery, and their greed for medals of honor.[37]

But leftist war memory, whether fictionalized or presented as authentic testimony, did not simply refute the myth of comradeship between

officer and men. It also produced a counter-myth. One must not forget
the officers' continuous breaking of the "unwritten rules of comradeship" and their gourmandizing at the expense of their hungry comrades,
proclaimed the *Reichsbanner* journal. Such people weren't worth being
called comrades anyway, the journal added. They and their phony attitude contrasted sharply with "real comrades" and real comradeship.[38]
Both featured in Adam Scharrer's war novel *Unpatriotic Companions*.
Drafted soldiers from the socialist working class demonstrated what "real
comradeship" was about – and what it was not. The novel mocked a lieutenant who would share a piece of sausage with his men only "when the
shells exploded above our heads" and would stop displaying this kind of
comradeship "as soon as we were off the beaten track" so that "the have-
nots, the proletarians once again had nothing to eat but dry bread," and
it described comradeship in war as "the greatest lie ever." And yet it conjured up a different type of comradeship, the one practiced by doomed
men, the proletarian soldiers. While under fire, one of the novel's proletarian anti-heroes, Daimler, fetches a box his loved ones had sent him just
the day before – and performs a classic ritual of comradeship. The skillfully finished wooden box contains three full glasses of schnapps which
Daimler naturally shares with his two proletarian-comrades. As soon as
they have gulped down their respective portions, Daimler is killed in
action, together with one of his comrades.[39]

The leftist myth of comradeship did not merely confine soldierly solidarity to the ordinary soldiers but rather filled it with a new meaning. While vertical comradeship in rightist stories served to fuel combat
morale, the leftist counter-myth gave birth to comradeship only in the
proletarian soldiers' "mutually shared sense of enmity against the war"
and the "warmongers" – the officers, that is.[40] In Ernst Johannsen's
1929 anti-war novel *Four from the Infantry* (which gave rise to the popular film *Westfront 1918* in 1930) none of the four comrades sought to
prove themselves heroic or anything of that kind. They simply wanted
to survive. To them, comradeship was the virtue of mutual protection,
not so much against the enemy across the lines but against those within
their own army, the officers. In this novel, comradeship translates into
solidarity among equals against the superiors and took drastic measures
when necessary. So the group decide to shoot a sergeant who had driven
an anxious private into the battle by threatening him with summary execution. A new member of the group takes over the subversive act of
"officercide" in order to be "considered worthy their comradeship."[41]

Alluding to socialist and communist traditions of international
working-class solidarity against capitalist exploiters, this type of comradeship included even the proletarian soldiers on the opposite side of

the trenches, according to the counter-myth. Most prominently, Remarque's famous anti-war novel rehearsed the fraternization of German and French soldiers against the warmongers on both sides. Facing a Russian POW, Remarque's boyish anti-hero, Paul Bäumer, who had volunteered for the army as a high-school student, is shocked, feels pity for the enemy, and shares his cigarettes with the POW rather than with one of his own troop. Later, Bäumer is hiding in a bomb shell-hole under fire when a French soldier suddenly drops in. Frightened, Paul stabs him. The enemy, gurgling endlessly, dies slowly. Paul has but one desire – "to get away" from that "dark figure." Ongoing machine-gun fire outside prevents him from jumping out. He is condemned to stay with a human being he has just killed. Hours pass. Suddenly the enemy-victim's eyes open and paralyze the perpetrator. Paul realizes his victim is not just any anonymous soldier, but an individual who had hopes and dreams of his own. Paul has killed all that. A person named Gerard Duval who had a wife and a daughter. Paul looks for the deadly wound, but there is nothing more to do than to whisper: "'I want to help you, Comrade, camerade, camerade, camerade' – eagerly repeating the word" – even in French – "to make him understand." When the Frenchman finally dies, Paul feels guilty: "Comrade, I did not want to kill you . . . Forgive me, comrade; how could you be my enemy? If we threw away these rifles and this uniform you could be my brother just like Kat and Albert."[42]

Fritz von Unruh, a former officer who had converted to pacifism, and a prominent member of the Reichsbanner, hailed this scene in a book review as "the gamete of a new community that will enable the nation, the people, the peoples to eventually build their real league of nations."[43] In fact, the birth of a "real" league of nations out of the spirit of a "comradeship in time of need and death" had been proclaimed before in order to establish a mythical ground for rapprochement between former German servicemen and their French and British equivalents.[44] The myth of reconciliation of enemies on the battlefield as depicted in Remarque's novel – and it certainly was a mythical inflation of extremely rare events in the reality of the war – supported the diplomatic reconciliation that had led to the Treaties of Locarno and to Germany's admission to the League of Nations. At the end of the 1920s, the "spirit of Locarno" needed such endorsement, as it stood on shaky ground. Gustav Stresemann, its German diplomatic promoter, died in 1929, without a successor in sight. Efforts of the leftist servicemen's associations to establish solid relationships with either their French or British counterparts were unsuccessful. In 1930 a grand reunion of German and French war veterans on the battlefields of Versailles, prepared for a long time and broadly advertised, fizzled out, much to the delight of the rightist veterans'

movement who had for some time viewed with suspicion the populariza-
tion of an antimilitarist and pacifist myth of comradeship.[45]

Yet the rightists did not stop worrying about Remarque's enormous
success which seemed to "plant an insurmountable horror of any kind of
soldiering in the hearts of adolescents," i.e. the future officers and troops
whose war enthusiasm was needed if the future war were to be won.[46]
Remarque's novel and the movie adaptation spread the pacifist reinter-
pretation of the comradeship myth most popularly but they were not the
only works to do so. Fictionalizing the 1906 mine disaster in the French-
German border town Courrières, G. W. Pabst's movie *Comradeship* conquered the hearts of German filmgoers in 1931 by extending the myth
of comradeship between German and French workers into the civilian
realm. Generously digressing from the historical truth, the movie shows
German workers rescuing their French miner comrades (in fact, the
mine *owners* had initiated the rescue) and eventually pledging to mutually respect each other in the spirit of comradeship – and to renounce
war once and forever. While this demonstration of the "unbreakable
comradeship" of the working classes beyond borders enthused the socialist press, the *Völkischer Beobachter* articulated the embarrassment of the
entire nationalist camp: Propagating the "solidarity of the nations" was
incommensurate with the "idea of comradeship."[47]

Such polemic only encouraged the Reichsbanner to further deploy
the idea of comradeship for a culture of reconciliation. In spring 1932
the association was admitted, in a "comradely" spirit, to the French-
dominated Ciamac, the international frontline soldiers' union, and a few
months later, a formal reunion of German and French veterans in Dijon
demonstrated the spearhead role of the working class in further spreading
the spirit of Locarno, and the crucial impact of the (counter-) myth of
comradeship, according to the leftist press. As one reporter claimed, it
was the personal exchange of war memories about trench fraternization
and the enthusiastic reception of the German anti-war movies *All Quiet
on the Western Front* and *Westfront 1918* in France that had made the
veterans' reconciliation possible.[48]

Indeed, the German anti-war movies landed on fertile soil in France.
French war memory revolved around comradeship, or brotherhood, as
it did in Germany. As the French historian Antoine Prost has said, in
post-World War I France too "all accounts of the war elaborated [on] the
theme of the brotherhood of the trenches. This was the norm," and "bad
comradeship" was remembered as an exception. As in Germany, "anec-
dotes of comrades rescued at the risk of one's own life were innumerable,
and daily life appeared to have been threaded through with copious inci-
dents of mutual care: sharing parcels or 'grog' wine, water or tobacco,

all the consolations of men prone to *le cafard*," as the French say when addressing anxieties, depressions, and worrisome moods.[49] In France as in Germany, veterans and society at large were helped to cope with their traumatic experiences of physical destruction, emotional depravation, and moral transgression by the notion of a sentimentalized or idealized, allegedly omnipresent, hallowed comradeship as the epitome of humanity. As with leftist and pacifist war remembrance in Germany, the myth of comradeship in France was embedded in a vision of international reconciliation and peace as the one lesson to be taken from the war. With rightist, fascist, and bellicose circles in France never gaining the power they had in Germany, French war remembrance followed the pacifist and reconciliatory line suggested during the war in Henri Barbusse's enormously popular novel *Under Fire* (1916). This novel describes the destructive panorama of mass slaughter in the trenches in order to unfold a socialist utopia of overcoming war and securing social fairness and peace throughout the world. The French veterans insisted on "their right and duty to fight against war, having seen its true face and realized its inhumanity." Rather than glorifying a past battle community and prolonging it into the present and future, French veterans memorialized a community of suffering, "unified by common pain and sorrow, bound together by horror, determined to prevent wars from ever happening again," thus envisioning a future without international conflict.[50]

Looking abroad, German leftists saw their own myth of comradeship endorsed. They easily detected more commonalities with their former French enemies than with their rightist fellow citizens in Germany. Truth was, however, that bellicose and pacifist veterans shared some common ground as well. The leftist myth of comradeship in Germany – and in France, for that matter – produced continuity where contingency ruled, as did its rightist counterpart. Both built continuity from the past to the present and onward to the future. The differences between the two lay in the type of continuity they envisioned. The rightist myth glorified a battle community fueled by mutual care between officers and men with various civilian identities, thus anticipating a grand *Volksgemeinschaft* that would overcome its internal antagonisms and be united by charismatic leaders and their loyal followers. By contrast, the leftist myth told of a past community in distress driven by the solidarity of peace-loving worker-soldiers on either side of the front lines. They fought their respective belligerent superiors, extended international class struggle into the battlefields of the Great War, and anticipated the agenda of the League of the Nations.

And there was even more common ground between rightist and leftist myths of comradeship. Both endowed the front soldiers' altruism and charity with a sacred aura. "Is there anything more beautiful, more holy in this world than selflessly given comradeship?" asked the social democratic *Reichsbund* journal in 1929, when Remarque's anti-war novel praised comradeship as "the finest thing that arose out of the war."[51] And so pacifist readers such as von Unruh felt reminded of Psalm 31:15 by Remarque's representation of comradeship. "Comrades, my future is in your hands," said the soldier, just as Christ had said, "Father, my times are in your hands."[52]

The essential message of the myth of comradeship as shared by rightists as well as leftists was this: The soldier who stood the test of comradeship was no barbarian. He embodied humanity per se. He succeeded Christ. By spreading this wisdom, the leftist myth helped the veterans coping with their violent legacy, as did its rightist counterpart. Both made mass violence morally bearable. And so the leftist myth of comradeship, while preaching pacifism, entangled itself in the belligerent claws of its rightist equivalent. This is even true of Remarque's bestseller, hated by nationalist readers for its declared pacifist and antimilitarist message. Remarque ridiculed military officers, and by denouncing the brutality of war he gave credence to the pacifist appeal "never again." And no product of German popular World War I memory managed so provocatively to overturn the message of the Uhland song as Remarque's famous Duval scene did. When the Frenchman dies, Paul mourns, just as Uhland's prototypical comrade does. To be sure, Paul mourns a foe-comrade, not a friend-comrade as in the Uhland song. But the story doesn't end with Paul's moral confusion, which might be read, and in fact was read, as a deliberate anti-war stance. Instead, the novel eventually renews the essence of the Uhland song: The good comrade keeps fighting, despite the loss of the comrade. Eventually getting out of the shell-hole and away from his new foe-comrade, Paul hurries to his old friend-comrades. They take care of him, comfort him, offer food and cigarettes to him, and calm him down. Paul feels relief. "I listen to them and feel comforted, reassured by their presence. It was mere driveling nonsense that I talked out there in the shell-hole." Back with his comrades, Paul overcomes the confusion his conscience had engendered and regains his strength, not to mutiny and to resist the war but rather to stick with it. Soon a comrade's "rifle cracks out sharply and dry." The war goes on, and the war will be waged together. Just as in the Uhland song, Remarque's novel, too, liberated the act of killing from human agency and responsibility. Stabbing Duval, Paul thinks, "I do not think at all, I make no decision." The battlefield generated "a sinister maelstrom" the individual soldier could not resist. Eventually it was the comradely We that killed, not the conscious I. "We have become wild beasts. We do not fight, we defend ourselves against annihilation... If we were not automatons at that moment we would continue lying there . . . But we are swept forward again power-less, madly savage and raging. We will kill, for they are still our mortal enemies."[53]

In Remarque's as in other anti-war novels, comradeship was the pri-vates' collective weapon against harassing drill sergeants and arrogant superiors in war. At the same time, however, it kept the war machine running. The good comrade went into battle with his buddies. He would never stay behind, trying to save his own life. In battle, Remarque's anti-hero Paul Bäumer lies in a shallow bowl and wishes nothing but "to stay lying there." But he knows he has to get out of it, "it is your comrades, it is not an idiotic command . . . They are more than my life." Wherever they are "is where I belong."[54] In a way, anti-war novels like this illuminated the workings of comradeship with historical accuracy: Collective hatred of officers, even symbolic acts of resistance, did not break the system but stabilized it, just as relief valves do in a pressure vessel.

This is why some critics refused to buy into the explicit, pacifist mes-sage of the anti-war novels and movies, notwithstanding the outcries precisely this message provoked in the nationalist and belligerent camp. Socialist critics such as Karl Sclutius suspiciously noticed young people's fascination with what he dubbed "pacifist war propaganda."[55] The truth is that there was indeed no distinct message in popular anti-war culture around 1930. Just as the Uhland song allowed different appropriations, the anti-war novels in late Weimar Germany radiated ambiguity and invited diverse interpretations, even contradictory ones. As another critic of Remarque put it, the secret of the novel's astounding success was that any reader could read out of it exactly what he was looking for.[56] The stories of soldiers suffering yet fighting bravely and performing humane comradeship may have suited pacifist ideologies, but they also spurred belligerent desires.

So it was with the stories about comradely fraternizations of enemy soldiers across the trenches. They served leftists to agitate against bel-ligerent plans for a future war to revise the Versailles Treaty. They also, however, opened a moral loophole in the net of guilt the war had laid over millions of civilian-soldiers who would not easily forget their roles in the machinery of mass death. Stories about humanity in war, most promi-nently about comradeship between enemies, were able to help them. So Bernhard Diebold published his *Book of Good Deeds, 1914–1918* in 1932. It gathered numerous eye-witness accounts of gestures of humanity in war, acts of comradeship between enemy soldiers, their sharing of the last cigarette, the rescuing of an injured soldier, and the like. What was the meaning of these stories? As Diebold explained – pathetically refer-ring to Genesis 18–19 – they altogether absolved the former soldiers from

their sins in war. For "as just ten righteous [persons], who would keep
us believing in the humanity of mankind, would have sufficed to absolve
Sodom from its thousand sins," just a few acts of comradeship sufficed
to canonize the perpetrator-soldiers, who had been forced into their evil
roles anyway.[57] Diebold's anthology was warmly welcomed – both in leftist and rightist milieus. Rightist speakers also learned to appreciate the
value of the myth of comradely fraternization when arguing for a morality of war as well and soon deployed, in their own memories, "many
thousand examples" of German soldiers selflessly comforting, helping,
and rescuing their French and English comrades, all of them contributing to a vision of paradisiac battlefields with no fights and no guilt, only
"primeval silence" and peace between friend and foe.[58]

War memory in Weimar Germany was divided along the lines of two
antagonistic ideological camps: pro-republican, leftist, pacifist, antimilitarist on the one side; and anti-republican, rightist, nationalist, and
belligerent on the other. Around 1930, however, with Weimar's democratic constitution being undermined by authoritarian governments and
increasing political violence, the boundaries between these camps started
to weaken and to fracture. The dispute about the meaning of comradeship in the past and in the future fueled these changes. Certainly, the idea
of closing class gaps through comradeship, as envisioned in the rightist
Volksgemeinschaft utopia, remained a sham in the eyes of most leftists. Yet,
the comradely frontline units in most of the leftist novels included soldiers of different social backgrounds, and at least some Social Democrats
were inspired by the experience of comradeship in war to welcome the
idea of overcoming antagonisms in a *Volksgemeinschaft*. At the same time,
the Reichsbanner – especially its vocal youth branch, the Jungbanner –
adopted elements of a leadership cult and a more authoritarian concept of comradeship as it had always been propagated in the nationalist
camp.[59]

Eventually it was the antagonism between democratic and anti-
republican visions and actions that led Weimar Germany into the abyss.
But under the surface of contest some agreement gained ground, visible more than anywhere else in popular culture. The reception of the
front novel *Krieg*, or *War*, published in 1928 under the name Ludwig
Renn, illustrates the convergence paradigmatically. Ludwig Renn was the
pseudonym of a former aristocratic officer who had joined the German
Communist Party in 1928. He understood his book as an indictment
of the inhumanity of war but, just as most anti-war novels around 1930
did, he did not level this indictment at the soldiers themselves. *Krieg*
presents them as war heroes, who would successfully overcome their suffering from the inhumanity of war by demonstrating manly toughness

and selfless dedication to their fatherland and their comrades. Renn's *Krieg* was enthusiastically welcomed in not only the leftist but also the rightist camp even after the pseudonym and author's communist affiliation were revealed. Even in the Nazi period literary critics praised *Krieg* for its contribution to the rise of the *Volksgemeinschaft* from the ashes of frontline comradeship.[60] Remarque was a different case, all too clearly profiled as an antimilitarist, an anti-Nazi, even (wrongly) denigrated as a Jew, and thus one of the first to see his books burned by the Nazis in May 1933. Earlier, however, he too had enjoyed some respect among rightist readers. One of them had praised him for "reviving the enormous power of male frontline comradeship," for serving as a "spearhead" of a Germany that would be rebuilt by "front soldiers marching into the realm of politics."[61]

NOTES

1 Victor W. Turner, "Myth and Symbol," in David L. Sills (ed.), *International Encyclopedia of the Social Sciences*, vol. X (New York: Macmillan, 1968), p. 577. Turner resumes, among other sources, Mircea Eliade's, Carl G. Jung's, and Bronislaw Malinowski's thinking about myths, and his own theory on liminality. See Mircea Eliade, *The Sacred and the Profane* (New York: Harcourt, 1959); Carl G. Jung, *Psychological Reflections: An Anthology of his Writings* (New York: Harper, 1953); Bronislaw Malinowski, *Magic, Science, and Religion, and Other Essays* (Boston: Beacon Press, 1948); Victor Turner, *The Ritual Process: Structure and Anti-Structure* (Ithaca, NY: Cornell University Press, 1977). See also Hans Blumenberg, *Work on Myth* (Cambridge, MA: MIT Press, 1985); and, for a thematically related appropriation of myth theory, Hellmann, *American Myth and the Legacy of Vietnam*.

2 *Mitteilungen des Reichsbundes der Kriegsbeschädigten und ehem. Kriegsteilnehmer*, Dec. 6, 1918. See also *Reichsbanner*, April 1, 1926, and Sept. 26, 1931.

3 *Kyffhäuser*, May 5, 1929, pp. 337–38.

4 See Chapter 1 above, notes 7 and 8.

5 Gunther Mai, "*Verteidigung* und *Volksgemeinschaft*: Staatliche Selbstbehauptung, nationale Solidarität und soziale Befreiung in Deutschland in der Zeit des Ersten Weltkrieges (1900–1925)," in Wolfgang Michalka (ed.), *Der Erste Weltkrieg: Wirkung, Wahrnehmung, Analyse* (Munich: Piper, 1994), pp. 583–602; Jeffrey Verhey, *The Spirit of 1914: Militarism, Myth and Mobilization in Germany* (New York: Cambridge University Press, 2000).

6 Franz Schauwecker, *The Fiery Way* (London: Dent, 1929), p. 57. Cf. Ann P. Linder, *Princes of the Trenches: Narrating the German Experience of the First World War* (Columbia, SC: Camden House, 1996), pp. 74–85.

7 Franz Schauwecker, *The Furnace* (London: Methuen, 1930), pp. 196–97. Similar claims came up immediately after the war: See Johann Wilhelm Mannhardt, *Schützengrabenmenschen* (Hamburg: Verlag des Deutschen Volkstums, 1919). Cf. also Hermann Pongs, "Krieg als Volksschicksal im

deutschen Schrifttum I," *Dichtung und Volkstum*, 35 (1934), 40–86 (at p. 61); Günther Lutz, *Das Gemeinschaftserlebnis in der Kriegsliteratur*, Ph.D. dissertation, University of Greifswald (1936), pp. 82, 91–92; Michael Gollbach, *Die Wiederkehr des Weltkrieges in der Literatur: Zu den Frontromanen der späten Zwanziger Jahre* (Kronberg: Scriptor-Verlag, 1978), pp. 154–59.

8 *Nachrichtenblatt der Offiziere des ehem. 6. Bad. Infanterieregiments "Kaiser Friedrich III.,"* Oct. 1, 1925, p. 3.

9 *Konstanzer Zeitung*, Aug. 31, 1925.

10 Lothar Burchardt, Dieter Schott, and Werner Trapp, *Konstanz im 20. Jahrhundert: Die Jahre 1914–1945* (Konstanz: Stadtler, 1990) p. 167. Note that the term "republican" in Germany (as in other European countries) in the nineteenth and first half of the twentieth century had a decisively liberal and democratic meaning; it must not be confused with the far-rightist party of the same name that emerged in Germany in the 1980s or with other conservative political traditions.

11 *Der Seehase*, May 15, 1926.

12 *Konstanzer Volksblatt*, May 12, 1921.

13 Ibid., Sept. 2, 1925.

14 Ibid., May 17, 1921.

15 *Deutsche Bodensee-Zeitung*, Aug. 31, 1925.

16 Kühne, *Belonging and Genocide*, pp. 15–20; Michael Wildt, "Volksgemeinschaft und Führererwartung in der Weimarer Republik," in Ute Daniel et al. (eds.), *Politische Kultur und Medienwirklichkeiten in den 1920er Jahren* (Munich: Oldenbourg, 2010), pp. 181–204.

17 Brian E. Crim, *Antisemitism in the German Military Community and the Jewish Response, 1914–1938* (Lanham, MD: Lexington, 2014); Tim Grady, *The German-Jewish Soldiers of the First World War in History and Memory* (Liverpool University Press, 2011); Derek J. Penslar, *Jews and the Military: A History* (Princeton University Press, 2013), pp. 166–94; on subjective experiences of Jewish soldiers during and after the war, see Michael Geheran, "Betrayed Comradeship: German-Jewish World War I Veterans Under Hitler," Ph.D. dissertation, Clark University (2016).

18 *Konstanzer Volksblatt*, Aug. 28, 1925.

19 Ibid., May 22 and 25, 1926; *Deutsche Bodensee-Zeitung*, May 26, 1926; Burchardt et al., *Konstanz im 20. Jahrhundert*, pp. 152, 169–74.

20 *Konstanzer Zeitung*, May 25, 1926.

21 Ibid., Dec. 8, 1927 (quotation); *Deutsche Bodenseezeitung*, Dec. 12, 1927; letter of the Association of the Former 114th Regiment to the mayor of Constance, Aug. 25, 1930; letters of the Constance branch of the Reichsbanner, Oct. 11 and 18, 1929 to the mayor, all Stadtarchiv Konstanz, S II 3859.

22 See, for instance, Eric D. Weitz, *Weimar Germany* (Princeton University Press, 2007), pp. 81–128.

23 Schauwecker, *Im Todesrachen*, pp. 57–58; Wilhelm Ritter von Schramm, "Schöpferische Kritik des Krieges: Ein Versuch," in Ernst Jünger (ed.), *Krieg und Krieger* (Berlin: Junker und Dünnhaupt, 1919), pp. 44–45. Cf. Theodor Bartram, *Der Frontsoldat: Ein deutsches Kultur- und Lebensideal*, repr. (Berlin: Verlag der Gegenseitigen Hilfe, 1934), pp. 14, 16–17, 20–22;

Lutz, *Das Gemeinschaftserlebnis in der Kriegsliteratur,* pp. 62, 88; Mannhardt, *Schützengrabenmenschen,* pp. 18–23.

24 Flex, *Der Wanderer zwischen beiden Welten,* pp. 13–15. Cf. Linder, *Princes of the Trenches,* pp. 82–84.

25 Werner Beumelburg, "Schaffensweg," *Blätter für Bücherfreunde,* 35/5 (1935), 3–4. Linder, *Princes of the Trenches,* analyzes the many facets of the idea of psychological and social transformation through war experience as played out in German war literature after 1918.

26 *Stahlhelm,* Nov. 25, 1928, p. 12.

27 Peter Fritzsche, *Rehearsals for Fascism: Populism and Political Mobilization in Weimar Germany* (New York: Oxford University Press, 1990); Frank Bösch, *Das konservative Milieu: Vereinskultur und lokale Sammlungspolitik in ost- und westdeutschen Regionen (1900–1960)* (Göttingen: Wallstein, 2002), pp. 66–85; Helge Matthiesen, "Von der Massenbewegung zur Partei: Der Nationalismus in der deutschen Gesellschaft der Zwischenkriegszeit," *Geschichte in Wissenschaft und Unterricht,* 48 (1997), 316–29; Claus-Christian W. Szejnmann, *Nazism in Central Germany: The Brownshirts in "Red" Saxony* (New York: Berghahn, 1999).

28 *Stahlhelm,* June 7, 1925, p. 13, and Feb. 9, 1930, p. 6; Ernst Hans Posse, *Die politischen Kampfbünde Deutschlands,* 2nd edn. (Berlin: Junker und Dünnhaupt, 1931), p. 31; Alois Klotzbücher, *Der politische Weg des Stahlhelm – Bund der Frontsoldaten in der Weimarer Republik,* Ph.D. dissertation, University of Erlangen-Nürnberg (1964), pp. 43–44; Berghahn, *Der Stahlhelm,* p. 107; Benjamin Ziemann, "Republikanische Kriegserinnerung in einer polarisierten Öffentlichkeit: Das Reichsbanner Schwarz-Rot-Gold als Veteranenverband der sozialistischen Arbeiterschaft," *Historische Zeitschrift,* 267 (1998), 357–98 (at p. 364).

29 Hermann Ullmann, *Das werdende Volk: Gegen Liberalismus und Reaktion* (Hamburg: Hanseatische Verlagsanstalt, 1929), p. 81, quoted in Hans-Ulrich Thamer, "Nation als Volksgemeinschaft: Völkische Vorstellungen, Nationalsozialismus und Gemeinschaftsideologie," in Joerg-Dieter Gauger and Klaus Weigelt (eds.), *Soziales Denken in Deutschland zwischen Tradition und Innovation* (Bonn: Bouvier, 1990), pp. 112–28 (at 117).

30 Gert von Klass, *Albert Vögler: Einer der grossen des Ruhrgebiets* (Tübingen: Wunderlich, 1957), p. 278. Cf. Peter Dudek, *Erziehung durch Arbeit: Arbeitslagerbewegung und freiwilliger Arbeitsdienst 1920–1935* (Opladen: Westdeutscher Verlag, 1988), pp. 83–87.

31 Cornelia Rauh-Kühne, "Hans Constantin Paulssen: Sozialpartnerschaft aus dem Geiste der Kriegskameradschaft," in Paul Erker and Toni Pierenkämper (eds.), *Deutsche Unternehmer zwischen Kriegswirtschaft und Wiederaufbau: Studien zur Erfahrungsbildung von Industrie-Eliten* (Munich: Oldenbourg, 1999), pp. 109–92.

32 "Discussion Between Comrades: Employer and Employee," *Stahlhelm,* April 6, 1930.

33 Dudek, *Erziehung durch Arbeit,* esp. pp. 15–17, 144; Klaus Kiran Patel, *Soldiers of Labor: Labor Service in Nazi Germany and New Deal America, 1933–1945* (Cambridge University Press, 2005), pp. 22–63.

34 Kurt Tucholsky, "Militaria" (1919), in Tucholsky, *Gesammelte Werke in 10 Bänden*, vol. II (Reinbek: Rowohlt, 1975), pp. 8–38.

35 Benjamin Ziemann, "'Gedanken eines Reichsbannermannes auf Grund von Erlebnissen und Erfahrungen': Politische Kultur, Flaggensymbolik und Kriegserinnerung in Schmalkalden 1926," *Zeitschrift des Vereins für Thüringische Geschichte*, 53 (1999), 201–24.

36 Hobohm, "Soziale Heeresmißstände."

37 Heinrich Wandt, *Etappe Gent* (Berlin: Freie Presse, 1921); Theodor Plivier, *Des Kaisers Kulis: Roman der deutschen Kriegsflotte* (Berlin: Malik, 1929); Erich Maria Remarque *All Quiet on the Western Front* (New York: Fawcett, 1982; German orig. 1929, 1st English edn. 1929); Ernst Johannsen, *Vier von der Infanterie: Ihre letzten Tage an der Westfront* (Hamburg-Bergedorf: Fackelreiter, 1929); Adam Scharrer, *Vaterlandslose Gesellen* (Vienna: Agis-Verlag, 1930).

38 *Reichsbanner*, Sept. 26, 1931, p. 310, and April 1, 1926, Gaubeilage (Krause).

39 Scharrer, *Vaterlandslose Gesellen*, pp. 93–95, and cf. pp. 143, 175–81.

40 "Jugend, Krieg und Frieden," *Reichsbanner*, Sept. 12, 1931; cf. *Reichsbund*, Dec. 6, 1918, p. 5, Oct. 10, 1920, p. 147, and Nov. 15, 1925, p. 170.

41 Johannsen, *Vier von der Infanterie*, pp. 11, 13–14, 48–49.

42 Remarque, *All Quiet on the Western Front*, pp. 192–94, 216–25.

43 Fritz von Unruh, "'Im Westen nichts Neues': Erich Maria Remarques Roman," *Vossische Zeitung*, Feb. 5, 1929, as in Bärbel Schrader (ed.), *Der Fall Remarque: Im Westen nichts Neues: Eine Dokumentation* (Leipzig: Reclam, 1992), pp. 28–32. Cf. *Stahlhelm*, March 17, 1929, p. 7. On Unruh, see Ziemann, *Contested Commemorations*, p. 156.

44 *Reichsbund*, Nov. 15, 1925, p. 170.

45 *Völkischer Beobachter*, April 18–19, 1930; *Stahlhelm*, March 17, 1929, p. 7; Rohe, *Das Reichsbanner Schwarz Rot Gold*, pp. 148, 152–53.

46 *Deutsche Wehr*, April 10, 1929, p. 270; cf. Schrader (ed.), *Der Fall Remarque*, p. 90.

47 *Arbeiterjugend*, Jan. 1932, pp. 22–23; *Völkischer Beobachter*, Dec. 1, 1931, quoted in Hermann Barth et al. (eds.), *Kameradschaft/La tragédie de la mine: Drehbuch von Ladislaus Vajda, Karl Otten, Peter Martin Lampel nach einer Idee von Karl Otten zu G. W. Pabsts Film von 1931* (Munich: edition text + kritik, 1997), pp. 186–87.

48 *Reichsbanner*, May 28 and Oct. 29, 1932 (cover pages); *Reichsbund*, June 20, 1932, pp. 129–30; Rohe, *Reichsbanner Schwarz Rot Gold*, p. 147.

49 Antoine Prost, *In the Wake of War: "Les anciens combattants" and French Society* (Providence, RI and Oxford: Berg, 1992), pp. 19–20. More details in Prost, *Les anciens combattants et la Société Française, 1914–1939*, 3 vols (Paris: Presses de la Fondation Nationale des Sciences Politiques, 1977), esp. vol. II, pp. 84–85, vol. III, pp. 25–32, 166–68.

50 Bartov, *Mirrors of Destruction*, p. 18.

51 *Reichsbund*, Oct. 10, 1929, p. 147; and Remarque, *All Quiet on the Western Front*, pp. 26–27. Similarly, see Johannsen, *Vier von der Infanterie*, pp. 14–15; Ludwig Renn, *Krieg*, repr. (Frankfurt: Societäts-Druckerei, 1931), p. 22. Cf. *Reichsbund*, Dec. 6, 1918, p. 5, Nov. 15, 1925, p. 170; *Reichsbanner*, April 1, 1926.

52 Unruh, "'Im Westen nichts Neues,'" p. 29. For similar comments, see Schrader (ed.), *Der Fall Remarque*, pp. 18–96; Johannes Brautzsch, *Untersuchungen über die Publikumswirksamkeit der Romane "Im Westen nichts Neues" und "Der Weg zurueck" von Erich Maria Remarque*, Ph.D dissertation, Paedagogische Hochschule Potsdam (1969), pp. 136–200.

53 Remarque, *All Quiet on the Western Front*, pp. 228–29, 113–15.

54 Ibid., pp. 211–12, 201. Cf. Scharrer, *Vaterlandslose Gesellen*, pp. 142–43.

55 Karl Hugo Sclutius, "Pazifistische Kriegspropaganda," *Die Weltbühne*, April 2, 1929, pp. 517–22; Sclutius, "Nochmals: Pazifistische Kriegspropaganda," *Die Weltbühne*, May 28, 1929, pp. 826–27.

56 *Welt am Sonntag*, May 27, 1929, quoted in Schrader, *Der Fall Remarque*, p. 82; Axel Eggebrecht, "Gespräch mit Remarque," *Die Literarische Welt*, June 14, 1929, repr. in Erich Maria Remarque, *Im Westen Nichts Neues: Roman. Mit Materialien und einem Nachwort von Tilman Westphalen* (Cologne: Kiepenheuer & Witsch, 1987), p. 311. Cf. Sabine Pamperrin, *Helmut Schmidt und der Scheißkrieg: Die Biografie 1918 bis 1945* (Munich: Piper, 2014), pp. 165, 204. Although taking issue with an earlier assessment of mine of the ambivalent message of *All Quiet on the Western Front* (Kühne, *Belonging and Genocide*, pp. 9–11) and highlighting instead the antimilitarist attitude of Remarque and probably most of his contemporary readers, Ziemann, *Contested Commemorations*, pp. 250–61, eventually acknowledges the "ambiguities" of Remarque's novel and the movie and their reception in pre-1933 Germany. My interpretation of "texts" like Remarque's novel and the respective movie is shaped by reception theory, according to which the meaning(s) of a "text" is not inherent in the text itself but the result of an ongoing negotiation between author and readers (such as critics); as the latter interpret and appropriate the text based on their respective, i.e. diverse, mind-sets and personal experiences, there is never one meaning of a given text. See Hans Robert Jauss, *Toward an Aesthetic of Reception* (Minneapolis: University of Minnesota Press, 1982); Jauss, *Aesthetic Experience and Literary Hermeneutics* (Minneapolis: University of Minnesota Press, 1982); Stuart Hall, *Encoding and Decoding in the Television Discourse* (Birmingham: Centre for Contemporary Cultural Studies, 1973). See also Thomas Becker, *Literarischer Protest und heimliche Affirmation: Das ästhetische Dilemma des Weimarer Kriegsromans* (Butzbach-Griedel: AFRA, 1994).

57 Bernhard Diebold (ed.), *Das Buch der guten Werke 1914–1918* (Frankfurt: Societäts Verlag, 1932), pp. 9, 17–18. Cf. *Reichsbund*, May 10, 1932, pp. 29–30. On the rare reality of such fraternization during the First World War, see Jay Winter and Blaine Baggett, *The Great War and the Shaping of the Twentieth Century* (New York: Penguin, 1996), pp. 96–99, 235–38; and Tony Ashworth, *Trench Warfare, 1914–1918: The Live and Let Live System* (New York: Holmes & Meier, 1980).

58 Friedrich Schmidt, *Der Wehrmann des XX. Jahrhunderts* (Berlin: Eisenschmidt, 1928), p. 104 (thousand examples); Josef Magnus Wehner, *Sieben vor Verdun: Ein Kriegsroman*, repr. (Munich: Langen, 1935), p. 95 (paradisiac silence), and cf. pp. 46–51; Friedrich Lehmann, *Wir von der Infanterie: Tagebuchblätter eines bayerischen Infanteristen aus fünfjähriger Front und Lazarettzeit*,

3rd edn. (Munich: Lehmann, 1934; 1st edn. 1929), p. 110; Werner Beumelburg, *Die Gruppe Bosemüller* (Oldenburg: Stalling, 1930), pp. 189–90.

59 *Reichsbanner*, Oct. 17, 1931, pp. 336–37, July 22, 1928, appendix "Jungbanner"; more material in Bundesarchiv-Lichterfelde, SAPMO Ry 12 II 113/7. Cf. Rohe, *Reichsbanner Schwarz Rot Gold*, pp. 136–37; Arndt Weinrich, *Der Weltkrieg als Erzieher: Jugend zwischen Weimarer Republik und Nationalsozialismus* (Essen: Klartext, 2013), p. 120. On the SPD, see Dieter Groh and Peter Brandt, *Vaterlandslose Gesellen: Sozialdemokratie und Nation 1860–1990* (Munich: Beck, 1992), pp. 204–06.

60 Pongs, "Krieg als Volksschicksal," p. 67; Renn, *Krieg*; cf. Ludwig Renn, "Über die Voraussetzungen zu meinem Buch 'Krieg,'" *Die Linkskurve*, 1/1 (1929), 13; Gollbach, *Die Wiederkehr des Weltkrieges in der Literatur*, p. 319.

61 Martin Stoss, "Die Front marschiert! Die Tragödie Remarque," *Die Tat: Monatsschrift zur Gestaltung der Wirklichkeit*, March 1929, quoted, next to similar voices, in Brautzsch, *Untersuchungen über die Publikumswirksamkeit*, pp. 166–67.

3   Steeling

The polyvalence of the comradeship myth grounded its popularity. Different people, different movements, and different regimes could derive belligerent or pacifist, authoritarian or subversive messages from it. The Nazis, once in power and eager to integrate Germany's conflicting sociopolitical camps, managed to run the whole gamut of meanings of comradeship most successfully. Before 1933, the leftists' efforts to effect reconciliation with former enemies on the basis of mutual experiences of comradeship had often been frustrated, and the rightists had simply loathed even to think of attempting it. From 1933 on, the Nazi regime promoted and achieved it. As early as fall 1933, Hitler publicly announced his intention to work on German–French reconciliation and consequently initiated reunions of both veterans and youth from either side. Inspired by the Berlin 1936 Olympic games – now dubbed the "festival of comradeship between the nations" – the Nazi regime pushed reunions of French and German veterans more spectacularly than any Weimar veterans' association would ever have been able to. The French partners evinced enthusiasm, at least for a while. It was only when Nazi Germany invaded the rump Czechoslovak state in March 1939 and no longer hid its disregard of any international treaty, that they learned that they had been duped.[1]

Hitler, of course, staged this reconciliation as a distraction from his rearmament program. In a meeting with journalists in November 1938, he dwelt on the "precarious implications of an ongoing peace propaganda" such as the one he had launched five years before. It might even be taken seriously "by many people," Hitler sarcastically explained. Hence the Nazis' propaganda of peace and reconciliation remained embedded in bellicose rhetoric. Reunions of frontline soldiers, the now Nazified old veterans' associations echoed, must never slide into "pacifist whimpering" and "feeble fuss" but radiate the martial aura of true soldiers' knightly "pride of an equal enemy."[2]

Although the cult of martial masculinity grew more vocal under the Nazi regime, it had been propagated before 1933 in response both to

70

the alleged feminization of men and the masculinization of women, phe-
nomena that were both perceived as a threat to established notions of
masculinity. Before 1914, and increasingly during and after the war,
women emerged from the private sphere they had traditionally occupied
and took on "male" jobs and terrains in the public sphere. After the war,
the democratic constitution honored this engagement on behalf of the
fatherland by granting women the right to vote and to enter parliaments
and governments, hitherto considered an exclusively male prerogative.
The "New Woman" embodied this female emancipation paradigmatically. No longer tied into any domestic restriction, independent from
men and children, she pursued her own career. Supposedly, she also
drove men out of their jobs. Unable to find a job, the men pushed the
prams while their wives took over as breadwinners, according to misogynistic scenarios spread as a result of the Great Depression.[3]

gender damage

The feminization of men as amplified in scenarios such as this had
a much larger dimension, however. Already before the war, scandals of
homosexuality, among both Germany's ruling elite and Germany's new
youth movement – arising from discontent over middle-class priggish-
ness – had confused seemingly unchangeable, biological definitions of
what made a man in the first place – heterosexuality, that is. The idea
that the war would bring the gender order back into its traditional balance proved an illusion, just as the hope to unify the nation and rid
it of class antagonisms through war soon faded away. Homosexual men
joined the army, many even volunteering, seeking and finding male love in
a deliberately un-effeminate environment, refuting their stigmatization,
strengthening their gay pride, and eventually demanding public recognition. After the war, homosexuals, previously condemned to oppress
or hide their identities, publicly established a veritable gay culture, at
least in big cities such as Berlin.[4] And it was not only homosexuality that challenged "true" masculinity. Innumerable heterosexual men
experienced unmanly "weakness" in the trenches and on the battlefields,
suffered from emotional depredations and raging "war neuroses," and
belied traditional notions of men as representing the strong, hard, and
self-controlled pole of the binary gender order on an even broader scale
than the homosexual minority could ever have done.[5]

In short, the polar gender order, contrasting strong, tough, and
aggressive men ruling over the public sphere, and weak, tender, and caring women restricted to family life – all this allegedly a biological given –
seemed to be in a state of ultimate dissolution. It needed to be fixed.
Conjuring up the virtues of true manliness and martial masculinity,
demanding pure virility, hardness, resoluteness, aggression, brutality,
coldness, and disdaining whatever smelled of femaleness, weakness,

porosity, fluidity, uncertainty, instability, was one way to re-establish the lost security about male and female roles. Although it was supported not only by military and paramilitary circles but also by parts of the Catholic and socialist youth movement, the cult of martial virility never gained as much popularity as its vociferous propagandists had hoped, at least not in Weimar Germany.[6] For too many men had learned that anonymous and mechanized warfare rarely allowed the performance of steely heroism, and too many men had wanted rather to survive the war and return to their civilian lives than to sacrifice them on the altar of perpetual war and perpetual warrior virtues. Under the emasculating effect of mass death, mass mutilation, and mass depravation, the certainties about "maleness being granted only to men and femininity only to women" vanished into thin air, as one observer stated. A confusing experience held sway: Each individual was made of masculine and feminine traits.[7]

Franz Schauwecker, proud of his manly career as a war volunteer, wondered in his early war memoir in 1919 about "a tender, womanlike sentiment" he had faced as soldier, "a desire to bestow love and to be loved." Talking openly about it was not easy, however. In war, he said, one would have "repressed it immediately" and "never admitted" it. For in the all-male army there was "no friendliness, no kindliness, no love," he lamented. "Empathy and warmth, both female traits, were lacking entirely."[8] And yet he articulated it publicly, even though only after the war. What Schauwecker was concerned with had nothing to do with real women, of course. He talked about male imaginations of women, imaginations of femininity within men. These imaginations allowed men to cope with ambivalent and contradictory emotions, desires, and deprivations. Like containers, these imaginations accommodated whatever did not fit into straight concepts of manliness and enabled men (and women) to visit those ambivalences whenever they needed.[9]

For revealing feminine sentiments was a dangerous path: It smelled of homosexual desires. Yet the need to cope with and to talk about these sentiments persisted, as the very fact of Schauwecker's public confession shows. Popular discourse on masculinity after the Great War therefore sought integrative concepts of manliness that gave meaning to the ambivalent, ambiguous, and complex desires, emotions, and experiences of men, and that could be adopted by different types of men as they fought together in modern mass armies. The myth of comradeship achieved exactly this: It built bridges between divergent experiences, united disrupted identities, showed how femininity and masculinity could be on good terms within one person. It offered a way to handle emotional ambiguity.

you can feel things and still be a man

In order to address those feminine sentiments legitimately, the concept of homoeroticism offered assistance. Homoeroticism was "that one very special vibration between two men that is somehow feminine," as the military psychologist Hans-Heinrich Grunwaldt stated in 1937.[10] Where did that vibration start and where did it end? The contemporary discourse separated platonic homoeroticism from physical homosexuality. During and after the war, various strands of the homosexual emancipation movement shared, as the historian Jason Crouthamel has shown, "a new image of a homosexual 'warrior' activist for whom 'friendship,' the widely used euphemism for homosexual love, and 'comradeship' were conflated." Magnus Hirschfeld, the famous sexologist and homosexual activist, even "argued that while physically erotic homosexual relationships remained largely hidden, same-sex bonding was to some degree encouraged under the guise of comradeship to promote cohesion and military strength." In his *Sexual History of the War* (1930), he quoted a letter written to him by a German officer confessing how he had fallen "in love" with a young soldier and had "engaged in sexual activity, but only rarely and in a thoroughly fine, aesthetic, but never punishable form."[11] Confessions like these confirmed, in a way, the dominant discourse of veterans, war novelists, and active soldiers. Homosexuality was forbidden. What was allowed was homoeroticism, "a sublimated (i.e. 'chaste') form of temporary homosexuality" that showed itself in "'idealistic,' passionate but non-physical 'crushes.'"[12] But legitimate eroticism was never entirely insulated from the "morass" of physical love, as Grunwaldt warned. There was always the risk of transgressing the "fluid boundary between homoeroticism and homosexuality." Approvable was what "remained within the limits of 'puppy love,'" such as the "irresistible" attraction sparked by the lieutenant's "charming" breeches or the "heartfelt and timid affection the junior youth felt toward the somewhat elderly youth." But "hugging and kissing" was already close to committing "felony," he stated.[13]

And even this elaboration, drawing on World War I, was an exception from the rule of homophobia and fear of homosexuality in the Third Reich.[14] "No one turning from the poetry of the Second War back to that of the First can fail to notice there the unique physical tenderness, the readiness to admire openly the bodily beauty of men, the unapologetic recognition that they may be in love with each other," stated Paul Fussell in his book on British World War I literature. It certainly applies to Germany as well. In the interwar period, talking about male homoeroticism was still common in both countries, although the chaste, non-physical character of male friendships and male love was the preferred theme of this talk. It would be wrong, however, to neglect the differences between the two countries. In Germany there was no equivalent to the Anglophone prewar tradition of respectable and prominent homoerotic poetry running "from Whitman to Hopkins to Housman," and even less to the established upper-class tradition of public-school homoeroticism. Hence, the British enthusiasm for male beauty, clothed or naked, for gloating about "crushes" between officers and men, for "soldiers bathing" scenes, only rarely met equivalents in German war literature. Of course, there was Thomas Mann, who may count as equivalent to Wilfred Owen, but Mann never served in the military, let alone in war.[15]

The different attitudes toward male homoeroticism in British and in German World War I literature respectively reflect a more general divide between both national discourses on the relation between friendship and comradeship. Although often conflated, the two concepts carried different meanings. You could choose your friends according to your sympathies and the needs of your self, and it was up to you to start and to end a friendship. Comradeship, by contrast, was embedded in destiny and coercion. You would be assigned to a group of comrades by some authority, often randomly, and at least in the military you would not be asked whether you liked them or not. This did not suit everyone. Before he became a prominent film critic, Siegfried Kracauer had served briefly as a soldier in World War I and had never seen action. He was still upset about comradeship, however. It was a nightmare to him. It "de-personalizes the individual mind, kneads it again and again, until it parallels the rhythm of the others," he said. Friendship, on the other hand, thrived on the individual's way of life and was based on personal choices. In Kracauer's view, friendship was the only truly modern social relationship, a view that has been confirmed since then many times by sociologists throughout the Western world.[16]

And most British World War I writers and memoirists would have agreed, too, as the literary scholar Sarah Cole has shown. Although the British discourse on male friendship and comradeship in war also tended to conflate both categories, two different concepts were yet visible, intimate "individualized relationships of amity and love between men," i.e. friendships, on the one hand, and "comradeship" as the concept to refer to "a corporate or group commitment" that is beyond individual choice but coerced, on the other. Most British soldiers and ex-soldier authors favored the concept of voluntary friendship over enforced comradeship and bemoaned the destruction of the first in war, "despite all its self-presentation as the site of male loyalty." Friends were "killed in the course of the day," and if not through death, friendships were terminated by "a bureaucracy that ceaselessly and arbitrarily" transferred soldiers from one unit to another and thus "separated friends from one another." This experience left many writers frustrated and troubled. To them, the "impersonal comradeship" held "no consolation or truth." The "figure of the bereaved male friend," says Cole about the English literature, "becomes a representative of the war par excellence."[17]

Of course, this experience was familiar to German soldier-writers as well, and they certainly mourned the loss of friends among comrades, just as the Uhland song had suggested already in the nineteenth century. But the German interwar military discourse on comradeship did not allow lingering over grief for lost friends; in fact, the Uhland song had not allowed it either but requested the soldier to continue fighting, which also meant to look out for new friends or comrades. Friendships were allowed as long as they did not question the priority of comradeship. Not by accident does the dying friend remain anonymous and abstract in the Uhland song. Comrades in the army could be substituted endlessly; the loss of a comrade did not undermine the pursuit of the task. Friendship served only to enrich the individual self and radiated egotism, suggested German military writers, while comradeship was a social tool to get assignments done. Friendship was soaked with "individual sentiments," thus unreliable, unstable, and ambiguous, explained the *Kyffhäuser* journal despitefully in 1932. By contrast, comradeship drew its strength precisely from being determined by destiny and from being reproducible.[18]

German war memory praised as virtue what its British equivalent bemoaned. Notwithstanding many parallels between the meaning of comradeship in German and British World War I memories, the British focus on the individual soldier and consequently on individual friendship – usually between two men – contrasts with the German fascination after 1918 and especially since the late 1920s with the squad, the platoon, the company, i.e. with groups of men who were ready to sacrifice themselves for their comrades or their fatherland.[19] While Lawrence of Arabia established a hero cult revolving around the aesthetic and eccentric male self and homoerotic relationships catering to this self, the hero worship of the German fighter pilot Baron von Richthofen drew on his outstanding military record and his comradely charismatic leadership.[20]

And one can draw the lines of comparison farther into the Anglophone world. While the ultimate bestseller among German war novels in 1929 was a hymn to comradeship, a similarly bestselling American war novel, published in the same year, shunned this military virtue. The hero of Ernest Hemingway's *Farewell to Arms* did not find much, and certainly did not dwell in, comradeship although it is not absent in the novel. But this story does not revolve around a fatalistic all-male bond but the love between the soldier and a women; its vantage point is the civilian world, not the battlefield. Only Hemingway's second and even more successful war book chose comradeship as its theme. But the comradeship depicted in *For Whom the Bell Tolls* (1941) is an entirely different one than Remarque's, not only in that it includes both men and women and allows romantic relationships between them. It is a comradeship that not just allows but is embedded in agency – in individual decisions and choices that start with the American Robert Jordan's volunteering for the Spanish guerrilla group, lead to inner dialogues about responsibility and personalities, and end with Jordan's request to die alone, on behalf of the group however.[21]

Not limited to German military discourse, the metaphor of the family, consisting of father, mother, and children, gained enormous popularity as it offered a respectable symbolic framework for communicating those strange feminine traits within men, sorting out the emotional chaos they caused, and highlighting the priority of military functionality over individual sentiments. The metaphor translated forbidden homoeroticism into respectable heterosexuality. The soldiers are "a great family lying in shell-craters and trenches," said Schauwecker.[22] In a platoon or company, then, the commander assumed the role of the father, called *Papa*, or Dad. He would rule over the unit rigorously and yet justly, and have an open ear for all and everyone, for his "kids." Occasionally showing empathy, which was coded feminine, he nevertheless represented the tough, manly side of the military. Obeying orders from the upper echelons and issuing orders to his men-kids, he represented, just like the middle-class family father, the hinge between the "public" sphere, the army as a whole, the world outside of the family, that is, and the "private" sphere, the family, the unit of his men-kids. The second in the hierarchy was the sergeant or a veteran private, clearly restricted to the inner world of the family. Just as the mother operated within the family, taking care of its physical and emotional health, the "sarge" served as the "mother of the company" and took care of its apparel and equipment. Representing the female part of family leadership, he combined, as does the mother in a real family, sensitivity and severity. In this way, he owned a "superfine sense" of whether one of his men-kids was unwilling or unable to do his job. Anyone who was unable could count on "motherly" care. Anyone who was just unwilling would be given "motherly" strictness.[23]

Werner Beumelburg's war novel *Die Gruppe Bosemüller*, or *Platoon Bosemüller*, published in the same year as Remarque's bestseller and widely considered its pro-military, nationalist equivalent, fleshed out family imagery and its homoerotic references most consistently. The hero of the novel, the middle-class volunteer Ernst Siewers, arrives at the front equipped with "Mom's sandwiches" and a "bouquet of violets," the insignia of a "mama's boy." Sergeant Bosemüller, the father of the company, always striving to protect his "family," and an experienced, elderly private named Wammsch, the mother of the company, sort of adopt him. None of the group shows embarrassment about comrades who suffer from emotional breakdowns and behave in unmanly ways. One of them does so when almost being buried alive in a collapsing trench, together with a few comrades. Like a toddler, he cries, "mummy . . . mummy . . . " Everyone in the group knows how fragile and weak the ideal of manly hardness is. Only Ernst, the novice, has a hard time digesting this comrade's unmanly behaviour and can't fall asleep the following night, after they had been rescued. He reaches for Wammsch's hand. Wammsch, of course, is ready to calm him down. "If he hadn't cried 'mummy, mummy,' we would have taken you all for dead," Wammsch explains. Then he runs his hand over the kid's hair and stays for another five minutes with him, until "the kid has closed his eyes."[24]

In the course of the story, Ernst grows up, becomes a real man, thanks to combined experience of the tough and hardening side of the war and his comrades' tenderness and empathy. As a real man Ernst is, even more than as a boy, allowed to perform tender masculinity and to act out homoerotic desires. Only within rigid limitations, however. On one occasion, he manages to rescue his comrade Esser from the line of fire, and so a close relationship starts, sanctioned by this ultimate act of heroic comradeship. "You saved my life," says Esser to Siewers, "I love you" – but only after he has asked him about the first time he kissed a girl, thus securing a heterosexual frame for their homoeroticism. And the novel produces even sharper boundaries to keep the homoerotic relationship under control. From the beginning, the story is imbued with melancholy foreboding its tragic end. Esser dies in action, alone, without a comforting hand, just as the comrade in Uhland's song. There had been enough tenderness, is the message of the story. A little homoeroticism was allowed, but it needed to be contained, to come to an end.[25]

In popular war memory, it was precisely the traumatic and destructive nature of the war that granted more leeway to homoeroticism (not homosexuality) than a civilian setting could have done, but it could do so only because death, or at least relocation, was at any point likely to end male love – to contain it, that is. Thus Hans Zöberlein's 1931 autobiographical novel *The Belief in Germany*, endorsed by Hitler as the authoritative war novel and a bestseller in the Third Reich, allowed tender body contact between men, developing the Uhland song. And yet their homoeroticism was as rigidly confined as in the song and in Beumelburg's novel. "Hans," lisps Zöberlein's comrade on his deathbed, "and our eyes burned into each other. More wasn't necessary between the two of us; we were used to understand each other without talking," and, one might add, without touching. But now, in face of death, different rules apply. "A pale hand fumbled for mine. And now I felt his blood running through his fingers." Death made sure that homoeroticism would be kept under control.[26]

Imaginings of femininity within men stored the complements to the symbolic world of tough or hard and violent masculinity. A real man knew how to stand his ground in this world. But in order to do so, he needed to know about the opposite. Tough manliness could not be imagined or exist without the blueprint of weakness, which, in a binary gender order, needed to be coded as feminine. A real man did not need to split off those feminine traits but he knew how to keep them under control. He deployed the "weak" side of comradeship to recover, to recharge the batteries of his fighting spirit. But he knew how to not get lost in the seductions of the femininity within men and male comradeship. He knew how to handle the tensions between manliness and male femaleness. He would accept the challenge of the unsettling effects of the latter because he knew how to settle or even draw strength from his feminine moods. He also knew that hardness was a temporary state that could not be achieved irreversibly and for good. Thus, a state of constant anxiety, of uncertainty – or inner disruption, of swinging back and forth between enthusiasm and melancholy – remained.[27]

The myth of comradeship was tied into an intense public communication about ambivalent masculinities, about male weakness and tenderness, and about male homoeroticism. Not all contemporaries welcomed this frank talk. Some worried about its effects on the youths who would have to fight the next big war, widely anticipated as being even more destructive than the previous one. The "emotionally robust and disciplined young man" was to keep all emotional challenges under control, stated Grunwaldt in his account on soldierly homoeroticism.[28] But would that man succeed in doing so? Wouldn't the "weak" or "feminine" moods undermine men's manliness and thus their functioning as soldiers? Nothing stirred up these fears in Germany's militarist and nationalist camps as much as the unprecedented success of Remarque's anti-war novel. Paul Bäumer's comradeship protected even the scared bed wetter, the epitome of an unmanly man. As such appeared first the recruit Tjaden, a natural subject of drill sergeant Himmelstoss's degradations which the comradely group collectively avenged; once at night, when the tormenter was drunk, the group ambushed him, pulled off his trousers, and thrashed him.[29] In the same spirit, Paul later empathically took care of a "fair-headed recruit," who, "in utter terror . . . had his pants full after the first bombardment." Instead of mocking at him, Paul reassures him, saying "that's no disgrace."[30]

As a response to Remarque's popularity and more generally to the civilian-soldier's soft notion of comradeship, the Stahlhelm's paramilitary branches and the NSDAP's Storm Troopers promoted a "comradeship of action" that was to overcome the comradeship of suffering as portrayed not only in Remarque's novel but also in Beumelburg's. After 1933, some intellectuals even blamed *Die Gruppe Bosemüller* for spreading the disease of a "weakly and cloudy humaneness," introduced by Remarque, which – in their view – did not comply with true comradeship.[31] They condemned it as un-German. French soldiers, one Captain Franz Hundeiker stated in a sophisticated inquiry into national differences between European military cultures, would resort to this kind of weak or defensive comradeship in order mutually to protect themselves, whereas German soldiers performed daring, offensive comradeship, a "community of action." As Hundeiker claimed to have observed in the war on the Western Front, French soldiers did not bother to bury their fallen comrades but rather left them to decay in the trenches so that eventually, if they had an opportunity, the Germans would fulfill this comradely duty. In other words, Germans practiced heroic and goal-oriented comradeship, whereas the social cohesion of French soldiers was that of an amorphous "mass," based on "talkativeness," herd instinct, the desire for security, and enjoying life.[32]

Loaded with aggression and willpower, comradeship in the Third Reich was promoted to being one of the key Nazi values. While the melancholy of the Uhland song had well suited the civilian-soldier, the Nazis' political soldier – the soldier who had internalized the Nazi racist ideology – adhered to the Horst Wessel song, the anthem of the NSDAP from 1930 on. Also known by its opening words "The Flag on High," it didn't end with the death of the comrade, in sharp contrast to the Uhland song. The song, written in 1929 by the Nazi Horst Wessel, carried a deliberately aggressive message that was enhanced when Wessel was murdered by a communist in spring 1930. The song was all about revenge, about transforming grief into aggression, and about comradeship as the virtue of waging war, not suffering from it, in this case civil war. "Comrades shot by the Red Front and reactionaries / March in spirit within our ranks," repeats the song four times. The fallen comrades "march in spirit within our ranks" in order to keep "the ranks tightly closed" and watch over the surviving comrades' fighting spirit, as the first verse of the song demands.[33]

As part of the Nazification of German politics, society, and culture from spring 1933 on, the new spirit of comradeship soon spread over the country. In Constance, for instance, the veterans had honored the comradeship of suffering from war and drawn peaceful lessons from it. In 1933, they understood that comradeship meant moving beyond "the zone of civilian security" and gearing up Germans for the next war. "Hardened in storms of steel, infused with infinite love for the German people and country," the soldiers of the Great War had built the Nazi movement on the foundation of comradeship, the Constance veterans claimed in November 1933, commemorating the "fallen heroes" for the first time under Nazi rule.[34]

The imagery of aggressive comradeship, exemplarily visualized in the *Comradeship* sculptures of Joseph Torak and Arno Breker, did not break with the mythical traditions of the concept that aimed to reconcile diverging emotions and diverse people.[35] The Nazis stressed a different aspect of the myth than mainstream war memory in Weimar Germany had emphasized; they did not revoke its ambivalences, the basis of its popularity, however. A little sentimentality was still allowed as long as it did not undermine the fighting morale comradeship was supposed to fuel. In the mid-1930s, the Storm Troopers memorialized the Nazi Party's *Kampfzeit*, the period before 1933. Now even "the warm heart, the helping hand," and the "emotional and spiritual harmony" that had filled their retreats, the "storm bars," was honored. This kind of "comradeship," they said, was "everything," "home and pleasure," that one "section of the front line that guaranteed repose and protection from the enemy."[36]

The truth was that comradeship included both soft and hard masculinities. Comradeship was the virtue of empathy, care, and tenderness in the military, but also the compound to convert weakness into hardness, to steel the men. The army's official training manual, the "Reibert" (named after its initial author), described comradeship as "the indispensable glue" that, next to discipline, "kept the army together. Without discipline [the army] would be a rampant crowd, without comradeship the soldier's life would be unbearable." But this comradeship was not at the discretion of the individual. It was a must. "The soldier *has to* get along with his comrades in peace." It was not a matter of choice. "He may not abandon them in battle, distress, or danger but has to support them as far as possible, whenever they are in need of him," declared the German military code unambiguously.[37] In other words, the warm, tender, and altruistic side of comradeship was tied into a system of mandatory reciprocity. In order to enjoy the group's comfort, help, and protection, you had to offer the same, and not only when you were in the

mood to do so, but at any time. Comradeship was the virtue of conformity. If one comrade failed in some task or just stepped out of line,
the entire group would be blamed and penalized. In order to avoid collective punishment, stronger or more experienced comrades might help
the freshmen and weaker ones to get along. Those however who didn't
conform could not count on comradely support. "Comradeship entails
strong discipline and oppresses the malicious, unreliable and uncomradely elements," stated the military pedagogue and World War I veteran
Erich Weniger on the eve of the Second World War and explained how
the machine of conformity worked. Back in the past war, he said, "one
would have felt ashamed not to match the standards of the community"
of comrades, and the fear of shame made you do what you were supposed
to do. You would never desert your comrade, he explained, "because you
would be scared of being shamed."[38]

The war novels widely illustrated what Weniger elaborated theoretically. The very "idea of being disgraced for falling behind," and the
possibility of "being called a shirker," led Hans Zöberlein to flog himself into battle, with his comrades, even though he was suffering from
a 104 degree fever and imminently to break down entirely.[39] Himself a
born soldier and a dedicated Nazi, Zöberlein was not the only one to
praise the fear of shame. Paul Bäumer, Remarque's anti-war hero, felt
and acted the same way, and, most significantly, he spread the same
morality in interwar Germany. In a safe shell-hole, Bäumer discards concerns about his own survival and runs into the battle again, knowing, "it
is your comrades, it is not an idiotic command." In fact, Bäumer had
already demonstrated the morality of sacrificing oneself for the sake of
the group in battle when he ran into their hated former drill sergeant (and
high-school teacher) Himmelstoss in a dugout at the front. Himmelstoss
turns out to be a coward, staying behind, "pretending to be wounded,"
while Bäumer naturally runs out. Bäumer has no pity for the coward.
"'Get out!' I spit," and again, when Himmelstoss still "crouches back to
the wall and shows his teeth like a cur," Bäumer shouts at him: "'You
lump, will you get out – you hound, you skunk, sneak out of it, would
you?'"[40]

Despite their ironic undertone, scenes like this in the anti-war literature
spread the same conformist morality, and picked up on cowardice in
much the same way, as did openly bellicose novels or military tutorials.
Whoever was not willing to sacrifice the I on the altar of the We was
threatened with an "unbearable existence," announced one officer at
the climax of the Remarque surge.[41] Typically, his comrades would give
him the "Holy Spirit," a euphemism for the vigilante justice common in
the German military. Preferably at night in the dormitory, they would

tear the outsider under the shower, pour a bucket of water in his bed, bash him, or punish him in other ways, usually quite brutally. Or they would just ignore and shame him. Having no one to talk to was a serious punishment in a social setting that left few choices for socializing.[42]

Even socialist veterans agreed that the individual who violated the laws of comradeship was to be shamed and isolated. In 1929, the *Reichsbanner* journal published a war story targeting the "egoist" in a group of working-class soldiers. The "egoist" was a peasant who refused to share the gift boxes full of butter, ham, and sausages his relatives had sent. His starving comrades tried to teach him comradeship by kicking him out of the dugout and violently forcing him to give some of his food to them, but he proved unwilling to learn. One day when his comrades couldn't resist eating the meat of a horse killed in battle, the "egoist" mockingly started singing the song of the good comrade, well knowing that soldiers looked on their horses as comrades as well. The unit took revenge, confiscating the "egoist's" food supply and making *him* eat the entire horse roast.[43] The message of such stories was always the same: Stick to the group and forget about your individual needs and desires, if you don't wish to be ostracized.

Around 1930, this conformist morality, promulgated in the spirit of comradeship, was no longer limited to discourse on past wars or the present military. It was also advocated by major parts of the youth move-ment, which had developed around 1900 and craved for community. For a long time youth groups had kept a balance between individualism and collectivism, or between friendship and comradeship. Often, they used the latter two terms synonymously. Sitting around a campfire or stay-ing overnight in a barn, they enjoyed a communal life on a voluntary basis, one that catered to their individual selves. However, when they came together, duties had to be shared on a fair basis; individual moods, preferences, and peculiarities had to be subordinated to the group. In other words, there was a need for comradeship, although not the com-radeship of soldiers facing death. Everybody was free to join or leave a group or to start another one. As a result, in the youth movement the concepts of friendship and comradeship were often used interchangeably. But in the late 1920s, as part of a profound militarization of the youth movement, the balance between friendship and comradeship changed. The community would always "recognize the outsider and know how to defend itself," threatened the *Reichsbanner*, looking to its own socialist youth associations. Whoever preferred to seek out solitude rather than joining the crowd was seen as uncomradely and was shunned. Mother's boy, the "chicken" who was solely concerned with his private longings, was destined to be an outcast. The tone of such language is very much to the point. The youth movement succumbed to the pressure of the mythical community, which required subordination and denied individual freedom. Before 1933, nobody was forced to join the youth clubs. Many youths, however, wanted to be "pressed" into a "community that was afraid of neither death nor devil."[44]

The activities of these groups, generally boyish games and tests of courage, seemed harmless enough, and the praise of friendship and individuality never died out entirely. In urban and intellectual settings they were favored anyway.[45] In 1924, Leopold von Wiese, an influential sociologist, published a memoir about his life as a young cadet, a member of an elitist military college in imperial Germany. The story paints a nasty portrait of the rituals of torture, pressure, and social isolation awaiting the individual who was either not able or not willing to accept his peers' social rules. Wiese's conclusion was that the individual carries a much higher moral value than does any community. And in the same year the young philosopher Helmut Plessner published an influential pamphlet on Germans' longing for community, which he observed with revulsion. The intellectual Plessner advocated the right to intimacy and individuality.[46] In the same spirit, another sociologist, Alfred Vierkandt, summarized in 1931 his and many of his colleagues' shared belief: Modern society revolves around the individual and the self, not the group. Modern meritocracy fostered personal ambition, personal responsibility, personal achievements, and personal sovereignty, Vierkandt stated. He contrasted modern society with tribal societies in Asia, Africa, and the Americas where these values seemed not to exist and where people constantly lived under public control: Their communities did not allow individual differences. Vierkandt anticipated the work of the American anthropologist Ruth Benedict. Her 1946 book on Japan, *The Chrysanthemum and the Sword*, called this the shame culture, opposing it to guilt cultures. Western ethics, Benedict said, grew out of a guilt culture. In guilt cultures, people are responsible for their own actions. They experience guilt individually and in dialogue with God or the superego. In shame cultures the community sets itself up as the highest moral authority. Shame is grounded in the fear of exposure, disgrace, and exclusion with which the community threatens the individual who does not submit to its rules. Shame culture trains one to be inconspicuous, to conform, to participate – and to be happy by being in the good graces of the group, by enjoying security and relief within the community.[47]

Not much interested in war memory or popular culture, Vierkandt failed to notice that an ethics of public control and containment of the individual was underway in Germany precisely at the time when he lectured about industrial society's individualism. There was admittedly still much ambiguity in the youth movement and in the popular memory of the Great War, as shown by Remarque's Paul Bäumer, who switches back and forth between comradeship and conscience. Thinking about these ambiguities in his *Confessions of the Youth* (1930), Franz Matzke resorted to the metaphor of the mask to describe the way individuals cope with the pressure to merge into community and to conform. "Silently we make ourselves subordinate, even if we know better and feel differently. Such subordination, however, will be limited to the outer districts of our selves, and never intrude into the nucleus of our mind, which always will be individual and distant from the community, even if longing for the community."[48] Inwardly, Matzke tried to say, one's individuality was safe under the mask. What Matzke did not consider was the self-dynamic the mask could develop. Performing subordination, conformity, comradeship, the external mask, the visible part of the self, demanded imitation and might lead the internal self also to conform. While Matzke, and also other advocates of the youth movement, may have been concerned about the dissolution of the I in the We, popular war memory, and even more so military tutorials, taught precisely this. As their homoerotic elements show, popular war novels such as Beumelburg's, Zöberlein's, or Remarque's did not dismiss concepts such as the self or friendship between individuals entirely. But ideas about sacrificing the individual for the sake of the community spread quickly, and the discourse on comradeship left no doubt that friendship – or peculiarities of the self, for that matter – were allowed only as long as they did not question the absolute priority of the group. This was the ultimate theme of the war novels from the political Right to the Left: how to transform individualism into collectivism, weakness into hardness, femininity into manliness.

At that time, around 1930, comradeship was no longer a male prerogative, however. Since the turn of the century the alleged feminization of men had been one factor contributing to confusing the gender order. The discourse on comradeship opened up the possibility that the other factor, the masculinization of women, might now also be addressed. Again the ambivalence of the concept of comradeship itself and the attention it drew from all sides of cleavages, from all ideologies and parties, was crucial in "healing" the social wounds of interwar Germany. Although eventually deployed to ensure male dominance, the concept was initially used by socialists and youths to reform the bourgeois nineteenth-century gender order according to which women's biology limited them to the private sphere while only men qualified to rule over the public sphere, whether as breadwinners, citizens, or politicians. In 1920, Elisabeth Busse-Wilson hailed a gender revolution, as boys and girls had shared comradeship in the Wandervogel movement since 1900; many young people rejected their parents' anxieties about pre-marital sex and enjoyed hiking together and camping together overnight, much to the horror of the Wilhelmine adults. Similarly, leftist pedagogues in the 1920s promoted more egalitarian relations between men and women in the spirit of comradeship. Comradeship in these terms was even understood as a vehicle of female emancipation.[49]

If so, it was a special type of emancipation, however. The concept of comradeship did not aim to facilitate sexual liberation but rather the opposite: a chaste or prudish control over lust and sexual desires, which was seen as a remedy for "brutal and blind sexual instincts," as the socialist feminist Clara Zetkin had noted already before 1914. Rooted in the military, comradeship demanded fierce relationships, even within civilian life. There, comradeship was to help couples cope with deprivation and demands, but not to enjoy lust and love.[50] It informed an instrumental type of intimacy that served a political cause, whether socialist class struggle or, in nationalist fashion, Germany's military resurrection. In fact, both socialists and nationalists promoted similar ideals of femaleness when promoting comradely marriages or partnerships. "We need women who stand like men, / not those who care for balls and baubles, / women who are ready to work hard for the German fatherland, / who are able to take action and not only to chitchat . . . " versified Otto Riebecke, a leader of the Kyffhäuser veterans, in 1927.[51] Female comrades would not sink into mourning for their fallen husbands or sons when the nation was at war but rather keep fighting, whether in munitions factories or war hospitals, as women had done in the Great War.[52]

However, fantasies about female comrades, especially those produced in the veterans' media, did not put women on an equal footing with men. When the veterans, or their tabloids, imagined female warriors such as the ancient Amazons, the Nibelungen Saga's Brunhild, or female trench soldiers in World War I, or when they scrutinized women workers in war factories or war administrations, they expected these women to step back into their traditional role as soon as they were no longer needed in those allegedly male jobs. Their "masculinization" was supposed to be a temporary or supplemental state. It would ensure but not question male dominance. "Our Reichsbanner is a male movement," stated its journal, even if it needs to be "complemented by women."[53]

Comradeship between men and women furthered a kind of female emancipation that aimed at gender harmony and hid gender conflict. Hence the youth movement could absorb the concept of comradeship between men and women and at the same time replace coeducation by sex segregation, thus granting girls space for themselves that still depended on the exclusionary strategies of men. Girls were invited to practice female comradeship, but only, in the view of men, to learn how to "respect male comradeship." Men would, in the meantime, "float in the collective and political realms of male society," that is, govern the state and the public sphere, as Fritz Klatt, a socialist sponsor and mentor of the youth movement, explained in 1930.[54]

The very fact, however, that youth and veterans' spokesmen felt urged to remind their audiences of a hierarchy of comradeships attests to the perturbation this concept caused. Just as comradeship oscillated in the military between hierarchy and equality, or between paternalism and solidarity, it did not simply introduce order into interwar gender trouble but also fermented trouble. Addressing women as comrades always meant to liberate them from the private sphere and to concede them a visible place in the public sphere. How far this liberation would reach, and what role women were to play in public, was subject to an ongoing dispute that would not stop during the Third Reich, although men never tired of stressing the subordination of women to men, and of female to male comradeship.[55]

The Third Reich pushed women more deliberately into the public sphere than any political regime in Germany had done before. To be sure, when the Nazis assumed power, they appealed to traditional gender stereotypes and took action to reverse women's emancipation, which they considered one of the innumerable errors of the liberal society. They did not, however, simply roll back progress in gender relations, which would have protected the private sphere of female identity. The family had no rights of its own in the Third Reich. The Nazis praised motherhood and family as biological resources of the militarized *Volksgemeinschaft* rather than as a retreat from it. As with boys and men, girls and women were drawn into a tight net of organizations that trained them to renounce individual lifestyles and devote themselves to the needs of the nation. Comradeship was the code word to address the Nazis' concept of femininity. The visible symbol of being someone was the uniform, the "dress of comradeship" for "all boys and girls of Germany," as the National Youth Leader Baldur von Schirach called it.[56]

Granting girls and women their own realms of comradeship was meant to harden women and to masculinize traditional notions of femininity, without questioning the superior role of men. As comrades, women were supposed to be tougher than the old-fashioned "Gretchen" type that drew happiness solely from her role within the private sphere of the family, not for the sake of their individual happiness but for the grandeur of the fatherland. In the Third Reich, explained Hitler, "the woman has her own battlefield. With every child she brings into the world, she fights her battle for the nation."[57] And Luise Fick, a leader with the Nazis' girls league, added that the ideal woman in Nazi Germany "lived neither for herself nor just for that 'one' man; she lived . . . for her Volk."[58] A woman could do so by assuming different roles. As a mother, she would be giving the Führer children. As an athlete, she would push other women to train their bodies. As a district nurse, she would make use of her position of trust in the local community to x-ray her fellow citizens physically and ideologically. For the nurse was "appointed to a post where she faces, similar in a way to close combat, all the hazards that threaten the people's welfare," explained a brochure on NS-Volkswohlfahrt, the Nazis' social service organization. Reminding nurses of how easily people bare their hearts and their physical problems to a caregiver, the brochure asked them to build up a "martial communal comradeship" to counter-act "whatever threatens it: local diseases, entrenched bad habits, occupational diseases, infant mortality, superstition, ignorance."[59]

The discourse on female comradeship and on comradeship between men and women, as it developed from the late 1920s, was also a discourse on the *Volksgemeinschaft* that the veterans' movement envisioned as the eventual outcome of trench comradeship – the extension of the mythical frontline community into the national realm that would inevitably also include women. This *Volksgemeinschaft* needed tough women, women as comrades, as junior partners of men fighting for the nation's grandeur, not housewives dedicated to merely private interests. Conceding or even praising comradeship among women and comradeship between men and women was in the Third Reich tied into the needs of the *Volksgemeinschaft* – understood as a racially cleansed, ideologically conformist, and highly militarized united nation.

In 1933, the veterans' vision seemed to become reality. The National Socialist movement had always presented itself as born in the trenches and aiming to transfer frontline comradeship to the entire German people. The veterans' movement was the first to welcome the apotheosis of comradeship as "the basis of the new *Reich*." "Our yearnings are fulfilled," exclaimed the *Kyffhäuser*, "finally, the bridge from frontline experience to state building is concluded."[60] Indeed, in the Third Reich the term comradeship was ubiquitous, now applied to women even more naturally than ever before. The basic unit of both the Hitler Youth, serving youths from the age of ten to eighteen, and the Labor Service, recruiting adolescents right afterwards, was called comradeship, or *Kameradschaft*, understood as an organizational unit, such as platoon or squad. Apprenticeships too were now organized into comradeships. College students would meet in comradeships instead of fraternities. All kinds of occupation were to be trained in comradeships. Even artists would no longer meet in art colonies but in comradeships.

Nazi Germany presented itself as a great "national comradeship," with a broad range of institutions and aids to do away with party struggle, class divisions, and any appearance of "egoism" or loneliness.[61] Comradeship was to oil the *Volksgemeinschaft* that would overcome the lacunas of an unfinished nation and guarantee social harmony throughout Germany. It was staged by the Third Reich's national leisure and welfare organization *Kraft durch Freude*, or Strength Through Joy, for instance at a big theater and theme night in the town of Singen in Baden in 1934. Affluence or prestige would no longer determine the allocation of seats or positions: These would be raffled so that the "blue-collar worker would be seated next to the CEO, and the public servant next to the craftsman." Consequently, "snobbishness and arrogance would be averted in these hours of informal comradeship."[62] In the same way, comradeship was to harmonize social relations anywhere in society, at the workplace, in school, in the neighborhood, and in holiday accomodation.

Historians have long argued that the Third Reich's promise of social harmony and happiness was part of a delusive propaganda. It highlighted the "splendid appearance" of the *Volksgemeinschaft* in order to distract from its downsides and insufficiencies. Despite its ubiquitous rhetoric against class divisions, the Nazi state did not seriously challenge, let alone eliminate, the gap between working and middle classes. By and large, the material basis of the working class, measured by income, wealth, and living standard, did not change at all.[63] The "splendid appearance" of the Third Reich was two-faced: On the one hand, it relied on promises, visions, and utopias of material well-being, mass consumerism, affordable cars, homes, and vacation trips for everyone, which only rarely became real experiences and yet indicated that change was on its way. On the other hand, the benefits and blessings of the Third Reich's grand national comradeship were tied into a system of obedience, coercion, and exclusion, just as comradeship in a platoon or a training camp was. Jews and other alleged enemies of the Third Reich were never to enjoy any of these blessings, and even the Aryan *Volksgenossen*, or People's Comrades, would do so only as far as they conformed to what the regime and its many local officials considered useful for the *Volksgemeinschaft*, the people's community.

Comradeship in Nazi Germany "meant effort and devotion" – effort on behalf of and devotion to Führer and *Volksgemeinschaft*. Only the person who served as a willing and efficient small cog in the machine of the *Volksgemeinschaft* could expect to be called "comrade." Anyone who made a mistake, or did not function appropriately, was consigned to outer darkness, labeled "uncomradely," and ostracized from the *Volksgemeinschaft*. For incapability could always be considered to be unwillingness.[64]

A fortiori, anyone expressing any sign of dissatisfaction with the regime was considered uncomradely. According to the Nazis' obsessions, the *Volksgemeinschaft* was threatened not only by alleged racial aliens such as the Jews, Sinti, or Roma, but also by a broad range of "community aliens" (*Gemeinschaftsfremde*) like homosexuals, whores, alcoholics, tramps, beggars, all of them considered unable or unwilling to adjust to the community. These too were to be eliminated, or at least sterilized, or taken into "preventive detention."[65] The hunt for this type of "enemy within" was so insidious because it spread uncertainty. What exactly was a "community alien"? Some categories were established, but this one only opened a vast grey area. "Whoever challenges our unity, will end up at the stake," announced Baldur von Schirach, the national leader of the Hitler Youth, in 1934.[66] Who exactly challenged the unity of the Hitler Youth? Might it be the boy who, instead of diving into the comradeship of the Hitler Youth, wasted his time with reading a book at home or strolling along the streets?

Nazi propagandists, jurists, doctors, pedagogues eagerly labeled all kinds of "community pests" in order to spread the fear of being ostracized. Among these labels were the "coward," the "shirker," the "troublemaker," the "griper," the "peacock," the "uncontrolled," the "schemer," and the "loner." Although the lone wolf was not necessarily a criminal, as a military psychologist noted uneasily, his behaviour could be considered as a "preliminary stage of desertion." Desertion, from whichever unit, was the epitome of treason, the ultimate betrayal of one's comrades and community.[67] It would be wrong to assume that the Third Reich left no space for individuality, as historians have noted. But individuality was allowed only so far as it did not question the absolute priority of the *Volksgemeinschaft* but conformed to its rules.[68] And whoever did not conform, or obey, but just tried to be himself, was considered a possible deserter – a traitor to the *Volksgemeinschaft*.

But not only shirking or opposing individuals seemed to threaten the *Volksgemeinschaft*. Comradeship itself, understood as the epitome of social cohesion, did have a downside, in the view both of military psychologists and the Nazi planners of a totalitarian state. Instead of serving the fighting morale and smoothing the military hierarchy, the social cohesion in small units was always at risk of undermining order and obedience. Erich Weniger in his 1938 book on military training warned explicitly of the "camaraderie" of "goldbrickers," "thieves," and plain "criminals" and other types of mistaken comradeship, especially those that served to cover up blunders of all kinds.[69] A little grumbling and griping was OK, as long as it served as a psychological relief valve to restore discipline, obedience, and fighting morale. But the mutinies at the end of the Great

War had shown the German military that minor collective recalcitrance, the comradeship of cliques, could mushroom into a veritable rebellion, as Max Simoneit warned in 1933.[70]

In order to curtail its subversive potential, comradeship was to be tied to charismatic leadership and mutual trust between officers and men, just as the myth of comradeship had praised it since the war.[71] In the larger *Volksgemeinschaft*, the Führer Adolf Hitler embodied the ultimate perfection of this type of leadership. Thus in the official glossary of the Third Reich, comradeship translated into "absolute obedience" to and "unconditional trust" in the Führer. "In the Third Reich the notion of comradeship has absorbed a new and deep meaning," explained *Trübners Deutsches Wörterbuch* authoritatively in 1943. It was now the code word for unconditional "belief and obedience that merged Adolf Hitler's allegiance into an indissoluble and irrevocable community."[72] Indeed, it was a new meaning. Previously, comradeship described the unity of men (or women) with different or even conflicting ideological identities. Comradeship hovered above and in fact neutralized ideological cleavages, according to the World War I myth about frontline communities. By contrast, the Nazis' notion of comradeship implied that there were no longer any cleavages. Comradeship denoted the unity and solidarity of ideologically standardized, Nazified soldiers and citizens.

But for the time being the complete Nazification of German soldiers and citizens was only a goal, not yet reality. Preparing for total war, the *Volksgemeinschaft*, a.k.a *Wehrgemeinschaft*, or martial community, could not afford to ostracize or detain too many people. Everyone was needed, at least those considered racially fit. Thus, the rhetoric of exterminating or ostracizing "community aliens" and "non-comrades" was tied into a program of converting the troublemakers, grumblers, and egoists into useful *Volksgenossen*, or at least into cannon fodder. And it was not only about the troublemakers. While the *Gleichschaltung*, or enforced coordination, of the state apparatus was concluded within a few years, the ideological and psychological side of the Nazi revolution would need a much longer "transitional period," as Heinrich Himmler once said.[73] Ridding Germans of class-consciousness and other civilian identities could not start too early in life. As Hitler explained in a speech in December 1938, "boys join our organization at the age of ten." Four years later, "they move from the *Jungvolk* to the Hitler Youth . . . And then we are even less prepared to give them back into the hands of those who create class and status barriers, rather we take them immediately into the Party . . . into the SA or into the SS," after which they "are polished for six or seven months" in the Labor Service. And if there "are still remnants of class consciousness or pride in status, then the Wehrmacht will take over the further treatment for two years' of basic training, and after that, to prevent them from slipping back into old habits once again, we take them immediately into the SA, SS etc., and they will not be free again for the rest of their lives."[74]

In order to build an ideologically united *Volksgemeinschaft,* the Nazi state forced young boys and also, less coercively, girls and adults, into a sophisticated training program. German boys from the age of ten to eighteen joined the Hitler Youth. In 1933 one in three did so, and from 1939 on almost everyone. As part of their training, they spent some time in a camp, usually a couple of weeks per year. Adults also were asked to join a training camp for a few weeks. From 1933 until 1939, about 70 percent of German teachers participated in at least one training camp. From 1935 on, the compulsory camps of the National Labor Service – Reichsarbeitsdienst or RAD – enforced a six-month work schedule on all males between the ages of eighteen and twenty-five. And from 1935 until 1945, the Wehrmacht drafted about 17 million men for military service, which began with a two-year training period in the barracks – a special kind of camp.[75] Girls and women were urged to join camps as well, for instance as members of the German Girls' League (Bund Deutscher Mädel, or BDM) or of the female Reichsarbeitsdienst.[76]

Unlike the pre-1933 youth movement, which had allowed boys and girls to leave a camp whenever they liked, the Third Reich organized camps militarily, or as "total institutions." This is the label the sociologist Erving Goffman coined for prisons, hospitals, monasteries, and military barracks where all the activities of the inmates occur in the same place with the same people answering to a single authority. And so it was in Nazi youth camps. All camp members wore uniforms as the symbol of their equality, all were required to work, sleep, and play together, and all were subjected to a tight daily schedule that included exercises, classes, meals, sleeping, but very little leisure time. Separated for weeks, months, or even years from their previous life as civilians, from their jobs, possessions, friends, and relatives, isolated from the rest of society in a "community of fate," these people had to get along, whether they liked it or not.[77] Separation from relatives and friends "condensed" social interaction in the camp, providing the optimal prerequisites for brainwashing or "assimilation," as a Nazi pedagogue, Ernst Krieck, wrote. The camp brought together young people so that they would "all adopt the same type [of personality] and a similar lifestyle."[78]

In many regards this "assimilation," or standardization, relied on elements of the male initiation rites that were known in many societies, pre-industrial as well as industrial, European as well as non-European.[79]

These rites, which were well known to Nazi anthropologists and pedagogues, separate boys from women and teach boys how to become a man, to think, feel, and behave like other men, to adopt and internalize manly social qualities. Boys are sent to the men's hut to learn male conformity and male solidarity. Sometimes homosexual practices are included, sometimes not. Usually, these rites are dramatically framed, torture and humiliation playing a major role. Only they seem to guarantee the desired result. As the cultural anthropologist Victor Turner has explained, male initiation rites are embedded in a "liminal" period of intended uncertainty, during which the characteristics of the ritual subject are ambiguous. "He passes through a cultural realm that has few or none of the attributes of the past or coming state." Social conventions are decisively disregarded during this transitional state, and even social hierarchies, authorities, and inferiorities are confused. The neophytes have left "society as a structured, differentiated, and often hierarchical system of politico-legal-economic positions." They enter a new society – actually an anti-society. The "anti-structure," as Turner names it, "emerges recognizably in the liminal period as an unstructured or rudimentarily structured community."[80]

Similar patterns of male initiation have governed youth gangs and youth cultures in Western societies; they have been crucial in the training period of soldiers in military cultures, and also in paramilitary settings. To become a real man, a "mother's boy" needed to erase any infantile, egocentric identities that were rooted in the female world of his family. To knock out his private identity and to give him a new, truly male identity, he was sent to the "school of manliness" – military service. Germany's interwar period differed from other European countries only insofar as the Versailles Treaty had interrupted the tradition of conscription until 1935, when the Nazis reintroduced the draft. But this interruption did not prevent military psychologists and veterans from discussing the workings and the benefits of military initiation rituals.[81] Pedagogues in interwar Germany justified and sought to organize military and paramilitary training as a "period to break up the wrong consciousness," to reshape completely the entire personality of a youth.[82] Max Momsen, a college director in Cottbus, explained in 1935 how camp training worked. "When camp service seizes the body and compels it to a certain concise performance, it also forces the body into certain mental and emotional habits, which consist first of all in relinquishing all that is individual and selfish ... The private self, the individual, will be broken. This might be a hard and painful procedure. It is inevitable, though, for the sake of a higher and larger community."[83] The boy who was to become a full member of this larger community had to start from scratch. Accepting his status as lowest on the pecking order was the first step. Only when he was there, on the lowest step of the ladder in the hierarchical structure of male bonding, could a new identity be ascribed to him. Mother's boy had "to go through an entire system of tortures" carried out by his comrades or his superiors in order "to be acknowledged as a real man and no longer be considered just a young whippersnapper."[84]

Devoid of women, the camp's or the barrack's "anti-structure" was not without the symbolic power provided by the dichotomies and hierarchies of a gendered system. The new recruit was made to do "things he would decisively have refused to do as a pampered mother's boy" – cleaning, mending, darning, making beds, peeling potatoes, folding the washing, all the things that "Mother" had done for him and that were "not at all a man's job."[85] Thus, ironically, for a boy to become a real man, he had to become a woman first. For the moment, he lost any gender identity but only so that he could soon regain an even clearer and more powerful one. For the humiliation of the male neophyte came with a promise: If you bear the humiliation, and play along, you too will soon be a fully-fledged member of our community – you will be a real man, and incidentally then also be entitled yourself to humiliate neophytes. Humiliation, thus, was designed as the starting point of a period of suffering, which would eventually lead to redemption.

The initiation was concluded when the "manly I" was completely absorbed by the "army's communal spirit" and felt happy in realizing that "I am no longer an I, the I is gone."[86] This obsession with erasing the individual identity and implanting a purely collective one is what distinguishes the Nazi ideas about community, comradeship, and camp training from similar programs and discourses in other countries. One example is the Civilian Conservation Corps (CCC) in the United States, introduced by the Roosevelt administration as one of the pillars of the New Deal. Just like the Reichsarbeitsdienst, the CCC was an instrument to fight youth unemployment, included a pedagogical component, was organized under the guidance of the army in a strongly authoritarian fashion, consisted of the same type of physically demanding outdoor labor, and lasted six months. The similarities were so obvious that con-temporary American critics of the CCC feared that their country would move into the direction of the Nazi dictatorship. But there were cru-cial differences, as the historian Kiran Klaus Patel has shown. Unlike the RAD, the CCC remained a voluntary service and restricted to men. While the CCC was not free of discrimination against African Ameri-cans, "access criteria were not defined fundamentally in völkisch-racist terms" as in Germany, where Jews were rigidly excluded. And while the CCC also aimed to "prepare individuals for their role as responsible members of society," to raise their ability to integrate themselves into a group, it left much more leeway for the preservation of individual identities. In sharp contrast to the RAD, the CCC education was only rarely praised for creating a sense of collective identity, and when so, it was bound to a different notion of citizenship than in Germany. While the pedagogical goal in Germany was a conformist one, the CCC aimed at a "differentiated contributing citizenship" that valued "an independent participation in a democracy, such as the ability to assume responsibility in a self-governing group" – precisely that kind of responsibility which the Nazi morals wanted to overcome. Characteristically, "nearly the entire educational program in the evenings was voluntary, which sets the CCC fundamentally apart from the RAD," where all activities were mandatory and regimented, precisely in order to deliberately destroy any individual niches. In addition, the CCC camps "were less rigidly closed off from the outside than were those in Germany . . . Protestant, Catholic, and also Jewish clergy conducted services," and the "teaching staff included women," thus weakening the "character of the Corps as a male society."[87]

The Nazi pedagogues' fascination with replacing the I with the We reflects the goal, not the reality of camp and youth life. Germans of all age groups were able to save niches of individuality in a dictatorship that aimed at but never achieved totalitarian control and indoctrination of its citizens. Yet many testimonies clearly show that the individualist felt an isolated outsider among a mass of comrades who were eager to join in. The cult of the We was not simply a woolly theory. Sebastian Haffner, who after the Second World War would become a popular political journalist and biographer of Hitler, is a good example. Born in 1907 into a left-liberal Berlin family, he emigrated in 1938 to London with his Jewish fiancée, tried to make a living as a journalist, and wrote a youth memoir that ended with an account on his own experiences in a Nazi training camp in 1933. As a civil service candidate, he had to join it for a couple of weeks before being permitted to take his legal exams. The camp was located in a village on the plains of Brandenburg, far away from urban pleasures and comforts, and Haffner was surprised to discover that it was not mainly a place of ideological indoctrination. Instead of learning about antisemitism, Nazi eugenics, the *Lebensraum* ideology, the leadership principle, or the heroic past of the NSDAP, adolescents such as Haffner were to internalize military order, and most importantly, the grammar of comradeship. If one's feet smelled, one was obliged to wash them "every morning and every evening. That is a rule of comradeship." Annoying others was to be avoided at all costs. And this did not just apply to body hygiene. More important were fitness exercises and paramilitary drill, bellowing "Heil Hitler," marching around the camp and singing military songs. Beyond obeying orders, even without supervision, the comrades practiced comradeship on their own.

Haffner did not deny the "happiness of comradeship," admitting frankly that "it was a pleasure to go for a cross-country run together in the morning, and then to go naked into the communal hot showers together, to share the parcels that one or another received from home, to share also responsibility for misdemeanours that one of your comrades had committed, to help and support one another in a thousand little ways." What embarrassed him, however, was the counter-world of comradeship, its anti-structure, as the anthropologist Victor Turner would later say, which official military assessments and popular war memory usually addressed only indirectly or covertly. "Civilian courtesy," Haffner observed, was scorned with the abundant use of crudities and profanity. The "ritual reciting of lewd songs and jokes" served to vilify bourgeois love. As he understood it, comradeship "actively decomposed" both "individuality and civilization" and elevated men above "civilized tenderness." A highlight of such decomposition was the boyish prank "of attacking a neighboring dormitory at night with 'water bombs,' drinking mugs filled with water to be poured over the beds of the defenders . . . A battle would ensue, with merry 'Ho's and 'Ha's and screaming and cheering. You were a bad comrade if you did not take part . . . It was taken for granted that comradeship prevented those who had been attacked from telling tales."

The lesson to be learned might have been entitled "The Sovereignty of the Male Bond." The group did not need a superior authority to run its internal affairs but restored order on its own. Individuals were powerless but comradeship offered empowerment. The night after a dormitory raid "we had to be prepared for a revenge attack." Revenge restored order just as ostracism did. "If someone committed a sin against comradeship" by acting in a superior way, showing off, or exhibiting "more individuality than was permissible, a nighttime court in the barracks would judge and condemn him to corporal punishment. Being dragged under the water pump was the punishment for minor misdemeanors." Someone who "favored himself in distributing butter rations," however, suffered a "terrible fate." He would be "dragged from his bed and spread-eagled on a table. 'Every man will whack Meier once, no one is excused,' the judge thundered." And the victim was well advised to accept what the group did to him. "By the dark laws of comradeship that governed us, independently of our individual wills, a complaint would have put him in danger of his life."

To be sure, Haffner's experience was by no means unique nor was it limited to Nazi Germany. Subcultural youth gangs in Weimar Germany and all kinds of fraternities and sororities in other countries, including democratic ones, have practiced similar and often much more brutal initiation rituals, known as hazing, since ancestral times and continue to do so still in the present.[88] Haffner, however, understood well the peculiarity of his experience in Nazi Germany. While hazing in gangs, fraternities, and sororities gains its momentum from operating in secret and against the rules of the respectable society, this opposition no longer existed in Nazi Germany. Here, the state orchestrated comradeship the way Haffner faced it in a training camp. With more acumen than many contemporary critics and later analysts of the Third Reich, Haffner, looking at Nazi Germany from his London exile, identified the code word of the moral, emotional, and ideological standardization of the German society the Nazis aimed at. Comradeship, he noted a few months before the Nazis started the war that would soon lead also to genocide, "can become a means for the most terrible dehumanization" as it "relieves men of responsibility for their own actions, before themselves, before God, before their conscience. They do what all their comrades do . . . Their comrades are their conscience and give absolution for everything." "Widely praised harmless male comradeship," he said, "completely destroys the sense of the responsibility for oneself." But what he had in mind was not only the training camps. Rather, he stated disgustedly, comradeship had become "demonic" as well as pandemic in Germany. The "whole nation, Germany" was, according to his diagnosis, infected "with a germ that causes its people to treat their victims" as if they were "wolves." The name of the germ was comradeship. Germans, Haffner said, "are 'comraded,' a dreadfully dangerous condition . . . They are terribly happy, but terribly demeaned; so self-satisfied, but so boundlessly loathsome; so proud and yet so despicable and inhuman."[89]

NOTES

1 Prost, *Les anciens combattants et la société française: 1914–1939*, 3 vols. (Paris: Presses de la Fondation Nationale des Sciences Politiques, 1977), vol. I, pp. 177–87; Heiko Haumann, "Eine inszenierte Friedensaktion: Freiburg i. Br. und Besançon als Schauplätze deutsch-französischer Frontkämpfertreffen 1937–1938," *Zeitschrift des Breisgau-Geschichtsvereins "Schau-ins-Land"*, 108 (1989), 289–316 (p. 311 on Hitler). On Nazi propaganda, see *Kyffhäuser*, Oct. 27, 1935, p. 1072; ibid., March 8 and 15, 1936, pp. 254, 283; ibid., Nov. 20, 1936, pp. 1117–18; ibid., March 21, 1937, p. 275; ibid., April 4, 1937, p. 331; ibid., Aug. 14, 1938, pp. 777–78; *Kriegsgräberfürsorge*, Aug. 1936, p. 117 (Olympics); P. C. Ettighofer, *"Wo bist du – Kamerad?" Der Frontsoldat im Reichssender Köln* (Essen: Essener Verlagsanstalt, 1938), pp. 7–8, 43–44, 163–200; and Friedrich Grupe, *Jahrgang 1916: Die Fahne war mehr als der Tod* (Munich: Universitas, 1989), pp. 43–45 on the reception among youth in the Third Reich.

2 Wilhelm Treue, "Rede Hitlers vor der deutschen Presse (10. Nov. 1938),"
   Vierteljahrshefte für Zeitgeschichte, 6 (1958), 175–91 (at p. 182); *Kyffhäuser*,
   Jan. 12, 1936, p. 30; *Kriegsgräberfürsorge*, Aug. 1936, p. 117.
3 Weitz, *Weimar Germany*, pp. 297–330; Ute Frevert, *Women in German
   History: From Bourgeois Emancipation to Sexual Liberation* (Oxford: Berg,
   1989), pp. 151–204. Man and baby carriage: Hermann Haß, *Sitte und Kultur im Nachkriegsdeutschland* (Hamburg: Hanseatische Verlagsanstalt, 1932),
   p. 77.
4 Robert Beachy, *Gay Berlin: Birthplace of a Modern Identity* (New York: Knopf,
   2015); Ulrich Geuter, *Homosexualität in der deutschen Jugendbewegung: Jun-
   genfreundschaft und Sexualität im Diskurs von Jugendbewegung, Psychoanalyse
   und Jugendpsychologie am Beginn des 20. Jahrhunderts* (Frankfurt: Suhrkamp,
   1994); Claudia Bruns, *Politik des Eros: Der Männerbund in Wissenschaft, Politik
   und Jugendkultur (1880–1934)* (Cologne: Böhlau, 2008); Jason Crouthamel,
   "'Comradeship' and 'Friendship': Masculinity and Militarization in Germany's Homosexual Emancipation Movement after the First World War,"
   Gender & History, 23 (2011), 111–29; Crouthamel, *An Intimate History of the
   Front*, pp. 41–64, 147–69.
5 Paul Lerner, *Hysterical Men: War, Psychiatry, and the Politics of Trauma in Ger-
   many, 1890–1930* (Ithaca, NY: Cornell University Press, 2003); and Jason
   Crouthamel, *The Great War and German Memory: Society, Politics and Psycho-
   logical Trauma, 1914–1945* (Liverpool University Press, 2010).
6 Irmtraud Götz von Olenhusen, "Vom Jungstahlhelm zur SA: Die junge
   Nachkriegsgeneration in den paramilitärischen Verbänden der Weimarer
   Republik," in Wolfgang R. Krabbe (ed.), *Politische Jugend in der Weimarer
   Republik* (Bochum: Universitätsverlag, 1993), pp. 146–82; more largely,
   George L. Mosse, *The Image of Man: The Creation of Modern Masculinity*
   (New York: Oxford University Press, 1996), pp. 133–80.
7 *Freideutsche Jugend*, March 1917, p. 81.
8 Schauwecker, *Im Todesrachen*, pp. 16–20, 68.
9 Silvia Bovenschen, *Die imaginierte Weiblichkeit: Exemplarische Untersuchungen zu kulturgeschichtlichen und literarischen Präsentationsformen des Weiblichen*
   (Frankfurt: Suhrkamp, 1979); Christa Rhode-Dachser, *Expedition in den dun-
   klen Kontinent: Weiblichkeit im Diskurs der Psychoanalyse* (Berlin: Springer,
   1991), pp. 95–100.
10 Hans-Heinrich Grunwaldt, "Das erotische Moment im Rekrutenleben,"
   Soldatentum, 4 (1937), 31–36.
11 Jason Crouthamel, "'Comradeship' and 'Friendship,'" p. 111, quotation at
   p. 116, referring to Magnus Hirschfeld, *The Sexual History of the War* (1941;
   repr. Honolulu: University Press of the Pacific, 2006), pp. 135–36. Cf. Harry
   Oosterhuis and Hubert Kennedy (eds.), *Homosexuality and Male Bonding in
   Pre-Nazi Germany: The Youth Movement, the Gay Movement, and Male Bonding
   Before Hitler's Rise* (New York: Routledge, 1991).
12 Paul Fussell, *The Great War and Modern Memory* (New York: Oxford University Press, 1975), p. 271.
13 Grunwaldt, "Das erotische Moment," pp. 35–36, quoting Georg Graben-
   horst, *Fahnenjunker Volkenborn* (Leipzig: Koehler & Amelang, 1928), pp. 43,
   155–56.

14 Burkhard Jellonnek, *Homosexuelle unter dem Hakenkreuz: Die Verfolgung von Homosexuellen im Dritten Reich* (Paderborn: Schöningh, 1990); for a nuanced assessment, see Crouthamel, *An Intimate History of the Front*, pp. 161–69.

15 Fussell, *The Great War and Modern Memory*, pp. 270–309 (quotation at pp. 279–80). Cf. Sarah Cole, *Modernism, Male Friendship, and the First World War* (Cambridge University Press, 2007); Gabriel Koureas, "'Desiring Skin': Eugenics, Trauma and Acting Out of Masculinities in British Inter-war Visual Culture," in Fae Brauer and Anthea Callen (eds.), *Art, Sex and Eugenics: Corpus Delicti* (Aldershot: Ashgate, 2008), pp. 163–87.

16 Siegfried Kracauer, "Über die Freundschaft," in Kracauer, *Schriften*, vol. V (Frankfurt: Suhrkamp, 1990), pp. 29ff., 33, 37ff. (first published 1917–21). Cf. Friedrich H. Tenbruck, "Freundschaft: Ein Beitrag zu einer Soziologie der persönlichen Beziehungen," *Kölner Zeitschrift für Soziologie und Sozialpsychologie*, 16 (1964), 431–56; Harry Blatterer, *Everyday Friendships: Intimacy as Freedom in a Complex World* (Basingstoke: Palgrave Macmillan, 2012).

17 Cole, *Modernism, Male Friendship, and the First World War*, pp. 139, 144–46, 148, 151, 155. See also Wolfgang Mann, "Englisches Kriegserleben aus 'War Letters of Fallen Englishmen,'" *Neuphilologische Monatsschrift*, 8 (1937), 462–67.

18 *Kyffhäuser*, July 24, 1932, p. 518; Till Kalkschmidt, "Kameradschaft und Führertum der Front," *Dichtung und Volkstum*, 39 (1938), pp. 183–84; Bruno H. Jahn, *Die Weisheit des Soldaten* (Berlin: Keil, 1937), pp. 37–38; *Stahlhelm*, Nov. 29, 1925. See also Ulrich Nassen, *Jugend, Buch und Konjunktur: Studien zum Ideologiepotential des genuin nationalsozialistischen und des konjunkturellen 'Jugendschrifttums'* (Munich: Fink, 1987), p. 63. This devaluation of friendship is only one aspect of a broader discourse on male relationships, of course. It did not question an older track of Western thinking about friendship as a political sentiment (i.e. the nucleus of political entities), see the survey of Danny Kaplan, "What can the concept of friendship contribute to the study of national identity?," *Nations and Nationalism*, 13 (2007), pp. 225–44. The above-mentioned "friendships" between "outlaws" of the Weimar Republic and early Nazis is part of this thinking, which, as may be noted, still affirms the voluntary principle of friendship, as opposed to comradeship.

19 Svenja Levsen, "Constructing Elite Identities: University Students, Military Masculinity and the Consequences of the Great War in Britain and Germany," *Past and Present*, 198 (2008), 147–98; and Levsen, *Elite, Männlichkeit und Krieg: Tübinger und Cambridger Studenten, 1900–1929* (Göttingen: Vandenhoeck & Ruprecht, 2006), pp. 189–251. Levsen has shown that university students in Germany in the 1920s translated war experience into group and community-oriented masculinities while British students, under the impression of material wealth and consumerism, indulged in individualized concepts of masculinity. See also Leo Braudy, *From Chivalry to Terrorism: War and the Changing Nature of Masculinity* (New York: Knopf, 2003), pp. 395–442, esp. 428.

20 Cole, *Modernism, Male Friendship, and the First World War*, p. 186; Graham Dawson, *Soldier Heroes: British Adventure, Empire, and the Imagining of Masculinities* (London: Routledge, 1994); Rene Schilling, *"Kriegshelden":*

Deutungsmuster heroischer Männlichkeit in Deutschland, 1813–1945 (Paderborn: Schöningh, 2002), pp. 252–315.

21 Ernest Hemingway, *A Farewell to Arms* (New York: Scribner, 1997); Hemingway, *For Whom the Bell Tolls* (New York: Scribner, 1968).

22 Schauwecker, *The Fiery Way*, p. 67.

23 *Kyffhäuser*, Nov. 17, 1929, pp. 839–40, and Feb. 23, 1930, pp. 134–35; Johannes Stepkes, *Wehrhaft – Mannhaft: Lebens- und Charakterschule für deutsche Soldaten* (Freiburg: Herder, 1936), pp. 8–9, 12–14; Kleo Pleyer, *Volk im Feld* (Hamburg: Hanseatische Verlagsanstalt, 1943), pp. 111–14; Beumelburg, *Die Gruppe Bosemüller*, pp. 38–39. On pre-1914 traditions, see Ute Frevert, *A Nation in Barracks: Modern Germany, Military Conscription and Civil Society* (Oxford: Berg, 2004), pp. 182–99; Thomas Rohrkrämer, *Der Militarismus der "kleinen Leute": Die Kriegervereine im Deutschen Kaiserreich* (Munich: Oldenbourg, 1990); and Rohrkrämer, "Das Militär als Männerbund? Der Kult soldatischer Männlichkeit im Deutschen Kaiserreich," *Westfälische Forschungen*, 45 (1995), 169–87.

24 Beumelburg, *Die Gruppe Bosemüller*, pp. 26, 36–37, 50, 114–15, 119–20.

25 Ibid., pp. 134, 136, 182–83.

26 Hans Zöberlein, *Der Glaube an Deutschland – Ein Kriegserleben von Verdun bis zum Umsturz* (Munich: Franz Eher, 1931), p. 718; Tobias Schneider, "Bestseller im Dritten Reich: Ermittlung und Analyse der meistverkauften Romane in Deutschland 1933–1944," *Vierteljahrshefte für Zeitgeschichte*, 52 (2004), 77–97 (at p. 87).

27 Obviously, my reading of Germany's interwar discourse on soldierly masculinity does not comply with Theweleit's interpretation in *Male Fantasies*. This is only in part the result of my consulting different sources. Theweleit's picture is, in my view, committed to simplifying and also to demonizing soldierly and Nazi, or pre-Nazi, masculinities, and eventually masculinities at large. This approach was common in older studies on the ideological, emotional, and social causes of Nazism. Since the 1980s, however, after Theweleit's study came into being, scholarship on the ideological and psychological roots of Nazism as well as research on masculinities have de-demonized their subjects and allowed acknowledgement of ambivalences. Although relying on Theweleit, Jeffords pioneered this approach in *The Remasculinization of America*.

28 Grunwaldt, "Das erotische Moment im Rekrutenleben," p. 32.

29 Remarque, *All Quiet on the Western Front*, pp. 45–46.

30 Ibid., pp. 61–62.

31 Josef Magnus Wehner, *Mein Leben* (Berlin: Junker und Dünnhaupt, 1934), p. 71 (quotation); Pongs, "Krieg als Volksschicksal," pp. 77–79.

32 Egon Hundeiker, *Rasse, Volk, Soldatentum* (Munich: Lehmann, 1937), pp. 44, 100–01.

33 Text: Internet Modern History Sourcebook, www.fordham.edu/halsall/mod/horstwessel.asp (accessed Oct. 14, 2013). Cf. George Broderick, "Das Horst-Wessel-Lied: A Reappraisal," *International Folklore Review*, 10 (1995), 100–27; and Daniel Siemens, *The Making of a Nazi Hero: The Murder and Myth of Horst Wessel* (London: I. B. Tauris, 2013).

34 *Konstanzer Zeitung*, Nov. 2, 1933; cf. *Der Seehase*, July 1937, p. 2.

35 Georg Bussmann et al. (eds.), *Kunst im Dritten Reich: Dokumente der Unterwerfung* (Frankfurt: Zweitausendeins, 1975), pp. 110–16.

36 Julius Karl von Engelbrechten, *Eine braune Armee entsteht: Die Geschichte der Berlin-Brandenburger SA* (Munich: Eher, 1937), p. 85.

37 Wilhelm Reibert, *Der Dienstunterricht im Reichsheer: Ein Handbuch für den deutschen Soldaten*, 6th edn. (Berlin: Mittler, 1934), p. 96; [K. L.] von Oertzen, *Deutsches Reichsheer-Handbuch (D.R.H.)*, (Charlottenburg: Offene Worte, 1923), p. 87.

38 Weniger, *Wehrmachtserziehung und Kriegserfahrung*, pp. 117, 135–36; Kurt Kreipe, "Der Rekrut der Allgemeinen Wehrpflicht," *Soldatentum*, 3 (1936), 136–41.

39 Zöberlein, *Der Glaube an Deutschland*, pp. 297–98.

40 Remarque, *All Quiet on the Western Front*, pp. 211–12, 131–32.

41 E. Jäger, "Der Krieg wandelt den Menschen," *Deutsche Wehr*, May 22, 1931, p. 526.

42 Kreipe, "Der Rekrut der Allgemeinen Wehrpflicht," p. 139; Erich Schwinge, *Militärstrafgesetzbuch nebst Kriegssonderstrafrechtsverordnung*, 2nd edn. (Berlin: Junker und Dünnhaupt, 1944), pp. 61, 93, 112.

43 *Reichsbanner*, Sept. 7, 1929, pp. 294–95.

44 Richard Braun, *Individualismus und Gemeinschaft in der deutschen Jugendbewegung*, Ph.D. dissertation, University of Erlangen (1929), pp. 35, 42, 45, 52, 88; Harry Pross, *Jugend – Eros – Politik: Die Geschichte der deutschen Jugendverbände* (Vienna: Scherz, 1964), pp. 67–68; Matthias von Hellfeld, *Bündische Jugend und Hitlerjugend: Zur Geschichte von Anpassung und Widerstand 1930–1939* (Cologne: Verlag Wissenschaft und Politik, 1987), pp. 33–34; *Das junge Deutschland*, 25 (1931), 398–403; *Reichsbanner*, Oct. 17 1931, pp. 336–37; *Arbeiterjugend*, 1926, p. 108. On the Catholic youth movement, see Irmtraud Götz von Olenhusen, *Jugendreich, Gottesreich, Deutsches Reich: Junge Generation, Religion und Politik, 1928–1933* (Cologne: Verlag Wissenschaft und Politik, 1987), pp. 69, 79–80, 87–88.

45 Moritz Föllmer, *Individuality and Modernity in Berlin: Self and Society from Weimar to the Wall* (Cambridge University Press, 2013).

46 Leopold von Wiese, *Kindheit: Erinnerungen aus meinen Kadettenjahren* (Hanover: Steegemann, 1924), pp. 77–78; Helmut Plessner, *Grenzen der Gemeinschaft: Eine Kritik des sozialen Radikalismus* (Bonn: Bouvier, 1924).

47 Alfred Vierkandt, "Sittlichkeit," in Vierkandt (ed.), *Handwörterbuch der Soziologie* (Stuttgart: Enke, 1931), p. 538; Ruth Benedict, *The Chrysanthemum and the Sword: Patterns of Japanese Culture* (Boston: Houghton Mifflin, 1948).

48 Franz Matzke, *Jugend bekennt: So sind wir!* (Leipzig: Reclam, 1930), p. 57.

49 Paul Krische, *Die Frau als Kamerad: Grundsätzliches zum Problem des Geschlechtes*, 3rd edn. (Bonn: Marcus & Weber, 1923); Elisabeth Busse-Wilson, *Die Frau und die Jugendbewegung: Ein Beitrag zur weiblichen Charakterologie und zur Kritik des Antifeminismus*, ed. Irmgard Klönne (Münster: Lit, 1989; 1st edn. 1920); Karen Hagemann, *Frauenalltag und Männerpolitik: Alltagsleben und gesellschaftliches Handeln von Arbeiterfrauen in der Weimarer Republik* (Bonn: Dietz, 1990), pp. 325–31.

50 Ulrich Linse, "'Geschlechtsnot der Jugend': Über Jugendbewegung und Sex-
    ualität," in Thomas Koebner, Rolf-Peter Janz, and Frank Trommler (eds.),
    "Mit uns zieht die neue Zeit": Der Mythos Jugend (Frankfurt: Suhrkamp, 1985),
    pp. 245–309 (Zetkin quotation at 281). Critical: Max Hodann, *Bub und
    Mädel: Gespräche unter Kameraden über die Geschlechterfrage* (Leipzig: Olden-
    burg, 1924), pp. 102–04. See also Ben B. Lindsey and Wainwright Evans, *Die
    Kameradschaftsehe* (Stuttgart: DVA, 1928), the widely debated translation of
    the American original *Companionate Marriage* (New York: Boni & Liveright,
    1927).
51 *Kyffhäuser*, March 20, 1927, poem and drawing.
52 *Kriegerzeitung*, Aug. 10, 1924, 1st appendix.
53 *Reichsbanner*, Sept. 26, 1931, p. 310; *Zentralblatt für Kriegsgeschädigte*, Nov.
    1, 1925, pp. 3–4.
54 Fritz Klatt, "Geschlechtliche Gruppierung der Jugend," *Das junge Deutsch-
    land*, 24 (1930), 166–69.
55 For a more detailed elaboration, see my *Belonging and Genocide*, pp. 138–44,
    from which the following paragraphs are drawn.
56 Baldur von Schirach, *Revolution der Erziehung: Reden aus den Jahren des Auf-
    baus*, 3rd edn. (Munich: Eher, 1942), p. 46, speech from April 19, 1938.
57 Hitler speech to the National Socialist Women's Congress in 1935, excerpted
    in George L. Mosse, *Nazi Culture: Intellectual, Cultural and Social Life in the
    Third Reich* (New York: Grosset & Dunlap, 1966), p. 40.
58 Luise Fick, *Die deutsche Jugendbewegung* (Jena: Diederich, 1939), p. 180.
59 Hanna Rees, *Frauenarbeit in der NS-Volkswohlfahrt* (Berlin: Eher, 1938),
    pp. 30–35.
60 *Kyffhäuser*, Sept. 3 1933, pp. 614ff.; *Stahlhelm*, Jan. 27, 1935, and Jan. 29,
    1933 (!), "We are creating the nation!"
61 Cornelia Schmitz-Berning, *Vokabular des Nationalsozialismus* (Berlin: de
    Gruyter, 1998), pp. 343–45.
62 Quotations from local newspapers as in Gerd Zang, *Die zwei Gesichter des
    Nationalsozialismus: Singen am Hohentwiel im Dritten Reich* (Sigmaringen: Jan
    Thorbecke, 1995), p. 182.
63 Ian Kershaw, *The Nazi Dictatorship: Problems and Perspectives of Interpretation*,
    4th edn. (London: Arnold, 2000), pp. 161–82; Richard Evans, *The Third
    Reich in Power, 1933–1939* (New York: Penguin, 2005), pp. 414–503.
64 See Kühne, *Belonging and Genocide*, pp. 34–37.
65 Michael Burleigh and Wolfgang Wippermann, *The Racial State: Germany
    1933–1945* (Cambridge University Press, 1991), pp. 75–197; Robert Gel-
    lately and Nathan Stoltzfus (eds.), *Social Outsiders in Nazi Germany* (Prince-
    ton University Press, 2001).
66 Baldur von Schirach, *Die Hitler-Jugend: Idee und Gestalt* (Berlin: Koehler &
    Amelang, 1934), p. 85.
67 Hermann Göring, *Reden und Aufsätze* (Munich: Eher, 1938), pp. 226–44;
    Karl Mierke, "Gefährdete Kameradschaft," *Soldatentum*, 6 (1939), 138–
    41, 188–95; Hermann Foertsch, *Der Offizier der deutschen Wehrmacht*, 5th
    edn. (Berlin: Eisenschmidt, 1941), pp. 56, 67; L. Schulz, "Loslösung und
    Einfügung im Soldatenleben," *Soldatentum*, 4 (1937), 2–10; Kurt Kreipe,

"Versager im soldatischen Friedensdienst," *Soldatentum*, 2 (1935), 79–82; Gerathewohl, "Eigenart und Behandlung des Einzelgängers," *Soldatentum*, 5 (1938), 163–68.

68 This is overlooked in the otherwise important and insightful study of Föllmer, *Individuality and Modernity in Berlin*, pp. 105–80.

69 Weniger, *Wehrmachtserziehung und Kriegserfahrung*, p. 122.

70 Simoneit, *Wehrpsychologie*, p. 129. Cf. Reibert, *Der Dienstunterricht im Reichsheer*, pp. 96–97; Friedrich von Rabenau, *Vom Sinn des Soldatentums: Die innere Kraft von Führung und Truppe* (Cologne: DuMont Schauberg, 1940), p. 7; Heinrich Himmler, *Geheimreden 1933 bis 1945 und andere Ansprachen*, ed. Bradley F. Smith and Agnes F. Peterson (Frankfurt: Propyläen, 1974), pp. 224–25. On the long shadow of the mutinies on military psychology, see Erich Schwinge, *Die Entwicklung der Mannszucht in der deutschen, britischen und französischen Wehrmacht seit 1914* (Berlin: Schweitzer, 1941).

71 Hans Ellenbeck, *Der Kompaniechef* (Leipzig: Detke, 1942), p. 19; H.Dv. [Heeresdienstvorschrift] 130/1, Sept. 1, 1936, No. 9, Bundesarchiv Freiburg, RHD 4.

72 Alfred Götze (ed.), *Trübners Deutsches Wörterbuch*, vol. IV (Berlin: de Gruyter, 1943), p. 84.

73 Felix Kersten, *Totenkopf und Treue: Heinrich Himmler ohne Uniform* (Hamburg: Mölich, 1952), p. 184.

74 Hitler speech, Dec. 4, 1938, in Jeremy Noakes and Geoffrey Pridham (eds.), *Nazism, 1919–1945: A History in Documents and Eyewitness Accounts*, vol. I (New York: Schocken, 1983), p. 417.

75 Michael Kater, *Hitler Youth* (Cambridge, MA: Harvard University Press, 2004); Jürgen Schiedeck and Martin Stahlmann, "Die Inszenierung 'totalen Erlebens': Lagererziehung im Nationalsozialismus," in Hans-Uwe Otto and Heinz Sünker (eds.), *Politische Formierung und soziale Erziehung im Nationalsozialismus* (Frankfurt: Suhrkamp, 1991), pp. 167–202; Gerhard Kock, *"Der Führer sorgt für unsere Kinder . . . ": Die Kinderlandverschickung im Zweiten Weltkrieg* (Paderborn: Schöningh, 1997), pp. 144–49; Patel, *Soldiers of Labor*, pp. 190–291. On the figures, see also Claudia Koonz, *The Nazi Conscience* (Cambridge, MA: Harvard University Press, 2003), p. 157; newspaper report on teacher camps from 1937, in Noakes and Pridham (eds.), *Nazism*, pp. 432–35.

76 Dagmar Reese, *Growing Up Female in Nazi Germany* (Ann Arbor: University of Michigan Press, 2006).

77 Erving Goffman, *Asylums: Essays in the Social Situation of Mental Patients and Other Inmates* (Garden City, NY: Doubleday, 1961).

78 Ernst Krieck, *Nationalpolitische Erziehung*, 4th edn. (Osterwieck: Spaeth & Linde, 1937), pp. 9–13.

79 The following paragraphs draw on Kühne, *Belonging and Genocide*, pp. 46–48.

80 Turner, *The Ritual Process*, pp. 95–96.

81 *Das junge Deutschland*, 1944, pp. 85–90 ("mother's boy"). Cf. on pre-Nazi Germany: *Arbeiterjugend*, 1926, p. 108; *Das junge Deutschland*, 1928, pp. 159–68. On "school of manliness": Frevert, *A Nation in Barracks*, p. 162; and Patel, *Soldiers of Labor*, p. 216.

82 Helmut Stellrecht, *Neue Erziehung* (Berlin: Limpert, 1942), p. 61.

83 Max Momsen, *Leibeserziehung mit Einschluß des Geländesports* (Osterwieck: Zickfeldt, 1935), pp. 19ff.

84 Lehmann, *Wir von der Infanterie*, p. 18.

85 *Wir Mädel*, 1940–41, p. 812; Jesco von Puttkamer, *Deutschlands Arbeitsdienst* (Oldenburg: Stalling, 1938), pp. 24, 41.

86 Pongs, "Krieg als Volksschicksal," p. 47; Friedrich Altrichter, *Die seelischen Kräfte des Deutschen Heeres im Frieden und im Weltkriege* (Berlin: Mittler, 1933), pp. 18–19, 29. Kalkschmidt, "Kameradschaft und Führertum der Front," pp. 180–92; Jäger, "Der Krieg wandelt den Menschen," p. 527 ("the I is gone").

87 Patel, *Soldiers of Labor*, pp. 3, 186, 263, 269, 274–75, 283–85. Cf. Olaf Stieglitz, *100 Percent American Boys: Disziplinierungsdiskurse und Ideologie im Civilian Conservation Corps, 1933–1942* (Stuttgart: Steiner, 1999).

88 See, e.g., Hank Nuwer, *The Hazing Reader* (Bloomington: Indiana University Press, 2004).

89 Sebastian Haffner, *Defying Hitler* (New York: Picador, 2002), pp. 258–96. Cf. Folker Schmerbach, *Das "Gemeinschaftslager" Hanns Kerrl für Referendare in Jüterbog 1933–1939* (Tübingen: Mohr Siebeck, 2008).

Part II

The Practice of Comradeship, 1939–1945

4   Assimilation

A few weeks before the Third Reich collapsed, Kurt Kreissler, a thirty-three-year-old NCO fighting in the East against the Red Army, seemed to be in the best of moods. Most of his comrades had been killed in action, but there was something that made up for mass death all around him, he wrote in a letter to his parents in Baden. Social life trumped physical death. Only recently the shrunken battalion – merely 150 soldiers – had successfully defeated a Soviet detachment of 1,000 men. The mood of his outfit "couldn't be better," he wrote. Although assembled only shortly before, they got along splendidly. Immediately becoming "the best of friends" with men one had never known before induced a feeling of great community that became stronger the more devastating the nation's future looked. Kreissler's conclusion in February 1945 was: "We want to stick together, we want to fight together, or we want to get wounded together – that's what we are longing for."[1]

Kreissler's enthusiasm seems to confirm a famous argument about the Wehrmacht's fighting morale. Determining "why the German army in World War II fought so stubbornly to the end" – even when the soldiers could have realized, and in fact did realize, that Germany would lose the war – two American sociologists, Edward Shils and Morris Janowitz, pointed to the soldier's "interpersonal relationship within the company – his primary group."[2] Shils and Janowitz used a term coined by Charles Horton Cooley in 1909. Looking at the family and the neighborhood, Cooley defined primary groups as "those characterized by intimate face-to-face association and cooperation." They enable "a certain fusion of individualities in a common whole so that one's very self . . . is the common life and purpose of the group . . . a 'we' that is built on 'sympathy,' 'mutual identification' and 'intimacy.'"[3] The primary group was opposed to larger, complex, and anonymous social entities – "secondary" groups, organizations, the population of a city, the entire army, or simply the entire society, entities that lacked the warmth suffused by primary groups. Cooley was not the first to explore this dichotomy. Various sociologists and philosophers had identified it at the turn of the century, when the consequences of industrialization and urbanization had become obvious in Western societies. Most famously, the German Ferdinand Tönnies, as early as 1887, had pitted the warm and organic "community" against the cold and anonymous "society" where "everyone is out for himself alone and living in a state of tension against everyone else" while the community was full of "mutual understanding or consensus," radiating cooperation, belonging, security, trust – the "intimate knowledge of another and willingness to share in his or her joys and sorrows."[4]

Exactly this judgmental juxtaposition allowed Shils and Janowitz in 1948 to challenge the depiction, popular among the Allied powers, of German soldiers as fanatical racists.[5] Relying on interviews with German soldiers in American captivity, conducted during the war, the American sociologists held that the German soldier had not fought out of hatred for "subhumans" but out of comradely ties to his fellow soldiers. Keen to avoid a repeat of 1918, the German army had, according to Shils and Janowitz, managed to satisfy the soldier's most basic physical and emotional "primary personality demands" almost until the end of the war, had "offered him affection and esteem from both officers and comrades, supplied him with a sense of power and adequately regulated his relations with authority." Although not entirely ignoring the impact of "secondary symbols" such as the Nazi ideology, the soldiers' "devotion to Hitler," and the widespread fear of Germany's destruction by the Red Army, Shils and Janowitz eventually "denazified" Hitler's soldiers. The implicit essence of the 1948 analysis was this: These soldiers were no monsters. They had fought not out of hatred against demonized enemies, but out of human sentiments, of affection to their comrades, just as soldiers in other armies had done and would do at all times. As parallel empirical studies on American soldiers showed, these had indeed been mostly apolitical characters, fighting not so much for patriotism, let alone nationalist fanaticism, but rather on behalf of their immediate buddies, their comrades – out of group loyalty. "The men seem to be fighting more for someone than against somebody," stated two Americans in 1945.[6]

For decades, the inquiries of Shils and Janowitz into the Wehrmacht's fighting morale remained unquestioned. The exculpation of ordinary German soldiers fitted too well into the ideological framework of the Cold War. After all, the Germans weren't evil Nazis but good comrades, they had kept their humaneness, and as such they easily qualified as partners in the new alliance of the civilized world against the real evil – communism. The influence of Shils and Janowitz, however, resulted from more than political expediency during the Cold War.[7] Their study also interfered in a debate within the American army about combat effectiveness. It identified a crucial "factor strengthening primary group solidarity": the

German replacement system. Unlike the US Army, the German Army deployed its divisions on a strictly regional basis, thus guaranteeing units with a common cultural identity, common accents, common cookbooks, and so on. While the American army refilled casualties in World War II individually (and still did so in the Korean and Vietnam Wars), the Germans made sure that "the entire personnel of a division" would be kept together as long as possible and "be withdrawn from the front simultaneously and refitted as a unit with replacements" from the same regions. This way, new soldiers had time to be assimilated into the group that then was sent to the front as a whole, a system that, as Shils and Janowitz rightly said, "continued until close to the end of the war." It was only from late 1944 that this replacement system broke down, and "hastily fabricated units" spurred the "deterioration of group solidarity."[8]

The enormous impact of the Shils and Janowitz study surprises if one considers its relatively poor empirical basis. The two sociologists had queried an undisclosed yet obviously small number of German soldiers captured in North Africa and at the Western front, so that it was not clear whether their theory applied only to these theaters or to the Eastern front as well. Examining the sociology, the motivation, and the indoctrination of the Wehrmacht at the Eastern front, the historian Omer Bartov presented in the 1980s the most decisive critique of the primary group theory, bristling not least at its quasi-sanctification of the Wehrmacht. Following the basic assumption of the theory, that primary groups generate solidarity only if group members know each other and live together over a longer time, Bartov pointed out the Wehrmacht's enormous casualties and subsequent personnel fluctuation from winter 1941–42 in the East. He held that the huge number of casualties interrupted the traditional replacement system, thus impeding primary group cohesion long before the end of the war. Bartov showed that other factors explain the troops' fighting morale: the internalization of secondary symbols, especially antisemitism and more generally the racist demonization of the enemy in the East; the harsh discipline; and "demodernization of the front" – the animal-like material conditions of the soldiers – which brutalized and barbarized them. In Bartov's view, the Wehrmacht was by no means an apolitical, "normal" army but exactly the opposite: deeply Nazified, a crucial engine of the Nazis' genocidal project.[9]

Many studies have confirmed Bartov's argument about the Nazification of the Wehrmacht and the popularity of antisemitism among the soldiers, although the ideological diversity of this army, which in total conscripted 17 million men from all parts of German society, is obvious too. But do soldiers – and did the Wehrmacht soldiers – fight *either* for their intimate comrades *or* for their fatherland? Do primary groups and secondary symbols really exclude each other as factors of fighting morale? Scrutinizing various armies since the Second World War, numerous sociologists, including Janowitz, have doubted the dichotomy between primary and secondary groups and suggested studying instead their interrelationship, and how different identities and objects of affection either do or don't work together: horizontal bonding between peers; vertical bonding between enlisted men and different ranks of authorities; bonding in face-to-face units and their embedding in or separation from larger organizations – the battalion, the regiment, the division – and even larger institutions, such as the entire army, or social entities such as the nation.[10] Primary groups do not operate in a cultural vacuum. Or as Janowitz put it some twenty-five years after the publication of the 1948 article: "The goals and standards or norms that primary groups enforce are hardly self-generated, they arise from the military environment and from the surrounding civilian society."[11] Patriotic and nationalist sentiments easily coalesce with emotional bonds to one's immediate comrades. But they don't need to. Small group cohesion can also undermine fighting morale. If a group rejects the military goal – the defense of the homelands, the destruction of other armies, the conquest of territories – "group solidarity could be detrimental to the institutional mission" and lead to "mass surrenders or group disobedience," stated Victor Madej, challenging Shils and Janowitz.[12] "The solidarity of the small group can lead to the refusal to fight, to disobey orders and even to mutiny," added the military historian Hew Strachan, looking at the "live and let live system" that undermined the "intentions of higher command" in the First World War.[13] In order to propel fighting morale, the primary group needs to be directed by secondary symbols. An army operates most effectively if both levels are synchronized.

Instead of reifying primary groups, one must take into account their potential inconsistency and changeability, the diversity of their concrete emanations.[14] Different wars (the First versus the Second World War, the US Korean War versus the Vietnam War), different societies (Nazi Germany versus the USA in World War II), different theaters of war (the Eastern and the Western fronts of the Wehrmacht), different periods (the Wehrmacht's advance and its retreat) and situations (front versus rear of the action), different types of army (elite troops such as the Waffen-SS in Nazi Germany, as opposed to draft-based mass armies such as the Wehrmacht), different social strata within one army (conscripted soldiers versus volunteers, rank-and-files versus officers) may generate, or adhere to, different types of primary group, and the whole variety of soldiers even within one army may practice and realize primary group cohesion in different ways – or not do it at all.

In a way, this is what the myth of comradeship in Germany from the time of the First World War was about: It conveyed polyvalence. Different people could appropriate it in different, even opposing ways. Comradeship as understood by many Germans in the interwar and Nazi period aligned and reconciled primary group bonding and secondary symbols of national unity. And its leftist representation, at least, had indicated the subversive potential of comradeship. No complete consensus has ever been established about the precise meaning of comradeship. It served as a popular synonym of national harmony, and yet its core semantic revolved around the small frontline unit, the face-to-face group in or even outside of the army. The term addressed the humane, tender and caring side of the soldier in war, and simultaneously it epitomized the social pressure that made men perform in a "manly" way in battle. It could denote vertical trust and cooperation between officers, NCOs, and enlisted men, or it could be limited to peer relationships, especially between rank-and-file soldiers.

Analyzing how the soldiers of the Second World War practiced comradeship is not possible without considering their cultural luggage, their mythical and experiential "knowledge" about comradeship, and more broadly about community, soldiering, and warfare. The German World War II soldiers did not enter their outlets, the army, the barracks, the battlefields, or the bunkers, as blank slates – without any idea of what they would face. Often already as children, even more as teenagers, adolescents, and adults, many of them, though not all equally, had been swamped with ideas and myths – "knowledge" – about the power of comradeship (or primary groups, for that matter). Images of comradeship and experiences of comradeship were omnipresent throughout the war that started in 1939.

Shils and Janowitz were aware of this type of knowledge when they inquired into the Wehrmacht's fighting morale. In fact, they honored the German myth of comradeship as a key factor of the perseverance of the primary groups in the Wehrmacht.[15] Ten to fifteen percent of all enlisted men, a "hard core" of young soldiers, mostly NCOs and junior officers in their twenties, were imbued with the "ideology of *Gemeinschaft* (community solidarity)" and facilitated the cohesion of the primary groups as charismatic "opinion leaders," Shils and Janowitz stated. These immediate combat leaders served as the engines of primary group cohesion in the Wehrmacht, just as the myth of comradeship since the Great War had praised "comradely leaders" such as Ernst Wurche. And these leaders also helped, according to Shils and Janowitz, "to minimize the probability of divisive political discussions." In other words, just as collective memory of the First World War had claimed, the comradely primary group was still elevated above ideological antagonisms between soldiers in the Second World War. Primary group (comradeship) trumped secondary symbols (class society in the First World War, or the division between Nazis and anti-Nazis in the Second), the American researchers assumed.[16]

But Shils and Janowitz got it wrong, at least in some crucial respects. First, they ignored the interwar controversy about the reality of men–officer relationships that had shaken the memory of the Great War. Instead, they took the myth's romanticized depiction of this relationship at face value and extended it into the Second World War, as if Hitler's Wehrmacht had only comradely leaders. Even more problematic was a second shortcut from myth to reality. Naturally, the German interviewees, all of them ordinary soldiers (up to lower officer ranks), had no clue about such sociological concepts as primary groups. As the interviews were held in German, neither interviewers nor interviewees talked about primary groups. They talked about comradeship and comrades, i.e. *Kameradschaft* and *Kameraden*.[17] Shils and Janowitz simply translated these German words into their primary group vocabulary, and omitted the fluid semantic of the German term altogether. The German concept was not limited to face-to-face relations but encompassed a multitude of ambivalences that arbitrated between horizontal and vertical relationships, between femininely coded tenderness and seemingly masculine toughness, between group pressure and group pleasure, and between the close military unit and national identities – in other words, between primary groups and secondary symbols.

Since Bartov's research, historians and archivists have hugely enlarged the body of accessible primary sources. These include innumerable private war letters and diaries, testimonies and memoirs of former soldiers and postwar interviews with them, and confidential conversations between German soldiers in American and British captivity, secretly recorded by their guards.[18] These sources cover both the ideological diversity of the German army and the change of experiences during the war. Taking advantage of these materials and also of a number of recent inquiries into the Wehrmacht's social and ideological conditions and its fighting morale,[19] the following chapters will explore the meaning of comradeship in two ways.

On the one hand, they examine the symbolism of comradeship: How did the Wehrmacht soldiers appropriate the myth of comradeship? How did they use the "social knowledge" about comradeship as it had been established in Germany in the interwar period? In what way did this knowledge influence the experience of the European war from 1939 to 1945? And conversely, how did the World War II experience shape the soldiers' understanding of the concept of comradeship? How did the rather different shape of the Second World War, especially its genocidal dynamic, change the meaning – the symbolism – of comradeship?

On the other hand, we shall complement this inquiry into comradeship as a *historical* concept – the historical semantic of the word – by scrutinizing comradeship as an *analytical* category, a signifier of the soldiers' social cohesion, their bonding, their group cultures in various settings, theaters, and time periods. Did the soldiers indeed, as Shils and Janowitz assumed, stick together until (almost) the end, and if yes, why? Was it because of comradely bonds in their units, or because they believed in Hitler, or were they driven by hatred (or fear) of Jews and Slavs, and by the utopia of a racially cleansed *Volksgemeinschaft*? Or did the soldiers, when they dwelled in the rhetoric about comradeship, simply obfuscate the reality of their social situation, a reality filled with individual isolation, egoism, and social dissolution rather than cohesion?

The Wehrmacht united 17 million German men of different, though mostly younger, ages; of urban and rural backgrounds, and of all social classes; of all political and ideological camps, from Nazis to conservatives, liberals, Social Democrats, and even communists; of all religious and non-religious creeds (including some Jews, who managed to hide in the Wehrmacht); and of course of enormously different personalities; men who had embraced the Hitler Youth or other sections of the German youth movement, and those who would have preferred to pursue their own careers and enjoy their private lives as husbands and fathers. To whom did comradeship matter, and in what ways?

This inquiry cannot cover the variety of nuances, personalities, military ranks, civilian backgrounds, war periods, and theaters comprehensively, only exemplarily, mainly by focusing on the Eastern front and on the fighting troops. I shall do so in three steps. This chapter analyzes the initiation of the soldiers into the army and the practice of comradeship – the base training and the time they spent with the reserve troops waiting for their deployment to the front lines. The following chapter analyzes the megalomania the soldiers on the Eastern front revelled in during the first year of Operation Barbarossa, the invasion of the Soviet Union. Although not entirely free of pessimistic moments, the soldiers were mostly intoxicated by the army's dramatic victories, the prospect of a glorious future of the German *Volksgemeinschaft* ruling over the European continent and colonizing its Eastern parts, and the experience of cooperation, solidarity, and harmony within the army. Occasional partisan attacks, hugely inflated by rumors and propaganda, did not challenge but reinforced the experience of a grand comradeship and allowed the German soldier to fight qualms about the obvious genocidal dimension of the war. The stronger the enemy in the East, including the Soviet partisan movements, grew, the faster doubts of the *Endsieg*, or final victory, and fears of the vengeance of the enemies in case of a defeated Germany, spread among the troops. This period is the subject of the third chapter of this section. In this stage of the war – from fall 1942, even more after the German disaster at Stalingrad – the soldiers lapsed into a fatalistic and yet resilient mood. It only occasionally allowed for the initial euphoric comradeship but instead nurtured a cynical comradeship in which moral transgressions became part of the daily routine. And yet, even then, soldiers had choices, and so they used the concept of comradeship in different, even opposing ways.

No doubt, numerous soldiers enthused about the experience of comradeship in Hitler's army. They expected it, because the mass media, newspapers, war novels, the movies, their fathers, grandfathers, even mothers and grandmothers, teachers, colleagues, and friends had taught them about it; and many of those soldiers had got a foretaste of comradeship in the youth associations before and after 1933, and in the training camps of the Nazi state. One of those soldiers was Kurt Kreissler, who volunteered for the Wehrmacht in 1940 at the age of twenty-eight, following a successful career as a salaried Hitler Youth leader. He had himself spread the gospel of comradeship in word and deed. Before joining the army, he had been made Deputy Banner Leader, overseeing roughly 3,000 German youth in the Lake Constance region. His prestigious position in the Hitler Youth, however, did not protect him from the humiliation and depersonalization rituals all Wehrmacht novices underwent. Entering the army as a "naïve civilian," as he said in a private memoir, he too had to start from scratch as did all other recruits. He had to suffer harassment, chicanery, and arrogance from the drill sergeants, randomly ordered roll calls, crawling endlessly through mud, dung, and puddles, and unfair punishments for ridiculously irrelevant misdemeanours. "Within four weeks," Kreissler wrote, "the poor *Landser* changed from fervent idealist to torrid hater of the German Wehrmacht and especially their officers."[20]

But youth leaders such as Kreissler had internalized the rationale of the military initiation rite long before joining the army. He knew that it served to "harden" them, to gear up the men for the fights they would have to endure. This hardening-up was widely recognized as a good thing in Germany at the time. Werner Gross, equally enthusiastic about the Nazi regime and its youth organization, and equally upset about the "unbelievably rude" and absurd degradation he faced as a Wehrmacht recruit in 1936 at the age of twenty-two, yet eventually found it "perfectly

OK . . . that we get this pressure, because the soldier, when it gets serious, needs to respond to even bigger challenges in a manly way. We just have to be hardened," he wrote proudly in a letter to his parents.[21]

Gross too knew what all this was good for: for building weak boys up into tough, "real" men – men who owned not only the biological but also the social attributes of manhood. Initiation into manhood meant changing selfish civilians into fully-fledged members of the male community, transforming "I" into "We." Recruits such as Gross or Kreissler eventually experienced the humiliation rituals not in a state of isolated desperation but in one of communal euphoria. Hatred for the tormentors had a conciliatory note. It ensured solidarity and even a certain harmony within the group. "By and by small circles of likeminded guys emerged, coalescing into an iron comradeship," Kreissler recounted. He and his twenty-three roommates soon "stuck together like peas and carrots. Nothing could shatter us any more, not even the worst blow-up of our first lieutenant. We no longer took him seriously." Instead, an "amazing spirit of comradeship outshone our basic training."[22] "Imperceptibly," another Wehrmacht recruit wrote to his Hitler Youth friend in 1942, "we have grown together into firm comradeship" through the harassment suffered in the first three weeks of serving together. They followed the slogan "nobody can get to us" and the motto "and should our arses turn to leather, never mind, we'll stick together" – the German equivalent of the American WETSU formula – "We eat this shit up."[23]

"Nothing welds men as much as shared anger at someone or something," stated a former soldier in his memoir, echoing common psychological wisdom. At the end of war, he had to weld a bunch of poorly trained recruits into an effective fighting force, driven by "heroic comradeship," and he knew that the best way to do that was to make them hate their superior.[24] Recruits established comradeship by mutually fending off the terror their superiors inflicted on them. Often, such comradeship issued in pranks and little conspiracies. Hans-Karl Vorster's unit took revenge on a "particularly malicious" drill sergeant; Vorster too had grown up in the youth movement, considered himself a member of the Walter Flex generation, as he called it, and he had been born into a family of soldiers. After the sergeant had got drunk and fallen fast asleep one night, his trainees, Vorster and his comrades, secured a padlock around his testicles and threw away the key. The next day, agonizingly, the sergeant had to carry out his duties with his hand in his trouser pocket to minimize his discomfort. His recruits, however, were delighted, and they stuck together when the sergeant demanded that the culprit reveal himself. Together they got through the inevitable punishment with conspiratorial indifference.[25]

Little conspiracies even protected the culprit trapped in the workings of the military subjugation machine. While Hans Lorenz was at a pub with his comrades – their first such excursion after three weeks in the military – his belt and his gun were stolen. Three days of detention awaited him; a soldier was responsible for his gear, and there were no excuses. His comrades, however, held "a council of war" and decided that one of them would report sick every day so that Hans could borrow the "sick" soldier's gun and a belt. They continued this scheme until they were permitted another pub visit, at which time Hans managed to procure a gun and a belt in the same way he had lost his own.[26]

There is no community-building without boundaries, without the Other. The group needs the Other in order to become a community. The Other could be the mean superior, but also a peer – an outsider, a maverick, in fact anyone who, as Sebastian Haffner put it, exhibited "more individuality than was permissible."[27] Sometimes a smart superior chose an outsider whom the group could terrorize. A "sniveller" who started trembling and howling and marched to a different drumbeat whenever reprimanded in formal drill was a welcome target. In one unit, a tank gunner of this kind received a symbolic burial. His sergeant made him lie in a hole and pull his steel helmet over his face, and his comrades covered him with a sheet of corrugated iron. Eventually, the sergeant shot three blank cartridges over the "grave." Shortly after, after making shooting errors, the gunner had to hold a cigarette that the sergeant pretended to shoot out of his hand. No army regulations prohibited such humiliation ritual. It pleased both the superior and his men.[28]

If there was no outsider, one had to be fabricated. "Nothing unites the members of a group like a common enemy," the sociologist Albert Cohen stated. External and internal enemies are, in a way, exchangeable. Either of them "arouses the sentiments of community and revives a waning solidarity." As an internal enemy, deviants "function as a 'built-in' outgroup, and contribute to the integration of the group in much the same way as do witches, devils, and hostile foreign powers," Cohen said.[29] Or, as George Herbert Mead wrote in 1918, "the attitude of hostility toward the lawbreaker has the unique advantage of uniting all members of the community in the emotional solidarity of aggression."[30]

Usually the group did not need the advice of a superior to identify an outsider. Anyone who failed to adapt to the expectations of his group, who resisted the demand to sacrifice himself on the altar of the We, could easily find himself in that role. It could be the eager beaver who tried to raise himself above the group norms, but mostly it hit the "incompetent" who failed to match them. The principle of collective punishment, of penalizing the entire unit for infractions of individual members, common in many armies, taught the group to police itself – and thus generated community-building of its own kind. "Comradeship entails strong discipline and oppresses the malicious, unreliable and uncomradely elements," said the army pedagogue Erich Weniger in 1938. "Comradeship," he went on, "also establishes a rigid hierarchy among its elements and puts the responsibilities for the weaker ones on the stronger ones."[31] A recollection of Dieter Wellershoff, who had volunteered for the elite Tank Division "Hermann Göring," illustrates what Weniger meant. An orphan from the countryside was "entirely incapable of keeping up with the mental and physical standards of our training group," Wellershoff remembered. "Because of him our group always attracted attention and was punished and degraded as a whole." Unavoidably the collective wrath turned upon the incompetent colleague. When the poor kid stole a sausage from one of his comrades, the group decided that enough was enough and relieved its frustration in a blanket party. At night, the "Holy Spirit," as the group's internal law enforcement agency was nicknamed in the German military, tore the culprit from his bed and forced him into a pack drill and then, because he never kept himself clean, pushed him under the shower until he was totally frightened.[32]

The culprit was taught to adjust to the group, and to give up his own individuality on its behalf. He had to learn that it was only together with his comrades, but never on his own, that he was able to bear the terror of the military as a "total institution." Not all soldiers took to this as easily as Kreissler or Gross. Willy Reese had just graduated from high school, fallen in love, and landed a job as bank clerk; he was dreaming of a career as a writer when he was drafted to the Wehrmacht in early 1941 at the age of twenty. It was a disaster for him. "Nothing could be more antithetical to my nature than having to become a soldier, to be anonymous among strangers, a toy at the whim of commands and moods," he wrote in a private autobiographical *Confession* in early 1944, shortly before he died in battle. Receiving the call-up was the end of his life as a "citizen of the world," "my abdication," he said. The only way to cope with the role of a soldier was to take it as "repentance," Reese wrote bitterly, deploying the Christian language of atonement, knowing that his suffering was a communal destiny. "We accepted it, like a monk the scourge. Under the mask of a soldier, we settled our debt, and to atone for past lives of deception, frivolity, and illusion, we consecrated ourselves to pain and danger." Although the very existence of this *Confession* and of related poems and private letters is proof of his efforts to save at least the idea of a civilian self from the We of the army, Reese eventually could only accept the "sentence" of "powerlessness" by indulging in apathy and indifference – by wearing the mask of a soldier, constantly vegetating in a state of "sadness and despair, emptiness and fear . . . helplessness and abandon . . . never being alone, but always a stranger among strangers, separated from the others by spirit and soul, manner of life and beliefs."[33]

If they had ever met, Reese would have found a like-minded friend in Heinrich Böll, who after 1945 indeed made a career as a writer and also became one of the icons of West Germany's pacifist movement. Born in 1917 into a Catholic family in Cologne, Böll was about to establish himself as a bookseller, trying to survive intellectually and mentally in one of the niches of the Third Reich, when he was conscripted in August 1939; his literary ambitions transpire from the letters he wrote to his fiancée and to his family during his humble career as a Wehrmacht private. He too was constantly looking for ways to save the civilian I from the soldierly We. The "sleazy rabble" of mean drill sergeants and the brawling, obscene, cynical, and misogynistic sociality of his roommates nauseated him. The army seemed to him the "ultimate institution of dullness." A mandatory "evening of comradeship" was the climax of the absurdities he faced on a daily basis: The individual had to sacrifice on the altar of the community even the minimal amount of private time he was entitled to. "The party last night again made me really aware of my individualism; a hundred and thirty men herded and squeezed together, sweating, all looking alike and ordered to be happy, boozing and gabbling and bawling . . . what a torture, these military exhilarations." It is clear that Böll either did not bother to, or could not, hide his disgust. He paid the price for prioritizing his Self over the We of the comrades. Barracks and uniforms ate up his "mind and spirit," he once said, referring to his constant fear of the suspicious, shaming, terrorizing gaze of superiors and comrades – of a community that could not tolerate the dissenter: "Often and massively I have been standing out in the most unfavourable ways these days, and now they all keep an eye on me," he recorded once; his superiors seemed "to have plotted to kill me," he suspected another time.[34]

Most soldiers tried to keep some sort of balance between the I and the We – a balance also between different concepts of manliness. Take Franz Wieschenberg, Helmut Wißmann, or Albert Neuhaus as examples, all of them drafted in 1940. Born into working-class families, Wieschenberg and Neuhaus in 1909, Wißmann in 1920, they grew up in the Rhenish-Westphalian industrial area, Neuhaus in a mining village in its rural foothills. Wieschenberg, the son of a carpenter who died in battle in 1918, became a carpenter too. As a Catholic, he was engaged in the social life of his church in his hometown of Düsseldorf. In 1935 he married his longtime girlfriend Hilde, who had converted from Protestantism to Catholicism. Wieschenberg died in action in March 1945. Wißmann, a Protestant, was rooted ideologically in the socialist movement. His father was a member of the Communist Party and was bullied by the Nazis from 1933 on. His mother came from a social democratic family. Wißmann himself, however, had somewhat distanced himself from these political traditions, not least as the result of a *Landjahr*, a nine-month-long Nazi boarding and training program, which he attended at the age of fourteen and which left him "brainwashed," as he said later in an interview. From the mid-1930s he was in a relationship with Edith Wulf, whom he married in 1943, and he survived the war. Neuhaus, also the son of a carpenter, grew up as a Catholic in Münster, Westphalia, where he established himself in the mid-1930s as a delicatessen merchant with his wife Agnes. Deeply engaged in local Catholic associations, he had also been a member of the local SA in the mid-1930s when it was no longer the violent spearhead of the Nazi party.[35]

As did almost all recruits, these three suffered during training from the drill and the harassment designed to change their civilian identities into soldierly ones.[36] Unlike model comrades such as Kreissler, individuals such as Wieschenberg and Wißmann had a hard time adjusting to the rules of comradeship. But unlike anti-comrades like Böll, they eventually made it. Thrown into a unit of mostly Catholics, the Protestant Wißmann wrote to his fiancée a few days after reporting for duty in the Rokitzan barracks in Bohemia (Rokycany in Czech), far away from home, "my comrades aren't worth a dime." Pondering his previously happy private life and thinking about the life that awaited him in the army, he concluded unambiguously: "I am much better off as a man on his own."[37] Wieschenberg similarly decided, after a short time in the remote barracks in East Prussia to which he was sent, that "All this comradeship is completely useless." Men like him despised the idea of trading in their individual identities for a collective entity as if this was the only way to become real men. To him, just as to Böll or Haffner, real men were those who coped with individual lives and careers. Still half a year later, he stated apodictically: "My family comes between the army and me . . . Truth is, by establishing a family I already made up my mind about which of the two worlds is mine." Unlike younger soldiers who longed to pass the test of manhood in war, he wasn't looking for "further adventures." Instead, "'home' has always been the slogan for me," he assured his wife in one of the daily letters he never tired of writing; sometimes he wrote twice a day, each time reaffirming that even though he was physically far from home, in spirit he was only with his wife.

Indeed this was how correspondence by letter with their families helped soldiers, whether the letters dealt with daily life at home, the desire for sex with the partner, their everlasting love, or visions of raising children once the war would be over: It allowed individuals to save parts of their civilian identities from being squashed by the army's We, at least for a while. Sometimes only for a very short while. Letter-writing was, for good reasons, seen as an escape from the group, and passionate letter-writers knew that their comrades were keeping an eye on them. Another recruit born in 1910, Erich Kuby, soon found this out when trying to settle into barracks in 1939, as he looked back on a career (jeopardized in the Third Reich, naturally) as a left-liberal writer. He made his debut with his roommates by switching off their radio: He found the noise intrusive and it didn't allow him to focus on the letters he wanted to write. His comrades took no pity on him; solipsistic letter-writing was not supposed to supersede comradely brawling. Kuby ended up being beaten up soundly – his first but not last encounter with the vigilante justice used by the group to correct the deviant individualist.[38]

Soldiers usually managed to avoid such escalations by keeping a low profile when writing their letters. It was not advisable to challenge the priorities of group life. Neuhaus, for instance, observed the appropriate priorities in order to not jeopardize the "nice comradeship" he enjoyed with his roommates in the barracks of Belgard in Pomerania, where he was sent as a recruit. "I have to finish now," he concluded a letter to his wife, "my comrades want to have their coffee party and need the table. We are 13 guys in one den – you can imagine what the vibes are like."[39] Neuhaus's letters suggest he took it easy, getting along well with his comrades and the drill sergeants. The conservative, nationalist milieu in his hometown had prepared him for the symbolic world of the military; Hans Zöberlein's World War I front novel was one of his favourite books. He knew that abandoning oneself to desires for privacy, tenderness, love, and care at home and fantasizing about a self-determined life would not heal the wound the army inflicted on the civilian self, but merely rub it in.[40]

Sometimes, soldiers' wives sensed the emotional desolation their men suffered and tried to help. Edith Wulf prescribed good comradeship. From early on, she worried whether her fiancé, Helmut Wißmann, would meet "true and nice comrades." When Helmut said No, she cheered him up: "After just one week, there is no way for you guys to get to know each other. Let's not be too pessimistic," she wrote in the first person plural, and encouraged him to take matters into his own hands: "Always be a good comrade to your comrades, and an obedient and willing subordinate to your superiors. Just don't talk religion to your comrades, just shut up," she urged him, being unhappy about his Catholic comrades. And Edith sent a cake – to be shared with his roommates.[41] She knew about the symbolism of the comradely ritual of sharing food parcels, and she appreciated it. The caring, tender, "soft" side of comradeship was the one that connected the emotional and moral world of the soldier with civilian society.

Comradeship, however, demanded not only mutual support but also inconspicuousness. Encouraging Helmut to be a good comrade and a willing subordinate, Edith addressed the most important attitude the soldier had to adopt – the virtue of staying under the radar, not by separating himself from the group but by joining in. "He always told me," Helmut reported about his drill sergeant, "if I really shout at you, just think: kiss my ass. Yet make sure you join in anyway. Then you may even get some fun out of it."[42] When the brass band struck up a song, for instance, you would naturally sing along, whether or not you were in the mood. "Woe betide him who won't open his mouth," or at least pretend to sing along, was a lesson learned by Wieschenberg also immediately after he was put into a uniform. Wieschenberg, eleven years older and even more deeply rooted in a civilian identity than Wißmann, mocked at this etiquette of sorts for quite a while. "Everything goes by numbers and according to the book, the individual doesn't count a bit and is just swept away by the crowd," he grumbled. Wißmann, by contrast, was more familiar with the ethics of joining in thanks to his *Landjahr*, and proudly reported to his fiancée after a couple of weeks about having kept a low profile and having been able to connect with his comrades. A few booze-ups had been beneficial, he confessed to Edith, who gave her approval. Comradeship as the virtue of smooth functioning in the military machine seemed the best guarantee that she would get her fiancé back in one piece and without mental damage. Of course, female adoration of soldierly manliness mattered too. On the day of his swearing-in he appeared to her in a dream, she wrote to him. She couldn't believe that he was such a "handsome" and "dashing" soldier, she wrote in a letter immediately afterwards, adding that now she was even more decided to bear the distress of separation as "brave military wife" in faithfulness.[43]

The latter was by no means guaranteed. Far away from home, soldiers never stopped worrying about the fidelity of their wives, fiancées, or girlfriends. Rumors suggested that some of them cheated on their men while they sacrificed life and limb for their loved ones at home. A lack of mail from home could give soldiers jealous nightmares about what was going on there. In truth, the soldiers knew what they were talking about when it came to adultery and debauchery. Their distrust toward their women at home reflected and was nourished by an all-male and misogynist culture that honored unfaithfulness as virtue – as long as it was the men who did it. "They" – the soldiers – "rake the women over the coals and consider all women as whores," noted private Albert Neuhaus indignantly.[44] "In each hotel and bar you find a brothel," wrote Wißmann to Edith about Rokitzan, expressing embarrassment too.[45]

No less appalled was Heinrich Böll, noticing how one of his comrades chatted up a girl in front of the barracks, and indeed she wasn't much better, as Böll stated in a letter to his fiancée. "Shamelessly, she gossips about being engaged to a soldier who is fighting in the East and has just sent her a letter. But, she says, you never know: Might he not be getting killed in action right now? And then she laughs joyfully and gives him [Böll's comrade] her address. Of course, he is married too and has even three little children at home," reported Böll, concluding: "these are just the things you get used to, like the rain, the sunshine, and the sleep."[46] What outraged moralizers such as Böll was that the soldiers deliberately transgressed the morality of the civilian world at home. "The crazier the adventures with women, the higher the individual scores among comrades," Wieschenberg soon learned too.[47] Showing off about sex demonstrated the social sovereignty of the comradely leagues of males, their superiority over women, family, and home – over civilian society and civilian morality.

By denouncing their comrades' sexual debaucheries in their letters, soldiers tried to assure their wives at home that their own conjugal morality was unstained. This tactic did not always suffice to calm the worries at home. It was common knowledge that the middle-class ideals of chastity and fidelity often fell into oblivion among soldiers. When Helmut was serving in Bohemia, Edith Wulf's friends gossiped over coffee that "venereal diseases will have infected a hundred percent of our soldiers in France if they stay there for another two years." Helmut's own reports left Edith in no doubt that Bohemia wasn't any better. Realizing that in Helmut's new environment "manners and morals are in a sorry state," Edith still tried to reassure herself as she wrote that "my Helmut will never feel comfortable over there." But the rhetoric of trust could not hide the reality of distrust. In order to avoid the worst, she urged her fiancé to not get "too intimate" with the natives in Rokitzan but to stick to his comrades instead.[48]

Edith's advice relied on the tender, caring, and homoerotic yet chaste depiction of comradeship that the interwar discourse had abundantly glorified. Men did re-enact this type of comradeship as soldiers, or they missed it if there was no chance to re-enact it. Another recruit, Peter Pfaff, first went through the National Labor Service in 1943 and then entered the Wehrmacht. Accepting that fate's grip on him was now "a little tougher" and had pulled him out of the "sphere of motherly security" at home, throwing him into an enforced community of men randomly shuffled together, he sought and soon found an equivalent for motherly tenderness and love – male sociability. "We are getting more and more used to each other, and slowly the sense of comradeship is emerging, even if only for practical reasons. It's not really fondness for each other but simple calculation: I support you, and you support me; I share with you, and you share with me . . . And so we at least overcome the tensions, the nasty and often mean tone." And soon afterwards, Pfaff enthused about the tenderness and empathy that poured into his tough military environment. In Pfaff's rhetoric, which reflected what the public discourse on comradeship had spread endlessly since the Great War, motherly love at home and male homoeroticism in the army were rooted in the love of God, thus were pure, pristine, straight – not only beyond any moral doubt but representing moral goodness per se.[49]

Tender comradeship was a relief valve in the emotional pressure vessel of the army, and simultaneously a lubricant for the build-up of the male bond. Either way, it served as the extended arm of civilian morality in the army. This way, homoerotic (not homosexual) love between soldiers was considered legitimate and even appreciated as a substitute for the love between men and women at home. In his letters to Edith, Helmut highlighted exactly this depiction of comradeship by reporting how he and his closer comrades spent their free time sharing their feelings of homesickness. They coped with it by decorating their rooms and singing "beautiful songs" that reminded them of their families at home. Implicitly or explicitly, these reports corroborated the pristine depiction of soldierly comradeship: comradeship as a safeguard against sexual adventures, debaucheries, and adultery. Thus Helmut reported how a senior soldier and close comrade of his had urged him "whatever you do, avoid dating any kind of women," and that he, Helmut, got along best with a roommate who was bound to his wife at home by deep and true loyalty – a comrade who would never fall into the trap of the amorous seductions that waited around the corner. This was exactly what Edith wanted to hear: "Now I no longer need to worry about you going out alone."[50]

The crux of comradeship was its Janus face. Military wives such as Edith Wulf and Hilde Wieschenberg received innumerable letters with endless love declarations from their husbands or fiancés. But what exactly these men were doing away from home was not under their control. Edith even had to bear her father's mocking about her fiancé "having fun with other girls" in faraway Bohemia. She knew that her father was just "teasing" her. But couldn't it be true? In February 1941, after he and Edith had discussed fidelity and infidelity in their letters, Helmut went with some close comrades on a Sunday trip to Pilsen, the only city of any size within reach for the Rokitzan recruits. He made the mistake of mentioning it in a letter to his mother but not to Edith.

Edith learned of it anyway through her future mother-in-law and could not hide her suspicions. Helmut played it down – "Darling, you can't seriously think your boy gets in touch with Czech women" – and tried to whitewash himself by sullying his comrades, distancing himself from *their* amorous adventures. By doing so he threw oil in the fire. "Since you wrote that Willi met this girl and you were present, I always get these thoughts ... Darling, always be on your guard when you go out with Willi. He might pick up a girlfriend of his girl, and then you would kind of be obliged to play the cavalier." Helmut asserted the innocence of this comradeship by sentimentally amplifying hiking trips together with Willi. Plus, not Willi but another comrade was the actual wrongdoer, who had even once kissed a girl, Helmut argued. "I always tease him about it. Then he is embarrassed and wonders whether he should confess it to his Ilse. Of course you should, I answer, and if you don't tell her, I will, because I am your comrade, and comradeship persists only if it is true and good."[51]

Depicting comradeship as per se morally good, Helmut referred to what Germans at that time loved about it. For most of them, the idea of an evil comradeship was a *contradictio in adjecto*. There were bad comrades who didn't stick to the rules of comradely solidarity and mutual support, and there was misunderstood comradeship. But voices such as that of Sebastian Haffner, who explicitly denounced comradeship as an engine of moral decay, were rare. At the same time, there was no doubt that male solidarity could venture into all kinds of wrong. Exactly this ambiguity fueled the conversation between Edith and Helmut. Months and even years later, when fighting on the Eastern front, Helmut still saw himself as needing to calm Edith's jealousy by conjuring the chaste face of comradeship and its allegedly private vanishing point. As a youth among male comrades, he had never really felt at home, he maintained. Rather, to him they were only weak substitutes for what really had mattered to him back then: his relationship with his beloved Edith, who was to become his "mother, friend, comrade, and advisor." As a youth, his male comrades had even teased him for his fixation on Edith, he wrote. How could Edith think he would fall into the quagmire of male debaucheries – of evil comradeship?[52]

We don't know whether Edith's worries about Helmut's fidelity were justified. They were overshadowed by even more serious concerns that also revolved around the practice of male comradeship. Edith worried not only about Helmut's moral integrity but even more about his physical integrity. Initially he had pledged to stay away from soldierly adventures and tests of courage. But the pledge didn't last. The longer he was away from home, the more his civilian male identity as a husband and future father crumbled. Instead, he adopted the opposite concept and rebuilt himself along the lines of martial masculinity. In a pathetic statement, Wißmann explained to his fiancée in January 1941 – a few months after pledging to remain a family man in his heart and to stay away from seeking to prove his virility in war – that it would be better to get back home having lost a few limbs than to be deemed a coward or "rear echelon motherfucker" (REMF) for the rest of his life.[53] A little later – in the letter that also included his confession about the Pilsen trip – he went into further detail: "everyone is blaming me for being such a coward. I am really hopping mad. Just now requests [to volunteer] for the colonies and the storm troops are coming in. We [he and his comrades] are determined to stay together. So far, I have always declined. What shall I do now? Honey, wouldn't it be better if I were a man too. I can't bear it any longer... Think for a moment, how would it look like if later on we are all sitting together around the table [at home] and everyone trades war stories and I am just the damn REMF and can't keep up."[54] Edith, holding this letter in her hands, was "beat, I couldn't think anymore," as she wrote back immediately, "angry at those people" – his comrades – "who call you a coward." She expressed some understanding for the pressure he was under, but she challenged the martial concept of manliness he was adopting and tried to steer him back to his earlier mind-set: "Helmut, a war is not an opportunity to get into adventures. Instead, everyone is to do his duty wherever he is ordered to be. My dear little Helmut, if the Führer needs you, you'll get to the front, don't worry. And think of us. Your Mom!.... And then there is your girl waiting for you at home."[55] In the subsequent communication, Helmut played down his comrades' impact on him. The truth was that he had made up his mind, and Edith could no longer ignore it. Only recently, Helmut had read a book on pregnancy and childbirth. He shared with Edith the lesson he took from it: "Female honor consists of chastity and motherly happiness. The honor of a man, however, consists of personality and heroism."[56]

Soldiers such as Kreissler and Gross internalized this identity long before they entered the army, in the Hitler Youth, in school, through their reading, and not least through their parents; both Gross's and Kreissler's fathers were proud World War I veterans and dedicated to the Nazi cause. The same was true of Karl Fuchs, born in 1917 and also brought up in a Nazi family. In spring 1940, having successfully completed his training period as a tank gunner and now an officer candidate, he wrote to his father – and not to his fiancée – that "we," that is, he and his comrades, wished nothing more than to be "transferred to the front soon." He knew "that our women don't understand this wish" but also knew that "that cannot matter... Women do not understand anything about the necessary struggle of a man . . . a man must prove himself in battle" if he didn't want to run the risk of being tagged "a coward," which was his biggest fear: "I couldn't live with the shame." Of course, his fiancée, then wife, was not unaware of these priorities, which he eventually explained to her in detail. While in wartime a woman had only one soul that feared "for the life of her husband," a man "has two souls in difficult times." One of them certainly wished "to be at home with his beloved." "The more important one," however, was the other one that "wants to be engaged in battle," because "he who avoids this struggle is a despicable coward and does not deserve to live."[57]

In the Third Reich, the martial idea of manliness dominated not only state propaganda but also private communication. It left little space for honoring family-oriented concepts of manliness. "I want to be and have to be a soldier," stated Helmut Wißmann apodictically. Eventually Edith gave in. Bedevilled by antisemitic stereotypes about deviant Jewish masculinities, she wrote in March 1941 that she wanted her fiancé to be "a German soldier rather than a Jew."[58] Letters exchanged between soldiers and their families could not be an adequate counterweight to the face-to-face communication among soldiers. Only the latter was tied into and paralleled by daily and incessant acting together, working together, altercating together, joking together, and relaxing together. "What we do here is done by all of us together. Either we all go to the movies, or no one does," Wißmann wrote to his fiancée.[59] Joining in was the maxim when it came to doing things, as it also was when it came to thinking, to imagination, to fear, and to enjoyment. Soldiers such as Wieschenberg, Wißmann, Böll, and Reese had grown up in environments that kept Nazism and militarism, including the Hitler Youth and the Nazi training camps, at a distance; Wißmann's *Landjahr* was an exception, but even that could not annul the influence of an anti-Nazi family. Only under the impact of comrades and comradely superiors in the Wehrmacht did they change their attitude. The soldiers even spent their leisure times together with, and under the control of, their comrades. Disconnected from the civilian world, the soldiers established their own consensus on what mattered and what did not. They created their own collective identity, and put aside the individual mind-sets that made their lives as soldiers so difficult. They understood that a man was someone who conformed and did what other men did.

Although the personal writings of the Wehrmacht recruits included numerous complaints about unfair, arrogant, harassing, or ignorant superiors, they also revealed that sooner or later the soldiers got along with them surprisingly well. "Thanks to the training and drill of the past couple of weeks the comradeship between rank-and-file soldiers and superiors has got much better," Neuhaus stated two months after becoming a soldier.[60] In fact, the novices were socialized into the military by their immediate superiors, senior privates, NCOs, and junior officers not only through malevolence and unfairness but also through competence, empathy, and patience – in other words, through comradely leadership. Wieschenberg was impressed by a lieutenant who took part in his men's booze-ups and pub crawls.[61] And Wißmann wrote in spring 1941, still in the Rokitzan barracks: "we are getting quite a lot of pressure," "but that's just fine. One might feel differently about it if there wasn't this amazing community. But if the first lieutenant himself doesn't bother taking part in any kind of exercise, I guess, then you have to just get along with it too. OK, he may not do so all the time, but still, you know, he means it and makes true what Hindenburg once said: 'Great combat community can be achieved only on the basis of comradeship between leader and ranks.'"[62] The comradely leader thus extended the soldiers' sense of comradeship from small face-to-face communities into an "imagined" community[63] of millions of German soldiers fighting all over Europe – all allegedly acting in concert, filled with the same spirit of comradeship, laying their individual I's on the altar of the We of the army and the fatherland. Realizing that they were part of this grand community completed both Wißmann's and Wieschenberg's military socialization and training as comrades. In late spring 1941, they were ready to volunteer to go to the front.

And so were soldiers such as Böll or Reese, although with much less enthusiasm. Occasionally they too enjoyed the pleasure of comradely togetherness, Reese for instance on a short trip from the training barracks in Cologne to the picturesque medieval town of Monschau. They hiked, and in the evening "lit a campfire" at the castle, emptied a small barrel of beer, smoked and sang songs of soldiers "lives, love, going to war, and death, full of the melancholy [but] beautiful bliss of death that I once felt when listening to Haydn's Military Symphony . . . In that hour I felt at ease with my company, one of many who shared the same destiny, the same garb." But for Reese, such sentiments were rare, and even then soaked in the melancholy of disruption. Only "for a few hours" did he feel like a soldier, "even in my heart." And yet he insisted on wearing only the "mask of a soldier." "Secretly, though, what I loved was the feeling of returning to myself." It was a self that would never internalize the role of the soldier as the selves of Wißmann and Wieschenberg did. Reese's "homesickness unrolled its carpets over all things and experiences," he wrote shortly before he died, after three years of "living in my own kingdom . . . , which, even in self-division, spiritual anxiety, despair, and questioning, I preferred to the soldierly world of masks."[64]

Böll too joined in, if only rarely: once, for instance, by boozing with his roommates, if only to feel embarrassed about himself the morning after. Inwardly and in the letters to his fiancée, he deliberately worked on staying clear from any sense of belonging to his unit. He always reminded himself of the deep gap between "our real life," the one of individuality, privacy, and family, and the enforced life in uniform that was all at the mercy of oppressors and comrades. They were to him only a "grey thick mush," kept together by "this endless babble, always the same, dumb and foolish, brainless, shallow as a stinking puddle."[65] The way Böll coped was twofold: He dreamed of martial individualism on the one hand, and re-enacted the sacrifice of Christ on behalf of humankind on the other. While Böll despised the obscene, brawling, and boozy type of male bonding and the underlying concept of conformist manliness – a man joins in and avoids being shamed among his peers for not doing so – he yet was not void of ideas of martial masculinity. Later during his service, he read Ernst Jünger, fascinated with the heroic warrior who fought ahead and above the mass of comrades, in Böll's words, "absolutely martially, truly the absolute soldier."[66] In Böll's view, as for other individualist outsiders, "male comradeship" seemed unmanly as it devalued the concept of individuality. Böll once in a letter called the all-male community of his comrades a "gathering of fishwives"; in his 1949 war novel *The Train Was On Time*, the soldier Andreas once fantasizes about travelling on civilian trains, where one would meet not "only men. It is terrible," Andreas states, "being among men only all the time. Men are so womanish."[67] In a similar way Sebastian Haffner feminized the all-male society, mocking the "soft cushions of comradeship" and contrasting it to the "hardness of civilian life," where individuals were responsible for themselves, while comradeship relieved them from precisely that burden.[68]

But soldiers such as Reese and Böll, who desperately sought to save themselves from the maelstrom of comradeship, joined in anyway, even if only in a cynical spirit and without enthusiasm. They understood well the rationale of all the drill, the humiliation, and the terror both during the training period and while they were in reserve positions. It was to make the soldier keen to get away to the front, where it could only get better, as Böll occasionally thought.[69] "Barracks life and drills seemed worse than war," stated Reese, noticing – explicitly including himself – how, through this life in the barracks, "the platoon was made into a machine, able to fight, to overcome hardship, to suffer privation, and to attack . . . and to die."[70]

NOTES

1 Letter of Kurt Kreissler to his parents, February 19, 1945, copy owned by author.
2 Shils and Janowitz, "Cohesion and Disintegration," p. 280.

3 Charles Horton Cooley, *Social Organization: A Study of the Larger Mind* (New York: Scribner, 1909), pp. 23, 26, quoted in part in Shils and Janowitz, "Cohesion and Disintegration," p. 283.

4 Ferdinand Tönnies, *Community and Civil Society* (Cambridge University Press, 2001; German orig. 1887), pp. 52, 32–34, 36, 66. For a different contemporary juxtaposition, see Émile Durkheim, *The Division of Labor in Society* (New York: Free Press, 1997; French orig. 1893), pp. 149–75.

5 Shils and Janowitz, "Cohesion and Disintegration," p. 281.

6 Samuel Stouffer et al., *The American Soldier*, 2 vols. (Princeton University Press, 1949). See vol. I, pp. 83–84, vol. II, pp. iii, 98, 108–09, 130–31, 136–38, 143–49, in conjunction with the evidence used by John McManus, *The Deadly Brotherhood: The American Soldier in World War II* (Novato, CA: Presidio, 1998), pp. 228–90. (But see, for a more nuanced view of the role of hatred, McManus, pp. 171–200, and Stouffer et al., *American Soldier*, vol. II, p. 158.) On the 1945 quotation, see Roy R. Grinker and John P. Spiegel, *Men Under Stress* (Philadelphia: Blakiston, 1945), quoted in Alexander George, "Primary Groups, Organization, and Military Performance," in Roger W. Little (ed.), *Handbook of Military Institutions* (Beverly Hills, CA: Sage, 1971), pp. 293–318 (at 294).

7 Simon Wessely, "Twentieth-century Theories on Combat Motivation and Breakdown," *Journal of Contemporary History*, 41/2 (2006), 275–86; Ulrich Bröckling, "Schlachtfeldforschung: Die Soziologie im Krieg," *Mittelweg 36*, 9/5 (2000), 74–92.

8 Shils and Janowitz, "Cohesion and Disintegration," pp. 287–91. Cf. Martin van Creveld, *Fighting Power: German and U.S. Army Performance, 1939–1945* (Westport, CT: Greenwood, 1982), pp. 74–79; Peter S. Kindsvatter, *American Soldiers: Ground Combat in the World Wars, Korea, and Vietnam* (Lawrence: University Press of Kansas, 2003), pp. 11–74. On the deterioration of group solidarity and military effectiveness at the end of war, see Andreas Kunz, *Wehrmacht und Niederlage: Die bewaffnete Macht in der Endphase der nationalsozialistischen Herrschaft 1944 bis 1945* (Munich: Oldenbourg, 2005); and the case study by Roger Beaumont, "A Different Perspective: Cohesion, Morale and Operational Effectiveness in the German Army, Fall 1944," *Armed Forces and Society*, 25 (1999), 97–130.

9 Bartov, *Hitler's Army*, pp. 5–9, 12.

10 Guy L. Siebold, "Key Questions and Challenges to the Standard Model of Military Group Cohesion," *Armed Forces & Society*, 37 (2011), 448–68; cf. Siebold, "The Essence of Military Group Cohesion," *Armed Forces & Society*, 33 (2007), 286–95; Darryl Henderson, *Cohesion: The Human Element in Combat: Leadership and Societal Influence in the Armies of the Soviet Union, the United States, North Vietnam, and Israel* (Washington, DC: National Defense University Press, 1985). Important historical applications include John A. Lynn, *The Bayonets of the Republic: Motivation and Tactics in the Army of Revolutionary France, 1791–94* (Urbana: University of Illinois Press, 1984); and James M. McPherson, *For Cause and Comrades: Why Men Fought in the Civil War* (New York: Oxford University Press, 1997).

11 Morris Janowitz and Roger W. Little, *Sociology and the Military Establishment*, 3rd edn. (Beverly Hills, CA: Sage, 1974), p. 94.

12 W. Victor Madej, "Effectiveness and Cohesion of the German Ground Forces in World War II," *Journal of Political and Military Sociology*, 6 (1978), 233–58 (at p. 243).

13 Hew Strachan, "Training, Morale and Modern War," *Journal of Contemporary History*, 41 (2006), 211–17 (at p. 213).

14 George, "Primary Groups," p. 299.

15 W. K. Pfeiler, *War and the German Mind: The Testimony of Men of Fiction Who Fought at the Front* (New York: Columbia University Press, 1941) introduced the Anglophone audience to German World War I literature and is quoted in Shils and Janowitz, "Cohesion and Disintegration," p. 284, n. 4.

16 Shils and Janowitz, "Cohesion and Disintegration," p. 286.

17 See the draft typescript of their 1948 publication, written in spring 1946, which still uses the German words: Edward Shils and Morris Janowitz, "Cohesion and Disintegration in the German Army in World War II," 114 pp., University of Chicago Library, Edward Shils Manuscript Series II/70.

18 In addition to the works listed and evaluated in Kühne, "Der nationalsozialistische Vernichtungskrieg," see, on the records of conversations in captivity: Sönke Neitzel and Harald Welzer, *Soldaten – On Fighting, Killing, and Dying: The Secret World War II Transcripts of German POWs* (New York: Knopf, 2012); and Felix Römer, *Kameraden: Die Wehrmacht von innen* (Munich: Piper, 2012).

19 Fritz, *Frontsoldaten*, esp. pp. 156–86; Rüdiger Overmans, *Deutsche militärische Verluste im Zweiten Weltkrieg* (Munich: Oldenbourg, 1999); Christoph Rass, *"Menschenmaterial": Deutsche Soldaten an der Ostfront: Innenansichten einer Infanteriedivision 1939–1945* (Paderborn: Schöningh, 2003); Michaela Kipp, *"Großreinemachen im Osten": Feindbilder in deutschen Feldpostbriefen im Zweiten Weltkrieg* (Frankfurt: Campus, 2014).

20 Kurt Kreissler, *Im feldgrauen Rock: Erlebtes und Gesehenes*, 2 parts, undated manuscript (c. 1947), part I, pp. 1–6 (copy owned by author).

21 Letters of Werner Gross to his parents, April 23, 1936, May 3, 1936, August 18, 1938, Landeshauptarchiv Koblenz, Best. 700, 153, nos. 286–91.

22 Kreissler, *Im feldgrauen Rock*, part I, pp. 1–3, 5–8.

23 Hermann Melcher, *Die Gefolgschaft* (Berg: Druffel & Vowinckel, 1990), pp. 112–13. Cf. Kindsvatter, *American Soldiers*, p. 29.

24 Hans Werner Woltersdorf, *Picknick zwischen Biarritz and Shitomir: Ein Schicksal der Generation, deren Jugend der Krieg war*, 3rd edn. (Remagen: Alverlag, 1988), p. 109.

25 Author's interview with Hanns Karl Vorster (pseudonym), 1994. Cf. Erhard Steininger, *Abgesang 1945: Ein Erlebnisbericht* (Leer: Rautenberg, 1981), pp. 95–96; Max Bauer, *Kopfsteinpflaster: Erinnerungen* (Frankfurt: Eichborn, 1981), pp. 100–02.

26 Hans Lorenz, *Graubrot mit Rübenkraut: Ein zeitgeschichtliches Schicksal* (Moers: Brendow, 1993), pp. 108–09, 117.

27 Haffner, *Defying Hitler*, p. 289.

28 Criminal Case against Sergeant-Major Wilhelm J., May 18, 1944, Bundesarchiv-Zentralnachweisstelle Aachen-Kornelimünster, W 11/M 59.

29 Albert K. Cohen, *Deviance and Control* (Englewood Cliffs, NJ: Prentice-Hall, 1966), pp. 8ff.

30 George Herbert Mead, "The Psychology of Punitive Justice," *American Journal of Sociology*, 23 (1918), 577–602 (at pp. 590–91).

31 Weniger, *Wehrmachtserziehung und Kriegserfahrung*, p. 119. Cf. Kindsvatter, *American Soldiers*, p. 20; Stouffer et al., *The American Soldier*, vol. I, pp. 414, 423–25.

32 Dieter Wellershoff, *Der Ernstfall: Innenansichten des Krieges* (Cologne: Kiepenheuer & Witsch, 1995), p. 48.

33 Willy Peter Reese, *A Stranger to Myself: The Inhumanity of War: Russia, 1941–1944*, ed. Stefan Schmitz (New York: Farrar, Straus and Giroux, 2005), pp. 7–8, 12–13.

34 Heinrich Böll, *Briefe aus dem Krieg 1939–1945*, ed. Jochen Schubert, 2 vols. (Cologne: Kiepenheuer & Witsch, 2001), vol. I, pp. 235, 249, 261, 271–72, 292, letters to fiancée, Aug. 1, 1941, Sept. 7, 1941, Nov. 3, 1941, Dec. 20, 1941, Feb. 5, 1942. For a similar example, see Siegbert Stehmann, *Die Bitternis verschweigen wir: Feldpostbriefe 1940–1945*, ed. Gerhard Sprenger (Hanover: Lutherisches Verlagshaus, 1992), e.g. pp. 73–74, letter to his wife, Nov. 30, 1940.

35 Interview of Helmut Wißmann with the author, 2001. Letters of Helmut Wißmann and Edith Wulf, later Wißmann, owned by their descendants, excerpted by author. Letters of Franz and Hilde Wieschenberg, Kempowski-Archiv, Nartum, now Akademie der Künste, Berlin. On Wieschenberg's biography, see letter of his daughter Hilde Drosser to author, Aug. 30, 1998. On Neuhaus, see Karl Reddemann (ed.), *Zwischen Front und Heimat: Der Briefwechsel des münsterischen Ehepaares Agnes und Albert Neuhaus* (Münster: Regensberg, 1996), pp. ix–xxix.

36 See Neuhaus's letters to his wife Agnes written during his training period, in Reddemann (ed.), *Zwischen Front und Heimat*, pp. 4, 12, 22, 40, 42–43, 47, 49.

37 Helmut Wißmann, letter to Edith, Oct. 22, 1940.

38 Erich Kuby, *Mein Krieg: Aufzeichnungen aus 2129 Tagen* (Munich: Nymphenburger Verlagshandlung, 1975), p. 33, diary entry, Feb. 19, 1940. See also Stehmann, *Die Bitternis verschweigen wir*, p. 166, letter to his wife, Feb. 4, 1942: "Continuously writing letters in my leisure time, I have almost made a fool of myself."

39 Reddemann (ed.), *Zwischen Front und Heimat*, p. 13, letter of Neuhaus to Agnes, June 23, 1940.

40 Ibid., p. 86, letter of Neuhaus to Agnes, Sept. 2, 1940.

41 Edith Wulf, letters to Wißmann, Oct. 14, 19, 21, 24, 26, 31, 1940.

42 Helmut Wißmann, letters to Edith, April 17, 21, 22, 1941, May 4 and 5, 1941.

43 Edith Wulf, letter to Wißmann, April 28, 1941.

44 Reddemann (ed.), *Zwischen Front und Heimat*, p. 561, letter of Neuhaus to Agnes, July 23, 1942.

45 Wißmann, letter to Edith, Oct. 3, 1940.

46 Böll, *Briefe aus dem Krieg*, vol. I, p. 235, letter to Annemarie, Aug. 1, 1941.

47 Wieschenberg, letters to Hilde, Aug. 4, 1940, Oct. 7, 1940.

48 Edith Wulf, letters to Helmut, Oct. 19, 21, 1940, Dec. 14, 1940.

49 Hans Graf von Lehndorff (ed.), *Die Briefe des Peter Pfaff 1943–1944* (Munich: Herbig, 1988), pp. 18, 48, letters to his mother, May 2, 1943, Sept. 22, 1943.

50 Helmut Wißmann, letters to Edith, Nov. 16, 1940, Dec. 3, 12, 1940, Jan. 9, 1941; Edith Wulf, letter to Helmut, Nov. 19, 1940.

51 Edith Wulf, letter to Helmut, March 14, 1941; Wißmann, letter to Edith, March 16, 1941.

52 Wißmann, letters to Edith, March 16, 17, 18, 20, 1941, July 27, 28, 29, 1941; Sept. 17, 24, 1941; Edith Wulf, letters to Helmut, Aug. 1, 2, 3, 1941, Sept. 23, 1942.

53 Wißmann, letter to Edith, Jan. 10, 1941; the German word for the soldier who dodges in the rear area is "Etappenhengst." Wißmann, otherwise comfortable with German orthography, wrote "Etappenhenkst," an unusual spelling error reflecting the pronunciation of the word and indicating that he had learned the word only via oral communication.

54 Wißmann, letter to Edith, Feb. 19, 1941.

55 Edith Wulf, letter to Helmut, Feb. 23, 1941.

56 Wißmann, letter to Edith, Feb. 25, 1941.

57 Karl Fuchs, *Sieg Heil! War Letters of Tank Gunner Karl Fuchs, 1937–41*, ed. Horst Fuchs Richardson (Hamden: Archon, 1987), pp. 50, 62, 104–05, letters to his father, Feb. 9, 1940, June 2, 1940, letter to his wife, May 24, 1941.

58 Edith Wulf, letter to Helmut, March 3, 1941.

59 Wißmann, letter to Edith, May 8, 1941.

60 Reddemann (ed.), *Zwischen Front und Heimat*, p. 70, Neuhaus, letter to Agnes, Aug. 21, 1940.

61 Wieschenberg, letter to Hilde, Dec. 18, 1940.

62 Wißmann, letter to Edith, April 12, 1941.

63 Benedict Anderson, *Imagined Communities: Reflections on the Origin and Spread of Nationalism*, rev. edn. (London: Verso, 1993).

64 Reese, *A Stranger to Myself*, pp. 17–18.

65 Böll, *Briefe aus dem Krieg*, vol. I, pp. 237, 260, letters to Annemarie, Aug. 3, 1941, Oct. 29, 1941.

66 Ibid., vol. I, p. 592, letter to Annemarie, Jan. 24, 1943, and vol. II, p. 1091, letter to Annemarie, July 19, 1944.

67 Ibid., vol. II, p. 899, letter to Annemarie, Sept. 22, 1943; Heinrich Böll, *Der Zug war pünktlich*, in *Werke: Romane und Erzählungen*, 5 vols., ed. Bernd Balzer (Cologne: Kiepeneuer & Witsch, 1978), vol. I, p. 108.

68 Haffner, *Defying Hitler*, p. 286.

69 Böll, *Briefe aus dem Krieg*, vol. I, p. 292, letter to Annemarie, Feb. 3, 1942.

70 Reese, *A Stranger to Myself*, p. 14.

5   Megalomania

Böll served with the reserve army in Germany and the occupational forces in France until the autumn of 1943 before he was sent to the Eastern front. Reese had already arrived there in August 1941 but only to feel even more a "stranger to myself." There is no statistical evidence on how many of the 17 million Wehrmacht soldiers shared the sentiments of these two. Anecdotal evidence, however, suggests that most German soldiers, even those who had been coerced into the army, were overwhelmed by an "impetuous German advance" that "cannot be stopped" and "has never been seen in the world," as Albert Neuhaus wrote. Being part of an invasion that within a few weeks advanced hundreds of miles into enemy country across a front line of almost two thousand miles, destroying thousands of enemy tanks and airplanes, capturing hundreds of thousands of POWs within a few weeks, all combined to instill in the soldiers a sense of megalomania.[1] The early victories confirmed the expectations the soldiers shared even before Barbarossa had begun: "We have been born into a fantastic time, and the world will soon know it," bragged Wieschenberg in May 1941. Soon afterwards, he too joined in the euphoria on the Eastern front.[2] The soldiers were not just witnessing this grand event, but making it happen, and it filled them with abundant pride. They knew, or thought they knew, that they would be assigned a privileged place in the society that would emerge from the conquest of *Lebensraum* in the East.

Basking in the euphoria of conquest, the soldiers forgot about the rifts between I and We that had haunted them before. "At the front line the sarge polishes his shoes himself, and he takes care of his uniform himself. He makes his bed himself and cleans his room himself. He is a true comrade," observed Kurt Kreissler, glad no longer to have to bother with the "cocky garrison idiots," as he put it.[3] "This is how true comradeship should be," Wieschenberg exclaimed, intoxicated by the joy of "sharing everything" with his comrades, of taking care of each other.[4] Wißmann was deeply impressed when a general and a colonel came along saluting the troops at the front line. "I have to say, there appears to be an excellent spirit of comradeship here."[5] The myth of comradeship, as told in World War I stories and promised by Nazi propaganda, seemed to be coming true. The soldiers experienced the best in comradeship in primary groups, and they felt equally at home in their secondary groups, the army, the *Volksgemeinschaft*.

Comradeship was a set of concentric circles, pulling men into face-to-face communities and into "secondary," anonymous and imagined groups such as the entire army, the mystic community of fallen soldiers, and the *Volksgemeinschaft*. The military discourse on social relations and social cohesion in interwar Germany had supported this notion of comradeship. It mediated between communities of different sizes and textures. Military psychologists may have devalued its smallest possible element, the dyadic relationship between friends or buddies rooted in personal sympathy, in emotional, intellectual, and physical attraction. But as middle and high school essays written in Nazi Germany suggest, friendship never lost its fascination for German youth. When asked to put their preferences in writing, they often chose friendship over comradeship, indicating the limited effect of propaganda and public rhetoric.[6] And so it was still in the army. Many soldiers sought for close friends in order to feel settled in the army, wherever it operated.

Fritz Farnbacher, who left an exceptionally detailed personal diary, may serve as an example. Born in 1914 and thus already grown up when the Nazis came to power and no longer subject to their mandatory youth training programs, he was a clerk in Nuremberg when he joined the army in 1937. As a soldier with the prestigious 4th Tank Division, he took part in the Polish and French campaigns, was promoted to lieutenant in 1940, and represented those parts of the Wehrmacht that willingly adopted the military identity – Farnbacher was a bachelor without a girlfriend waiting at home – and yet kept the Nazi ideology at distance. Farnbacher was a Protestant believer and as such not always safe from being teased by less religious comrades. In fact, for most of his time with the army – he fought with his front division in the East until the end of the war and survived it – he felt an outsider. It was having a close friend among the comrades that made his soldiering bearable, sometimes enjoyable – and difficult when he had to do without one. During the Wehrmacht's advance on the Soviet Union in summer 1941, one of the radio operators of his unit caught Farnbacher's attention. It made him happy to watch "Bobbi" relaxing like a kitten in a warm corner of the radio car. "When I look at him, he always smiles back so boyishly and innocently. You just gotta love this boy," he confessed to his diary.[7] Even more meaningful was an officer friend of his, Peter Siegert, who served with a neighboring unit.

With him, "We often sit together in front of the tent... We enjoy being together so much." Peter was more than a "comrade," he was a "friend, in whom I can confide, who understands me, and who comes along with me." Each single meeting was enchanting. "We would shake hands again and again, and then not stop asking 'How are you' and 'How have you been.'" Like a mother would do with her child, Farnbacher popped "a cookie into Peter's mouth; but he doesn't notice it, he is so sound asleep, sitting up straight, so that I have to put a few more on his arm." When it was time to say good-bye, Peter was given chocolate, "which I still have from mom."[8]

Homoeroticism entrenched intimate relationships between comrades; as close friends, they rejoiced in the "sunny" mood of the other, his shiny eyes, his beaming face, his way of walking, and in deep conversations. Such intimacy necessarily needed some distance from the rest of the unit. "We like to dissociate ourselves from the rest of the crowd, at least a little" Farnbacher wrote about Peter and himself. Yet they were careful to stay in touch with the "crowd" and to avoid being seen as snobs or mavericks. When Farnbacher dished up a festive dinner for his friend – "a wonderful roast with potatoes," and plums from home as dessert – other comrades were welcome to join in; in the end, seven rather than two comrades enjoyed the meal in "brotherly" harmony.[9] This way, friendships opened up to the larger community, the platoon, the company, the battalion, the regiment, and the division. Friendships within the comradely fabric of a unit established a balance between intimacy and anonymity, and by extension also between the civilian I and the soldierly We. And yet the comradely fabric of the enforced community ruled the military culture, not the friendships driven by mutual sympathy. Sentimental accounts of the latter as they appear in the private writings of soldiers like Farnbacher or Kreissler – the list could be easily extended for less enthusiastic soldiers like Heinrich Böll, Erich Kuby, or Willy Reese – should not be mistaken for the rule. The very fact that they took the time to write about their sensations and frustrations put them at a distance from the bawling, misogynist, and hypermasculine, hegemonic sociability of the less literate, less intellectual soldiers. They always knew about their outsider status, as did Siegbert Stehmann, a Protestant pastor (and member of the Nazi-resisting Confessing Church), born in 1912. Serving with the occupational army in Norway, he experienced a "gruesome Christmas eve" in 1940. "In one hour the entire battalion (800 men) was so dead drunk that you would see only bawling beasts rolling senselessly on the floor." Luckily, he had a few closer comrades, believers like him, who allowed him to stay away from the rest, "but otherwise...? Horrible," he wrote in a letter.[10]

Like their civilian counterparts, friendships between soldiers were based on individual sympathy and on emotional and spiritual exchange between individuals. Yet these friendships never enjoyed the sense of freedom characterizing those between civilians. It was not only that the suspicious gaze of the larger group of comrades constantly watched over the intimate friendship, but also that the military hierarchy and the contingency of war made its very existence subject to the blows of fate and the decisions of superiors rather than the control of the friends themselves. Helmut Wißmann arrived at the Eastern front with his crony Willi, but after a couple of weeks they were separated; Willi stayed with the combat unit, while Helmut was ordered to join the baggage in a unit made up mostly of "bullheaded East Prussians". As a Westphalian, he despised these and didn't get along with them. The third of three musketeers who had enjoyed each other's company during the training period, Walter, had been sent to a different unit long before. After losing Willi, Helmut suffered from loneliness among his comrades for a long time.[11] "It's always the same," noted another private, Jochen Klepper, in his diary, "you happily get to know someone, and after a spell you are in pain over the loss of him. The soldier has no control over anything."[12] Tenderness between soldier-friends was a crucial force in an organization that demanded cohesion and yet destroyed tenderness constantly – through relocations, furloughs, casualties, and death.

It was learning to accept the recurrent loss of precious friends, and to embrace the fate that caused the loss instead of questioning it by wondering about missed choices, that shaped the soldier – and the good comrade. On November 20, 1941, Farnbacher's friend Peter was fatally injured in combat. Farnbacher relived the Uhland song, spending time with his dying and then dead friend, letting his mind wander between the front line and "our mothers" at home, and mourning the "part of myself" he had lost, as the Uhland song put it. "Everything around me is so empty, so useless," Farnbacher bemoans, loaded with survivor guilt: Why him, not me? But the battle went on, just as in the Uhland song. Indeed it was this song, together with Walter Flex's words in the face of the death of his friend Ernst Wurche, that helped Farnbacher to cope. Action was called for, not paralysis; rejoining the comrades in combat instead of lonesome suffering. Two comrades took care of him. They showed empathy, "shake hands with me heartily because they know how close friends we were." They didn't leave him alone, however. Soon after, he was reunited with them in battle and proud of his unit: "Our men put up a good fight . . . A page of honor!"[13]

Such losses accompanied the soldiers throughout the war. The longer the war went on, the more soldiers anticipated the loss of a relationship, permeating it with melancholy from the start. For a while, Kurt Kreissler was blessed by a deep, homoerotic friendship with a younger soldier named Schwania. "I hope I never have to let go of his hand," Kreissler thought when they met, desiring to be with him "for ever." But he had seen too many scenes of mass death to harbour any illusions. Schwania was killed in action soon after. "Why" wondered Kreissler, but only for a short time. There was no answer. "The only thing you can do is to put up with destiny. As soldiers, we have to resign ourselves to our fate."[14] A soldier was one who had learned routinely to swallow personal hurts and losses – the loss of one's own self, as in the Uhland song. It was the crucial step of merging the I into the We. He who achieved it had gained a precious attribute. He knew that "I match the men," as Klepper put it.[15] He was a fully accomplished member of the all-male society. His emotional well-being – and his functioning as a soldier – no longer depended on one particular friend. Instead, he knew that his large community of comrades provided an unlimited reservoir of new friends.

Thus Wißmann found a new friend in March 1942. Flattmann's home was in the Ruhr area, like Wißmann's – a solid basis for mutual sympathy. Gestures of mutual caring and sharing, and especially the exchange of secrets, strengthened the friendship. Back home Flattmann had fathered an illegitimate child, about which his wife did not and must not know. He was coping with a legal quarrel about this, which he had to handle while serving in the East, and he spoke about it with Wißmann, who provided helpful advice and appreciated it as a proof of trust, as he expressed in a letter to Edith: "He was so happy to unburden himself and bare his heart... I too was really glad to find someone to share with deeply. I am so excited about having someone I can really talk to." The friendship between them was based on mutual sympathy, emotional unison, and intimate trust. Yet it remained tied into the concept of comradeship understood as a coercive community that existed to resolve common tasks and challenges rather than to please individual selves. His friendship with Flattmann helped Wißmann to get over his long-standing problems in getting on with the East Prussians who dominated his unit. Having formerly held himself aloof from them, he now grew closer to them by "playing" at the rituals of sharing comradeship. He provided breakfast for everyone, decorated postcards for them, and joined in their boozy evenings. Recently, he wrote in a letter, they had enjoyed "an evening of true comradeship. Life is good." And the friendship with Flattmann had an even more serious impact on Wißmann's performance as soldier. In May 1942 the two of them were ordered to carry out a night-time intelligence mission, a suicide action through mined and marshy territory

along the main front. When they came under heavy fire, Wißmann urged
Flattmann – who unlike Wißmann was a father – to stay behind or back
out. But Flattmann declined. "He came along with me. If we have to,
we'll fall together," Flattmann said, a reaction that made Wißmann see
him as a model comrade.[16]

Comradeship was a social resource that gained momentum from pressure, menace, and destruction, or rather, from resisting or overcoming
havoc and mayhem, paradigmatically on the battlefield. On 22 September 22, 1941 Farnbacher experienced "the most memorable" day of his
life so far, as he put it in his personal diary less than twenty-four hours
later in a thirty-page long entry on one combat day. The 4th Tank Division took part in the battle for Kiev, which eventually brought Hitler
and the Wehrmacht another monumental victory, with 665,000 Soviet
soldiers captured.[17] But the victory wasn't guaranteed from the beginning. In fact, the battle revealed a new, "dramatic" side of the war, the
increasing strength of the enemy, as Farnbacher also noted. For him in
particular, things started badly that morning. His car needed to be tow-
started once his unit had already set off, so that he only caught up with
his men later. Then everything seemed to go wrong; he didn't know what
to do, there was "no assignment for me." "Helpless, I kick my heels," he
noted in his dairy. What he saw were the new Soviet tanks, the T-34s,
a "heavy chunk" superior to any of the German tanks, a real shock to
the German soldiers who had expected an enemy inferior to them on
all measures. More than anything else, the T-34 proved how wrong the
Germans and the German anti-Soviet propaganda had been. The Soviets struck Farnbacher's battalion, a truck was destroyed, and the first
fatalities and casualties occurred – Farnbacher's comrades. And it was
comradeship that turned the tide. "Barely any of our soldiers backed
off," noted Farnbacher, "they all stood rooted to the ground," men and
machines working together as one. The combat unit showed its mus-
cle and excelled itself. Suddenly a tank rolled towards Farnbacher. He
was hiding in a ditch, hoping the tank wouldn't hit him, but one of its
caterpillar tracks entered the ditch. Farnbacher managed to jump out
at the last moment, "the tank two centimetres away from my left foot."
The comrades all had to be this cold-blooded. They interacted perfectly,
Farnbacher noted, cooperating, helping out, protecting, and encouraging each other – the perfect combat community, textbook comradeship.
Running out of ammunition for his ordnance, one sergeant ran to the
next anti-tank gun to help operate it, so that it was able to continue firing
until the last bullet. Eventually a bull's-eye hit the emplacement, and a
tank ran over it. The brave sergeant, fatally wounded, asked: "Captain,

when I get back, and I hope it'll be soon, can I continue to serve as a soldier?" to which the captain responded "Of course, I've no doubt you'll soon be one of us again."[18]

Nothing could express the radiance of combat comradeship better then this wish – articulated in the face of death – to stay with the comrades, to join in again as soon as possible. Physical death lost its cruel face when social death was overcome and symbolic life as a hero was guaranteed. Whereas the coward attracted the shaming gaze of the community for questioning its very existence, the hero gloried in the adoring gaze of the community for raising it beyond itself. The epitome of this type of hero was the charismatic leader who put his men under his spell and drew them magnetically into battle. One such was Lieutenant Colonel Lüttwitz, the commander of Artillery Regiment 103, in the mid-August 1941 advance on Smolensk, 200 miles west of Moscow. Awestruck, Farnbacher noted in his diary the "majestic" scenario. "While all men are on the ground, taking cover from shrapnel and missiles . . . Lieutenant Colonel Lüttwitz stands upright in the midst of it all under the attack, stoically assessing the situation, pondering the options, and eventually taking his decisions . . . a true leader of sweeping power . . . None of his men ever saw him dither or yield," Farnbacher recorded. "He stays upright in the midst of all the shooting and detonations and doesn't stop issuing clear and positive orders. An amazing leader."[19] Lüttwitz, who embodied both charisma and comradeship in combat, soon after initiated a dramatic liberation operation. A German fighter pilot had bailed out behind the front line and fallen into Soviet hands. Whichever way it was carried out – various options were pondered in the regiment headquarters, to which Farnbacher belonged – this action was likely to cost more German lives than the one who was to be rescued. But this action was not about saving physical lives; it was about enhancing social life. It was about realizing the very idea of comradeship. Farnbacher was "enthusiastic about it." These "dashing men," compared to whom Farnbacher felt "like a rabbit," "really pep the battalion up," he noted. In a surprise coup the operation was concluded successfully within a few hours, with no fatalities.[20]

The soldiers experienced this kind of ultimate comradeship in many ways. Charismatic leadership in battle, with the officer or NCO moulding the soldiers into a cohesive, effective fighting unit through the force of his personality, represented one type; the altruistic and heroic act of saving a soldier, the rescue of wounded or missing comrades from the battle zone by risking one's own life, was another type. Witnessing or participating in any of these acts awarded the soldiers a unique and sacred sense of belonging. Re-enacting the myth of comradeship, the soldiers inserted their momentary experience of belonging into the eternal stream of the martial community. "It is this comradeship and the support that we are able to give each other that is, in my opinion, the secret behind our incredible successes and victories," stated Karl Fuchs in October 1941 in a letter, now serving as a tank gunner on the Eastern front. "We can depend on each other unconditionally...I have always known of this loyalty," he added echoing the myth of comradeship as the nucleus of the *Volksgemeinschaft*, "but today it burns in me like a holy flame. Let this loyalty which I have experienced out here in comradeship be the foundation of our future life."[21]

But there was no inclusion without exclusion. From the beginning of the war in the East, the enthusiasm and megalomania was challenged – yet eventually confirmed – by disgust and horror. The poor living conditions of the Slavic peoples the German soldiers faced in the East seemed in fact to confirm the Nazi propaganda they had long been fed about the absence of culture and civilization in the East. "These people here live together with the animals, indeed they live like animals," wrote Karl Fuchs in a letter. "Hygiene is something totally foreign to these people. You folks back home in our beautiful fatherland cannot imagine what it's like," he informed his mother. Seen from the East, the German fatherland took on its most magnificent shape, thanks to the contrast with what the soldiers found when they invaded the Soviet Union. Sitting together, acting together, practicing comradeship, the soldiers produced this fatherland. In a letter to his wife, Fuchs praised an evening with comrades "under the Russian sky" singing German folk songs. "While we sang, our native Germany materialized in front of us. Our homeland seemed more magnificent and beautiful than ever before...No matter where you look, there is nothing but dirty, filthy cabins...We now realize what our great German fatherland has given its children. There exists only one Germany in the entire world."[22]

Anti-Slavic and antisemitic stereotypes merged into apocalyptic visions, instigated by Nazi clichés about the diabolic mind-set of the peoples in the East. "If these beasts who are our enemies here had come to Germany, murders would have occurred such as the world has never seen," wrote a corporal in mid-July 1941. "They all look emaciated and the wild, half-crazy look in their eyes makes them appear like imbeciles," echoed Karl Fuchs. "And these scoundrels, led by Jews and criminals, wanted to imprint their stamp on Europe."[23] Caught up in clichés such as these, Wehrmacht soldiers widely approved of the terror against the Jews, led and carried out primarily but not only by the SS Einsatzgruppen, German police units, and local collaborators. Albert Neuhaus agreed that "up here in former Lithuania there is quite a lot of Jewishness, and of course they are given no quarter."[24] Both the way they reported on the murder of the Jews (and other mass crimes) in their private letters during the war and the way some of them talked about it as POWs in American and British captivity – where their guards secretly recorded their conversations – suggest that the majority of the soldiers knew about the mass shootings in the East.[25]

And the soldiers not only knew about them. Detailed historical research has widely documented the Wehrmacht's complicity in, and the shades of its responsibilities for, the murder of the Jews and other German mass crimes in Eastern Europe and the Soviet Union.[26] Individual soldiers and entire units had committed atrocities already during the invasions of Poland and France, but at this early stage these crimes could still be categorized as mere aberrations from the rules regulating "regular" warfare.[27] The advance on the Soviet Union changed the rules. The Wehrmacht was being asked to give up age-old traditions and ignore international war treaties that demanded the sparing of enemy civilians and POWs, and to join in a genocidal war intended to achieve not only the occupation and annexation of territories and the enslavement of subjugated peoples but also, and primarily, the annihilation of an unspecified number of non-combatants and the destruction of their social and cultural structures.

Arguably the Wehrmacht's "biggest crime" was the planned death of millions of Soviet POWs, for which the army was exclusively responsible.[28] Soviet prisoners were to be sent to forced labor in Germany, to work for the Wehrmacht and thus against their homelands, or they were to be shut up in overcrowded compounds, left without shelter, without sufficient food, and cut off from possible Red Cross aid. Tens, possibly hundreds of thousands of Soviet POWs were "liquidated" immediately after capture; many more perished later in prison camps. In all, more than half of the 5.7 million Red Army soldiers captured by the Wehrmacht did not survive.[29]

Roughly 2.8 million civilians and POWs were forced into abusive labor service. Recruiting them was the job of German labor authorities, who relied on army and police support. Often acting like colonial slave hunters, Wehrmacht soldiers were responsible for the seizure of about half of these. With Germany's World War I hunger crises and the strikes on the home front in mind, the Wehrmacht High Command (OKW) and leading Nazi officials had decided already in spring 1941 that the army would not only live off the occupied land itself, but also send huge amounts of foodstuffs back home to Germany. What that meant for Russia was that "umpteen million people will starve to death, if we extract from them the least we need."[30] In this way, Army Group A, for instance, one of the four major sections of the Wehrmacht, robbed the civilian population within ten weeks of 187,000 cattle and 434,000 sheep. About half of the Soviet civilians under German occupation suffered from hunger.[31]

Without the Wehrmacht's support, the Einsatzgruppen – the SS and the police – often in conjunction with local collaborators, could not have killed more than a million Jews. Wehrmacht headquarters registered the Jews of a conquered region or city, forced them to wear visible identification, and concentrated them in ghettos. Wehrmacht units rounded them up and herded them to the execution sites, which the soldiers then shielded from public view, or they took bizarre pleasure in watching the spectacle. Individual soldiers or entire units joined in when the shootings started.[32] Alternatively, a unit would initiate mass murder itself. In Serbia, in some parts of Belarus, and in other theaters, Wehrmacht units operated independently from the SS and carried out the Holocaust on their own.[33] Some Wehrmacht soldiers took pleasure in murdering civilians, or at least they carried out the tasks they had volunteered for as cynically and cold-bloodedly as SS men, police officers, and local collaborators did. In Russia in March 1942, Private Erich Kuby bumped into a lance corporal who excitedly announced, "Tomorrow, it's a butcher's party." "The entire families!" he added. Everybody around understood what he meant. One hundred and eighty Jews were to be killed. Kuby felt "abysmally nauseated about those whom I have to call my people" who so "easily intertwined middle-class norms and barbarism . . . They play the role of decent soldiers, and in fact they are criminal accomplices."[34]

Kuby himself represented the minority of the Wehrmacht soldiers who would rather have opted out than belong to them and actually spoke out against his comrades' lust for murder.[35] Although his diagnosis about the soldiers' complicity was true – few did opt out; most of them applauded or looked the other way – the army never achieved ideological uniformity. Of the 17 million soldiers who served with the Wehrmacht, and even of the approximately 10 million who at some point served in the Eastern theater, few actually joined in murdering the Jews.[36] The Wehrmacht soldiers were from all levels of German society – the middle class, the working class, peasantry, and some from the aristocracy. They were Catholics, Protestants, or atheists (plus a very few "part Jews" who managed to hide in the Wehrmacht). They ranged from apolitical – including those who kept some distance from the Nazi regime because of their religious, socialist, liberal, or even conservative background – to fanatical Nazis. Despite all indoctrination efforts by the regime, this ideological, political, and cultural diversity still survived in Third Reich society, and subsequently also in the Wehrmacht, which reflected society.

When it came to taking action against Jews or other civilians, it was often the ideological disposition of the commanding officers and the choices they made that decided whether or not a Wehrmacht unit collaborated in mass murder. So it was with the two regiments of the 707th Infantry Division, a security division sited in the occupied rear areas and comprising mostly elderly soldiers, as opposed to the front units. One of the two regiments, IR 727, under Lieutenant Colonel Pausinger, developed outstanding success in "Jew-hunting" in the autumn of 1941, but its "actions" stopped when Pausinger was promoted and replaced in January 1942 by Colonel von Louisenthal, who did not want his soldiers shooting women and children and forbade them from participating in massacres of Jews. Colonel Carl von Andrian, the commander of the parallel IR 747, had done the same earlier. Although Andrian was convinced "that the Jewish race is an alien element within our people and thus needs to be exterminated" and was eager to carry out reprisals against Jews in a village where three of his men had died during a partisan attack, he "condemned" the indiscriminate shootings by SS and police units as "not acceptable for a civilized people [*Kulturvolk*] such as we wish to be," as he noted in his diary.[37]

Two opposing value systems directed the Wehrmacht soldiers' choices: on the one hand, the universal virtues of human compassion and pity for the weak, enjoining mercy for the unarmed civilian and a defeated enemy; on the other hand, the harsh racist ideology that denounced the idea of universality and demanded, as Himmler put it, an "ethics" that complies "solely with the needs of our people. Good is what is useful for the people, evil is what damages our people."[38] While the first morality honored the traditional distinction between combatants and noncombatants, this distinction was obsolete for the Nazis. To them, the Jews and all kinds of "subhumans" represented a much bigger threat to the Aryan *Volksgemeinschaft* precisely because they did not carry their weapons openly, as combatants do, but hid them in order to attack in ambush or to fight in even more hideous ways, such as by infecting their enemies with their poisoned blood, as the Nazi racist propaganda claimed. Of course the Nazis, advocating these particularistic morals, knew that even their most dedicated followers could not lightly and quickly dismiss traditional compassionate morality; hence the propaganda emphasizing the need for hardness in overcoming sentiments of mercy and pity.[39]

But even the persuasive rhetoric of hardening, of designating "weaklings" as feminine, met a brick wall. When the commanders of three parallel companies of Infantry Regiment 691, each of them in charge of securing large areas north of Minsk, were ordered by their superior to kill the Jews in their respective districts, only one of them, Reserve

Lieutenant Sibille, a forty-seven-year-old teacher, refused to carry out the order, explaining that he "could not expect decent German soldiers to soil their hands with such things" as the killing campaigns of the Einsatzgruppen. Asked by his superior when he would finally become "hard," Sibille answered: "in such cases" – when it was to murder Jewish civilians including women and children – "never."[40] Though the boundaries between the two value systems were blurred, they were not erased.

Open defiance as demonstrated by Lieutenant Sibille or Colonel von Andrian was rare in the Wehrmacht, however. Many more soldiers kept to themselves their disagreement with the Nazi genocidal project promoted by the SS and supported by the army, or only wrote of it in their diaries or private letters. Fritz Farnbacher is one such example. From the beginning, he felt uneasy about the "strange war" in Russia, as he noted in his diary on June 22, the day of the attack. It wasn't so much the "pictures of death" and the mutilated bodies in the battlefields that worried him, for he had seen them before in Poland and France. He was at first confused by the enemy civilians. They weren't as horrible-looking as the Nazi propaganda had made him expect. "Actually, they are not disagreeable," he wrote. Instead, he found them "astonishingly decent." Even more distress was caused by his German comrades. Though he agreed that the troops had to be "fed off the land," it bothered him that "all manner of things are being 'pinched.'" His comrades did not waste time before "requisitioning," the units jealously competing with each other for the bigger and more valuable hauls. In late July, 300 miles closer to Moscow, he encountered something even more "unpleasant," which he "had not thought possible." His unit picked up a string of Russian deserters, among them a Jew whom they "somehow suspect to be a commissar or some such . . . They decide to shoot the Jew because commissars are to be shot, according to a higher order. That is extended to Jews." First, though, the "very dashing" Major Hoffmann interrogated the suspect. By means of his "Jew comforter," a sturdy stick, the major tried to beat out of the suspect information on the whereabouts of other commissars. Farnbacher found it "terribly spine-chilling." After all kinds of mistreatment the Jew was led off to be shot, and, "as I learnt later on, the Jew actually was bumped off."[41]

Attitudes such as Farnbacher's made the Nazi and the Wehrmacht leadership in the autumn of 1941 – when the Wehrmacht's advance in the East had almost reached its peak but had also revealed the failure of the Blitzkrieg plan – worry about "the conduct of troops toward the Bolshevistic system" as Field Marshal von Reichenau wrote in an influential order. It was issued on October 12, 1941 to the troops of the Sixth

Army, and soon afterwards extended to all parts of the army, upon the request of Hitler. In late August, the General Staff Officer of one of the divisions of Reichenau's Sixth Army, Lieutenant-Colonel Groscurth, had tried to save ninety-one Jewish children from being executed by the SS. In an official report he had protested against "measures" like this "that in no regard differ from the atrocities of our enemy" – and pointed to his army training in soldierly decency and mercy toward defenseless civilians.[42] Upset at this protest, Reichenau, a close friend of Hitler's and one of the most decisive Nazis among the top Wehrmacht leaders, reminded the troops what the "most essential aim of war against the Jewish-Bolshevistic system" was: "a complete destruction of their means of power and the elimination of Asiatic influence from European culture." This goal could be achieved only by exceeding "the one-sided routine of soldiering," Reichenau explained, ranting against the troops' "humanitarian" attitude toward enemy civilians and POWs. "Treacherous, cruel partisans and degenerate women are still being made prisoners of war, and guerrilla fighters dressed partly in uniform or plain clothes and vagabonds are still being treated as proper soldiers, and sent to prisoner-of-war camps," Reichenau noted indignantly. "The soldier in the Eastern territories," he pointed out, "is not merely a fighter according to the rules of the art of war but also a bearer of ruthless national ideology and the avenger of bestialities which have been inflicted upon German and racially related nations. Therefore the soldier must have full understanding for the necessity of a severe but just revenge on subhuman Jewry."[43]

Such inflammatory rhetoric against the "one-sided routine of soldiering" guided the planning of Operation Barbarossa from its inception, and in fact it was embedded in the Nazi regime's general attack on universalistic ethics rooted in Christian (and Jewish) traditions and Enlightenment philosophy. At the heart of the military part of this struggle of moralities stood the concept of comradeship, which restrained the dynamic of violence in modern warfare, if not through the idea of solidarity then at least because of respect between enemies. Comradeship, in its traditional meaning, inhibited the genocidal radicalization of warfare desired by the Nazis. This notion of comradeship was what Hitler meant when, in a secret meeting on March 30, 1941, more than two months before the Soviet campaign, he urged some 250 Wehrmacht generals to "forget the concept of comradeship between soldiers. A communist is no comrade before or after the battle," he said. Operation Barbarossa would be the ultimate "clash of two ideologies," a "war of extermination."[44]

Two orders were issued on May 13 and June 6, 1941 – now described as the Criminal Orders – and they went into more details. Carrying the seal "top secret," they were given to the lower ranks only verbally and only a couple of hours before the June 22 attack began. The "Instructions on the Treatment of Political Commissars" accused the commissars of the Red Army, who were actually in charge of political indoctrination, of being the originators of "barbaric, Asiatic methods of warfare," so that to consider them "in accordance with international rules of war is wrong and endangers both our own security and the rapid pacification of conquered country." They were not to be "treated as soldiers. The protection afforded by international law to prisoners of war is not to be applied in their case. After they have been segregated they will be liquidated." As soldiers such as Farnbacher understood, pervasive anti-semitism in the Wehrmacht meant that Jews were considered to be the same as commissars. Hitler's "Decree on the Conduct of Courts-martial in the District of 'Barbarossa' and for Special Measures of the Troops" went much further. It stated that in a country full of enemies attacking German soldiers from behind, "guerrillas" were "to be killed ruthlessly by the troops in battle or during pursuit," and even after their capture, once they had become POWs. The decree went on to order "collective punitive measures by force to be carried out immediately" against villages from which the Wehrmacht was "insidiously and maliciously attacked." Stipulating that "for offences committed by members of the Wehrmacht and its employees against enemy civilians, prosecution is not compul-sory, not even if the offence is also a military crime or violation," it gave "every soldier the right to shoot from in front or behind any Rus-sian he takes to be – or claims that he takes to be – a guerrilla," as a high-ranking Wehrmacht leader noted after reading it. What was at stake here was not just a change of military tactics. The goal was a change of the moralities of warfare. In the Soviet Union, German soldiers were to internalize mercilessness and to share in a distinctive community from which traditional moral considerations had been eliminated. "In the east, harshness today means leniency in the future," explained the Jurisdiction Decree, hence "commanders must make the sacrifice of overcoming their personal scruples."[45]

Speeches such as Hitler's in March 1941, and orders such as those of May and June 1941, reveal goals and visions, not the actual state of mind in the German army. In summer 1941, the majority of ordinary soldiers had not yet adopted the racist and exclusionary moral order the Nazis propagated, and they had not yet left behind the popular concept of comradeship, the symbolic, moral, and emotional extension of civilian society into the world of warfare. In fact, even in 1942 public discourse in the Third Reich still permitted deliberate criticism of the Nazi ethics of mercilessness. In spring of that year, the Catholic moral philosopher Joseph Pieper, often subject to censorship in the Third Reich, urged in an official Wehrmacht journal that German soldiers should not forget about the virtue of chivalry "toward defenseless and weak" enemies. Of course, there was no shortage of opposing voices. Soon afterwards, Kleo Pleyer, a Bohemian Nazi who served during the war as a company commander on the Eastern front, published a bellicose pamphlet that limited the idea of comradeship between enemies – among a "transnational" community of front soldiers – to those who were on a par. "Subhumans" such as Bolsheviks and Jews did not qualify, Pleyer made clear, conjuring up Nazi stereotypes of their animalistic, bloodthirsty nature.[46]

In order to make the soldiers "overcome their personal scruples," the propaganda on mercilessness was tied into the imagery of revenge. The concept of revenge is embedded in the morality of honor and shame.[47] Shame is a social correction mechanism designed to make the members of a group observe its standards, secure its reputation, and uphold its power. Honor is a code that establishes and secures moral and social identity and integrity. The code exerts a communal force against those who wrong the group or its members. Revenge ensures justice; tied into the ethics of honor, it strikes the whole group the wrongdoer belongs to, not him or her as individual. The harmed group reconstitutes itself by taking revenge on the wrongdoer's group, even for acts anticipated in the future or that happened long before. It must exact retribution to secure its own identity. Revenge, shame, and honor deny individual choices; it is the collective that is challenged and that takes action even if only one individual did wrong or was wronged.

In this thinking, comradeship mediated between the abstract, "secondary" imagery of national honor, or the army's honor, and the experiential space of military face-to-face groups. It could do so in different ways. By acknowledging the mutual suffering of soldiers on both sides of the front lines, comradeship could counter the radicalization of violence. Understood as a mechanism of in-group cohesion and small-group identity, however, it spurred this radicalization. The Nazis had long worked on stressing this aggressive side of comradeship, paradigmatically in the Horst Wessel Song, the song about revenge, about transforming grief into aggression, and about comradeship as the virtue of waging war, not suffering from it.[48] Taking revenge was an obligation toward one's comrades. This notion of comradeship inspired the Plenipotentiary Commanding General of Serbia, Franz Böhme, in the fall of 1941, when he entreated his soldiers to "proceed with all means available and with maximum ruthlessness . . . into a strip of territory where, thanks to the treachery of the Serbs, both men and women, rivers of blood flowed in 1914. You are the avengers of those dead. We must deliver a warning that will make the greatest possible impression on the population. Anyone who shows compassion will be sinning against the lives of his comrades."[49]

Not only in Serbia but all over the Eastern front, and soon also in other European theaters, the morality of revenge and retribution lured Wehrmacht soldiers into the Nazi genocidal project. This morality gained violent dynamism from the entwining of obligation and permission. Taking revenge was a moral duty but also an emotional valve. You had to take revenge on your enemies for their misdeeds, but you were also allowed to do so. Retributional violence was morally sacrosanct – as long as one believed in the code of honor, and as long as the revenge was exacted against a wrongdoer, or more precisely, against his group. Who was considered as such was contingent. Since the nineteenth century, the German army had established a normative culture of anti-partisan warfare that demanded the most brutal retaliation against actual or suspected guerrilla fighters, dubbed "franc-tireurs" – not only against convicted individuals but also against the communities they belonged to, or were suspected to belong to, and even against enemy communities that had not yet supported guerrillas, but might or were about to. In this way the German military entrenched a doctrine of preventive retaliation, hyperbolized as "war necessity" or "military necessity." In order to win a war, the theory of "war necessity" urged the army to ignore concerns about collateral damage among enemy civilians; the distinction between them and enemy soldiers; and eventually international laws on armed conflicts.[50]

Fear of guerrillas was fear of one's own weakness – of the dissolution of troop unity. Such fears could be countered only by demonstrating absolute strength. Any kind of civilian resistance, real or imagined, would be taken as a provocation that automatically required violent counteraction to re-establish the honor and the identity of the troops. "Military necessity" left no choices. All had to stick together to perform strength through brutality. When the attack on Poland began, propaganda hammered into the minds of Wehrmacht soldiers a derogatory image of the Poles as inferior but fanatically angry and capable of sabotage and other vicious attacks. Minor or even alleged partisan attacks and a very few Polish atrocities stimulated fear and overreactions among the troops. A "guerrilla-psychosis" spread through the troops, as one officer noticed. Resistance cast doubt on the alleged racial, moral, and physical superiority of the occupiers. "Courteous treatment will be seen as weakness," the soldiers were advised. "Military necessity" commanded brutal retaliation.[51]

In the Nazi war of annihilation, terrorizing enemy civilians became the pre-emptive German response to fear of guerrilla resistance, in particular when such fear was intensified by rumors of mutilated or tortured German soldiers. This does not mean that partisans did not threaten the Wehrmacht. Stalin called for a "people's war against the fascist oppressors" immediately after the German invasion. But only from autumn 1941 on, and indeed only in earnest from 1942, did the Soviet partisan movement gain momentum and represent a threat to the German forces.[52] In summer 1941, just as in Poland earlier, it was only occasionally that dispersed Soviet soldiers attacked Germans – or, when picked up by Germans, were suspected of guerrilla activities – and were consequently shot on the spot, sometimes in conjunction with brutal retaliation against the local population that had, or seemed to have, supported and hidden them. It was not the actual partisan threat but the German invaders' obsession with it that fueled the spiral of brutality in summer 1941. Orders such as those of May 13 and June 6, 1941 exacerbated the level of threat from the partisans in the Soviet Union, and instigated a climate of fear of and anger among soldiers in order to dull their inhibitions about mistreating, terrorizing, or killing civilians and POWs – and Jews. At a meeting with his entourage on July 16, 1941, Hitler welcomed the first Russian partisan attacks, which were still minor: "This partisan war . . . has some advantage for us. It enables us to eradicate everyone who opposes us."[53] Jews were declared to be partisans per se, as for instance in a Wehrmacht and SS seminar on "Fighting Partisans" in Mogilew, Belarus in late September 1941. Everywhere partisans showed up there were Jews, thus the Jews were the partisans, was the basic lesson the students learned. And Jews lived in almost every town, village, and hamlet. The murder orders to the 1st battalion of IR 691 in early October 1941 were part of increased efforts in autumn 1941 to include the Wehrmacht in the Nazi genocidal project. So was a decree of OKW chief Keitel on September 16, 1941 that justified and demanded the most extreme reprisals thus far. From now on, fifty to one hundred "Communists" – that is, Jews – were to be killed as "atonement" for one German soldier's life, the order requested. Previously, it had been five for one or ten for one.[54]

Not all German soldiers and occupiers bought into the alleged identification of partisans with Jews, as the choices made by Wehrmacht officers such as Groscurth, Sibille, von Louisenthal, and von Andrian show. Probably most soldiers followed the line of Andrian. They despised, and tried to stay away from, indiscriminate killings of civilians, especially women and children, and were also embarrassed about the mass death of Soviet POWs. But a broad range of diverse evidence – personal diaries, private letters, secretly recorded private conversations in American and British captivity – suggests that most soldiers approved of what they saw or passed it off as response to partisan activities.[55] Revenge and atonement seemed not only legitimate responses to partisan attacks but in fact a moral duty toward comrades killed in ambush or mutilated after being taken prisoner. In July 1941, "seventeen comrades" of Private Herbert Veigel were "murdered in the most cruel way," he wrote in a letter. "When we arrived shortly after the attack, some of them were still alive. All of them were horribly mutilated. They had cut out the heart of one of them and put it on his stomach; they had stripped the face and pulled off the skin of another . . . As reprisal, some soldiers went and burned the entire village down where the Russians had come from."[56] Whether any of the inhabitants had supported the partisans didn't matter. Wehrmacht officer Udo von Alvensleben was greatly concerned about the genocidal tendency of the war in the East from 1939. In principle, he noted in his diary in August 1941, "German soldiers are inclined to be good-natured to POWs." But after seeing the corpses of 150 Wehrmacht soldiers murdered and mutilated by Russians, he found it understandable that "the desire for revenge is unlimited."[57]

An army in war had the right to take measures against guerrilla attacks; laws and customs of international war at the time of World War II defined the range of these measures only vaguely and left ample leeway for even brutal counter-insurgency. But the Wehrmacht went far beyond even these customs by categorizing all kinds of resistance as irregular, even just arduous or desperate ones in battle. Partisans did not enjoy the protection of the Geneva Convention or other war laws. But often it was not clear who had done what. The Jurisdiction Order effectively encouraged German soldiers to not wonder about individual responsibilities, and the obsessive exaggeration of the malicious nature of the Bolshevik enemy in the East justified unlimited brutality against anyone and any group perceived as a threat to one's own comrades.

When the Germans invaded the Ukraine in late June 1941, they revealed the massacres of thousands of local civilians committed by the NKVD (*Narodnyy Komissariat Vnutrennikh Del*, or People's Commissariat for Internal Affairs), Stalin's political police, before the Red Army withdrew in face of the German invasion. Nazi propagandists and SS men immediately saw their chance, and guided Wehrmacht soldiers to piles of mutilated corpses and blamed the Jews for the communist cruelty.[58] The Wehrmacht Sergeant-Major Christoph Banse reported to his wife in July 1941, "You get an idea of the chosen people. The Jews here also organized the cruelties against Ukrainians." Conflating large-scale NKVD massacres of Ukrainians before the German invasion with rare

Russian partisan attacks on the German invaders, Banse went on: "And German soldiers have also been victimized by the deviousness of these dirty bastards. Thus we Germans no longer have any reason to spare these creatures. Currently, they count less for us than a dog."[59]

Not all soldiers joined in this easily. Fritz Farnbacher was one of those German soldiers who cared about international war laws and age-old traditions of chivalry toward defeated enemy soldiers and of mercy toward enemy civilians, even when in autumn 1941 the Soviet partisan movement grew and threatened German soldiers more seriously. In late November 1941, his unit brought in some civilians who were suspected of being commissars or partisans and were "bumped off right away," as Farnbacher learned, still trying to keep his inner distance from the ongoing brutalization. "All these executions," he noted, "are really not my thing; I am glad that I am not in charge of that stuff." He also refrained from setting Russian villages afire when retreating. "Anischino is in flames; every house was burning when the troops left. However, I don't set fire to the places we have been, whatever other people do, and the commander doesn't like doing so either." Knowing that he had "not shot a single time nor slaughtered a chicken or a goose nor ever ordered the execution of a Russian or even attended an execution" provided some relief, as his diary shows.[60]

Yet the diary also reveals a moral and emotional roller-coaster. Sometimes the Russians looked "decent," he noted, and yet "they are nothing but a bunch of motherfuckers." When he heard "how some of our men" were "brutally mutilated by the Russians, the skulls smashed and pierced by bayonets," he too thought Germans "should not be too lenient," and agreed with his comrades that they should take no more prisoners. In the face of acts of sabotage by enemy civilians, and other kinds of "mischief," he too cast off his scruples about excessive requisitions of food. In one of these actions, a comrade hit a mine. "Three comrades dead, one seriously injured, one slightly injured," he found out and thought, "Well, then let's rob them of the last cow they have left." "The Russians strip German prisoners to the butt, tie them on a sledge, pour water on them, and let them freeze to death or push the entire sledge into a river," he learned in November 1941. "Beasts in human guise!" he wrote. "As a matter of course, such brutish murder of German comrades provoked countermeasures. We did not take any prisoners," he recorded, no longer keeping his I at distance from the We of the comrades. The comradely We swallowed the moral self. "What have we come to!" he wondered in late December 1941 when he heard what his comrades had done when in charge of transferring a group of thirty or so captives to a collection point. "They have bumped off all of them, they told us later; the assembly point was so far away. What I hear is an almost animal laughter," Farnbacher noted. "Five months ago we wouldn't have even said that, let alone dared do it! And today it's a matter of course, which, on reflection, every one of us approves. No mercy for these predators and beasts!"[61]

Farnbacher made this somber assessment on December 30, 1941, at a time when the initial enthusiasm of the soldiers about their victories, the grandeur of the *Volksgemeinschaft*, and the glory of comradeship had given way to "depressing visions," as he said.[62] From late autumn 1941, rain and then snow had shown up the poor equipment of the German army; neither weapons nor uniforms withstood the frost. The Wehrmacht seemed to be sinking in the quagmire. The Soviet counter-offensive in December 1941 forced the soldiers back hundreds of miles. The Wehrmacht had suffered from only a few casualties in the first months of Operation Barbarossa, but they escalated during the winter crisis. By spring 1942, more than a million German soldiers were dead, injured, or missing in action. Russia was a "cruel experience," groaned Wißmann as early as October 1941, haunted by nightmares of close combat, death, and mutilation.[63]

But the soldiers' daily routine, in the East or indeed anywhere else in Europe, was shaped not only by combat, crime, or comradeship, but instead, most of the time, by marching and riding, building posts, gathering food, recovering from exhaustion, and waiting for orders. The real world of the soldier looked totally different from what he had read in war literature, a war volunteer observed as early as August 1941: It was "full of egotism and baseness."[64] "The all-male society is made of jealousy and machinations," echoed Udo von Alvensleben many years later. Rooted in the aristocratic tradition of German militarism and fraught with melancholy over the demise of chivalrous soldiering in the Nazi war, he bemoaned early on also the decline of "true comradeship."[65] Often enough, however, simply the miserable living conditions on the Eastern front made it difficult to practice, let alone enjoy, comradeship. "Bunker tantrum" spread over the German troops in the East, noticed Wieschenberg, lamenting the culture of petty jealousies, harassment, and gripes instead of solidarity and tenderness.[66] "Dwelling all the time in bunkers and in the woods really ticks you off," echoed Albert Neuhaus in August 1942, looking back longingly to the "old Russian sheds" they had lived in the year before – and enjoyed lively comradeship. But now everyone was weary and fatigued. "All that oomph and the resilience we had when the campaign started is gone."[67]

Over long sections, Farnbacher's diary too reads as a chronicle of dysfunctional orders, logistical shortcomings, childish machinations, petty jealousies, and egotistic thoughtlessness. Sometimes a soldier dozed off and let his comrades do the job, or a soldier chickened out when he heard a shot; Farnbacher's unit noticed that "comrades" from a neighboring unit had pilfered important devices; the MO "wants to be pampered like a toddler and doesn't know how to kill time other than by being a fussy troublemaker"; or a "ruthless" officer comrade thought of nothing but "to satisfy his desire for medals of honor." Farnbacher himself felt constantly challenged, doubted, excoriated by his superiors, and treated as one of those "who are considered as good for nothing." A conforming believer, who abstained from alcohol and preferred to write diligently in his diary rather than join alcohol-fueled gatherings, he was a prime target for mockery, not knowing how to position himself or where to belong. He felt "pooped," "paralysed," and even "outcast." Shunted into roles of no obvious use, and serving as dogsbody, he felt like a fool – a wimp in the manly society.[68]

But he wanted to belong too. He wanted to be a good comrade and a comradely leader. The Wehrmacht's entanglement in the Nazi genocidal project and the army's blurring of the boundaries between regular, anti-partisan, and genocidal warfare gave him a chance to do so. In early 1942, his unit was given a rest. Occasionally some Russian partisans interrupted the collective boredom. A patrol fell into a trap and was carried off; a command in charge of requisitioning was attacked; a supply unit was slaughtered. A German attempt to destroy a partisan base of a thousand men failed. Instead Farnbacher's unit caught Russian civilians poisoning the food supply. Farnbacher no longer stood aside. A daunting requisitioning foray in the locality was initiated under Farnbacher's leadership and gave him a chance to catch up – and to enjoy a boy-scout-like experience of community in the vast Russian wilderness. Fifty soldiers formed an impressive force. They did not run into partisans but discovered sumptuous booty in one of the villages. Under the eyes of the frightened residents, potatoes, greens, fifty chickens, grain, three sucking pigs, "and above all a cow" were loaded onto thirty sledges. "Then I put myself at the head of my forces, once I had assured myself again that they were all present . . . and marched off homewards. The evening was as beautiful as the morning had been. The wind was at our backs and we raced along." The soldiers were in the best of humor. "On our expedition, when I asked whether the cow had been paid for, they just said 'Yessir!' To my question, how had they paid, came the answer 'with cigarette coupons!'"[69]

NOTES

1 Reddemann (ed.), *Zwischen Front und Heimat*, p. 221, Neuhaus, letter to Agnes, June 25, 1941. On the "megalomaniac extravagance of National Socialist political thinking," see the comments of Friedrich Paulus, the field marshal who commanded, and surrendered with, the Sixth Army in

Stalingrad, in a 1946 memorandum, quoted in Walter Görlitz, *Paulus and Stalingrad* (London: Citadel Press, 1963), p. 106.

2 Wieschenberg, letter to Hilde, May 4, 1941. For more general accounts, see Sven Oliver Müller, *Deutsche Soldaten und ihre Feinde: Nationalismus an Front und Heimatfront im Zweiten Weltkrieg* (Frankfurt: S. Fischer, 2007).

3 Kurt Kreissler, *Im feldgrauen Rock*, part I, p. 18.

4 Wieschenberg, letters to Hilde, July 29, 1941, Aug. 15, 1941, Sept. 6, 26, 1941.

5 Wißmann, letter to Edith, Sept. 30, 1941.

6 See, for instance, Iring Fetscher, *Neugier und Furcht: Versuch, mein Leben zu verstehen* (Hamburg: Hoffmann und Campe, 1995), p. 37; my assessment is based on the large collection of such school essays at the Walter Kempowski Archive, formerly Nartum, now Akademie der Künste, Berlin, Germany.

7 Farnbacher, War Diary, Aug. 2, 1941 (copy of typescript owned by author; a copy is also accessible in Bundesarchiv-Militärarchiv Freiburg, Msg. 1/3268).

8 Ibid., June 23, 27, 1941, July 6, 9, 10, 22, 29, 30, 1941, Aug. 16, 1941, and Introduction (to transcript of diary, written after the war), pp. 122, 124, 131.

9 Ibid., July 22, 1941.

10 Siegbert Stehmann, *Die Bitternis verschweigen wir*, p. 77, letter to his wife, Dec. 24, 1940.

11 Wißmann, letter to Edith, Feb. 28, 1943 (retrospectively); cf. letters to Edith, Oct. 28, 1941, Nov. 6, 1941.

12 Jochen Klepper, *Überwindung: Tagebücher und Aufzeichnungen aus dem Kriege* (Stuttgart: Deutsche Verlagsanstalt, 1958), p. 131, diary entry, Aug. 8, 1941.

13 Farnbacher, War Diary, Nov. 20, 1941, and Introduction, pp. 132–33.

14 Kurt Kreissler, *Im feldgrauen Rock*, part II, pp. 95, 107; Kreissler, letter to parents, Jan. 3, 1944.

15 Klepper, *Überwindung*, p. 211, diary entry, Sept. 23, 1941.

16 Wißmann, letters to Edith, March 13–14, 1942, April 3, 1942, May 28, 1942.

17 Christian Hartmann, *Operation Barbarossa: Nazi Germany's War in the East, 1941–1945* (New York: Oxford University Press, 2013), p. 51; Hartmann, *Wehrmacht im Ostkrieg: Front und militärisches Hinterland 1941/42* (Munich: Oldenbourg, 2009), pp. 286–91; David Stahel, *Kiev 1941: Hitler's Battle for Supremacy in the East* (Cambridge University Press, 2012).

18 Farnbacher, War Diary, Sept. 22, 1941.

19 Ibid., Aug. 14, 1941, and cf. Sept. 8, 1941. Cf. David Stahel, *Operation Barbarossa and Germany's Defeat in the East* (Cambridge University Press, 2009), pp. 260–305.

20 Farnbacher, War Diary, Aug. 30, 1941.

21 Fuchs, *Sieg Heil*, pp. 147–48, letter to his wife, Oct. 26, 1941.

22 Ibid., pp. 123–25, 146–47, letters to his wife and parents, Aug. 3, 15, 1941, Oct 20, 1941; cf. Ortwin Buchbender and Reinhold Sterz (eds.), *Das andere Gesicht des Krieges: Deutsche Feldpostbriefe 1939–1945* (Munich: C. H. Beck, 1982), pp. 68–79; Historisches Archiv des Erzbistums Köln, CLB, Kriegsbriefe Zweiter Weltkrieg, letter by Guenther H., Aug. 19, 1941; Wißmann, letters to Edith, Aug. 16, 1941, Oct. 13, 1941. This and the following

paragraphs draw on Kühne, *Belonging and Genocide*, pp. 106–09. See also Kipp, *Grossreinemachen im Osten*, pp. 47–182.

23 Letter of an anonymous corporal, July 10, 1941, in Buchbender and Sterz, *Das andere Gesicht des Krieges*, p. 74; Fuchs, *Sieg Heil*, p. 122, letter to his wife, Aug. 3, 1941; cf. letter of Stefan Schmidhofer to his wife, Sept. 30, 1941, privately owned.

24 Reddemann (ed.), *Zwischen Front und Heimat*, p. 222, Neuhaus, letter to his sister Johanna, June 25, 1941.

25 Neitzel and Welzer, *Soldaten*, pp. 120–63; Bernward Dörner, *Die Deutschen und der Holocaust: Was niemand wissen wollte, aber jeder wissen konnte* (Berlin: Propylaen, 2007); Kühne, *Belonging and Genocide*, p. 106.

26 Hartmann, *Wehrmacht im Ostkrieg*, pp. 469–698; Dieter Pohl, *Die Herrschaft der Wehrmacht: Deutsche Militärbesatzung und einheimische Bevölkerung in der Sowjetunion 1941–1944* (Munich: Oldenbourg, 2008); Jeff Rutherford, *Combat and Genocide on the Eastern Front: The German Infantry's War, 1941–1944* (Cambridge University Press, 2014); Hamburger Institut für Sozialforschung, *Verbrechen der Wehrmacht: Dimensionen des Vernichtungskrieges 1941–1944. Ausstellungskatalog* (Hamburger Institut für Sozialforschung, 2002).

27 Jochen Böhler, *Auftakt zum Vernichtungskrieg: Die Wehrmacht in Polen 1939* (Frankfurt: Fischer Taschenbuch Verlag, 2006); Alexander B. Rossino, *Hitler Strikes Poland: Blitzkrieg, Ideology, and Atrocity* (Lawrence: University Press of Kansas, 2003); Raffael Scheck, *Hitler's African Victims: The German Army Massacres of Black French Soldiers in 1940* (Cambridge University Press, 2006).

28 Christian Hartmann, *Operation Barbarossa*, p. 89.

29 Christian Streit, *Keine Kameraden: Die Wehrmacht und die sowjetischen Kriegsgefangenen 1941–1945*, new edn. (Bonn: J. H. W. Dietz, 1997); Rüdiger Overmans, "German Policy on Prisoners of War, 1939–1945," in Jörg Echternkamp (ed.), *Germany and the Second World War*, vol. IX/2: *German Wartime Society 1939–1945: Exploitation, Interpretations, Exclusion* (Oxford University Press, 2014), pp. 804–29.

30 Memorandum on a Conference of Under-Secretaries, May 2, 1941, in *Trial of the Major War Criminals Before the International Military Tribunal, Nuremberg, 14 November 1945 – 1 October 1946* (Nuremberg, 1946), vol. XXXI/84, Doc. 2718-PS. Cf. Alex J. Kay, *Exploitation, Resettlement, Mass Murder: Political and Economic Planning for German Occupation Policy in the Soviet Union* (New York: Berghahn, 2006).

31 Hartmann, *Operation Barbarossa*, p. 103.

32 Wolfram Wette, *The Wehrmacht: History, Myth, Reality* (Cambridge, MA: Harvard University Press, 2006), pp. 90–138. For a sophisticated case study on the complicity of Wehrmacht bystanders, see Michaela Christ, *Die Dynamik des Tötens: Die Ermordung der Juden von Berditschew, Ukraine 1941–1944* (Frankfurt: Fischer Taschenbuch Verlag, 2011), pp. 100–28.

33 For an excellent case study, see Waitman Beorn, *Marching into Darkness: The Wehrmacht and the Holocaust in Belarus* (Cambridge, MA: Harvard University Press, 2014). On Serbia, see Christopher Browning, "The Wehrmacht in

Serbia Revisited," in Omer Bartov, Atina Grossman, and Mary Nolan (eds.), *Crimes of War: Guilt and Denial in the Twentieth Century* (New York: New Press, 2002), pp. 31–40; Walter Manoschek, "'Coming Along to Shoot Some Jews?': The Destruction of the Jews in Serbia," in Hannes Heer and Klaus Naumann (ed.), *War of Extermination: The German Military in World War II, 1941–1944* (New York: Berghahn, 2000), pp. 39–54.

34 Kuby, *Mein Krieg*, pp. 228–29, diary entry, March 25, 1942.

35 Kühne, *Belonging and Genocide*, pp. 126–28.

36 Christian Hartmann, "Verbrecherischer Krieg – verbrecherische Wehrmacht? Überlegungen zur Struktur des deutschen Ostheeres 1941–1944," *Vierteljahrshefte für Zeitgeschichte*, 52 (2004), 1–75.

37 Peter Lieb, "Täter aus Überzeugung? Oberst Carl von Andrian und die Judenmorde der 707. Infanteriedivision 1941/42," *Vierteljahrshefte für Zeitgeschichte*, 50 (2002), 523–57 (at pp. 529, 537–43). For further examples and a convincing assessment of the crucial role of the unit leaders, see Beorn, *Marching into Darkness*, pp. 119–34, 216–17.

38 Speech to SS Generals, Jan. 23, 1939, quoted in Josef Ackermann, *Heinrich Himmler als Ideologe* (Göttingen: Musterschmidt, 1970), p. 141.

39 Kühne, *Belonging and Genocide*, pp. 55–62. See also Wolfgang Bialas, "Nazi Ethics: Perpetrators with a Clear Conscience," *Dapim: Studies on the Holocaust*, 27/1 (2013), 3–25.

40 Letter by Sibille, Feb. 2, 1953; and statements by other witnesses interrogated in the early 1950s for the trial against Nöll et al., Hauptstaatsarchiv Darmstadt, H 13 Darmstadt, 979, Ks 2/54, against Nöll, Zimber, and Magel at pp. 207–10, and verdict from March 10, 1956 at pp. 756ff. See Beorn, *Marching into Darkness*, pp. 119–34; and Thomas Kühne, "Male Bonding and Shame Culture: Hitler's Soldiers and the Moral Basis of Genocidal Warfare," in Olaf Jensen, Claus-Christian W. Szejnmann, and Martin L. Davies (eds.), *Ordinary People as Mass Murderers: Perpetrators in Comparative Perspectives* (Basingstoke: Palgrave Macmillan, 2008), pp. 55–77 (at 55–56).

41 Farnbacher, War Diary, June 22–24, 30, 1941, July 1, 1941, July 20, 1941; cf. Kühne, *Belonging and Genocide*, pp. 95–96.

42 Helmuth Groscurth, *Tagebücher eines Abwehroffiziers 1938–40. Mit weiteren Dokumenten zur Militäropposition gegen Hitler*, ed. Helmut Krausnick and Harold C. Deutsch (Stuttgart: Deutsche Verlagsanstalt, 1970), pp. 534–42; Kühne, *Belonging and Genocide*, pp. 110–11.

43 English translation: United States Office of Chief Counsel for Prosecution of Axis Criminality, *Nazi Conspiracy and Aggression*, 8 vols. (Washington, DC: United States Government Printing Office, 1946), vol. VIII, pp. 585–87; cf. Bartov, *Hitler's Army*, pp. 129–31.

44 No minutes were taken at this secret meeting; our knowledge of Hitler's speech is based on private notes taken from memory by OKH chief Franz Halder; see Franz Halder, *The Halder War Diary*, ed. Charles Burdick and Hans-Adolf Jacobsen (London: Greenhill, 1988), pp. 345ff.

45 Translation of the Commissar Order in Hans-Adolf Jacobsen, "The *Kommissarbefehl* and Mass Executions of Soviet Prisoners of War," in Helmut Krausnick et al. (eds.), *Anatomy of the SS State* (New York: Walker, 1968),

pp. 505–63 (at 532–34); translation of the Jurisdiction Decree in United States Office of Chief Counsel for Prosecution of Axis Criminality, *Nazi Conspiracy and Aggression*, vol. III, pp. 637–39. Facsimiles of the originals: Hamburger Institut für Sozialforschung, *Verbrechen der Wehrmacht*, pp. 43–55. On the widespread application of the Commissar Order, see Felix Römer, *Der Kommissarbefehl: Wehrmacht und NS-Verbrechen an der Ostfront 1941/42* (Paderborn: Schöningh, 2008).

46 J[oseph] Pieper, "Gedanken über Ritterlichkeit als soldatische Haltung," *Soldatentum*, 9 (1942), 40–43; Pieper, *Noch wusste es niemand: Autobiographische Aufzeichnungen, 1904–1945* (Munich: Kösel, 1976), p. 175; Kleo Pleyer, *Volk im Feld* (Hamburg: Hanseatische Verlagsanstalt, 1943), pp. 11, 26, 28, 33.

47 Thomas J. Scheff and Suzanne M. Retzinger, *Emotions and Violence: Shame and Rage in Destructive Conflicts* (Lexington, MA: Lexington Books, 1991); Thomas Scheff, *Bloody Revenge: Emotions, Nationalism, and War* (Boulder, CO: Westview Press, 1994).

48 See above, Chapter 3, p. 000.

49 Directive from Sept. 25, 1941, quoted in Walter Manoschek, "Serbien ist judenfrei," *Militärische Besatzungspolitik und Judenvernichtung in Serbien 1941/42* (Munich: Oldenbourg, 1993), p. 60.

50 Manfred Messerschmidt, "'Völkerrecht' und 'Kriegsnotwendigkeit' in der deutschen militärischen Tradition seit den Einigungskriegen," *German Studies Review*, 6 (1983), 237–69; Isabel V. Hull, *Absolute Destruction: Military Culture and the Practices of War in Imperial Germany* (Ithaca, NY: Cornell University Press, 2005), pp. 117–26.

51 Rossino, *Hitler Strikes Poland*, pp. 176 (guerrilla-psychosis), 25ff. (quoting OKH Guidelines on Peculiarities of Polish Warfare, July 1, 1939); Böhler, *Auftakt zum Vernichtungskrieg*, p. 189; Kühne, *Belonging and Genocide*, p. 100.

52 Historians have not yet agreed on how effective and powerful the Soviet partisan movement against the German invasion was, especially in summer and fall 1941. Whereas Hannes Heer, "The Logic of the War of Extermination: The Wehrmacht and the Anti-Partisan War," in Heer and Naumann, *War of Extermination*, pp. 92–136, claimed that the Wehrmacht invented the partisan threat, more recent research has stressed its reality from as early as summer 1941 on: See Bogdan Musial, *"Konterrevolutionäre Elemente sind zu erschiessen": Die Brutalisierung des deutsch-sowjetischen Krieges im Sommer 1941* (Berlin: Propyläen, 2000); Ben Shepherd, *War in the Wild East: The German Army and Soviet Partisans* (Cambridge, MA: Harvard University Press, 2004); Alexander Hill, *The War Behind the Eastern Front: The Soviet Partisan Movement in North-West Russia, 1941–1944* (London: Frank Cass, 2004); Hartmann, *Wehrmacht im Ostkrieg*, pp. 699–764; Pohl, *Die Herrschaft der Wehrmacht*, pp. 283–304; Rutherford, *Combat and Genocide on the Eastern Front*. Its dynamic from 1942 on, however, is beyond doubt and well documented, for the Soviet Union as well as for most other theaters. See, in addition to the aforementioned, e.g., Peter Lieb, *Konventioneller Krieg oder NS-Weltanschauungskrieg? Kriegführung und Partisanenbekämpfung in Frankreich 1943/44* (Munich: Oldenbourg, 2007); Ben Shepherd, *Terror in the Balkans: German Armies and Partisan Warfare* (Cambridge, MA: Harvard University

Press, 2012); Carlo Gentile, *Wehrmacht und Waffen-SS im Partisanenkrieg: Italien 1943–1945* (Paderborn: Schöningh, 2012).

53 Minutes of a meeting at Hitler's headquarters, July 16, 1941, Nuremberg Document 221-L, translated in *Documents on German Foreign Policy, 1918–1945: Series D (1937–1945)*, selected by British FCO and US Department of State, 13 vols. (Washington, DC: United States Government Printing Office, 1964), vol. XIII, Document 114, 149–56.

54 Facsimile in Hamburger Institut für Sozialforschung, *Verbrechen der Wehrmacht*, p. 515. Translation in United States Office of Chief Counsel for Prosecution of Axis Criminality, *Nazi Conspiracy and Aggression*, vol. III, pp. 597–99.

55 Neitzel and Welzer, *Soldaten*, pp. 44–163; Römer, *Kameraden*, pp. 404–66.

56 Herbert Johannes Veigel, *Christbäume: Briefe aus dem Krieg* (Berlin: Dietz, 1991), p. 60, July 6, 1941.

57 Udo von Alvensleben, *Lauter Abschiede: Tagebuch vom Krieg* (Frankfurt: Propyläen, 1971), p. 195, diary entry, Aug. 16, 1941.

58 Musial, *"Konterrevolutionäre Elemente sind zu erschießen,"* pp. 98–171.

59 Quoted in Martin Humburg, *Das Gesicht des Krieges: Feldpostbriefe von Wehrmachtsoldaten aus der Sowjetunion 1941–1944* (Opladen: Leske + Budrich, 1998), p. 198; cf. Walter Manoschek (ed.), *"Es gibt nur eines für das Judentum: Vernichtung": Das Judenbild in deutschen Soldatenbriefen 1939–1944* (Hamburger Edition, 1995), p. 33.

60 Farnbacher, War Diary, June 23, 1941, July 12, 20, 21, 1941, Aug. 3, 1941, Nov. 24, 1941. Similar: Armin Böttger, *Durchkommen war alles: Mit der Kamera bei der 24. Panzerdivision, ein authentischer Bericht vom Arbeitsdienst bis zur Gefangenschaft* (Berg: Vowinckel, 1990), p. 60; Michael Sager, *Jugend in der Mühle des Krieges: Russlandfeldzug und Gefangenschaft 1941–1949: Erlebnisse, Tagebuch und Briefe des Soldaten Michael* (Munich: private print, 2001), pp. 31, 252.

61 Farnbacher, War Diary, July 2, 30, 1941, Aug. 13, 27, 1941, Oct. 5, 27, 1941, Nov. 8, 9, 13, 24, 25, 1941, Dec. 7, 30, 1941. These and the following references to this source follow Kühne, *Belonging and Genocide*, pp. 95–97, 122–24; see also Hartmann, *Wehrmacht im Ostkrieg*, pp. 317–18, 354–61, 415–16, 477–79, 620–21, 668.

62 Farnbacher, War Diary, Oct. 9, 1941, Nov. 6, 1941.

63 Wißmann, letters to Edith, Dec. 1, 1941, Sept. 6, 11, 29, 1942, Oct. 7, 1942, Nov. 10, 22, 1942, Dec. 3, 1942.

64 Walter Bähr and Hans W. Bähr (eds.), *Kriegsbriefe gefallener Studenten 1939–1945* (Tübingen: Wunderlich, 1952), p. 74.

65 Alvensleben, *Lauter Abschiede*, pp. 436, 51ff., Dec. 13, 1944, March 31, 1940; cf. pp. 86, 423, June 4, 1940, Aug. 5, 1944.

66 Wieschenberg, letters, March 28, 1943, and earlier, June 11, 1942, Sept. 15, 1942, Oct. 5, 1942.

67 Reddemann (ed.), *Zwischen Front und Heimat*, p. 599, Neuhaus, letter to Agnes, Aug. 29, 1942.

68 Farnbacher, War Diary, July 15, 1941, Aug. 14–16, 1941, Sept. 22, 1941, Oct. 3, 1941, Dec. 10, 21, 1941, Jan. 15, 1942, Feb. 7, 1942.

69 Ibid., Feb. 21, 1942, March 7, 18, 21, 27, 1942; cf. Kühne, "Male Bonding and Shame Culture," pp. 68–69. On German soldiers' plundering, see Götz Aly, *Hitler's Beneficiaries: Plunder, Racial War, and the Nazi Welfare State* (New York: Metropolitan, 2006), pp. 98–117; and Klaus Latzel, *Deutsche Soldaten – nationalsozialistischer Krieg? Kriegserlebnis, Kriegserfahrung 1939–1945* (Paderborn: Schöningh, 1998), pp. 133–56.

6   Nemesis

In 1942, Nazi Germany's rule over Europe was at its height, while a static front immobilized the army in the East. Offensives in summer and autumn 1942 were ineffective or led to disaster, as did the battle for Stalingrad in January 1943. When in summer 1943 Operation Citadel, the battle for Kursk, known as the biggest tank fight in history, failed as well, the retreat of the Wehrmacht was sealed. And while the soldiers withdrew from the *Lebensraum* they had previously conquered, they also lost more comrades than ever before. In 1941, the Wehrmacht fatalities amounted to 357,000, but in 1942 the rate jumped to 572,000, then to 812,000 in 1943, and to 1,802,000 in 1944 (of which about 350,000 occurred during the major Soviet offensive at the "central front" in summer 1944), and finally to the dramatic number of 1,540,000 in the first months of 1945 until the Wehrmacht capitulated.[1] Only in these very last months was the Wehrmacht no longer safe from social dissolution; only then, in spring 1945, did the number of deserters increase significantly. But through winter 1944–45, no such signs of deterioration challenged the army's fighting morale, contrary to the German army's experience in 1918, and contrary to what other armies have experienced in similar situations of obviously looming defeats.

Why did the Wehrmacht soldiers continue to fight? What made them stick together, stick to their commanders, and stick to the orders they were given? Why did the Wehrmacht not fall apart? This chapter tracks the changing meaning of comradeship in the second half of the war, from 1942 and especially 1943 onward, when doubts about the "final victory" began to worm their way into the soldiers' minds. Comradeship, I argue, never entirely lost its traditional meaning as the epitome of solidarity in face-to-face units, and as the humane counterweight against the obvious brutalization of warfare, and yet it lost ground to a new concept of comradeship, the "grand," national comradeship of the Nazi *Volksgemeinschaft*, united through the soldiers' knowledge of the crimes against humanity committed in the name of Germany. The fabric of this new type of comradeship was no longer the warmth of cooperation, security, trust, and tenderness; instead, it was the coldness of mutual desperation, forlornness, and cynicism.

It was a capital crime in the Third Reich to doubt Nazi Germany's final victory – it could cost you your life. Private letters or diaries only rarely address such doubts, and yet they reveal the spread of pessimism throughout the army, conflated with trauma from the sight and the threat of death and mutilation; with physical exhaustion from months or years of bestial living; with emotional deprivation from separation from loved ones at home; and last, but not least, with moral confusion about the criminal war they were engaged in. The soldiers feared for their physical lives, for their emotional selves, for their moral identities. "You just want to get back home, and nothing else," wrote Albert Neuhaus as early as August 1942, bemoaning the loss of the euphoria that had driven him before. In May 1943 he stated, "I don't like being a soldier anyway."[2]

A frontline soldier could renounce his own leave on behalf of a comrade, and this was counted a touching gesture of comradeship. But it happened rarely, indeed less and less as the war went on. "When it comes to leaves," Wieschenberg noted in 1943, "it's over with comradeship . . . The *Landser*'s alpha and omega is the leave. Leave, nothing but leave."[3] He knew what he was talking about. As an older man and a father, he was entitled to more frequent leaves than most of his comrades, who didn't hide their envy. Once on leave and back home, or at least away from the combat lines, soldiers may have welcomed a minor medical condition "forcing" them to delay their return to the zones of death. Paul Kreissler, Kurt's slightly elder brother, was much less dedicated to the Nazi cause and to the martial community than Kurt, and was instead deeply concerned about the criminal dynamic of the war in the East, doubtful of a final victory from early on, and continuously bothered by arrogant, uncomradely superiors even in combat zones. "Suddenly suffering from tooth-ache" when on a short leave at home in June 1942, he didn't feel in a rush to return to his comrades and gladly welcomed another ten days of leave.[4]

But eventually he returned anyway. Yearning for privacy and security, the soldiers longed to be back home. Yet they wanted to belong to the community of men. They felt betwixt and between. Almost all of them stayed on duty, and they stayed with their comrades. Backing out was an option, but only a theoretical one, as even married men such as Neuhaus, Wieschenberg, and Wißmann told their wives when they urged their men to secure a safe post in the rear or in the reserve army at home. This war "needs men not book-keepers," Neuhaus advised his wife as early as autumn 1941, and there he left it. Soldiers such as him may have yearned to return home, at least on leave. But separated from their comrades, be it only for a short while, they decided sooner or later that "it is not right not to be with your crowd," as Neuhaus noted at one point in his diary.[5]

Suffering from psychosomatic diseases, both Helmut Wißmann and Kurt Kreissler spent long periods in hospitals in the rear and at home. Kreissler was sent back home after only two weeks of frontline service in the summer of 1941, Wißmann in late May 1942. Kreissler was to return only after two years in June 1943, Wißmann in early 1944. Kreissler could have applied for a safe position at home and continued his career as Hitler Youth leader; Wißmann too would have had the chance to stay away from combat. But neither took advantage of these options. Even in the hospital, both were afraid of being seen as cowards. He "would not get over it," said Kreissler, even after the Stalingrad disaster. On sick leave, his manly self-esteem relied on the war stories he could present to younger men and boys. But the longer he stayed away from combat, the more his heroic image faded. Or so he worried. The prospect of recovering too late to join in again – after the war was over – haunted him more and more. Finally back with a frontline unit in June 1943, he wasn't sent to the main front right away and observed that "everybody" felt as he did – eager for combat. "For God's sake, everyone wants to face the enemy. An elderly corporal, father of two children, steps forward and demands to be admitted to a combat unit – and succeeds. Many want the same." Kreissler himself had to wait for another two months.[6]

Coming from a socialist working-class family, Wißmann was less of a Nazi and less dedicated to martial ideals. And having been exposed to combat much longer than Kreissler, he was even more haunted by what would later be called Post-Traumatic Stress Disorder (PTSD).[7] "These terrible thoughts about the front are destroying me," he wrote to Edith while hospitalized in Austria. "Stupid" nightmares involving close combat, death, and injuries haunted him and were kept alive by trading war stories with fellow patients. At some point Edith tried to calm him down by reminding him of the privilege he enjoyed in the hospital – being far away from the killing fields. She opened an old wound. As Helmut wrote back, "exactly this proves that you'll never ever understand what this all is about. When I only think of it" – being hospitalized in safe Austria – "I [feel I] should report back to the front right away. I can if I want. It's only because of you" that he didn't, he advised her, yet unable to hide the inner frictions he suffered from: "if I called myself a 'shirker' it wouldn't be wrong [now in Austria]. But I am no coward, for God's sake. Nobody can call me a coward."[8]

As their private writings show, the Wehrmacht soldiers' loyalty to the army was not especially due to the draconian martial law that threatened the deserter with execution. Rather, the soldiers had internalized the public gaze that, in a militarized culture, deters the one who is about to break ranks. The entire *Volksgemeinschaft* was on the lookout for the individual who tried to shirk his duty to sacrifice himself for the martial community. He who shrank from serving the people's community and sacrificing himself for it was to be ousted from any community. A whole diversity of soldiers – of different military ranks, different generations, and different ideological imprints – feared they would be labelled "shirker" or "coward" not only during the war but also after it, for the rest of their lives. Many of these men, especially after Stalingrad, may no longer have believed in the final victory of Germany. But they all knew about the power and persistence of soldierly values. They had grown up in a country that had been terribly defeated before and yet had kept, in fact intensified, its militarist culture, the adoration reserved for men who choose death before dishonor. Whether young or old, the men of the Wehrmacht could not anticipate that after the end of the Second World War militarism would be devalued in an increasingly pacifist society. They had to assume that the paradigms of martial masculinity would survive, even if Germany lost the war.

These prospects explain why even younger Germans, and even those who kept their distance from Nazi ideology, worried that the war would end before they had the opportunity to prove their manliness in combat. "Otherwise you won't have the right to live afterwards," stated the young Peter Pfaff, who came from a family of Christian believers, in 1943.[9] And so students of Catholic theology too thought that it was only at the front line that you would meet real men. "Isn't it legit that I too yearn to prove myself" on the battlefield, wondered one of them a few days after the news about the Stalingrad disaster had spread all over Germany.[10]

What drew these men to combat, however, was not only the idea of joining, or rejoining, a specific group of comrades. Often an abstract and even mystical notion of comradeship was even more powerful. "My fallen comrades," Wieschenberg said, "oblige me to hang on."[11] They must not be allowed to have died in vain. Kurt Kreissler saw himself as part of a "single warrior family" united by "common destiny, common joy, and common suffering," one that included the soldiers of the Great War as well. In his mind, the war novels of Zöberlein, Dwinger, Beumelburg, and Ettighofer, which he had read as a youth, were always present. "Shivering" in face of the "greatness of the experiences of these frontline soldiers," he didn't doubt his destiny. It was at the front. When he came back to his "old crowd," he met barely any of his former comrades. They were "dead, missing, or wounded," he learned. The primary groups no longer existed. But that did not challenge his combat motivation. Within a short time, new primary groups, or equivalents, had been welded together – under the rules of comradeship. As a skilled NCO he knew what to do. He had to establish trustful and intimate relationships with his men. They had to be sure that he cared about them. He chatted "with each single man of my unit individually" so that he knew everything about his life, career, and personality – and "looked at him in a different way." As a consequence, "we are not just an organizational unit; we have become a strong community, ready to prove itself in the forthcoming fights," he wrote in a letter to his parents.[12]

It did not unsettle him that these fights almost immediately destroyed the newly established communal bonds. The myth of comradeship, and his own experience as a Hitler Youth leader and a Wehrmacht soldier, had taught him about the fragility of personal relationships in the army at war – "you happily get to know someone, and after a spell you are in pain over the loss of him," in Jochen Klepper's words.[13] And so Kreissler knew that comradeship was not a matter of long-term personal relationships but unfolded its power as a mythical concept over multiple re-enactments. Whenever he was sent back to the reserve troops, as in late 1944, Kreissler longed to be with the old crowd again at the front. What he craved, however, was not the primary group of specific individuals but the idea of a community that was made of a certain type of soldier, one that was exchangeable – the comrade. Private Bertold Paulus, unlike Kreissler a simple drafted soldier and a blue-collar worker in his civilian life, explained to his loved ones in a letter why it didn't really matter whether one, as a front soldier, met old friends: "It is all the same, whether we know each other or not, we are all comrades here who all depend on each other. And in fact those you know least are the best ones."[14]

To be sure, there was no shortcut from the idea to its re-enactment. The Wehrmacht's replacement system enabled the type of social engineering that was needed to make comradeship real even if massive casualties decimated the units and the bonds that had kept them together. In the Wehrmacht, such units were not refilled individually but withdrawn from the front line as a whole and then, in the rear, "reconstituted with new men and the remaining survivors of the old unit."[15] This way, the veterans served as the "stays" (*Korsettstangen*) of the army, at least until winter 1944–45. These "old geezers" may have been "stubborn" but you couldn't "unnerve" them, stated a soldier in a letter as soon as 1942. "You can always rely on them . . . they spread a magical and powerful spirit that imbues us and makes us vanquish everything."[16] The *Korsettstangen* constituted a nucleus of social continuity in the repeated destruction of the primary groups, as the historian Christian Rass has shown in his study on the 253rd Infantry Division, a typical front division deployed in the

East from 1941 to 1945. About 20 percent of all of its soldiers stayed with this division either the entire time (and survived) or for most of the four years. This does not mean, however, that they stayed with one face-to-face unit (such as a platoon) all the time. Rather, they transferred repeatedly from one unit to another, but only within the division or the regiment. Typically, intact units yielded some of their veterans to decimated units so that the experience of the veterans remained equally distributed among the various units. Rass's statistical analysis also confirms what the soldiers reported in their private writings. The training units did not stay together until they were involved in combat but were torn apart many times in between. The rationale of the training period was not to constitute coherent and long-lasting primary groups; instead, the soldiers were taught how to build and rebuild primary-group relationships again and again, whenever necessary. This was specifically the job of the veterans, mostly senior privates, lance corporals, and NCOs: They were to introduce the novices into the mystery of comradeship and familiarize them with how to realize the idea of comradeship.[17]

Take Karlheinz Ziegler as an example. Born in 1924, he wanted to belong in Nazi Germany but had a hard time proving that he qualified. As a youth, he applied to a NAPOLA, the Nazis' elitist boarding schools, but was declined. At the age of eighteen, he volunteered for the Wehrmacht and was accepted as an officer candidate. But already during the basic training he couldn't do without consuming his iron ration, the emergency food supply, although there was no emergency. He was demoted and was sent to the Eastern front as a simple private. From spring 1943 to his death in action three days before the German capitulation in May 1945, he took part in the heaviest battles, including the one for Kursk in 1943, and was with the Army Group Center when it collapsed in summer 1944. Often appalled by comrades from northern Germany with whom he, a southern German, didn't get along, he was still shocked to see them dying in large numbers. It was only thanks to his sergeant, Feldwebel Jahn, that he hung on. Jahn, the model of a "stay," a veteran comrade, covered up for Ziegler when he again ate his iron ration. More important, Jahn showed him how to survive amidst the landscapes of death. "It is only thanks to Feldwebel Jahn that I am still alive," Ziegler wrote in August 1943. Ten days later Jahn was seriously injured and sent to hospital. Ziegler lost "not only a comrade but also my best friend. Without him I don't want to rush into the battle again," he wrote. Thanks to a minor injury, he spent some time with the baggage and at the casualty station, safe from the front line but not from the sight of "mutilations you simply can't describe." Before, he had dreamed of going on leave and heading back home. But now he was "looking forward to getting back to my comrades" and being comfortable with his comrades, although they were replaced time and again. Actually back with his comrades at the front line in early September 1943, he no longer experienced surprise at meeting only three of them. Promoted to NCO in January 1944 and to lieutenant a year later, he adopted the role of a "stay" himself and worked eagerly at modeling himself on Lieutenant Ernst Wurche, the comradely character in Walter Flex's famous World War I novel. As his private letters show, it was only then – when the final defeat of Germany drew closer – that he overcame the depressive and desolate mood he had previously been prey to, even though the Wehrmacht was no longer fighting in (or retreating from) Russia but was being pushed into Silesia in East Germany. After a boozy night – "We roistered the entire night" – Russian machine-gun fire woke them up, and instantly "we mustered all men," and "together we brought the Ivans to a halt," he recorded on January 29, 1945. After a few days in the rear, he headed back to the front line on February 9, "not that I would expect anything good" there "but it is just where you belong."[18]

Kurt Kreissler and Helmut Wißmann were just two further examples of the "stays," the veterans who worked diligently on including the novices in the mystical bond of comradeship. After two years of sick leave and training in reserve units, Wißmann, promoted to corporal, returned in spring 1944 to his old unit at the Eastern front. Not much was left of the "old crowd" except its name. It was filled with new men, far fewer than before. But he wasn't bothered. He knew that "in a few days, I'll have settled in; first you have to dig yourself in, that's how it is anywhere." And that way it worked well. He still didn't like the East Prussians who dominated his division but he was enough of a veteran simply to ignore the frictions. With the Eastern front line receding dramatically and Germany's defeat looming, Wißmann's social horizon narrowed down to the unit he led as NCO. The fights against "Ivan" provided excitement and tightened the bonds. "We had only two casualties," he wrote in August 1944. "I was the last to get back to our post. My comrades were pretty worried about me. But then we laughed and were happy to be back together."[19] In the same fashion Kurt Kreissler noted in January 1945, after returning to the front: "none of my old comrades are still here." He hadn't expected anything else. Worrying about "how few are left" only encouraged him to put even more effort into "getting to know the men and their leaders as fast as possible, so that we get used to each other and gear up for the hard fights and uneasy missions that are ahead of us." Soon after, he wrote the letter to his parents quoted above, bragging about the splendid comradeship and fighting spirit in his "small community": "We want to stick together, we want to fight together, or we want to get wounded together – that's what we are longing for."[20]

Physical destruction, or the risk of it, fueled social life. In this way, the soldiers re-enacted and enlivened the myth of comradeship many times throughout the war. Once back with their units, the soldiers resorted to tender, "motherly," family-like comradeship in order to fight depression and deprivations and to enjoy homoeroticism in an all-male society. When decorated with flowers and pictures or even a small garden, the all-male household looked as if it had a sugar mommy.[21] None of these comforts would last long; they had to be recreated all the time. All these efforts were not about physical harvest, but about social yield. The social dynamic that generated "comradely love" benefited from the destruction of its physical resources. "Just as at home with mom," noted a soldier on Christmas in Stalingrad 1942. "Harmonica, fiddle, singing, happiness, and everything is done together . . . And we all felt so emotional . . . Some became teary-eyed." The soldiers were ending the party with a bottle of champagne when a bomb hit the bunker. "One dead and four casualties. . . . I can't help the one who died," noted the writer, a doctor, taking up the melancholy of the Uhland song.[22]

Those who survived moved even closer together. Death fueled comradeship. Terror generated tenderness. At the same time, the imagery and the experience of motherliness and family life produced solely by men also helped the soldiers to cope with the world of destruction. Getting together at night and sitting around a bonfire, chatting and eating, allowed the soldiers to enjoy the "only thing that holds you up – good and honest comradeship," noted Private Kreissler in his diary in late October 1942 when the mood in his unit was "somber" and they "clearly realized that the war wouldn't end any time soon." While Kurt enthused about comradeship as the high point of sociality per se, Paul appreciated it only as the very last haven, the sheet anchor of humanity midst in a sea of inhumanity. And while his brother Kurt worked eagerly on embodying the ideal of a vertical comradeship, with the platoon leader as the engine, Paul's experience of comradeship, much rarer anyway, was a deliberately horizontal one, defined by antagonism to superiors. To them, Paul noted once, "the war is the perfect means to get by with the inferiority complexes they suffer from as civilians."[23]

Paul's comradeship was the type of comradeship resorted to – only temporarily if at all – by the *Unsoldaten*, or "un-soldiers," those who never became acclimatized to the impositions of the army and who, throughout their military careers, tried to preserve their civilian identities. One of them was Kurt Napp, a blue-collar worker based in Hamburg, born in 1905, who had been a socialist activist and been sent to prison after 1933. He had been declared "unworthy to do military service," and yet in 1943 was drafted into Bewährungsbataillon 999, or Correction Unit 999, a Wehrmacht unit consisting solely of criminals – including political criminals – who were used either directly as cannon fodder or for suicide missions such as mine detection; Napp died in action in 1944 on the Eastern front.[24] At first, he tried to survive physically and emotionally via comradeship, albeit a defiant comradeship, deployed not to fuel fighting morale but to foster the soldier's self. Just like more conforming soldiers, he had a hard time finding "comrades" of the type he was looking for, but he too managed to handle repeated transferrals and the need to find new comrades or even friends. Mocking the official notion of comradeship, however, Napp watched out for comrades with whom he could talk about family idylls and about ideological issues. The focus of this type of comradeship was civilian life at home, and the values of civilian society, not how to contribute to the war efforts.[25] And yet even this type of comradeship – self-chosen friendship within the larger enforced community – did not undermine the institutional mission of the army but rather supported it. Offering a haven for mutual griping and whining, where one could articulate a desire to chuck the uniform, it made the army bearable. It made the soldiers function.

Either way, whether experienced euphorically as the heyday of homo-eroticism or somberly in a mood of forlornness, tender, family-like com-radeship was endowed with an aura of humanity. As comrades in war, the soldiers elevated themselves above the maelstrom of barbarism engen-dered in zones of mass death. Or so they pretended. And so did their loved ones at home and the home front at large. Lore Walb, a member of the Bund Deutscher Mädel (BDM) fascinated by the Nazi *Volksge-meinschaft*, was deeply moved when she learned about the tenderness of the "great spirit of comradeship and community" demonstrated by the famous air fighter Werner Mölders even in the last moments before he was killed in an air battle in November 1941. "His boys loved him so much," she noted.[26] And Christel Beilmann, engaged in the Catholic youth movement, understood as late as July 1944, when the Wehrmacht finally broke down in the East, that "the front experience does not really numb" the soldiers. Rather, she wrote in a letter to a soldier, it was "the beauty of humanity manifesting itself in comradeship," even in greatest danger, that prevented soldiers from emotional and moral numbing.[27]

Or so she and other women at home thought, influenced by books, papers, and propaganda, and the letters of their men at the front line. The truth was that this type of ultimate solidarity in the face of death, like tender and homoerotic male togetherness, remained throughout the war what it always had been – a rare exception from the rule of daily frustrations, boredom, and egoism. Paul Kreissler serves as an example. While his brother Kurt worked diligently on emulating Ernst Wurche as a comradely leader, Paul suffered most of the time from uncomradely superiors. Once in February 1943 he was ordered to bring a bottle of petroleum to the command post at the front line, in the middle of the night and in highly risky circumstances. What for? "Sirs" were celebrating a birthday and wanted to party through the night, playing card games. The following day, his unit was suddenly attacked by the Russians and needed to escape in short order. Only the officers had cars waiting for them so they could seek shelter instantly. Paul's anger didn't abate when, the next day, rank-and-files were ordered to risk life and limb to procure a velvet pillow for a medal of honor – for a major who was killed in action.[28]

It got worse. "Woe betide him who is not with his unit," Kreissler thought during one of the many hurried retreats in spring 1944, still appreciating the face-to-face comradeship, and yet bemoaning its erosion. Who was not with his unit "was beyond hope if hit . . . All are busy running. Nobody cares for anyone except himself . . . What has happened to the much-praised comradeship?" Only a "wretched abjection and powerlessness" was left. While he got away this time, he was less lucky a few months later, in July 1944, when the Red Army crushed the entire Wehrmacht Army Group Center in Operation Bagration. A sudden attack took him by surprise and separated him from his closest comrades. He found himself "all alone." A few comrades had sought shelter in a shell-hole but there was no more room for him. Eventually a shell hit him, leaving one of his feet all but severed. He was unable to stir, paralyzed by agony. "Seven feet away a soldier shouts and calls for help. And so do I when two vehicles flash by. In vain! Nobody gives a dime for us. Comradeship! Everyone just runs away," he noted a few weeks later in hospital, having had both of his legs amputated at the thigh.[29]

Kurt Kreissler was only one of millions of soldiers who died forlornly or were left alone, seriously injured. The rest, and hundreds of thousands of newly recruited soldiers, kept fighting – against enemy soldiers and enemy civilians. As historians have often noted, the Wehrmacht responded to the looming prospect of defeat by increasing rather than diminishing terror. "The more hopeless their military position became, the more radical were the orders issued from the high command, although it was easy to see by 1943/44, at the very latest, that these measures no longer had any military justification, to say nothing of any moral and legal defensibility," states the historian Christian Hartmann.[30] Somewhere between 300,000 and

500,000 people were killed during the Wehrmacht's anti-partisan war in the Soviet Union. From spring 1942, millions of Soviet citizens were coerced into forced labor service for Germany; Wehrmacht soldiers in the role of colonial slave-hunters played their part in destroying families, societies, and lives all over the occupied countryside.[31] In the retreat that began in 1943, the troops engaged in marauding, murder, and plunder throughout Eastern Europe. The Wehrmacht's scorched-earth policy concluded the destruction of the Eastern half of the European continent. The German invasion and occupation left huge territories of the Soviet Union devastated, deserted, and depopulated. Approximately 3 million Soviet citizens lost their homes and all their belongings. Other European theaters such as Greece and Serbia suffered from Wehrmacht occupation and anti-partisan fights in similar ways and, from 1943, with the Allies rolling up southern and western Europe, Italy, France, and the Low Countries were also drawn into the maelstrom of Wehrmacht terror.[32]

In the last two years of the war, comradeship did not vanish but it was altered. Solidarity, humanity, and tenderness in the face of mass death gave way to a new, Nazified idea of collective identity. There may still have been a few efforts by soldiers to preserve humanity in the midst of the violence but this kind of comradeship was increasingly overshadowed by a new type of bond, one that was driven by cynicism rather than care and tenderness. Willy Peter Reese's bitter autobiographical *Confessions*, written in 1944, looks back on what the Nazi war in the East had done to the soldiers' emotional and moral state. "Just as our winter gear ended up leaving only our eyes uncovered, so soldierliness left minimal room for the expression of human traits. We were in uniform. Not just unwashed, unshaved, full of lice, and sick but also spiritually ravaged – nothing but a sum of blood, guts, and bones. Our comradeship was made of mutual dependence, from living together in next to no space. Our humour was born out of sadism, gallows humour, satire, obscenity, spite, rage, and pranks with corpses, squirted brains, lice, pus, and shit, the spiritual zero ... The fact that we were soldiers was sufficient basis for criminality and degradation, for an existence in hell."[33] In this assessment, comradeship is expressed only in remnants of humane sociability. Here, the soldiers' cynical We is mired in "criminality and degradation." Pristine comradeship had become the social engine of this very inhumanity. It was the "We" of the soldiers that executed this inhumanity, and Reese was well aware he was part of it.

Reese had given an earlier account of his complicity in criminality. In 1942 he depicted in a poem a gang of soldiers guzzling and whoring, boasting and lying, cursing and crowing. "As a bawling crowd," they had "marched to Russia, gagged people, butchered bloodthirstily," and "murdered the Jews . . . We wave the banners of the Aryan ancestors. They suit us well . . . We rule as a band." And looking at the Wehrmacht's retreat from the Soviet Union and its scorched-earth tactics, he added in 1944: "Russia was turning into a depopulated, smoking, burning, wreckage-strewn desert." "On the way we torched all the villages we passed through and blew up the stoves . . . The war had become insane, it was all murder, never mind whom it affected." Outbursts "of rage and hate, envy, fistfights, sarcasm, and mockery" replaced "whatever may have remained of comradeship," he wrote, sentimentalizing the warm side of soldierly togetherness. As the Germans were forced to retreat further and further, a new, very different collective identity emerged, based on "heroic nihilism" and pure cynicism.[34]

Reese's literary treatment of the Wehrmacht's drowning in collective cynicism was no distortion of reality. To be sure, in the midst of all the frictions and miseries, comradeship did not vanish, but once the heyday of megalomania was gone, it lost its glory and its Janus face became ever clearer. As the anecdote of Farnbacher's seemingly funny, but in fact cynical requisition tour in spring 1942 suggests, comradeship now signified the tenuous solidarity of soldiers who, overwhelmed by fatigue, apathy, and numbness, escaped into sarcasm and no longer cared for the humane morality of their civilian selves. Farnbacher was only one of many cynics. Taking a short break from the front in spring 1942, Albert Neuhaus and his comrades strolled through a Russian village where "our *Landsers* had hanged from a tree a woman who had agitated against German soldiers. We make no bones about these people," he explained to his wife. "Well, initially you might find it strange, but eventually you just laugh at it."[35] So did Willy Peter Reese's comrades in 1943, when the visions of glory and victory evaporated. At one moment, they enjoyed marching "through an idyllic landscape of villages and fields." The next moment they saw "two hanged men" swaying "from a protruding branch. A musty smell of decomposition hung around their stiff forms. Their faces were swollen and bluish, contorted in grimaces. Their flesh was coming away from the nails of their tied hands. One soldier took their picture; another gave them a swing with stick. Partisans. We laughed and moved off."[36]

Comradeship denoted inclusion, belonging, solidarity, and togetherness, but its reality depended on its opposite, the Other, the foe – exclusion. The Other could be the overwhelming enemy soldier or the denigrated enemy civilian. Terror generated tenderness, destruction enabled cohesion. And vice versa. Producing togetherness, even if only once in a while, enabled the soldiers to cope with the omnipresence of death and devastation they faced in their war of annihilation. Lieutenant

Werner Gross joined the NSDAP before they came into power. Like Kurt Kreissler, the allure of male communities fueled his dedication to the Nazi cause and to the war in the East. Born in 1914, he made a living as a professional youth leader with the Labor Service and became a professional Hitler Youth leader soon after 1933, before pursuing a career as a Wehrmacht officer from 1936. Serving as lieutenant at the Eastern front from 1942, he basked in the glory of being the comradely leader, modeled on Ernst Wurche, always concerned about the health, the mood, and the cohesion of his unit. "As officers, we are to precede our men" and "to sweep them along," he once explained to his parents, turning down his father's suggestion that he seek a safe assignment. "I belong to my men," he said, whether on the battlefield facing death, in the field hospitals nursing his men, at a sentimental Christmas celebration enacting a "motherly" sense of home far away from real homes and families, or in the rear areas fighting partisans, or bandits, as the Nazis described them. With horses and carts, his troop roamed through occupied lands in the spring of 1943. Proudly he reported how they "searched villages, combed woods and cleared the area of gangs." To Gross, "gangs" was a synonym for partisans but it did not matter whether these people actually were partisans or were just civilians whom the German soldiers considered suspicious. Enemies were interchangeable. In fighting them, Gross and his men revelled in the happiness of comradeship: "We lived like gypsies and vagabonds," he boasted. He and his men were above civilian society and indeed the rest of the world.[37]

By showing feminine qualities and staging family-like settings, exclusively male societies freshened their ties to the civilian world at home; they demonstrated, to themselves and others, that they had preserved these ties and would continue to do so. At the same time they demonstrated their independence from real women and real families – from civilian society and civilian morality. The message was: Being on our own, we men are able to generate a warm sense of family, even if we fight cold-bloodedly a few seconds later; we are emotionally independent. Demonstrating the independence of male society from the world at home went far beyond performing family-like sociability and solidarity in the face of lethal danger. Paradoxically, it culminated in violating the very morality the comradely community claimed to honor. Jovial cooking, a sentimental Christmassy idyll, and melancholic singing could easily become a dreadful brawl. Lifting a glass together strengthened comradeship, just as did sharing food parcels, communal singing, or storming into battle. The booze made soldiers forget about frictions, frustrations, and catastrophes. Boozing together was one of the many rituals of comradeship that demonstrated the male bond's social sovereignty. Comradeship lived off a collective breaching of the norm. Drinking bouts and little riots mediated a sense of elevation above the rules of military discipline and civilian decency. Official orders banning boozy excesses were issued but not taken or even meant seriously. Military authorities usually turned a blind eye even to serious crimes committed out of comradely drunkenness. The male bond was stronger than external expectations and orders.

A comrade was someone with whom "you could get up to something now and then," as police lieutenant Gerhard Modersen put it in his diary in 1943. For countless soldiers, "getting up to something" meant one thing: adventures with women. Modersen was married. But it was precisely adultery, which he constantly practiced along with his comrades, that made life as a soldier attractive to him. Innumerable carry-ons did not jeopardize male comradeship but strengthened it. He got along particularly well with an officer comrade from Hamburg. "As there were the two of us, we made sure we got hold of two women" simultaneously, "of course." "In order to avoid any frictions between us, we agreed that as a matter of principle he would take the slender one whereas I would get the more voluptuous one." Male solidarity meant ruling over women, and as a power tool it rested on dividing the female world, on isolating women. Beyond the matter of sexual needs, sexual adventures served the male bond even more once they were history. Sexual boasting fed male solidarity, not least by establishing informal hierarchies. He who traded the most bloodcurdling adventures was the star. Another "good comrade" of Modersen had "wangled things in terms of women . . . my hair stood on end when he told his stories, and this although I am not exactly a choirboy in these regards." What made this comrade a big gun was that "he had a real knack for hiding things at home. His wife wouldn't doubt his fidelity although he cheated on her with a neighbor for one and a half years."[38]

Comradeship needed the Other in order to flourish. The Other could be the mean drill sergeant, the egotistic outsider, the enemy in combat – or the civilians at home, and first among them, the women. Bad-mouthing women, cracking dirty jokes, and dwelling on obscene talk helped the soldiers to get along together; and so did conspiring against, cheating on, or abusing women, the Other of the male society par excellence. Visiting a bordello was a collective act, just as boozing or obscene jokes were, and another proof of the power of the male bond. It was dingy, but it wasn't done secretly, and often it remained tied into the military hierarchy. When a Wehrmacht major in the East announced the opening of a new brothel and ordered his unit collectively to visit it, he did so in front of a few female military aides. Ilse Schmidt, one of them, felt deeply denigrated by this obvious misogyny.[39] But it wasn't an accident.

Instead, this demonstration of male solidarity against and power over women was deliberately staged when these aides – the female Other – were watching.

Whether fueled by misogyny or motherliness, by brutality or charity, the "anti-structure" of comradeship relied on challenging the "structure" of the civilian world outside. Abusing women in the occupied areas was the ultimate assertion of the all-powerful male bond.[40] Shortly after the Germans invaded her home town Pskov in early August 1941, Genia Demianova, a Russian teacher, was tortured and raped by a Wehrmacht sergeant. He did so not only for sexual gratification but also to position himself among his comrades, as the victim's account reveals. Immediately afterwards, he started boasting. "There is a roar of cheering, the clinking of many glasses. The sergeant is standing in the open doorway: 'The wild cat is tamed,' he is saying. 'Boys, she was a virgin. What do you say to that?' Another burst of cheering," and the sergeant closed the door, but Demianova was not left alone. "The others came in" and "flung themselves upon me, digging into my wounds while they defiled me . . . Then everything passed. The Germans kept coming, spitting obscene words towards me, guffawing as they tortured me."[41] Notwithstanding official bans, recurrent worries about the impact of sexual debaucheries on the troops' discipline, and the occasional judicial prosecution of perpetrators, the Wehrmacht by and large maintained a lax attitude toward the daily sexual violence and abuse of women committed by German soldiers in the occupied territories. After an evening of boozing in early December 1943, an infantry soldier of the 253rd Division and his comrade wanted to conclude the pleasant night with a Russian woman. They strolled around, finding only unwilling women. Eventually they broke into a home where they found eight women and three toddlers. They chose the youngest of the women, who happened to be the mother of the toddlers, abused, and raped her. In this case, a military court took action and sentenced the two soldiers to three years in prison and demotion. The court was concerned not about the plight of Russian women but about the discipline of the German troops. The two soldiers were pardoned after serving a symbolic three-month term in prison.[42]

At a meeting of high-ranking SS officers in 1943 several commanders expressed concerns that SS men were increasingly disregarding the laws on racial defilement (*Rassenschande*); it was assumed that "at least fifty percent of all men in the SS or police were breaking the rule" that forbade "intercourse with women of other races." Although a few offenders were punished, standard procedure in the SS was to disregard the order. Sepp Dietrich, commander of SS Leibstandarte Adolf Hitler and an old friend of Hitler, stated that this "order had been issued by theoretical experts" and would not apply to his troops. In 1940 Hans Frank, the Governor-General for the occupied Polish territories, even made it "obligatory to take some account of the physical state of those charged with carrying out executions." As the German historian Hans Buchheim rightly observed in the early 1960s, the lax handling by the SS of the rules on intercourse with racially alien women – a key feature of Nazi racist politics – contrasted sharply with the official SS "worship" of hardness and stoicism. Officially, the SS man was above ordinary human emotionality. And yet there was a consensus that those who proved their "hardness" by carrying out genocide in order to save the German nation were eligible for exemptions from the rule of hardness and stoicism, for instance when it came to meeting sexual needs. This "tendency toward moderation in practice," as Buchheim called it, "made it possible to live with the harshness," as "the strict copybook SS requirements could be met by no mentally or morally normal man."[43]

Buchheim was well acquainted with the social psychology of this "moderation in practice" and its closeness to the logic of comradeship; he had served with the Wehrmacht on the Eastern front from 1941 to 1945. The Wehrmacht's training manuals and pedagogical literature stereotypically stressed that "comradeship must not be taken as a mutual assurance to cover up one's own or somebody else's misconduct."[44] In official language, the term comradeship epitomized the morally good side of soldierly solidarity. Its evil side was called *Kameraderie*, or camaraderie.[45] So, for instance, Erich Weniger in his 1938 book on military training warned against the "camaraderie" of "goldbrickers," of "thieves," or of plain "criminals," and other types of mistaken comradeship that all served to commit or to cover up misconducts of various types.[46] Comradeship that "serves to cover up all kinds of stuff," echoed Heinrich Himmler, was "false comradeship."[47] And so Buchheim, even in the 1960s, explained that

"comradeship" implies a sense of soldierly solidarity between men and a readiness to share each other's burdens; *camaraderie*, on the other hand, implies no store is set by individual qualities and men are simply prepared to make mutual concessions to each other's weaknesses. In the name of *camaraderie* increasingly serious failings become acceptable, offences can be covered up, communal dereliction of duty can be concealed both from the authorities and the outside world. All this can be made to appear as a military virtue, as proof of loyalty, solidarity and mutual readiness to share one another's burdens; but as a result a man can lose all objective standards and come to model his behaviour simply upon that of his fellows. So the common level of morality sinks imperceptibly. A community already well on the way to degeneracy can keep itself alive by appealing to its "communal spirit," even though the standards are a mockery of heroism or idealism.

Buchheim's intention was to save the holy military virtue of comradeship from the moral quagmire into which the SS drew the German nation. Confirming the popular myth in post-1945 Germany, according to which only the SS but not the Wehrmacht had been responsible for the mass crimes against the civilian populations in the East, Buchheim held that "true comradeship," the morally good type of soldierly solidarity, had been untainted in military settings whereas its degenerated, evil version, camaraderie, had prospered only "in those SS organizations which had no true military role" and had not seen combat.[48] What Buchheim called the "tendency toward moderation in practice," however, is in fact misunderstood if simply ascribed to evil camaraderie. Instead it was a crucial element of all male bonding, at least in the Nazi war of annihilation, whether or not this bonding was called comradeship. The distinction between camaraderie and comradeship establishes a moral antagonism that serves to obfuscate the conflation if not interdependence of both in social and emotional practice. Both generated cohesion, solidarity, and a sense of unity. Such solidarity needed the Other to come into being and to last. The Other could be the enemy soldier, the racial enemy, the mean superior, the wives and girlfriends at home, or, more abstractly, the military code book, or the norms of chastity at home. What precisely the group or their leaders chose in order to achieve cohesion was contingent. Nazi soldiers may have chosen as the Other the traditions and laws of warfare that protected the civilian and the POW, including Jews and communists. Anti-Nazi soldiers, not a small minority in the Wehrmacht, may have chosen as their Other the official propaganda on the *Endsieg*, or final victory, which nobody was allowed to doubt in Nazi Germany, or idolatry of Adolf Hitler, the Führer.

According to traditional German military codes, the army was above political partisanships and the struggle between civilian political parties, social classes, and religious communities. Often, reality belied this idea. In imperial Germany, and still under Weimar, the officer corps, handpicked from the aristocracy and the educated upper middle classes would not accept socialists, working-class or even lower middle-class men, and it resented Jews, and even Catholics. The notion of a non-political army did not translate into support of leftist Weimar governments. It implied, after 1918, a certain distancing from governments, both from democratic governments before 1933 and thereafter from the Nazi regime, and the priority of military professionalism over political exploitation. For the troops, it meant that military effectiveness, including military cohesion, was not to be questioned by ideological disagreements, especially not within the face-to-face units. Unavoidable as they were in a drafted mass army, such arguments could not be allowed to undermine the social cohesion of the troops. As they could not be suppressed consistently, the idea of some sort of freedom of speech, or mutual indifference toward political arguments, was needed. If they were to trust each other in battle, soldiers needed to know that they would not be ostracized for expressing ideas and opinions with which not all comrades, or the superiors, agreed.

Soldierly comradeship trumped civilian ideologies – this was the ideal that had been nowhere realized more than in the trenches of the Great War, according to the myth. And it was not just a myth. Many soldiers still enjoyed this freedom of speech in Hitler's army. "Among comrades, different opinions are openly discussed. It is the uniform that allows diversity," observed Private Jochen Klepper in August 1941 on his way to the Eastern front. To Klepper it meant the world. In the Third Reich, he was a popular Christian writer, conservative and full of admiration for the Prussian military tradition but at odds with and ostracized by the Nazis. Klepper was married to a Jewish woman. But the army seemed to be safe from the totalitarian goals of the Nazi dictatorship, Klepper found. In the army, "German men" still got along, "apart from all partisanship issues," he noted after meeting a traveling soldier in need of accommodation, with whom he shared his bed, a demonstration of comradeship. Klepper enjoyed deep nightly talks with this "very sensible, warmhearted, and bright young man," although – or because – he was an SA man.[49]

Klepper's experience was not an exception. Many Wehrmacht soldiers, especially those distant from Nazism, appreciated this kind of freedom of speech among comrades especially as it no longer existed outside the army. Comradeship may have been for many soldiers a safe haven that shielded them against the Nazi regime's totalitarian aspiration. But it did not shield everyone, as Klepper also realized. "I can talk freely to anybody about everything. But not about the Jewish question . . . I always see that propaganda has been almost completely successful. Nobody questions it. The Jews have to go," he noted in the autumn of 1941 before being discharged due to his Jewish wife. The "beautiful human touch" of all the "talks with comrades" that enthused Klepper was was tainted.[50] As the historian Bryan Mark Rigg has shown, numerous Wehrmacht soldiers of Jewish or partly Jewish descent, so-called *Mischlinge*, managed to stay in the army for a while, thanks to inconsistent application of the Nazi racial laws or to protection by comrades; the latter, however, was rare, and, crucially, notwithstanding shortages of manpower in the second half of the war, the racial loopholes were closed.[51]

And it was not only the antisemitic consensus that perforated the shield that protected soldiers who kept a distance from the Nazis or feared per-secution. Issued in 1938 and publicly announced a few days before the attack on Poland in 1939, the *Kriegssonderstrafrechtsverordnung* (KSSVO), or Special Wartime Penal Code, considered any "public" expression of discontent with the regime, including doubt about Germany's final victory, as a subversion of the fighting power, or *Wehrkraftzersetzung*. It was considered a capital crime, to be punished with death. The term "public" was crucial. While the KSSVO did not define it, the Reich Court Martial, the military supreme court of the Third Reich, decided to take it in its extreme sense and to prosecute any statement or utterance that *could* have become public. Rigidly applied, this interpretation would have destroyed privacy altogether. It complied with – indeed was a consequence of – the Nazi goal to purify the *Volksgemeinschaft* not only racially but also ideologically, in other words to realize the totalitarian vision of a society in which each individual acted, thought, and felt as a Nazi. In this vision, the idea of an apolitical soldier was obsolete, and so was the concept of a politically indifferent comradeship. The apolitical soldier was to be substituted by the "political soldier." He absorbed, internalized, and dedicated himself to, the Nazi ideals. One of the first steps the Third Reich took to Nazify the soldiers was the Hitler oath, or oath of allegiance, sworn by Reichswehr, then Wehrmacht, soldiers from 1934 on; it pledged personal loyalty to the Führer instead of to the constitution. As one of the last steps toward "politicizing" the Wehrmacht, the regime introduced in December 1943 the *Nationalsozialistische Führungsoffizier* (NSFO), or National Socialist Cadre Officer, to ensure the indoctrination of the soldiers.[52]

In an army of "political soldiers" the concept of comradeship was subject to a fundamental change. It could no longer protect political dissidents or even those who were prey to momentary resentment or distrust of the regime. Only Nazified or "political soldiers" were to benefit from soldierly solidarity. As a dictionary explained in 1943, in the Third Reich comradeship had become the code word for unconditional "belief and obedience that merged allegiance to Adolf Hitler into an indissoluble and irrevocable community" of ideologically standardized or Nazified soldiers and citizens.[53] Hitler outlined this concept of comradeship in a big speech in Berlin in September 1942. Concealing neither the military setbacks in the East nor the plan to exterminate the Jews, he bragged about the "one great, bright side" of the war: "the great comradeship," the "National Socialist Volksgemeinschaft" united through the bloodbaths of the war. It would not allow for any dissidence. There was no longer any comradeship outside the Nazi mind-set.[54] Consequently, the Reich's Supreme Court (*Volksgerichtshof*) decided in 1943 in its judgment against a member of the "White Rose" that individuals who subverted the *Volksgemeinschaft*, or aimed to do so, had excluded themselves from any comradeship. There should be no comradeship that did not serve the racially and ideologically purified and homogeneous Nazi *Volksge-meinschaft.*[55]

It was not by accident, however, that these decisions and definitions dated from the time when the popularity of the regime dwindled. They articulated goals and ideals, not the actual state of Nazification. Although tainted by totalitarian claims of the regime, comradeship never lost its traditional, "apolitical" meaning entirely. Numerous conservative Wehrmacht officers, including prominent Nazi jurists such as Erich Schwinge, otherwise advocated draconian military laws but opposed the Supreme Court's totalitarian interpretation of the notion of "public" as used by the KSSVO. Random talk between friends, within the family, or among comrades in "closed," intimate settings should not be prosecuted, they recommended. They were not worried about privacy or freedom of speech in general. However, they feared the mushrooming of a culture of denunciations and, subsequently, of distrust within the army. Such a culture would destroy the very basis of the Wehrmacht's fighting power – the "comradely cohesion of the army."[56]

Denunciations still occurred within and outside the German army. Germans served as accomplices of the Gestapo. They spied into the privacy of their neighbors, friends, and families and resorted to whistle-blowing, or simply bad-mouthing in order to settle personal accounts.[57] In total, some 30,000 to 40,000 soldiers were found guilty of *Wehrkraftzersetzung.* Many of them ended up on the gallows of the Third Reich, often as victims of denunciation by their neighbors, relatives, or comrades.[58]

One of these victims was submarine commander Oskar Kusch, born in 1918 into a Berlin liberal and nationalist but not Nazi upper middle-class family; his father was a freemason and had volunteered to serve in World War I. As a teenager, Kusch became involved in the *bündisch* youth movement, which for a short time after 1933 maintained some independence until it was put under pressure by the Hitler Youth. Kusch's *bündisch* youth leader was sent to a concentration camp in 1937. After graduating from his *Gymnasium,* Kusch did the same as many Germans with his political background – national, liberal, and distant from the Nazis. He joined the Wehrmacht, pursuing a career as navy officer. The navy was known as the least Nazified part of the Wehrmacht, a haven for Kusch. Promoted to lieutenant in 1939 and first lieutenant in 1941, he then served as submarine commander. In early 1943, when the German navy had lost most of its effectiveness, he took over the command of U 154, a U-boat with an experienced crew. He got on well with his crew of around 50 men, although he did not bother hiding his fondness of the English language and his contempt for the Nazi regime. Kusch introduced himself to the crew by removing a photo of

Hitler from the wardrobe and announcing "We don't do idolatry here." Repeatedly, he called the Führer "insane" and told his men that only overthrowing Hitler could save Germany. But not even the two Nazis among his officer comrades, First Lieutenant Ulrich Abel and Lieutenant Kurt Druschel, took any action, or at least not for the first nine months. Nothing happened to Kusch, or so it seemed. Indeed, an "atmosphere of comradely solidarity" bridged the political gaps, as one of the sailors later testified, referring to one of the crucial elements of comradeship. Kusch's crew appreciated him as an excellent leader and a "born comrade," and Kusch felt safe with his comrades. Earlier, in a different ship, he had clashed with Nazi soldiers and was not denounced. At least in the navy, he once told an army comrade, the denunciation of a comrade was entirely out of the question. "Any superior," he said, "would throw a report denouncing an anti-Hitler comrade instantly into the bin, where it belongs, and bawl him out."

But blindly relying on comradeship was a fatal error, at least in Hitler's armed forces. For a long time, Abel and Druschel indeed dismissed Kusch's opinions as "private hogwash." But when Kusch refused to recommend his deputy Abel for a submarine command of his own, Abel, who was six years senior to Kusch and had waited a long time for this promotion, was deeply humiliated, felt betrayed (from his point of view, Kusch had violated his "comradely" obligation to protect his subordinate), and took revenge by denouncing him. In January 1944 Kusch was convicted of *Wehrkraftzersetzung* and sentenced to death; on May 12, 1944 he was executed.[59]

After the war, Kusch's case was reopened. His former comrades, peers, and men unanimously confirmed that Kusch had fallen victim to a personal rivalry, an exception from the rule of covering for anti-Nazis and anti-Nazi comments, even if these constituted *Wehrkraftzersetzung*. According to the recollection of the witnesses interviewed after 1945 and many other Wehrmacht veterans, comradeship, the small-unit cohesion, had provided a "haven of freedom" sheltering soldiers from getting caught by the Nazi spy and terror apparatus.[60] While the rhetoric of "freedom" may reflect memory's tendency to romanticize the past, there is no doubt that numerous dissenters survived Nazi terror thanks only to this comradely protection. Helmut Schmidt for instance, who after the war became a leader of the Social Democratic Party and West German Chancellor from 1974 to 1984, was conscripted in 1937, a year after he had been discharged from the Hitler Youth because of anti-Nazi patter. Still railing against the Nazi leaders as a soldier, he put himself at great risk. Once in 1944, bitching against Göring and the Nazi elite, Schmidt found himself accused of *Wehrkraftzersetzung*. But his superiors transferred him to a different unit and thus saved him from court-martial. They were "good and elderly comrades," as Schmidt acknowledged later.[61] A similar cover-up saved the life of Dirk Heinrichs, son of a liberal merchant family. Attending a training program for reserve officers in 1944, he lamented in an essay Germany's looming defeat, a capital crime in Nazi Germany. His sergeant gave him a dressing-down and told him he might just shoot himself – and yet allowed him to write a new essay.[62]

But not all soldiers were as lucky as Schmidt and Heinrichs. "Abhorrent denunciation proliferates amidst and among us," Hans Scholl found as early as February 1942. Scholl, a member of a Wehrmacht company of medical students in Munich, faced court-martial for mocking a Nazi professor. He got off lightly that time. The following year, however, he and his friends were arrested, convicted, and finally executed for having distributed the famous White Rose flyers.[63] The "heaven of freedom" that comradeship provided was entrenched in a quagmire of distrust and fear of denunciation, even in elitist circles, as also shown by the example of a small group of officers in the aristocratic Infantry Regiment 9. One of the officers was Richard von Weizsäcker, who would become a Federal President of West Germany in 1984. He and his comrades, raised in conservative militarist and nationalist but not National Socialist traditions, felt embarrassed about the Wehrmacht's entanglement in criminal warfare and yet caught in the oath to Hitler they had given. Occasionally they vented their anger even though they knew that if caught they were likely to be sentenced to death. Once, in a reserve position, "emotions ran high, and one of us, excited beyond reason, drew his gun and shot at a picture of Hitler hanging on the wall. It was a dangerous shot, straight from the sharpshooter's heart, requiring protection with a demonstration of solidarity. I therefore immediately aimed a second bullet at the picture, and the others followed suit. None could and none wanted to be excluded from the event and what might follow."[64]

Although there are no reliable statistics on Wehrmacht denouncers, the available data and rich anecdotal evidence confirm Scholl's diagnosis. The longer the war dragged on and the more doubts arose about Nazi Germany's final victory, the more soldiers gave way to their frustration about the regime, and the more soldiers, on the other hand, felt urged to prove their loyalty to the regime by denouncing the dissenters. From mid-1942 to mid-1944 alone, the number of documented cases of *Wehrkraftzersetzung* increased by more than 56 percent, from 4,080 in 1942–43 to 6,397 in 1943–44. In 1940, before the attack on the Soviet Union and under the impression of the sensational *Blitzkrieg* victories over France and other countries, only 926 people were court-martialed for this crime.[65]

What made Germans hand over their neighbors and comrades to the mercy of the Gestapo and a draconian court-martial? Inquiries into trial records and preliminary police investigations allow for some generalization of the tragic fate of Oskar Kusch. Political disagreements certainly mattered. Nazis denounced anti-Nazis. Personal strife, jealousies, mortifications, and suchlike played a crucial part, however. Under a political regime that valued denunciation as political loyalty, it was easy to use the articulation of political resentment as a means to settle old (or new) personal scores.[66] So it was in a special case of subversive comradeship that reminded the Reich Court Martial in 1944, after the conspiracy had been denounced, of the "most somber" chapter in the history of the German military, the naval mutinies in the fall of 1918. The affair took place in late summer 1943 in the rear of the Russian front line at Orel. Two soldiers of Sturmpanzerabteilung 216, or Storm Tank Unit 216, decided to launch a "Workers' and Soldiers' Council" modeled on those in 1918, and compiled a "black list" of those superiors whose insignia they wanted to tear off, just as the rebelling soldiers had done in 1918. After the revolution, announced one of conspirators, the CO of the company was to be deployed as cleaner and latrine constructor. For a while, the group was left alone to indulge in their subversive fantasies. In October, during one of their regular booze sessions, they enthused about a pamphlet of the Nationalkomitee Freies Deutschland (NKFD, National Committee for a Free Germany), the organization of German officers in Soviet captivity who had foresworn the Nazi state and supported Soviet anti-German propaganda.[67] The subversive *Sturmpanzer* soldiers constituted their cell as an NKFD branch, elected a president, and sang the famous German communist anthem "Brothers, to the sun, to freedom." As usual, the mood was rumbustious, and as the highlight of the evening, they set light to an official Führer photo. In the following days, the group attracted new members, and their nightly drinking sessions were occasionally joined by Russian and Ukrainian women. Führer photos were either burned or shot at, and doing so was considered a test of courage and a proof of solidarity with the group. However, the group admitted applicants only after they successfully passed a rigid hazing. One of those who didn't pass the test and was refused took revenge, and it was his denunciation that brought the revolutionists to court. Eleven were sentenced to death, and four more ended up in prison.[68]

A contemporary, born in 1926, the military historian Manfred Messerschmidt, served with the Wehrmacht at the end of the war, and stated in a 1987 assessment of the Wehrmacht's judicial system, that "the number of non-denouncers was still many times higher than the number of the denouncers."[69] While this assessment lacks direct statistical evidence and the total number of denunciations – some 30,000 to 40,000 – may seem dramatic, it must be considered in the light of the roughly 10 million soldiers who fought till the end, and in the light of the certainly smaller yet still huge number of soldiers who continued to believe in Hitler's quasi-supernatural power even at a time when Germany's looming defeat was obvious.

A plethora of anecdotal evidence from private letters and diaries indicates that most soldiers despised the July 1944 complot, the failed attempt by a group of conservative mostly aristocratic Germans around Colonel Stauffenberg to kill Hitler; in fact, the soldiers, like the regime, condemned it as hideous treason.[70] "A blaggard who doesn't join in now," stated a soldier in view of the destruction of the Army Group Center by the Red Army and only a few days before the failed July complot. When the news of the complot spread, he added: "No mercy for traitors!" and was echoed by another soldier who wrote: "No shortage of wimps here; I can only despise them."[71]

According to polls of German POWs in American captivity conducted by US sociologists, a strong majority of soldiers – about 60 percent or more – "trusted the Führer" up until January 1945, with few deviations, depending on the place and time of capture. Slightly fewer, but still up to 40 or 50 percent, believed at that time that "Germany is winning the war." These are surprisingly high rates, especially if one considers that the soldiers in American captivity were no longer subject to Nazi propaganda or jeopardized by the KSSVO and Gestapo terror (although some terror continued within the American camps, exercised by Nazi fanatics). In other words, we may assume that the rates were even higher, maybe much higher, among those millions of soldiers who kept fighting till the end. Only in March 1945 did these rates drop significantly. Then, only 31 percent still believed in Hitler, and only 11 percent believed in German victory.[72]

In part, belief in Hitler and Germany's final victory was fed by ongoing rumors about and hopes of the "miracle weapons" the regime was allegedly about to launch – an illusion, yet one that remained powerful till the end of the war, as is confirmed by private letters of soldiers.[73] These voices, however, also show the fragility and ambiguities of the soldiers' belief in Hitler, in the "wonder weapons," and in Germany's final victory. A private, deployed with the Wehrmacht's 210th Infantry Division in northern Norway, wrote on August 1, 1944 that he expected the end of the war to come soon, "within a few weeks," and then went on encouraging himself and the addressee of the letter to not give up anyway. For "if the Führer says that we have the weapons and the means to drive off the enemy out of our lands, and that we will eventually bear the palm, I know very well that we need unlimited trust and strong, unbending belief in our Führer to endure the difficult time we face now, and which has yielded only setbacks now for a long time," he said. But the rhetoric of steely belief in Hitler was soaked in too many "ifs" and "buts" to be taken at face value. It was a belief driven by desperation. There was no alternative to indulging in this belief. This is what Helmut Wißmann expressed in mid-July 1944, after the Soviet offensive Operation Bagration had destroyed the German Center front and in fact decided the war in the East: "Nothing can go wrong, otherwise everything would have been in vain," Wißmann driveled. And a few weeks later, Franz Wieschenberg echoed: "The entire situation is so knotty and strained that you just have no other option than blindly relying on the leadership."[74]

Seesawing between horrible fatalities during the retreats and blind belief in Hitler, the soldiers couldn't and yet had to suppress doubts about a cause and a war that was altogether lost and cruelly tainted. In this dilemma, the soldiers escaped into fatalism, euphemized as devotion to duty. "We stayed on duty... Trying to make sense of anything, was out of consideration," remembered a soldier later.[75] "Out there," said another soldier to his family before returning to the Eastern front, "you don't think much about what all that murder is good for. You are with your comrades and you do your duty, that's it."[76] If you let yourself be guided by duty alone, you renounced choices, agency, and responsibility, resigned yourself to an unknown fate, and went with the crowd. Soldiers learned to do this early on. "You are no longer the master of yourself," Wieschenberg noted as soon as autumn 1941. "You just do your job, compliantly and mindlessly... I surrender to lethargy and just don't care."[77] And Erich Kuby's father, a returning World War I veteran and a more dedicated soldier than his left-liberal son, advised the latter at about the same time to indulge in "the unrestricted couldn't-care-less attitude," or *Wurstigkeit*, as the German *Landser* called it. If one did so, Kuby's father said, "there is no longer anything remarkable about this war." What he wanted to say was that one no longer wondered what to do about the criminal war in which both father and son saw themselves as entrapped. One gave up on thoughts of individual responsibility and followed the crowd.[78] Grasping "the meanness all around us of dying and having to kill," wrote Willy Reese sarcastically in 1944, "I still got over things very quickly," by adopting a couldn't-care-less attitude. As he put it: "Individual details went under in a vast ocean of apathy and never took shape."[79]

In the last two to three years of the war, *Wurstigkeit* replaced the euphoria the soldiers had shared at the beginning of Operation Barbarossa. "You get more and more apathetic, you live for the moment, and you no

longer care how all this may end," said Wißmann in 1944, trying to cope
with the looming disaster.[80] In a state of *Wurstigkeit*, a soldier resigned
himself to whatever his fate might bring of terror, murder, and death,
and abandoned himself to the "camaraderie" of cynics, as Heinrich Böll
wrote after the war, looking back on his experiences among comrades in
war. Cynicism, he explained, meant "to enjoy everything ruthlessly, and
to be driven by destiny: from the bathroom in a French cantonment to
the murderous reality of war as it was in Russia. Deflecting the pain from
oneself, and observing the pain of others in the untouched, business-like
way an undertaker does, who isn't a murderer, after all."[81] "I couldn't
care less" was a phrase that made it easier to storm into battle and to
surrender to shellfire. It also made it easier to indulge in debauchery,
wild togetherness, and terror inflicted on enemy civilians.[82]

Sarcastic though Böll's postwar assessment sounds, it yet radiates the
empathy with his fellow soldiers he developed from late 1942 when the
Sixth Army's catastrophe in Stalingrad turned the megalomaniac utopias
into angst-ridden dystopias and the uselessness of all their sacrifices
began to dawn on the soldiers. Generalizing from his own suffering in
the army, Böll understood that his fellow soldiers' cynicism was a result
of their mourning for the selves that the war had not allowed them to be.
This sense of loss increased the longer the war went on and the bleaker
its eventual outcome appeared. Once browsing a pile of soldiers' IDs and
CVs, he found himself "amazed" at seeing the civilians – some photos
showed them with wife and children – behind the "grey faces" of the
soldiers he knew only as cynics and brasses. Their "own real lives" – as
civilians – as Böll thought, "in truth was what they were longing for,"
even if they tried to hide this desire behind a façade of brassiness. "They
are all so terribly sad and depressed," he said, and "the war assumes
a grey and hopeless shape . . . hard and bitter it is, and we are infinitely
forlorn." Sensing a parallel between his own forlornness in the army and
the fate of the millions of his fellow soldiers, he was able to identify
himself as part of the comradely We, though he was certainly far away
from glorifying comradeship as the virtue of enforced all-male society. In
October 1943, he was thrown into a new unit and initially lamented the
bother of adjusting to a group of soldiers who had already known each
other a long time. However, he found after only a few days "a really nice
platoon leader, an NCO, and also nice comrades, really," as he wrote
to his family in Cologne.[83] It was – and this is the point – only the suffering, depressed, and cynical community of soldiers facing the looming
defeat that allowed Böll, the epitome of an individualistic anti-soldier,
to join in, at least a bit. In other words, the soldiers may, at the end of
war, have been more concerned than before about their selves and the

destruction of them, and yet their social cohesion, whether or not it was called comradeship, lasted and even deepened.

In the state of *Wurstigkeit*, the soldier conformed. He demonstrated comradeship – a type of comradeship, however, that rested on what political scientists have called the spiral of silence, and social psychologists have designated "pluralistic ignorance." This occurs when a person, in spite of privately rejecting a norm, abides to it publicly because they assume that most others support it, and that to reject it would lead to isolation.[84] Soldiers may have wondered about how to save a remnant of their Selves from the maelstrom of conformity, duty, and apathy. Heinrich Böll certainly did, and so did Private Franz-Josef Langer, an artist in civilian life, who served from 1937 to the end of war and tried always to save "a tail of humanity," being unwilling, he said as late as 1944, "just to give in as most of those around here do." And yet he knew that he had to keep up appearances. Soldiers like him learned to hide their fantasies about eventually being "liberated" from the army to be themselves. They wore the mask of conformity.[85] They did what everyone else did – joining in. As one soldier said: "It is as if you build a husk around your self," and yet within that husk "you are absorbed by the crowd around you; you are only a piece of a relentless entity that soaks you up and foists its shape on you. You become barbarous and numb. You are no longer yourself."[86] Eventually, it was not the masked self but the mask that determined the choices the soldiers made, and the actions they performed, whether they laughed at sexist jokes or terrorized enemy civilians.

Whether worn as a mask or fully internalized, the culture of conforming gained momentum the more the disaster loomed, tied into the Germans' sense of belonging to the *Volksgemeinschaft*, no longer one of utopian megalomania but of dystopian desperation, abysmal fear, and stirring qualms. As early as summer 1941, somber ideas about "what would happen if we ended up as the defeated ones" made soldiers occasionally "shudder," as Fritz Farnbacher noted in his diary in September 1941, considering how the Germans treated the enemy population.[87] Another soldier witnessed the SS massacres of 5,000 Jews in Paneriai, Lithuania in July 1941, together with his comrades, and thought: "May God grant us victory because if they get their revenge, we're in for a hard time."[88] But as long as the Wehrmacht continued to advance or at least to hold the enormous territories conquered in 1941 and 1942, these qualms could be kept under control; the soldiers were used to looking the other way.[89] A group of comrades decided this in March 1942. One of them, Lieutenant Eugen Altrogge, reported in a letter to his family:

Last night, we got together and talked about things that you have to feel ashamed of, as a German. What you learn here, what they do with the "chosen people." This is not just antisemitism, this is inhumanity as you would not have thought possible in the twentieth century, the "enlightened modern time." How that will be avenged at some point! You might just run mad and despair of the meaning of this war, hearing such things . . . But what we can do? We have to shut up and stay on duty."[90]

These qualms were never entirely suppressed, however, and they began fueling angst and fear when doubts increased about the *Endsieg*, the final victory. The Nazi regime, and the Wehrmacht, had set up a cult of secrecy surrounding the murder of the Jews and of non-Jewish civilians: talking openly about it, or taking photos at the murder sites, was prohibited; sometimes soldiers were ordered to stay away from the Einsatzgruppen actions; and the two Criminal Orders, for instance, were explicitly classified. But the secret was an open one. The SS operated closely behind and often within sight of the Wehrmacht's front line, and rumors about large-scale massacres such as the one in Babi Yar "spread like wildfire."[91] The Commissar Order was carried out by the Wehrmacht itself and practiced in most units. And even those soldiers who only joined the army later, in 1942 or 1943, and were sent to the East, could barely avoid learning about what had been done shortly, or even a long time, before. Private Paul Riedel returned to his unit in Kharkiv in the Ukraine in May 1942 after being hospitalized in Germany for some time. His comrades' accounts of German misdeeds were abhorrent. "Thirty thousand Jews have been murdered in Kharkiv," he was told. "The bullets splash through the heads of children, mothers are yelling and – fall silent. They collapse on hills of corpses, blood steams . . . and the murderers wade through blood . . . Now, there are no more Jews in Kharkiv. In Kiev they have murdered seventy thousand; in all towns they have been exterminated . . . There were twenty thousand Russian POWs in the prison at Kharkiv. A few hundred are still alive."[92]

As the secretly recorded confidential conversations between German soldiers in American and British captivity suggest, these soldiers did not talk often about the Holocaust or other German mass crimes. Only in 0.2 percent of these conversations is the Holocaust touched upon. "But the absolute numbers are of limited relevance," Sönke Neitzel and Harald Welzer rightly state in their analysis of these records. It is not how often but how they talked about German crimes against humanity that is relevant. The result is unambiguous: "The soldiers' conversations make it clear that practically all Germans knew or suspected that Jews were being murdered en masse . . . Undoubtedly, not everyone had knowledge of everything. Nonetheless, the surveillance protocols are full of Holocaust specifics, from the asphyxiation of Jews using the exhaust fumes of motorized vehicles to the exhumation and burning of bodies as part of 'Action 1005' in which Jewish concentration camp inmates were forced to dig up bodies and burn them. Moreover, soldiers traded rumors so furiously that we must assume nearly all of them knew that massive numbers of Jews were being murdered."[93]

Evidence from private letters and diaries corroborates these findings. A striking example are the private writings of Captain Wilm Hosenfeld, who served with the army of occupation in Poland, in charge of sport and training programs for German soldiers in Warsaw. A member of the NSDAP and the SA, and fascinated by Hitler before the war, he was deeply ashamed of the German annihilation programs and put his knowledge on record. As early as March 1941, he anticipated that "after Hitler, there will no longer be a single Jew in Europe." In spring 1942, he learned about the gas chambers in Auschwitz; "notwithstanding all secrecy," he noted, such knowledge was widespread. Two years later, "the extermination of a couple of millions Jews" was simply a matter of fact.[94]

The soldiers did not keep their knowledge to themselves. They shared it with their friends and relatives at home. From the beginning of Operation Barbarossa in summer 1941, Germans at home learned about the murder of the Jews in the Soviet Union through soldiers' letters, oral accounts, gossip, and rumor.[95] As Neitzel and Welzer put it, the "spreading of rumors is an effective means of communication, especially when the subject matter is inhuman, secrecy is supposed to be maintained, and information is restricted."[96] The aura of secrecy did not contain the knowledge of the mass crimes but rather propelled its circulation. In spring 1942, Hilde Wieschenberg learned about them from photos passed around by friends in Düsseldorf. She was "horrified" at the "piles of corpses" in the photos, as she wrote to her husband in Russia, wanting to know more, not least about his own role in these actions. He waved her off. "Such things should not be sent home. Only rear units are doing this," he wrote, no longer remembering that he had earlier informed his wife about the murder of the Jews in the Soviet Union, without hiding his approval.[97]

Hilde was no exception. In January 1942 during a vacation in Austria, a staff judge from Berlin mentioned to a waitress in a coffee shop that the Jews in Germany would be notified of their deportation and would then be shipped to Poland where their graves were already prepared. Asked not to talk about such things, he said, "this is an open secret, any intelligent person knows about it, only the fools don't."[98] Probably few Germans knew about the entire monstrous dimensions of the death machinery of Auschwitz or Majdanek. But some did know, and some worked it out. Wilm Hosenfeld is one example. Another is Victor Klemperer, a German Jewish literature professor, who lost his tenure in 1935 and survived the Holocaust in his hometown Dresden only by chance and thanks to his marriage to an "Aryan" woman. On October 24, 1944 he noted in his diary that "six to seven million Jews . . . have been slaughtered (more exactly: shot and gassed)." How would he have known? It was the "reports of Aryans" that provided the intelligence, as his diary reveals. In fact, it states that this news "has now been reported too frequently and by too many consistent Aryan sources for it to be a legend." What happened at "Auschwitz" was, in 1944, no longer unknown to Klemperer either.[99]

How did the soldiers deal with this knowledge? As said before, most of them had been drafted into the Wehrmacht from rather diverse ideological and social milieus. Not all of these cultural imprints fell victim to Nazification. Private Stefan Hampel, born in 1918, made a radical decision after witnessing in May 1942 the mass execution of 2,000 Jews close to his Polish hometown where he happened to be spending some time on leave. Realizing that his German uniform made him complicit, he deserted and joined the Polish-Lithuanian underground movement.[100] Wilm Hosenfeld too was shocked by the "blood-guilt we have saddled ourselves with" and knew that his uniform, indeed his German citizenship, made him complicit in the murder of the Jews and Poles. Unlike Hampel, he kept his uniform on and used his position to rescue Jewish and non-Jewish Poles, including the Jewish pianist Władysław Szpilman, from Nazi terror.[101]

Private Paul Kreissler, who would lose both of his legs in action in July 1944, had been "ashamed" of being a "German soldier" from early on when he first learned, in Galicia in May 1941, about the "inhuman" treatment of Jewish forced laborers, and even more when, later on, he saw his comrades mistreating, abusing, and murdering Jews and "liquidating" emaciated Russian POWs. Paul resorted to symbolic gestures to fight his guilt feelings. In Galicia he visited Jewish families in their humble homes, exchanging food with them, and engaging in "many interesting conversations." But there he left it. "Of course, we have got to be very careful to not be caught. For German soldiers must not get in touch with the local people." A few months later in the Ukraine, he too learned about the hatred of gentile Ukrainians against Jews, and the acts of vengeance the Jews fell victim to, but unlike many other German soldiers, he stayed, at least in his diary, clear of German triumphalism. On Christmas Eve 1942 in the Caucasus, there were no longer any Jews but many Russian forced Wehrmacht aides with his unit. They too got a Christmas gift – and "are delighted as little children. They are now our comrades too," Paul noted. And there he left it. Nothing more could be done. He wondered about the authorities' "right to send people into such an insane war" but felt unable to do much about it and resorted to regretting the "deep tragedy" of it all. "We keep still and stand by helplessly... The bitter law of war wants it that way."[102]

Occasionally, the soldiers' pangs of conscience indeed allowed for symbolic gestures of peace and respect for their captured, abused, and exploited enemies in the East. Thus did Private Franz-Josef Langer, the artist, enthused neither about the war nor about Nazism, with his closer comrades at the Easter feast of 1943 in the East: They laid on an "Easter table with spirits, cake and the like" for the "Russians that are employed with us." The Russians, of course, were POWs and enforced laborers. Gestures such as this revitalized the idea of comradeship with the enemy that the Nazi war of annihilation so deliberately questioned. The idea never disappeared entirely, as these examples show. In fact, it may even have been reinforced at the end of the war amidst the ongoing destruction. Both Paul Kreissler's and Langer's reports date from a time when soldiers like these two no longer really counted on a victorious end to the war. After Stalingrad, the mind-set of the German soldiers in the East changed, as Erich Kuby noted sarcastically in November 1943. "I've gotta laugh when I recall the summer of 1941. Then they all pretended they'd rather sleep on a dunghill than under one roof with the Russians. Now they treat the Russians as dear household aides," and if they are female, "they can't get close enough... Facing defeat, they even give up on racism. Losing the complete equipment of a division in Kharkiv makes them a little human."[103]

Kuby, of course, was not unaware that the opposite consequence of the retreat – Germans becoming "even more brutish" – was at least as strong a reality. He understood well that this new friendliness toward the Russians served first and foremost to fight German soldiers' qualms about their own or their comrades' misdeeds and the fears about what those very same Russians would do to them once they came out on top. The truth was that soldiers such as Hampel or Jew-rescuers like Hosenfeld, whom Yad Vashem eventually recognized as Righteous Among the Nations, were extremely rare in Hitler's army.[104] And they acted in isolation. Afraid of being denounced, they could not rely on even a small network of solidarity. Comradeship, or any other type of solidarity, in the Wehrmacht did not support actions on behalf of the Jews, but those against them.

Certainly many more soldiers deserted at some point. They were isolated just as the Jew-rescuers were; no reliable figures exist but at

least about 35,000 to 40,000 were court-martialed; the actual figure
was maybe ten times higher, but the bulk of desertions occurred only
during the last year, especially the last half year, of the war. At that
time many soldiers tried somehow to get lost, without obviously deserting. This was much easier once the Wehrmacht was fighting only on
German homelands, rather than thousands of miles away from home.
Detailed inquiries into the motives of Wehrmacht deserters, however,
have consistently shown that they were driven less by indignation about
German crimes against enemy civilians or soldiers than by embarrassment about their own suffering from soldiering, not least the enforced
communal life, which did not allow them to live the desired life of a
"wild and fanatic individualist," as Heinrich Böll put it in a letter to
his fiancée.[105] They simply wanted to get back to their families, to their
wives or girlfriends; they wanted to return to civilian life, especially when
they felt continuously harassed by superiors and at the same time isolated from, or annoyed by, their peers – their comrades. Although not
always entirely immune to the mystique of comradeship, they experienced the virtue of male bonding primarily as restraint, as the historian
Magnus Koch has shown.[106] Alfred Andersch, after 1945 like Böll a figurehead of the antimilitaristic literary scene, deserted in 1944 because
he was, he said retrospectively, "sick and tired" of his comrades and of
comradeship.[107]

Even the increasing numbers of deserters at the end of the war leave no
doubt about what defined normality in the Wehrmacht: the comrades,
those who joined in and stuck it out, whether enthusiastically or in a spirit
of depression and desperation. It is impossible to estimate the number
of those soldiers who, like Paul Kreissler, kept some inner distance from
Nazism and the Nazi war but joined in anyway, even if only by wearing
a mask. A whole diversity of anecdotal evidence, however, warns against
overrating their significance. What kept the army together, even when
the bonds of comradeship loosened, was the racial foe. Antisemitism,
whether it manifested itself as murderous hatred of Jews or mere indifference toward their annihilation, was one of the most powerful ideologies
fueling the German army's consensus machinery and securing its cohesion, as is clearly suggested by the soldiers' conversations in the POW
camps.[108] There were a few soldiers who articulated shame and regrets
when talking about the plight of the Jews, and contempt for the way they
were treated. But often the regrets were tactically motivated, not morally.
One Colonel Erwin Jösting, for instance, related in April 1945: "I quite
agree that the Jews had to be turned out, that was obvious, but the manner in which it was done was absolutely wrong, and the present hatred is
the result. My father-in-law, who certainly couldn't stand Jews," Jösting

added, almost apologizing to his interlocutor for articulating concerns about the persecution of the Jews,

said: "That will not go unpunished, say what you like!" I'd be the first to agree to getting rid of the Jews... But why massacre them? That can be done after the war, when we can say "We have the power, we have the might; we have won the war; we can afford it!" But now! Look at the British government – who are they? The Jews. Who governs America? The Jews. While Bolshevism is Judaism in excelsis.[109]

It was the fear of revenge that gave German soldiers doubts about murdering the Jews. In fact, Nazi propaganda stirred up this fear from early on. "If we lose the war, you will be annihilated," Hermann Göring threatened his German audience in a public speech, and he continued: "The Jew is behind everything, and it is he who has declared a fight to the death, and to ruin, against us." Germans should not feel safe from Jewish revenge just for having kept some distance from the Nazis. If Germany lost the war, no German should think he might say afterwards: "'I always have been a good democrat against these mean Nazis.'" The Jews will take revenge on all Germans, Göring claimed, "whether democrat, plutocrat, Social Democrat or communist doesn't matter."[110]

The propaganda confirmed what many soldiers had thought before. In fact, fear of revenge by Jews (or Soviet communists or American capitalists) was felt by different types of soldier and, in a way, united them: those who felt pangs of conscience as well as the stubborn antisemites. The Allied air bombardments of German cities and, in 1944, rumors about Ilya Ehrenburg's call for the murder of German men and the rape of German women by the Soviet Army confirmed the stereotypes of the latter and the qualms of the former. And whether hatred, shame, or qualms dominated the soldiers' emotions, they were united by increasingly apocalyptic visions of Germany's fate. If we don't win the war, stated a private as early as May 1942 (not leaving in any doubt his admiration for the "great job" the SS had done) "we would be badly off. This foreign Jewish rabble would take horrible revenge on our people, given the fact that here hundreds of thousands of Jews have been executed in order to eventually establish calm and peace in the world."[111] And Helmut Wißmann echoed in early 1943: "Either we lose totally or we win. If these beasts savage Germany and I can't be with you... I am horrified at that very idea."[112] In the same fashion even Hosenfeld stated a few weeks later: "We all know, that there is no other choice for us than fighting... to ban the horrible threat from the East."[113] The Germans – the soldiers in particular – knew that they had entangled themselves, or had been entangled, in a huge crime of hitherto unthinkable dimensions, and whether they found it abominable or warrantable, they knew that they – the entire people, not only individuals – would be held responsible for it.

When it comes to illuminating the complex reasons for the Wehrmacht's fighting morale in the last two years of the war, the fear of revenge can barely be overestimated. Horrified by what would happen to themselves and to their loved ones if "these beasts savage Germany," keeping fighting seemed to be the only choice the soldiers had left. They would die either way, by fighting or by capitulating, on the battlefield or in captivity. Stressing the soldiers' fear of revenge is not a new idea in Wehrmacht studies. Shils and Janowitz in their 1948 attempt to explain "why the German army in World War II fought so stubbornly to the end" understood that the soldiers "projected on the Russians . . . the guilt feelings generated by the ruthless brutality of the Germans in Russia during the occupation period."[114] In compliance with the public opinion of their time, however, Shils and Janowitz subsumed the crimes against the Jews (the terms Holocaust and genocide were of course not yet in common use) under war crimes or "crimes against humanity," as the Nuremberg judgments put it at that time, and just as the Nuremberg tribunal declared only the SS, the Gestapo, and the SD as inherently criminal organizations but acquitted the Wehrmacht as an organization, Shils and Janowitz exonerated the mass of ordinary soldiers from "crimes against humanity" (but not from war crimes). The point here is not so much the obvious gap between SS and Wehrmacht but rather the fact that the soldiers of the latter may have *felt* even more guilty than the first. Unlike the thoroughly Nazified SS and police, traditional morals and ideals of warfare, based on respect of and mercy toward civilians and POWs, remained strong in the Wehrmacht and subsequently propelled remorse and pangs of conscience much more than among Himmler's troops. To use the juxtaposition of primary and secondary group identities as suggested by Shils and Janowitz, the fear of revenge is part of the latter. Yet the various facets of face-to-face comradeship, whether materializing as tender sociability and humane solidarity or as cold-blooded and morally indifferent brotherhood in crime, worked toward the same end. The soldiers kept fighting because they feared for their entire fatherland, and at the same time they saw no other choice than sticking to their comrades whatever these did.

"Fleeing – the sauve-qui-peut (every man for himself) – isolates men, the attack unites them," wrote Hannah Arendt in 1970. Violent action, she found, makes "individualism" disappear. A "kind of group coherence" emerges "which is more intensely felt and proves to be a much stronger, though less lasting, bond than all varieties of friendship, civil or private."[115] At the end of the Nazi war, Wehrmacht veteran Paul Kreissler, who, abandoned by comrades, lost both of his legs in action, would certainly have endorsed the first part of Arendt's statement, and many soldiers would have concurred, even if they had been luckier and somehow survived without major injuries. By contrast, Paul's only slightly younger brother Kurt remained enthusiastic about the "intensely felt" bond generated by even minor attacks amid the retreat, escape, and disastrous defeat through the end of the war. While the number of soldiers who belonged to the first group increased during the last months of war, the vast majority of them stuck it out till the end. Why? Why did the soldiers fight on? Obviously, not all did so for the same reason. Soldiers like Heinrich Böll or Erich Kuby would have dropped out as soon as possible if they had not been forced to stay with the army. The experience of social cohesion, whether caused by attack or by flight, did not appeal to them; their goal as soldiers was to save as much as possible of their physical, emotional, and moral identities as civilians, and to return to their civilian lives as soon as possible. No statistical data exist to establish the number of these or other types of soldier. But an entire range of subjective evidence – the soldiers' private letters, diaries, memories, and other private voices – warns us not to overestimate the impact of the Reich's comprehensive apparatus of coercion as an engine of fighting morale, even if the number of deserting, lingering, and shirking soldiers increased dramatically at the end of war and may have reached a mid-six-figure number – some 2 or 3 percent of all Wehrmacht soldiers.[116] In comparison, about 4 million out of 35 million Red Army soldiers, i.e. 11 percent, were charged with desertion or other forms of shunning military service, notwithstanding much more brutal coercion and draconian court-martial.[117] And an unknown dark figure would have to be added to the 4 million in order to compare it properly to the Wehrmacht deserters.

Coercion does not explain why so many German soldiers stuck it out and stayed with their comrades till the end. Certainly not all did so as wholeheartedly as Kurt Kreissler or Werner Gross, who eagerly merged their individual selves into a real or imagined group of comrades. Probably most of the soldiers oscillated between euphoria and reluctance. Soldiers like Franz Wieschenberg and Helmut Wißmann switched back and forth between soldierly and civilian selves, always trying, but never succeeding, to reconcile the two extremes. While both extreme groups, the deliberate "anti-soldiers" and the dedicated, quasi-"born" soldiers, represented significant minorities, the bulk of the 17 million Wehrmacht soldiers who were drafted (or of the more than 10 million that survived the war) belonged to the ambiguous middle group. They kept fighting, so this study suggests, because they were caught in a net of emotional inducements, moral motives, ideological dispositions, and practical interests that seemed to leave no other option. They wanted to survive the war and return to their civilian lives, although not as deserters or cowards; instead they wanted to serve their country, as soldiers did in other countries and in other wars as well. At the same time, they believed in the Nazi vision of a grand *Volksgemeinschaft* – a German nation that would rule over Europe, led by the charismatic, quasi-supernatural Führer. Not all of them supported the Nazi genocidal project unambiguously; many had qualms, some were ashamed of the murder of civilians and POWs from the beginning of the war in the East or acquired these qualms when the Nazi utopia merged into the dystopia of a German nation being held responsible for its mass crimes and haunted by the vengeance of its enemies. While it is impossible to quantify the diversity of opinions and attitudes represented in the army, letters and diaries show that Germans from all social and cultural milieus shared some sort of antisemitism and anti-communism. These ideological dispositions allowed them first to approve of the genocidal project, be it by looking the other way, by remaining silent, or by other ways of conforming; and later, when the ideologies of hatred merged into obsessions of fear, they pressured the soldiers to persevere till the bitter end.

Inquiring into the Wehrmacht's combat cohesion from 1943 on and listening to German POW war stories, the American sociologists Shils and Janowitz replaced the German mythical term *Kameradschaft* with the analytical concept of the primary group. This way, they sacrificed the German word's semantic polyvalence. While the concept of primary group reduces military cohesion to the soldiers' actual social interaction, the concept of comradeship draws attention to the conditioning of this action through "social knowledge," through collective myths, ideas, and fantasies established long before the military socialization of the Wehrmacht soldiers started. It was continually reworked.[118] This appropriation needs to be understood as a multi-layered learning process that intertwined doing, feeling, and thinking. Conceived of as a system of concentric circles of different identities – from the small group to the army to the nation – comradeship enabled the soldiers to reduce the complexity of the destruction the soldiers produced, encountered, and apprehended. As understood by Germans in the twentieth century, comradeship belies the juxtaposition of primary and secondary group identities and suggests considering them as a unity. In the

Wehrmacht, comradeship denoted dyadic friendships as well as the soldiers' loyalty to larger face-to-face units, such as the company, and even
larger, imagined units such as the division, the entire army, the Nazi
Volksgemeinschaft or the German fatherland, and not least the idealized
community of fallen soldiers. When making sense of their role in the
war, individual soldiers chose between, or combined, any of these vari-
ants. While the loyalty of the bulk of the soldiers to close buddies or
face-to-face units never expired entirely, the fear of revenge by the enemies – a secondary symbol in Shils and Janowitz's language – dominated
fighting morale as war drew to a close. The more the final defeat and
disaster loomed, the more comradeship changed its face. No longer did
the euphoria about male solidarity prevail. Instead, a somber community
emerged, tied together by a dire fate that left no choice but escaping into
the cynicism of fatalism and moral apathy, the renunciation of individual
responsibility, a couldn't-care-less attitude, or *Wurstigkeit* in the *Landser*
language. This fatalism became most powerful only during the war, but
it had been a core of the concept of comradeship before. The myth of
comradeship, popularized during the interwar period by the veterans'
movement and popular culture, and later by Nazi propaganda, praised
as virtue the absolution of the self by collective unities, especially the
community of soldiers in war.

The primary group theory juxtaposed two allegedly opposite types of
collective identity: small face-to-face communities and large, anonymous
social formations like the army, and especially the nation or the fatherland. The theory proposes that the soldiers' fighting morale depended
on the functioning of the first type of identity, and much less so of
the latter type, the secondary groups. But instead of juxtaposing primary and secondary groups, one has to unravel their intertwined relationships and examine how different types and layers of social bonding
and social identity enforce, replace, or blockade each other, and one
must assess the respective functional, cultural, and emotional contexts
of that bonding. In order to propel fighting morale, the primary group
needs to be directed by secondary symbols, as Edward Shils conceded
in 1950, reviewing Samuel Stouffer's ambitious "GI Survey" of 1949.[119]
When asked, "What was most important to you in making you want
to keep going and do as well as you could?" only 5 percent of the
enlisted men and 3 percent of the officers surveyed prioritized "idealistic reasons," "patriotism," the desire to protect their own country,
or fighting for a "better world." These responses grounded the World
War II sociologists' praise of the primary group as the crucial factor for
American, and by extension German, soldiers' fighting morale – and

their downgrading of both patriotism and enemy stereotypes. But this conclusion was premature, as this very same survey indicated. Only 14 percent of the enlisted men referred to "solidarity with the group" when asked what made them "keep going." Many more, 39 percent, of the enlisted men simply thought of "ending the task" and "getting the war over," another 10 percent mentioned "thoughts of home and loved ones," and a few more minorities reasoned in similar pragmatic ways.[120]

The problem with this survey was that it forced the interviewees to isolate quite vague and overlapping motives, and that it captured subjective attitudes of returning soldiers, not of fighting soldiers. While the American soldiers, at least those fighting in Europe, may have been relatively safe from blatant enemy stereotypes and aggressive patriotism (both being much more common among soldiers fighting in the Pacific theater), they yet adhered to what has been named "tacit patriotism."[121] A survey conducted in 1942 even suggested that 65 percent of the soldiers wanted to "fight until we can guarantee democratic liberties to all people in the world."[122]

The truth was that motivations and goals such as these did not work separately but in relation to each other. The "soldiers who thought first of getting the job done must," Shils explained in 1950, "have accepted the legitimacy for the 'job'"; "their identification with the United States" must have "made for an acceptance of specific commands of their officers"; and those 39 percent who wanted to be finished with the task "might have been reluctant if they had not been subject to the pressure of their comrades who, more or less hiding the same belief, added the autonomous weight of their approval and affection for those who conformed and disapproval for those who were deviant."[123] In fact, an even broader range of social pressures was at work when it came to making the soldiers fight, including not only the comrades of his military unit but also neighbors, friends, and relatives at home, all of them working toward the same end, namely generating the fear of being shamed as a coward.[124]

In order to gain cohesive power, to establish trust, affection, and esteem, to guarantee loyalty and solidarity, primary groups need significant time to develop, preferably starting with the training period. Or so assumed their first students in the 1940s and many successors. They praised the German replacement system for meeting this goal and criticized the American equivalent for failing to meet it. But the social life of an army in war does not depend only on the stability and longevity of relationships. It can also draw fighting power from the opposite, from the destruction and contingency of these relationships. Relationships of soldiers in war are not only "less lasting" than civilian bonds, as Arendt put it. They also need less time to come into being. Social life, especially in the Wehrmacht, was, paradoxically, nourished by social disruption, be it through the death of comrades or one's own transferral or other blows of fate, and by the never-ending intermixing and rearrangement of social groups. Soldierly solidarity may have grown over time, but it also grew ad hoc in battle, or shortly before, and often it was the result, not the prerequisite, of shared combat experiences.

This is not an entirely new insight, and it is certainly not limited to the Wehrmacht. Popular accounts of the psychology of soldiers and the sociology of armies in war have long vaunted those "intense bonds." Glenn Gray, for instance, drew on his "own experience" in World War II as an American soldier, when he said in his 1959 book *The Warriors* that the "physical proximity of men can do no more than create minimal conditions of comradeship" and instead pointed to the actual battle experience: "As any commander knows, an hour or two of combat can do more to weld a unit together than months of individual training."[125] While there is no doubt that social bonds benefit from the length of shared experiences, in particular if these do not allow for much privacy, the intensity of these experiences needs to be taken into account as well. Echoing Gray's assessment, another former US serviceman, who fought with the 96th Infantry Division in Okinawa in 1945, states: "The time spent together is apparently not important, but the circumstances, the experiences shared, the conditions under which one meets an individual exert influences which quickly cement warm relationships."[126]

Inquiring into the US First Marine Division's operation against imperial Japan, the historian Craig Cameron has pointed to the limited value of the "old conventional theory" about primary groups for explaining "the dynamics that kept infantry troops together" through even the heaviest battles. Similarly to the Wehrmacht, the fighting power of this marine division relied for some time indeed on stable personal bonds, but in the later stages of the war the primary groups "crumbled under the unremitting pressures of costly attritional warfare" and the turnover in personnel. The division's fighting morale did not crumble, however. Instead, the division gained "greater resilience and destructive power than it had ever had before," because, as Cameron explains, the interpersonal model of group cohesion was backed and, in the course of the war, increasingly replaced by "an institutionally defined relationship based on the subordination of the Marine spirit to, or its identification with, the technocratic functionalism of the larger American war machine." This "sense of servicewide homogenization" was shared by veterans and

replacements alike and fostered by a variety of factors, including intensified indoctrination as well as an informal system of leadership that helped
neutralize formal authorities that had lost their credibility.[127]

"A sense of servicewide homogenization" is what united the Wehrmacht soldiers too, and it did so increasingly as the war went on. As in
the American army, this sense allowed for solidarity on the battlefields
even among soldiers who barely knew each other. Notwithstanding its
problematic juxtaposition of primary and secondary groups, the empirical insights of the primary group theory indicate that the social cohesion
of small units in the American army – and in many other armies – followed
a similar mechanism as in the German army: informal, "interpersonal
ties" in the face-to-face units "supported and sustained the individual
in stresses he would otherwise not have been able to withstand." At the
same time, these units "set and enforced group standards of behaviour"
including the sacrifice of one's life and limbs in battle. Comradeship
implied comfort and support of the individual, but it also exerted pressure on the individual to conform. As in the Wehrmacht, comradeship
in the American army offered support and solidarity preferentially to
those soldiers who themselves were ready and willing to provide such
support and solidarity.[128] Like the German *Landser*, the American GI
was expected to internalize the "fear of being thought less than a man
by one's buddies." The eyes of the comrades watched over the individual
soldier's performance from the barracks to the battlefield, enforcing the
iron law of comradeship – "death before dishonor" – and the apotheosis
of soldier-saving acts in battle as the ultimate expression of comradeship.[129] As in the German army, combat morale in the American army
depended largely on comradely attitudes and the competence of the platoon leaders, on NCOs and junior officers "who knew and cared about
the men, shared jokes and hardships with them."[130]

As was true for the German army, the social culture of the American
army drew – as one of its academically trained members stated in 1945 –
some momentum from an "ideal of virility" that was derived from "pread-
olescent gangs" and honored not only griping but brawling togetherness,
aggressive misogyny, profanity, "rowdyism," a cynical attitude to the rest
of world – the signatures of the male bond's strength and "independence"
from the civilian moralities at home.[131] As students of military cultures
and atrocities in war have observed many times, looking at the US and
other armies of the twentieth century, it was this culture that provided the
moral ground for assaults on civilians and POWs.[132] It did so in rather
different ways, contingent upon the secondary symbols and the institutional settings. In contrast to their German opponents, the American

soldiers, when indulging in comradeship, knew that they were backed and controlled by, and would return to, a functioning civilian society. This society honored the individual pursuit of happiness and individual responsibility, democratic procedures of political decision-making, and a moral order that demanded mercy for the weak, the defenseless, and civilians, notwithstanding civilian society's and the army's racist traditions and the crimes against civilians committed by the American World War II army, especially in the Pacific theater.[133]

Comradeship could motivate such crimes. A friend of marine Edgar Shepard – "we were attached to each other like no other people could ever be," said Shepard – had given his life to save him in fending off a Japanese attack. Shepard felt urged to fight the Japanese more than ever before. He wanted "to avenge the death of the best pal I ever had," as he wrote to his parents.[134] But while the desire for vengeance was no stranger in the American army, especially in the Pacific war, spurred by the national humiliation at Pearl Harbor, there was no army-wide propaganda that inflated the sense of vengeance into a genocidal war strategy as the Criminal Orders to the Wehrmacht did. Unlike the deeply mystified concept of comradeship that dominated the Wehrmacht, its American counterpart was designed functionally and remained tied into civilian values. American "combat soldiers did not view the war as a great crusade in which they must willingly sacrifice their own lives," the military historian John McManus states. "These citizen-soldiers brought a uniquely American business-like attitude to combat. Everything from cleaning out a stubborn machine-gun nest to going on patrol was a 'job' that had to be done."[135]

In both the German and the American armies, comradeship denoted tenderness. "The soldiers' macho environment precluded an open discussion of any essential need for mothering but the more honest and reflective soldier-authors admit to it," observed the military historian Peter Kindsvatter.[136] The setting that allowed them to articulate and satisfy this need was, similar to the Wehrmacht's social culture, not so much the unit at large but the individual friend among the comrades. In Kindsvatter's words: "The GIs considered themselves part of the squad and the platoon but beyond that had one or two buddies with whom they were especially close. These buddies shared a foxhole, as well as letters, hopes, fears, and interests." They "became therapists for one another," said the military sociologist Roger W. Little.[137] While Little, studying American soldiers in the Korean War, tended to juxtapose dyadic buddy relations and unit cohesion in order to challenge the classic primary group theory, more recent students have stressed that these complemented each other – just as among Wehrmacht soldiers, as we have seen.[138]

And yet they didn't do so in the same way. The devil is in the details, or, more precisely, the contexts – the secondary symbols that guided the workings of the primary group. Neither the German nor the American army fostered the stature of the individual but demanded that he subordinate his self to the tasks and the cohesion of the group. But whereas Wehrmacht recruiters were to enforce this subordination with no restriction, the authorities in America knew that they had to render at least some respect to the autonomy and individuality of each soldier and that military service had to "achieve a balance between personal accomplishments and the type of teamwork that many had experienced in playing various sports. This tension between independence and submission lingered throughout the war," as private writings of the soldiers, as well as a powerful debate during and after the war, stressed.[139] That the claim for individuality could be articulated so powerfully indicates the difference from Germany, where the opposite happened. Comradeship in the American army was not distinct from but instead equalled friendship; it was the leitmotif of military units that considered themselves as teams collaborating in order to get the job done – and then to move on and return home; it was understood as a tool for individual survival, not for collective death.[140] The German military discourse played off comradeship, the apotheosis of the enforced, dutiful, and fateful community, against friendship, the model of individualistic, voluntary, and ultimately civilian relationship. The soldiers may still have worked on reconciling them – just as their American opponents did. But the Americans did not have to fight, or escape from, a powerful discourse that pressured individuals to sacrifice themselves on the altar of a racially purified and ideologically united genocidal *Volksgemeinschaft*.

NOTES

1 Overmans, *Deutsche militärische Verluste*, p. 266.
2 Reddemann (ed.), *Zwischen Front und Heimat*, p. 599, Neuhaus, letter to Agnes, Aug. 29, 1942.
3 Wieschenberg, letters to Hilde, June 17, 1943, Nov. 19, 1943.
4 Paul Kreissler, War Diary (copy owned by author), June 22, 1942, July 6, 22, 1942. Paul was born on Jan. 4, 1912, Kurt on Dec. 27, 1912.
5 Reddemann (ed.), *Zwischen Front und Heimat*, pp. 351, 559, Neuhaus, letter to Agnes, Nov. 14, 1941, diary entry, July 21, 1942.
6 Kurt Kreissler, letters to his parents, Sept. 11, 1941, Oct. 23, 1941, Dec. 2, 1941, Jan. 27, 1942, March 2, 1942, July 10, 1943; Kreissler, *Im feldgrauen Rock*, part II, pp. 76–80.
7 Edgar Jones and Simon Wessely, *Shell Shock to PTSD: Military Psychiatry from 1900 to the Gulf War* (Hove: Psychology Press, 2005).

8 Wißmann, letter to Edith, Oct. 8, 1942.

9 Lehndorff (ed.), *Briefe des Peter Pfaff*, pp. 13, 41 (April 24, 1943, Aug. 1943).

10 Historisches Archiv des Erzbistums Köln, Best. Collegium Carolinum Bonn, Kriegsbriefe Zweiter Weltkrieg, J. B., Feb. 21, 1943; cf. ibid., A. K., letter to his theology teacher, July 31, 1942.

11 Wieschenberg, letters to Agnes, Feb. 17, 1942, March 10, 1942.

12 Kreissler, *Im feldgrauen Rock*, part II, pp. 96–99, 107–08, 149, 153–58; Kreissler, letters to his parents, Dec. 29, 1943, Jan. 14, 1944, Nov. 5, 1944.

13 Klepper, *Überwindung*, p. 131. Cf. Farnbacher, War Diary, Feb. 14, 1942.

14 Wolfgang Wiesen (ed.), *Es grüßt Euch alle, Bertold: Von Koblenz nach Stalingrad: Die Feldpostbriefe des Pioniers Bertold Paulus aus Kastel* (Nonnweiler-Otzenhausen: Burr, 1991), p. 87, letter to family from "Russia," Oct. 27, 1942.

15 McManus, *The Deadly Brotherhood*, p. 260; Kindsvatter, *American Soldiers*, pp. 11–14.

16 Adelbert Ottheinrich Rühle, *Die Feldpostbriefe des Adelbert Ottheinrich Rühle 1939–1942: Briefe und Gedichte eines Frühvollendeten*, ed. Brunhild Rühle (Heusenstamm: Orion-Heimreiter, 1979), p. 80.

17 Rass, *Menschenmaterial*, pp. 138–41, 148–49, 193–204, 404–06.

18 Hans Ziegler, *Im Glauben an den Endsieg: Kriegstagebuch und Briefe eines Gefallenen* (Freiburg: Poppen & Ortmann, 1995), pp. 23, 30–32, 35, 53, 60, 63, 69, 75–79, 85, 90, 108–09. For a similar case, see Martin Humburg, "'Ich glaube, dass meine Zeit bald gezählt sein dürfte': Feldpostbriefe am Ende des Krieges: Zwei Beispiele," in Jörg Hillmann and John Zimmermann (eds.), *Kriegsende 1945 in Deutschland* (Munich: Oldenbourg, 2002), pp. 239–62.

19 Wißmann, letter to Edith, Aug. 9, 1944.

20 Kreissler, letters to his parents, Feb. 2, 19, 1945; Kreissler, *Im feldgrauen Rock*, part II, pp. 159–64. Cf. Sager, *Jugend in der Mühle des Krieges*, p. 181, letter, Feb. 13, 1945.

21 Rühle, *Feldpostbriefe*, pp. 74–75; Farnbacher, War Diary, April 18, 25, 1942.

22 Bähr and Bähr (eds.), *Kriegsbriefe gefallener Studenten 1939–1945*, pp. 193–95, letter of Kurt Reuber, Dec. 25, 1942 (Stalingrad).

23 Paul Kreissler, War Diary, Sept. 17, 1942, Oct. 18, 21, 1942; see also Sept. 9, 30, 1942, Oct. 12, 16, 22, 30, 1942, Dec. 24, 1942, Jan. 17, 1943, May 10, 1943, Nov. 19. 1943, Dec. 24, 1943. For a similar case – a soldier who eventually deserted – see Magnus Koch, *Fahnenfluchten: Deserteure der Wehrmacht im Zweiten Weltkrieg – Lebenswege und Entscheidungen* (Paderborn: Schöningh, 2008), pp. 87–103.

24 Gertrud Meyer, *Nacht über Hamburg: Berichte und Dokumente 1933–1945* (Cologne: Röderberg, 1971), p. 205; Hans-Peter Klausch, *Die 999er: Von der Brigade "Z" zur Afrika-Division 999: Die Bewährungsbataillone und ihr Anteil am antifaschistischen Widerstand* (Cologne: Röderberg, 1986).

25 Letters of Kurt Napp to his wife Elly (copies owned by author), March 3, 1943, April 4, 25–26, 1943, May 2, 17, 1943, June 26, 30, 1943, July 6, 1943, Aug. 8, 1943. See also Stehmann, *Die Bitternis verschweigen wir*, p. 297, letter to his wife, July 25, 1944, on a "friend and comrade" with whom

he, Stehmann, a Protestant believer, could talk religion; and more generally, on the concept of brotherhood, instead of comradeship, between Jesuit soldiers, Antonia Leugers, *Jesuiten in Hitlers Wehrmacht: Kriegslegitimation und Kriegserfahrung* (Paderborn: Schöningh, 2009), pp. 43–46.

26 Lore Walb, *Ich, die Alte, ich die Junge: Konfrontation mit meinen Tagebüchern 1933–1945* (Berlin: Aufbau Verlag, 1997), p. 234, diary, Nov. 22, 1941.

27 Christel Beilmann, *Eine katholische Jugend in Gottes und dem Dritten Reich: Briefe, Berichte, Gedrucktes 1930–1945. Kommentare 1988/89* (Wuppertal: Peter Hammer, 1989), p. 154, July 25, 1944; cf. p. 135, letter to a military chaplain, Nov. 30, 1942. See also Humburg, *Das Gesicht des Krieges*, p. 229. For a more detailed analysis of female appropriations of the concept of comradeship, see Kühne, *Belonging and Genocide*, pp. 137–59.

28 Paul Kreissler, War Diary, Feb. 9–11, 1943.

29 Ibid., July 26–27, 1944.

30 Hartmann, *Operation Barbarossa*, p. 79.

31 Markus Eikel, "'Weil die Menschen fehlen': Die deutschen Zwangsarbeitsrekrutierungen und -deportationen in den besetzten Gebieten der Ukraine 1941–1944," *Zeitschrift für Geschichtswissenschaft*, 53 (2005), pp. 403–33.

32 The crimes of the Wehrmacht during its retreat from the Eastern territories have not been as thoroughly researched as the initial phase of Operation Barbarossa, but see Stephen G. Fritz, *Ostkrieg: Hitler's War of Extermination in the East* (Lexington: University Press of Kentucky, 2011); Robert M. Citino, *The Wehrmacht Retreats: Fighting a Lost War, 1943* (Lawrence: University Press of Kansas, 2012); Karl-Heinz Frieser (ed.), *Das Deutsche Reich und der Zweite Weltkrieg*, vol. VIII: *Die Ostfront 1943/44* (Stuttgart: DVA 2007); Pohl, *Die Herrschaft der Wehrmacht*, pp. 321–35; Dirk W. Oetting, *Verbrannte Erde: Kein Krieg wie im Westen: Wehrmacht und Sowjetarmee im Russlandkrieg 1941–1945* (Graz: Ares, 2011). Important case studies include Jürgen Kilian, "Wehrmacht, Partisanenkrieg, und Rückzugsverbrechen an der nördlichen Ostfront im Herbst und Winter 1943," *Vierteljahrshefte für Zeitgeschichte*, 61 (2013), 173–99; Rass, *Menschenmaterial*, pp. 348–402. On southern and western Europe, see Michael Geyer, "Civitella della Chiana on 29 June 1944: The Reconstruction of German 'Measure,'" in Heer and Naumann (eds.), *War of Extermination*, pp. 175–216; Gentile, *Wehrmacht und Waffen-SS*, pp. 80–403; Mark Mazower, *Inside Hitler's Greece: The Experience of Occupation, 1941–1944* (New Haven, CT: Yale University Press, 1993), pp. 155–261; Madelon de Keizer, *Razzia in Putten: Verbrechen der Wehrmacht in einem niederländischen Dorf* (Cologne: Dittrich, 2001); Lieb, *Konventioneller Krieg*, pp. 448–83.

33 Reese, *Stranger to Myself*, p. 98.

34 Willy Peter Reese, *Mir selber seltsam fremd: Die Unmenschlichkeit des Krieges: Russland 1941–44*, ed. Stefan Schmitz (Berlin: List, 2004), pp. 242–43. (Not in the English edition.)

35 Reddemann (ed.), *Zwischen Front und Heimat*, p. 431, letter of Neuhaus to Agnes, Feb. 28, 1942.

36 Reese, *A Stranger to Myself*, p. 135.

37 Letters of Werner Gross (pseudonym), July 28, 1942, Sept. 25, 1942, April 4, 1943, Landeshauptarchiv Koblenz, Best. 700,153, no. 286–291. Cf. Kühne, *Belonging and Genocide*, pp. 124–25.

38 Diary of Gerhard Modersen (pseudonym), 1935–1949 (copy owned by author), Jan. 29, 1943.

39 Ilse Schmidt, *Die Mitläuferin: Erinnerungen einer Wehrmachtsangehörigen* (Berlin: Aufbau, 1999), pp. 47–48. On compulsory collective bordello visits, see, for instance, Fetscher, *Neugier und Furcht*, p. 188. On Wehrmacht bordellos, see Insa Meinen, *Wehrmacht und Prostitution während des Zweiten Weltkriegs im besetzten Frankreich* (Bremen: Edition Temmen, 2002); and Birgit Beck, *Wehrmacht und sexuelle Gewalt: Sexualverbrechen vor deutschen Militärgerichten 1939–1945* (Paderborn: Schöningh, 2004), pp. 105–16.

40 For a general assessment, see Madeline Morris, "Rape, War, and Military Culture," *Duke Law Journal*, 45 (1996), 651–781.

41 Regina Mühlhäuser, "Between 'Racial Awareness' and Fantasies of Potency: Nazi Sexual Politics in the Occupied Territories of the Soviet Union, 1942–1945," in Dagmar Herzog (ed.), *Brutality and Desire: War and Sexuality in Europe's Twentieth Century* (Basingstoke: Palgrave Macmillan, 2009), pp. 197–220 (at 201); and with more detail in Mühlhäuser, *Eroberungen: Sexuelle Gewalttaten und intime Beziehungen deutscher Soldaten in der Sowjetunion 1941–1945* (Hamburger Edition, 2010). The authenticity of this story is not guaranteed (see Mühlhäuser, *Eroberungen*, p. 93), but Mühlhäuser's research as well as the previous studies of Wendy Jo Geertjejanssen, *Victims, Heroes, Survivors: Sexual Violence on the Eastern Front During World War II*, Ph.D. dissertation, University of Minnesota (2004), Beck, *Wehrmacht und sexuelle Gewalt*, pp. 236–41, and David Raub Snyder, *Sex Crimes Under the Wehrmacht* (Lincoln: University of Nebraska Press, 2007), pp. 190–205, leave no doubt of the Wehrmacht's sexual violence in the East. (In the West, different rules applied.) For an even more brutal case of collective rape, see Bernhard Chiari, *Alltag hinter der Front: Besatzung, Kollaboration und Widerstand in Weißrussland 1941–1942* (Düsseldorf: Droste, 1998), pp. 146–47.

42 Rass, *Menschenmaterial*, p. 269. See also Beorn, *Marching into Darkness*, pp. 164–73.

43 Hans Buchheim, "Command and Compliance," in Helmut Krausnick et al., *Anatomy of the SS-State* (New York: Walker, 1968), pp. 303–96, at 317 (Frank), 343–45 (Dietrich).

44 [Friedrich] von Rabenau, *Vom Sinn des Soldatentums: Die innere Kraft von Führung und Truppe* (Cologne: DuMont Schauberg, 1940), p. 7. Cf. Reibert, *Der Dienstunterricht im Reichsheer*, pp. 96–97.

45 Note that the English words comradeship and camaraderie may be used synonymously whereas the German equivalents, *Kameradschaft* and *Kameraderie*, denote opposing moralities.

46 Weniger, *Wehrmachtserziehung und Kriegserfahrung*, p. 122.

47 Heinrich Himmler, secret speech to the officer corps of a grenadier division, July 26, 1944, in Himmler, *Geheimreden*, p. 224.

48 Buchheim, "Command and Compliance," pp. 343–45.

49 Klepper, *Überwindung*, pp. 157, 132, diary entries, Aug. 22, 1941, Aug. 8, 1941.

50 Ibid., pp. 206, 213, diary entries, Sept. 20, 25, 1941; see also p. 160, Aug. 23, 1941.

51 Bryan Mark Rigg, *Hitler's Jewish Soldiers: The Untold Story of Nazi Racial Laws and Men of Jewish Descent in the German Military* (Lawrence: University Press of Kansas, 2002).

52 Manfred Messerschmidt, *Die Wehrmacht im NS-Staat: Zeit der Indoktrination* (Hamburg: R. v. Decker, 1969), pp. 361–90; and Messerschmidt, *Militärgeschichtliche Aspekte der Entwicklung des deutschen Nationalstaates* (Düsseldorf: Droste, 1988), pp. 127–50, 197–220. A nuanced assessment of the impact of the NSFO is provided by Kunz, *Wehrmacht und Niederlage*, pp. 240–48.

53 Götze (ed.), *Trübners Deutsches Wörterbuch*, p. 84.

54 Max Domarus, *Hitler: Speeches and Proclamations 1932–1945 and Commentary by a Contemporary: The Chronicle of a Dictatorship*, vol. IV (Wauconda: Bolchazy-Carducci, 1992), pp. 2681–82.

55 Judgment of the *Volksgerichtshof* (National Court) against Kurt Huber, April 28, 1943, Bundesarchiv Berlin, NJ 1704, vol. VII, fol. 132. I am grateful to Detlef Bald, Munich, for sharing this material with me.

56 Erich Schwinge, *Militärstrafgesetzbuch nebst Kriegssonderstrafrechtsverordnung*, 6th edn. (Berlin: Junker und Dünnhaupt, 1944), pp. 432–34. Cf. B. Leverenz, "Der Begriff der Öffentlichkeit in § 5 Abs. I Ziff. I KSSVO, I," *Zeitschrift für Wehrrecht*, 8 (1943–44), 399–41; and Gwinner, "Der Begriff der Öffentlichkeit in §5 Abs. I Ziff. I KSSVO, II," *Zeitschrift für Wehrrecht*, 8 (1943–44), 411–13; Messerschmidt, *Wehrmacht im NS-Staat*, pp. 377–78.

57 Robert Gellately, *Backing Hitler: Consent and Coercion in Nazi Germany* (Oxford University Press, 2001), p. 198.

58 Manfred Messerschmidt and Fritz Wüllner, *Die Wehrmachtjustiz im Dienste des Nationalsozialismus: Zerstörung einer Legende* (Baden-Baden: Nomos, 1987), pp. 132–68; Bernward Dörner, "'Der Krieg ist verloren!': 'Wehrkraftzersetzung' und Denunziation in der Truppe," in Norbert Haase and Gerhard Paul (eds.), *Die anderen Soldaten: Wehrkraftzersetzung, Gehorsamsverweigerung und Fahnenflucht im Zweiten Weltkrieg* (Frankfurt: Fischer Taschenbuch Verlag, 1995), pp. 105–22.

59 Heinrich Walle, *Die Tragödie des Oberleutnants zur See Oskar Kusch* (Stuttgart: Franz Steiner, 1995), esp. pp. 30, 38, 44–54, 70–76, 93, 131, 135, 139. See Thomas Kühne, "Vertrauen und Kameradschaft: Soziales Kapital im 'Endkampf' der Wehrmacht," in Ute Frevert (ed.), *Vertrauen: Historische Annäherungen* (Göttingen: Vandenhoeck & Ruprecht, 2003), pp. 245–54.

60 Hans Georg Hess, *Die Männer von U 995: Gespräche mit ehemaligen Besatzungsangehörigen des Bootes von Laboe* (Oldenburg: Stalling, 1979), p. 48. Cf. Günter Kießling, *Versäumter Widerspruch* (Mainz: Hase & Koehler, 1993), pp. 54–55; Sigrid Bremer, *Muckefuck und Kameradschaft: Mädchenzeit im Dritten Reich* (Frankfurt: R. G. Fischer, 1988), p. 40; Rudolf Prahm, *Ungehorsam im Dienst der Wehrmacht: Als Soldat im Zweiten Weltkrieg* (Bremen: Donat, 1998), pp. 19–20.

61 Helmut Schmidt, "Politischer Rückblick auf eine unpolitische Jugend," in Schmidt et al., *Kindheit und Jugend unter Hitler* (Berlin: Siedler, 1994), pp. 209–82 (at 232). Pamperrin, *Helmut Schmidt und der Scheißkrieg*, pp. 256–60.

62 Letter of Dirk Heinrichs to the author, July 17, 1999.

63 Hans and Sophie Scholl, *Briefe und Aufzeichnungen*, ed. Inge Jens, rev. edn. (Frankfurt: Fischer Taschenbuch Verlag, 1988), p. 99; cf. pp. 98, 324–35.

64 Richard von Weizsäcker, *From Weimar to the Wall: My Life in German Politics* (New York: Broadway, 1999), p. 66. Cf. Mainhardt Graf von Nayhauß, *Zwischen Gehorsam und Gewissen: Zum Kämpfen verdammt: Das Leid der deutschen Soldaten im Zweiten Weltkrieg* (Bergisch Gladbach: Bastei-Lübbe, 1995), pp. 272–90; and Fetscher, *Neugier und Furcht*, pp. 152–53.

65 Messerschmidt and Wüllner, *Die Wehrmachtjustiz*, p. 132; for a subtle analysis of the data and the delict itself, see pp. 132–68.

66 See Gellately, *Backing Hitler*; Gellately, *Consent and Coercion in Nazi Germany* (Oxford University Press, 2001); Vandana Joshi, *Gender and Power in the Third Reich: Female Denouncers and the Gestapo (1933–45)* (Basingstoke: Palgrave Macmillan, 2003); and Gisela Diewald-Kerkmann, *Politische Denunziation im NS-Regime oder die kleine Macht der "Volksgenosssen"* (Bonn: Dietz, 1995).

67 Gerd R. Ueberschär (ed.), *Das Nationalkomitee "Freies Deutschland" und der Bund Deutscher Offiziere* (Frankfurt: Fischer Taschenbuch Verlag, 1996).

68 Judgments in Hermine Wüllner (ed.), *". . . kann nur der Tod gerechte Sühne sein": Todesurteile deutscher Wehrmachtgerichte* (Baden-Baden: Nomos, 1997), pp. 59–86.

69 Messerschmidt and Wüllner, *Die Wehrmachtjustiz*, p. 144.

70 Buchbender and Sterz, *Das andere Gesicht des Krieges*, pp. 141–48.

71 J. Dollwet, "Menschen im Krieg, Bejahung – und Widerstand?" *Jahrbuch für Westdeutsche Landesgeschichte*, 13 (1987), 279–322 (at p. 318), letters from July 16, 23, 1944; cf. Buchbender and Sterz, *Das andere Gesicht des Krieges*, pp. 151, 154, 157.

72 M. I. Gurfein and Morris Janowitz, "Trends in Wehrmacht Morale," *Public Opinion Quarterly*, 10 (1946), 78–84.

73 According to the polls quoted ibid., between 37 and 66 percent of the German POWs in American captivity polled from June 1944 to Jan. 1945 "believe[d] that Germany still has 'decisive' Secret Weapons." See Buchbender and Sterz, *Das andere Gesicht des Krieges*, pp. 132–41; and Ralf Schabel, *Die Illusion der Wunderwaffen: Die Rolle der Düsenflugzeuge und Flugabwehrraketen in der Rüstungspolitik des Dritten Reiches* (Munich: Oldenbourg, 1994).

74 Private B., Aug. 1, 1944, quoted in Buchbender and Sterz, *Das andere Gesicht des Krieges*, p. 154; Wieschenberg, letter to Hilde, Aug. 28, 1944, and Sept. 3, 1944; Wißmann, letter to Edith, July 15, 1944.

75 Wilhelm Raimund Beyer, *Stalingrad: Unten, wo das Leben konkret war* (Frankfurt: Athenaeum, 1987), p. 13.

76 Bremer, *Muckefuck und Kameradschaft*, p. 40.

77 Wieschenberg, letter to Hilde, Nov. 10, 1941.
78 Kuby, *Mein Krieg*, p. 186, letter from his father, Sept. 13, 1941.
79 Reese, *A Stranger to Myself*, pp. 18, 44.
80 Wißmann, letter to Edith, Feb. 25, 1944, July 1, 1944. Cf. Fritz, *Frontsoldaten*, pp. 125–27.
81 Heinrich Böll, *Brief an einen jungen Katholiken* (Cologne: Kiepenheuer & Witsch, 1961), pp. 15ff., 28.
82 Günther Cwojdrak, *Kontrapunkt: Tagebuch 1943–1944* (Berlin: Aufbau, 1989), p. 49, diary entry, Oct. 6, 1943.
83 Böll, *Briefe aus dem Krieg*, vol. I, pp. 573, 662, 770, vol. II, pp. 913, 929, letters to his wife and parents, Dec. 14, 1942, Feb. 21, 1943, May 16, 1943, Oct. 3, 21, 1943.
84 Deborah A. Prentice, "Pluralistic Ignorance," in Roy F. Baumeister and Kathleen D. Vohs (eds.), *Encyclopedia of Social Psychology* (Thousand Oaks, CA: Sage, 2007), pp. 673–74.
85 Letter of Franz-Josef Langer to his wife (copy owned by author), March 16, 1944.
86 Birke Mersmann, *"Was bleibt vom Heldentum?" Weiterleben nach dem Krieg* (Berlin: Reimer, 1995), p. 34, quote from a letter of the author's father from 1942.
87 Farnbacher, War Diary, Sept. 1941.
88 Testimony given in 1959 for the West German trial of the perpetrators, extracted in Ernst Klee, Willi Dressen, and Volker Riess (eds.), *"The Good Old Days": The Holocaust as Seen by its Perpetrators and Bystanders* (New York: Konecky & Konecky, 1991), p. 43.
89 Michaela Christ, "'Das wird sich alles einmal rächen': Gewalt und Verbrechen in den Gesprächen deutscher Kriegsgefangener im amerikanischen Verhörlager Fort Hunt," in Harald Welzer, Sönke Neitzel, and Christian Gudehus (eds.), *"Der Führer war wieder viel zu human, viel zu gefühlvoll": Der Zweite Weltkrieg aus der Sicht deutscher und italienischer Soldaten* (Frankfurt: Fischer Taschenbuch Verlag, 2011), pp. 266–98.
90 Letter of Eugen Altrogge, March 24, 1942, quoted in Kipp, *Grossreinemachen im Osten*, p. 101.
91 Reinhart Koselleck, "Glühende Lava, zur Erinnerung geronnen," *Frankfurter Allgemeine Zeitung*, May 6, 1995.
92 Diary of Paul Riedel, May 7, 1942, Bibliothek für Zeitgeschichte, Stuttgart. Cf. Andrej Andrick, "Massenmord unter deutscher Besatzung," pp. 117–24, and Norbert Kunz, "Das Beispiel Charkow: Eine Stadtbevölkerung als Opfer der deutschen Hungerstrategie 1941/42," pp. 136–44, both in Christian Hartmann, Johannes Hürter, and Ulrike Jureit (eds.), *Verbrechen der Wehrmacht: Bilanz einer Debatte* (Munich: Beck, 2005).
93 Neitzel and Welzer, *Soldaten*, p. 101.
94 Wilm Hosenfeld, *"Ich versuche jeden zu retten": Das Leben eines deutschen Offiziers in Briefen und Tagebüchern*, ed. Thomas Vogel (Munich: DVA, 2004), pp. 455 (letter to his son, March 7, 1941), 607 (diary, April 17, 1942), 628 (letter to wife, July 23, 1942), 631 (diary, July 25, 1942), 800 (letter to wife, March 25, 1944).

95 Herbert Obenaus and Sibylle Obenaus (eds.), *"Schreiben, wie es wirklich war!" Aufzeichnungen Karl Dürkefäldens aus den Jahren 1933–1945* (Hanover: Fackelträger, 1985), pp. 108, 106, 110–11, 113–114, 117, 127. Cf. Frank Bajohr and Dieter Pohl, *Der Holocaust als offenes Geheimnis: Die Deutschen, die NS-Führung und die Alliierten* (Munich: C. H. Beck, 2006), pp. 60–61.

96 Neitzel and Welzer, *Soldaten*, p. 101.

97 Letters of Hilde and Franz Wieschenberg, March 30, 1942, April 19, 1942.

98 Dörner, *Die Deutschen und der Holocaust*, pp. 336–40.

99 Victor Klemperer, *I Will Bear Witness: A Diary of the Nazi Years, 1933–1941*, vol. II (New York: Random House, 1998), pp. 371 (Oct. 24, 1944), 377–78 (Nov. 26, 1944).

100 Wolfgang Oleschinski, "Ein Augenzeuge des Judenmords desertiert: Der Füsilier Stefan Hampel," in Wolfgang Wette (ed.), *Zivilcourage: Empörte, Helfer und Retter aus Wehrmacht, Polizei und SS* (Frankfurt: Fischer Taschenbuch Verlag, 2004), pp. 51–59.

101 Hosenfeld, *Ich versuche jeden zu retten*, pp. 771 (diary, Dec. 5, 1943), 834 (letter to his wife, Aug. 23, 1944); Kühne, *Belonging and Genocide*, pp. 113–14; Władysław Szpilman, *The Pianist: The Extraordinary True Story of One Man's Survival in Warsaw, 1939–1945* (New York: Weidenfeld & Nicolson, 1999), pp. 209–22.

102 Paul Kreissler, War Diary, May 17, 21, 1941, July 5–8, 1941, Dec. 24, 1942, Jan. 22, 1943, Feb. 8, 1943. Similarly, Sager, *Jugend in der Mühle des Krieges*, pp. 104–05, diary, April 2, 1943.

103 Erich Kuby, *Mein Krieg*, pp. 355–57, diary, Nov. 18, 1943. See also Andreas Jasper, *Zweierlei Weltkriege? Kriegserfahrungen deutscher Soldaten in Ost und West 1939–1945* (Paderborn, Schöningh 2011), pp. 199, 211, 214.

104 On Hosenfeld, see www.yadvashem.org/yv/en/righteous/stories/hosenfeld .asp (accessed Dec. 14, 2014). For further case studies, but also on the scarcity of Jew-rescuers among Wehrmacht soldiers, see Wolfram Wette (ed.), *Retter in Uniform: Handlungsspielräume im Vernichtungskrieg gegen die Wehrmacht* (Frankfurt: Fischer Taschenbuch Verlag, 2002); Beorn, *Marching into Darkness*, pp. 173–81, 231–32, 241–42; Michael Good, *The Search For Major Plagge: The Nazi Who Saved Jews* (Fordham University Press, 2005); and Kuno Kruse, *Dolores & Imperio: Die drei Leben des Sylvin Rubinstein* (Cologne: Kepenheuer & Witsch, 2000), a fictionalized account.

105 Heinrich Böll, *Briefe aus dem Krieg*, vol. I, p. 335, letter to Annemarie Böll, May 17, 1942. The best general account is Benjamin Ziemann, "Fluchten aus dem Konsens zum Durchhalten: Ergebnisse, Probleme und Perspektiven der Erforschung soldatischer Verweigerungsformen in der Wehrmacht 1939–1945," in Rolf-Dietrich Müller and Hans-Erich Volkmann (eds.), *Die Wehrmacht: Mythos und Realität* (Munich: Oldenbourg, 1999), pp. 589–613.

106 Koch, *Fahnenfluchten*, pp. 69–352, based on highly original sources, as opposed to Lars G. Petersson, *Hitler's Deserters: When Law Merged With Terror* (Stroud: Fonthill, 2013).

107 Alfred Andersch, *Kirschen der Freiheit: Ein Bericht* (Zurich: Diogenes, 1971; 1st edn. 1952), p. 63. Cf. Andersch, pp. 65–69, 86, 100–01; and Jörg Döring, Felix Römer, and Rolf Seubert, *Alfred Andersch desertiert: Fahnenflucht und Literatur (1944–1952)* (Berlin: Verbrecher Verlag, 2015).

108 More recent accounts of the workings of antisemitism in Nazi Germany during the war and in face of the Holocaust include Saul Friedländer, *Nazi Germany and the Jews*, vol. I: *The Years of Persecution* (New York: Harper-Collins, 1997); Friedländer, *The Years of Extermination: Nazi Germany and the Jews* (New York: HarperCollins, 2007); Peter Fritzsche, *Life and Death in the Third Reich* (Cambridge, MA: Harvard University Press, 2008), pp. 225–307; Thomas Kohut, *A German Generation: An Experiential History of the Twentieth Century* (New Haven, CT: Yale University Press, 2012). On the Wehrmacht, see Bartov, *Hitler's Army*; Bartov, *Germany's War and the Holocaust: Disputed Histories* (Ithaca, NY: Cornell University Press, 2003); Bartov, *Mirrors of Destruction*; furthermore, Fritz, *Frontsoldaten*, pp. 195–200; Kühne, *Belonging and Genocide*, pp. 80–81, 98–99, 105–07, 126–32, 149–72.

109 Neitzel and Welzer, *Soldaten*, pp. 125–26.

110 Speech by Hermann Göring, Oct. 4, 1942, quoted in Jeffrey Herf, *The Jewish Enemy: Nazi Propaganda During World War II and the Holocaust* (Cambridge, MA: Harvard University Press, 2006), pp. 168–69. For further evidence, see Kühne, *Belonging and Genocide*, p. 131.

111 Letter of Private Heinz S., May 20, 1942, quoted in Müller, *Deutsche Soldaten und ihre Feinde*, p. 223.

112 Letter of Wißmann to his wife, Jan. 26, 1943.

113 Hosenfeld, *Ich versuche jeden zu retten*, p. 697, diary, Feb. 19, 1943.

114 Shils and Janowitz, "Cohesion and Disintegration," p. 301.

115 Hannah Arendt, *On Violence* (San Diego: Harcourt, Brace, 1969), p. 67, for the second quotation; the first one is only in the German edition, *Macht und Gewalt* (Munich: Piper, 1970), p. 68.

116 Midst the plethora of topics the soldiers routinely addressed in their letters, the coercion factor scores surprisingly low, although the soldiers knew how to handle censorship linguistically or didn't care. However, the focus of this assessment is the fighting troops, not civilian society or the home front; the latter showed significant signs of social corrosion, isolation, and dissolution at the end of and certainly during the last half year of the war, as a substantial body of research has documented, including Ian Kershaw, *The End: The Defiance and Destruction of Hitler's Army, 1944–45* (New York: Penguin, 2011); Neil Gregor, "'Is he still alive, or long since dead?' Loss, Absence and Remembrance in Nuremberg, 1945–1956," *German History*, 21 (2003), 183–203; Wolfram Wette, Ricarda Bremer, and Detlef Vogel (eds.), *Das letzte halbe Jahr: Stimmungsberichte der Wehrmachtpropaganda 1944/45* (Essen: Klartext, 2001); Kunz, *Wehrmacht und Niederlage*; Stephen G. Fritz, *Endkampf: Soldiers, Civilians, and the Death of the Third Reich* (Lexington: University Press of Kentucky, 2004). But see, for instance, Kathrin Orth, "Kampfmoral und Einsatzbereitschaft in der Kriegsmarine," in Hillmann and Zimmermann (eds.), *Kriegsende 1945 in Deutschland*, pp. 137–55.

117 Roger R. Reese, *Why Stalin's Soldiers Fought: The Red Army's Military Effectiveness in World War II* (Lawrence: University Press of Kansas, 2011), p. 20.

118 Berger and Luckmann, *Social Construction of Reality*.

119 Joseph W. Ryan, *Samuel Stouffer and the GI Survey: Sociologists and Soldiers During the Second World War* (Knoxville: University of Tennessee Press, 2013).

120 Stouffer et al., *The American Soldier*, vol. II, p. 108.

121 Kindsvatter, *American Soldiers*, p. 138. On racism in the Pacific theater, see John W. Dower, *War Without Mercy: Race and Power in the Pacific War* (New York: Pantheon, 1986).

122 Stouffer et al., *The American Soldier*, vol. II, p. 432.

123 Edward Shils, "Primary Groups in the American Army," in Robert K. Merton and Paul F. Lazarsfeld (eds.), *Continuities in Social Research: Studies in the Scope and Method of "The American Soldier"* (Glencoe: Free Press, 1950), pp. 16–39 (at 22, 24).

124 Kindsvatter, *American Soldiers*, pp. 136–41, 8–9.

125 Gray, *The Warriors*, pp. 41, 45.

126 Donald E. Seibert, "The Regulars," manuscript, 1988, quoted in Craig M. Cameron, *American Samurai: Myth, Imagination, and the Conduct of Battle in the First Marine Division, 1941–1951* (Cambridge University Press, 1994), p. 195.

127 Cameron, *American Samurai*, pp. 192–201.

128 Stouffer et al., *The American Soldier*, vol. I, pp. 410–29.

129 Kindsvatter, *American Soldiers*, pp. 18, 20, 24, 130–31; Stouffer et al., *The American Soldier*, vol. I, pp. 412, 420, 423–25.

130 Lee Kenneth, *The American Soldier in World War II* (New York: Scribner, 1987), p. 142; Stouffer et al., *The American Soldier*, vol. I, pp. 401, 408–10, vol. II, pp. 118–30; Kindsvatter, *American Soldiers*, pp. 229–34.

131 Henry Elkins, "Aggressive and Erotic Tendencies in Army Life," *American Journal of Sociology*, 51 (1945), 408–13 (at pp. 409–10); Kindsvatter, *American Soldiers*, p. 23.

132 See the literature survey in Morris, "Rape, War, and Military Culture."

133 Dower, *War Without Mercy*.

134 Andrew Carroll (ed.), *War Letters: Extraordinary Correspondence from American Wars* (New York: Scribner, 2001), pp. 197–98.

135 McManus, *The Deadly Brotherhood*, pp. 279–80.

136 Kindsvatter, *American Soldiers*, p. 96.

137 Ibid., p. 126, referring to Roger W. Little, "Buddy Relations and Combat Performance," in Morris Janowitz (ed.), *The New Military: Changing Patterns of Organization* (New York: Russel Sage, 1964), pp. 195–223 (at 200).

138 Frederick J. Kviz, "Survival in Combat as Collective Exchange Process," *Journal of Political and Military Sociology*, 6/2 (1967), 219–32. For a biographical example, see Katherine I. Miller, *War Makes Men of Boys: A Soldier's World War II* (College Station: Texas A&M University Press, 2013), pp. 71–88.

139 John Bodnar, *The "Good War" in American Memory* (Baltimore, MD: Johns Hopkins University Press, 2010), p. 27, based on Samuel P. Huntington, *The Soldier and the State: The Theory and Politics of Civil–Military Relations* (Cambridge, MA: Harvard University Press, 1957), pp. 90–91; Gerald Linderman, *The World Within War: America's Combat Experience in*

World War II (Cambridge, MA: Harvard University Press, 1997), pp. 185–87. See also Andrew Huebner, *The Warrior Image: Soldiers in American Culture from the Second World War to the Vietnam Era* (Chapel Hill: University of North Carolina Press, 2008), pp. 15–93.

140 McManus, *The Deadly Brotherhood*, pp. 237–38. Cf. George, "Primary Groups," p. 299; Stouffer et al., *The American Soldier*, vol. I, pp. 284–361; Miller, *War Makes Men of Boys*, pp. 71–88; Paul Fussell, *Wartime: Understanding and Behavior in the Second World War* (New York: Oxford University Press, 1989).

Part III

The Decline of Comradeship, 1945–1995

7 Privatization

On May 9, 1945, Grand Admiral Karl Dönitz, Hitler's successor, gave the soldiers of the German armed forces a final assignment. The catastrophe was obvious, and the victors' previous conferences and proclamations had left no doubt that the Nazi state would be crushed. "We don't know what the enemy will do with us," said Dönitz. And yet simply giving in was not an option. The Nazis' vision was not to die. "We know what we have to do." Unlike in 1918, Dönitz held, "our Volk is not yet disrupted." Instead the lasting "unity of our *Volksgemeinschaft*" was "the most beautiful and best of what National Socialism has given us," and the soldiers were to salvage it. They were, "under any circumstances, to uphold the comradeship that has been established by our people during the war, at the front lines and during the bombing raids at home. Only if we do this can we surmount the hard times ahead and ensure that the German people remain immortal."

What would remain after 1945 of the comradeship that had driven the Germans to fight a criminal war for a criminal regime? By renewing the myth of comradeship, Germans would find strength after the total defeat, suggested Dönitz. Addressing German crimes, of course, would not serve the goal. Instead, Dönitz lauded Germans' willingness to self-sacrifice in order to imbue the myth of comradeship with seminal significance. "We have nothing to be ashamed of. What the German Wehrmacht and the German people have accomplished amidst the suffering of these six years is unparalleled in history and in the world," Dönitz boasted. After the dream of world domination was shattered, Germans were to unite in a great community of suffering.[1]

And indeed, the idea of such a community of suffering was not a fantasy. Germans had already suffered during the war, and when the war was over, their suffering continued. Germany mourned the loss of over 7 million war dead, including 2.8 million civilians. To this were added millions of mutilated soldiers, and women who were raped by the invading Soviet soldiers. Close to 3 million civilians lost their lives when they tried to escape the invasion of the Red Army and afterwards during the expulsions from the East. Unmeasured further millions were missing with no notice of their whereabouts until eventually in the 1950s 1.3 million declarations of death were issued.[2]

Maybe more than anything else, it was the captivity of soldiers in the East that traumatized and agitated German society for years if not decades after the capitulation, and encapsulated the suffering. Roughly 11 million soldiers went into Allied captivity or were already prisoners of war when the Reich capitulated. Approximately two-thirds would return home by early 1947, but their release depended on the goodwill of the victorious nations and these acted rather differently. The West released all of their prisoners by the end of 1948. The Soviet Union, however, still held more than 450,000 in early 1948, and by early 1950 some 30,000 remained, not as prisoners of war, but as war criminals. Every third soldier died in Soviet captivity; in contrast, the mortality rate in Western camps was marginal. While the Western Allies held 70 percent of the German POWs and the Soviet Union only 30 percent, the 2 billion working days served in total by POWs were in the opposite proportion: 70 percent were served in the East, the rest in the West. Hard physical labor and miserable living and clothing conditions ruined the health of many prisoners in the East. These hardships were less the result of hunger plans by the Soviets (who might have revenged the Germans' earlier methodical neglect of the Soviet POWs) than a consequence of the German war of annihilation, which had left the Soviet Union devastated and widely unable to feed its own people.[3]

Existential misery and ubiquitous fear in Soviet and other POW camps in the East left little room for comradeship. Innumerable POWs suffered from tuberculosis, pneumonia, and especially from dystrophy, a hunger disease that destroyed the POWs physically as well as mentally, leaving them in a long state of apathy and depersonalization before eventually killing them. "Human beings turned into animals," was an oft-cited refrain used to explain the collapse of solidarity and the conditions in camp society.[4] The story about the doctor, who, as a prisoner, let his own brother starve to death because he stole his food rations, was not an uncommon one.[5]

But it was not only the physical misery that made the soldiers' solidarity collapse. The symbolic order of the soldiers also imploded, when they fell into the hands of the allegedly "subhuman" enemies, and even more when they realized what kind of hierarchy in the camps was to replace the military order they had been used to and had learned to accept. While not all superiors in the Wehrmacht may have matched the ideal of a paternalistic, comradely military leader, those who didn't could still be seen as the exception to the rule. In captivity, there was no longer any ideal. Former soldiers who, through either conviction or opportunism, cooperated with their Soviet captors ruled over the rest. At the pinnacle of the camp hierarchy stood the mess hall workers and the distributors of food rations, whose well-nourished bodies were easily distinguishable from the masses of walking skeletons. Other positions also offered opportunities to obtain better clothing and nourishment, as well as the possibility of returning home much earlier than the others. In the minds of the disenfranchised, the camp leadership was the focal point of social egotism. The new masters were distinguished by riding boots, leather coats, white shirts, and neckties from the masses of emaciated, ragged *Landser*, who shuffled about in their wooden shoes. In place of the iron war community, "lies, intrigues, selfishness, and underhanded business dealings" were the shaping forces in camp society.[6]

One particular threat to the renewal or continuation of the soldiers' wartime comradeship was the Soviet attempt to recruit Nazi-critical soldiers and to brainwash others for the communist cause and the reconstruction of Germany. Those charged with this task in the Soviet camps ran the Antifascist Committees, or Antifas. Not surprisingly, the *Lagerprominenz*, or "camp notables," as their former comrades disrespectfully called the privileged POWs, comprised most of the Antifas. Apart from communist education programs, the Antifas organized an informant system in Soviet camps, designed to gauge National Socialist sentiments and uncover involvement in war crimes. These spies often decided on life and death. It was their assessment that facilitated or blocked the release of the German POWs. They embodied the collapse of wartime comradeship more than anything else. To be sure, denunciation had not been unknown in the Wehrmacht either. But there it was still countered by a comradeship that prioritized military unity over civilian partisanships. Such comradeship was not to last in the Soviet POW camps, or if so, only rarely. There was no longer a common military goal, only the individual desire to survive and return home.[7]

Comradeship absolved a person from "responsibility for himself and before God, his conscience" as much as from "worry about his own existence," Sebastian Haffner had said in 1939, contrasting the weakness of comradeship to the hardships of "individual bourgeois life," which advocated "everyone for himself," and required individual decision-making and personal responsibility.[8] German POWs increasingly saw themselves as adapting to the reality of these "hardships." In captivity, soldiers experienced the complete reversal of their value system, in which comradeship had been deeply imbedded. Collaboration and conformity no longer guaranteed survival and prestige. Ruthlessness and self-assertion did.[9]

And yet, in the midst of distrust and atomization, prisoners attempted to build trust and establish a semblance of community. "Comrades had not existed for quite a long time, the last ones had fallen at Stalingrad, so the saying went, a bit ironically," wrote a POW in his memoir.[10] Yet a few were left. They resisted the grandiose words of comradeship. But when it came to the very qualities that had made comradeship so attractive, the mutual welfare and feeling of security it provided, also its conspiratorial side, they were committed. Outwardly, this comradeship assumed a private, almost civilian appearance. It had shaken off the chains of military discipline and become based on personal sympathy. Where military units had been broken up, professional and regional affinities grounded a sense of belonging. Swabians, Saxons, Rheinlanders, Prussians – all recognized each other from their dialects. Amidst the social austerity, encountering the native vernacular awakened memories of childhood, family, and friends at home. It created trust. Especially under the conditions of general distrust of all against everyone, it was vital to have at least one friend, an acquaintance, a comrade, with whom a POW could express himself.[11]

Now and then, a close group would test the comradely quality of an individual by subjecting him to a ritual, to which only the inner circle was privy. The "bread test," invented by a group of officers, was one of them. "The little bread we received in our provisions was divided up and offered to the new comrade," remembers one of them. "If he did not take the closest-lying piece without hesitation, but chose the largest one instead, he did not pass the test" – and remained excluded from the group of comrades and their solidarity.[12] Not surprisingly, the aura of conspiracy nourished this type of "small" comradeship. It provided protection and support, albeit only a little, against the Soviet authorities and their German collaborators. Anton Neufischer sat in solitary confinement for three weeks, living off 300 grams of soggy bread and a half-liter of barley coffee daily, when one day a hitherto unknown comrade began sliding a few extra pieces of bread through the grate.[13]

Conspiratorial comradeship was especially helpful when it came to "requisitioning," the military's equivalent of theft, which was now considered honorable among POWs as it not only benefited the group but also harmed the enemy (in this case the Russian camp administration). When the "hunger communities" became "requisitioning communities," their unity was grounded not merely in the battle for food, but also in the pride of collectively duping the enemy. These collective requisitions allowed POWs to regain agency, albeit only for a moment. They won back a small piece of their selves, which they had lost during their confinement.[14]

Although the social culture of the prisoners did not cut off their military traditions entirely, it gradually regained the civilian touch that comradeship always engrained. Comradeship had always been the elongated arm of civilian society in the army and in the death zones of the war. It represented humane solidarity in the midst of inhumane destruction, although it also served as the motor of this destruction. With this ambivalent and integrative concept in their cultural baggage, the soldiers had gone to war. When it was over, in captivity, the former soldiers once again adopted the patterns of civilian society. Their social life was no longer overshadowed by killing and avoiding being killed. Instead, it was about eating, cooking, and the "household business" of the camp. And when circumstances were just right, it culminated in a "bourgeois," in fact truly feminized, "idyll" – the "coffee party."[15]

But unlike coffee parties at home, these included only men. Women were missed, of course, not just sexually, although sexual desires were aroused when food was no longer the primary concern. Only for a few inmates did homosexuality provide an escape. Far more common, however, were homoerotic, platonic, often marriage-like friendships.[16] Like its military counterpart, the camp as a "male society par excellence" relied on mimicking femininity. Kurt Böhme, an early student of German POWs, observed that the missing "influence of the feminine" was not lost on the prisoners. They searched for "loopholes." Theatrical plays, for instance, allowed men, "skillfully or unskillfully made up as women, to play the female roles." In any case, "the feminine, physically non-existent, nevertheless occupies the intellectual world of the male society," Böhme said.[17] Plays provided only poor substitutes. German POWs were in fact, more so than other nationalities, "tired of the uniform and any other kind of military life," a senior official of the Soviet camp administration found in 1948, casting doubt on Soviet plans to recruit POWs for the newly established paramilitary police of the communist part of occupied Germany. "They want to be free and to live with their families, and not be bound by specific rules of behaviour," he explained.[18] This desire also affected the POWs' attitude toward comradeship. Longing for "civilian forms of interaction," explained a collaborator of Böhme, the POWs in the camps tended to avoid calling each other "comrade."[19] Instead, the *Kumpel*, or "buddy," became popular.[20] Friendships based on individual sympathies and similarities replaced the enforced community of comradeship. In captivity, the former soldiers distanced their solidarities from the coercive patterns of military communities and rehearsed individualized and self-chosen, civilian models instead.

This was also true for those former soldiers who were lucky enough to avoid internment altogether or who were released early, returned home, and then tried to get in touch with former war comrades. Immediately after the capitulation, no organized veterans' culture was yet on the agenda. Directive No. 2 of the Allied Control Council, which went into effect on September 20, 1945, forbade former German soldiers from establishing any organizations devoted to cultivating military traditions. Weimar Germany's militarism with its anti-democratic veterans' associations, a stepping-stone for Hitler, would never be resurrected. Yet informal, private networks came into being not long after the capitulation, facilitated by the Wehrmacht's regional recruitment system. Former soldiers from the same unit encountered each other in the streets of their hometowns after returning from war or POW camps. The desire to trade war stories may have been limited following total defeat and destruction of their fatherland, yet ex-servicemen looked out for each other to help establish or restore civilian lives and professional careers. A former soldier of the 78th Infantry and Storm Division, for instance, returned from French captivity to his hometown of Tübingen in 1946. Having been highly decorated in Hitler's army, he was not welcome at home. The local university administration, still under the supervision of the French military occupational regime, refused to reinstate him in his old position. So he resorted to founding a cleaning firm, together with the CO of his former Wehrmacht unit. The business went well, and soon they were able to extend into a retail shop of sorts, thanks to yet another former comrade, who managed to smuggle clothes from the American occupation zone into the French zone, i.e. to Tübingen, where they were most urgently needed. When the company expanded, war comrades were the first to be hired.[21]

Mutual support for each other in coping with minor or major challenges in their postwar lives kept alive the memories of wartime comradeship. Wartime comradeship, it turned out, had not been in vain but would be a life-long asset. And in addition to mutual support and solidarity in making ends meet, the old comrades began to socialize for fun. In Celle in northern Germany former soldiers of the "Nebler" Division met in the back rooms of local bars; sometimes they had to escape from the British military police through the windows or the restrooms. But as early as 1947 almost 100 former Nebler servicemen met for a clandestine reunion.[22] War veterans throughout modernity have met for similar reasons. Grand social, political, or military visions did not really suit their agenda. What held them together was their desire to exchange war stories, to talk about their military pasts, and to make sure that the years of serving, fighting, suffering, and sacrifice would not be forgotten. "Do you remember when . . . " was the phrase the old comrades saluted each other with when they met for their reunions. The soldiers had risked limb and life to earn the right to be seen as "real" men who "had been there." This was how Helmut Wißmann had explained to his fiancée in early 1941 why he would not stay behind. He wanted to be one of the heroes who "later on" would sit around a table with others and "trade war stories," instead of being seen as a "damn" coward who "can't keep up."[23] Trading war stories validated a crucial piece of one's identity as a man and as a citizen. The ex-servicemen wanted to keep alive the memories of those parts of their biographies that were supposed to prove their manliness in the first place.

The political climate in post-Nazi Germany, however, did not support naïve heroism and bravado. Not that it was entirely absent. A critical observer of a veterans' meeting of the 7th Tank Division in 1956 disgustedly noted: "What you can hear there makes you despair of Germany. The old buzzwords, the old songs, the old rhetoric. All that was missing was a 'Sieg Heil' to the most glorious of all Field Marshals."[24] Such critical voices, or the anticipation of them, did at least discourage the veterans from publicly using martial tones. Martial rhetoric was rare even in popular culture. The so-called *Landser* booklets did persist, however. Occasionally, they dwelt on outright glorification of the war, and this led to their inclusion in the government's index of publications that "endangered" youth. Available at every kiosk by the 1950s and still popular through the 1970s, these fictionalized, first-hand depictions of the front lines catered to an adolescent subculture (and as such they were certainly not a German peculiarity).[25]

More popular, including among adults – in fact the one bestseller in war fiction after 1945, and the biggest box office hit of the 1950s – was Hans Hellmut Kirst's trilogy, *08/15*. Between 1954 and 1956, 15 to 20 million people in Germany went to see the three-part film; by the 1970s 1.8 million copies of the book had been sold.[26] In addition, a series of highly acclaimed, popular war novels, including Theodor Plivier's *Stalingrad*, Willi Heinrich's *The Willing Flesh*, Heinz G. Konsalik's *The Doctor from Stalingrad*, Heinrich Gerlach's *The Betrayed Army*, and Fritz Wöss's *Dogs, Do You Want to Live Forever?*, some of which were subsequently turned into feature films, firmly established in the popular mind the image of the German World War II soldiers. They spread the same message as the veterans did in their public speeches and newsletters. They presented the war as the place where German soldiers had sacrificed themselves for the fatherland and had known little about the criminal wartime policies of the National Socialists, much less possessed any means to oppose them. As Peter Bamm's influential autobiographical novel claimed, war crimes and crimes against humanity were the doings of "others," namely the SS and the rest of Himmler's troops.[27] This was the underlying consensus in

West German war literature, even among writers such as Heinrich Böll, who had never cared much for soldierly honor or comradeship. Böll and his characters escaped from the "enforced community," and by despising "masculine absurdity during the war," they represented the other face of the West German memory of war.[28] Alfred Andersch did so even more radically when, in 1952, he condemned the one thing coveted by mainstream war literature – comradeship – and broached "a taboo of postwar society" by elevating desertion to an individual act of salvation.[29]

But Andersch remained a voice in the wilderness, and Böll's influence was restricted to the intellectual Left. The consensus in postwar society was that soldiers had had no choice other than to participate. None of the bestselling books glorified the deserter, the defector, or mutiny.[30] Instead, these novels and subsequent movies confirmed the image of the patient, tenacious, and determined German *Landser*. Their moral dilemma – the duty to keep fighting for a fatherland that was ruled by a criminal regime – merely reinforced the hopelessness of their actions, affirming their status as victims in a barbaric and senseless war.[31]

The remembrance of their suffering in war, and their stoicism in enduring all the pain, allowed former soldiers to suppress their knowledge of the criminal dynamic unfolded by "their" war and yet to celebrate the heroic manliness they had demonstrated on the fields of death. It was a defensive type of manliness, not an aggressive one, and one dedicated to the group, not one that served the individual. "O, what is man," lamented Tim Gebhardt during the memorial service for his regiment's war dead in Ludwigsburg in 1955, "what is virility, when death intervenes and obliterates everything?" Of course, being hurt, physically and mentally, had always been part and parcel of the construction of military masculinity. Initiation into the ranks of "real" men began with the indignities and humiliations of the training period, and they did not end there. Once you had made it this far, you knew that you would never be fully sure of your "virility." The cement of the male community was the shared knowledge of this uncertainty. You were not the only one. You knew that your comrades were with you. This was precisely what Tim Gebhardt meant when he apodictically invoked the memory of soldiers' self-sacrifice in Russia: "The best thing in the life of a man is comradeship." Just as the 1925 Constance altar had evoked the image of comradeship thirty years before, Gebhardt explained in his memento mori that comradeship meant empathizing with "the hardships and worries of others," and risking one's life "when it comes down to rescuing a wounded soldier, so that he won't fall into enemy hands. And when this wounded man, now a rescued comrade, feels his rescuer gently stroke his hair, just as a mother would, then he is able to die in peace." In the face of death, manliness was never guaranteed, especially when death "took one of our comrades." And yet, in death one experienced comradeship. Tender comradeship emerged in the melancholy of the farewell. Tender manliness became respectable in the presence of death. The sphere of death ensured that the symbolic hierarchies were operative. For it was not the soft side of man that defined him, but his ability to overcome it, not just once and for all, but again and again.[32]

Tim Gebhardt's memorial sermon recalled the demise of his "glorious" 260th Buckhorn Division and the 470th Grenadier Regiment in Russia. Along with other units of the Wehrmacht, they were destroyed in July 1944 during the collapse of Army Group Center. And yet they lived on, at least in the imagination: Memories of them remained intact. In the midst of a seemingly hopeless situation, there were some survivors who did not give in to the enemy but fought their way back to friendly lines, in ever smaller groups, over a period of weeks and even months. One of the "unprecedented accomplishments" of the "glorious regiment" was the breakout of roughly twenty officers from a Russian prisoner-of-war camp. None of the participants in this particular undertaking survived. The last one died after a forced march that lasted over three months, severely wounded, and "in the arms of his comrades."[33] Yet feats like this were not unique, regardless of how few their numbers. Through them, the ideal of comradeship and of the independent male community endured, coalescing in an image of martial masculinity and male femininity. The great retreat of the Wehrmacht, which had been transfigured in the memories of the veterans of the Russian campaign, did not contradict this notion; rather, it confirmed it. In fact, exactly this retreat offered a tableau of countless stories that spoke of perseverance, of defeat and resurrection, and of injury and recovery.

Without comradeship, such perseverance and endurance would not have been possible, the veterans claimed in post-World War II Germany. Within the context of comradeship, endurance was first practiced and then rewarded. One veteran recalled in the ex-soldier's newspaper *Alte Kameraden* (Old Comrades) how he fortuitously encountered his former comrade, Debo, seventeen years after the end of the war. Debo had been a corporal in August 1944, barely experienced enough to command an infantry squad, when he was awarded the German Gold Cross. Four times he had been wounded. "But he never remained in the field hospital longer than necessary." Rising up again and again was ingrained in him, soul and body. It was his comrades, however, who provided the impetus for his endurance and bravery; because of them, "he always made his way back to his old outfit." Debo did not land a successful career after the war. But for him as for many highly decorated officers, men who "amidst the desperate situation had never lost their faith or given up fighting," social decline was juxtaposed with heroic bearing.[34] At first, Debo found work in a wine distillery. Then he became a train conductor, finally the driver. On the side, he became a landlord, and decided to become an emergency first-responder with the Red Cross. A recurring strand running through his adult life was his nature as "a respectable and vigilant comrade." Debo had proved as much during the war; now, without fanfare, he helped the blind navigate their way through street traffic and placed himself at the disposal of the Red Cross as a volunteer. From the "comrades of yore" emerged the "men of today," who now "often stand among us unrecognized in the modern day," this story concluded.[35]

These men had stuck together, and they would stick together again whenever needed, as their testimonies confirmed. These spoke of men who had unimaginable hardships behind them, yet stuck together, men who were always there for others, for society in general. Women and children, however, were relegated to the periphery of these stories. As he said goodbye to his wartime comrade, Debo coincidentally "mentioned that he was married and had an apartment close to the train station." Wife and apartment were lumped together; they constituted a place of refuge, but they were not the center of his life. Even the blind person whom Debo helped was a male, blinded during the war, a comrade therefore. Tim Gebhardt honored "our mothers," "our wives," and their "children" only at the end of his long speech and in passing. Women had sacrificed and endured on behalf of their men, or so it appeared to the male narrators at the veterans' meetings. When men performed bravery, they did so for and under the eyes of their comrades. Yet the benchmark for *female* bravery was not other women, but men, warriors, the fallen. "How often mothers feared for their sons, our wives for their husbands, and children for their fathers," remembered a former soldier in the journal *Der Heimkehrer* (The Homecomer) in 1954 – respectfully, but not without reminding the reader of the patriarchal gender order.[36]

In 1946, a prisoner in the Werschetz POW camp in Yugoslavia wrote a poem dedicated to women that would be quoted again and again in the veterans' culture of the Federal Republic:

> However painful our fate as hostages,
> no man, no matter what he has endured, can complain,
> as the letters from home tell us
> that our Volk, our women, are suffering in our stead.
> What is it, that still distinguishes women from men?
> Who acquitted themselves most bravely during the war?

Who dealt with their fortunes in the most manly way?
Nothing but muted respect still cloaks us.
When one day we meet you again,
we'll appear slight
next to such greatness, that had been left alone![37]

Recited at the reunions of the survivors of the Werschetz camp, this poem also served to justify the admission of women to these meetings in the 1960s. Notwithstanding the veterans' focus on male comrade-ship, their social culture paid homage to the ex-servicemen's wives. They had waited for their men to come home, so went the tale, then helped them complete prisoner-of-war pension forms, participated in charity drives for those still being held in captivity, and even contributed to the prisoner-of-war memorials. In the light of these accomplishments, vet-erans' and homecomers' associations established women's departments, and appointed female consultants and committees so that the women could "join in the conversation" and become part of "our comrade-ship."[38] The Heimkehrer (Homecomer) League, an organization specif-ically dedicated to the needs of former POWs, even openly embraced equal rights for men and women. These moves were not made to erase femininity. The ideal mission for women functionaries was the Depart-ment of Family Affairs, so woman representatives in the Heimkehrer League were responsible solely for women's and social welfare issues.[39] Neither the Heimkehrer League nor any other ex-servicemen's associa-tion was drawn to practices in the USSR, where women were employed as construction workers, masons, city planners, and atomic research scien-tists. This kind of "over-emancipation," the Heimkehrer League lectured its West German audience, promoted the "masculinization" of women, and destroyed their "specifically feminine qualities."[40] This was not what the former soldiers wanted. Instead, their concept of including women in their comradely circles rested on older traditions that had already been in place in the interwar period. It promoted a kind of social harmony that never even brought the patriarchal hierarchy into question.

Not all women lived up to this high reputation. Men's suffering from the war and from postwar captivity stemmed, at least in part, from not knowing whether their wives or fiancées at home were indeed being "silent heroines" or rather were indulging in promiscuity. Some women had "gone fishing" for stronger, more virile men, not least former ene-mies who were now part of the occupation force. Many more women were suspected of having done so. And women emerged from the rubble landscapes, which they had cleared away, with an ever-growing sense of self-assurance. At the same time, the soldiers or POWs themselves often found it difficult to readapt to family life and civilian responsibilities.

Many ex-servicemen arrived home debilitated, marked by the symptoms of dystrophy, anxiety, and depression, and not least of all, the noticeable physical effects of emasculation and desexualization. Having been drafted into the army, or volunteered, immediately after completing school, many of them had no professional training or expertise, and they had got to know their wives and fiancées only fleetingly, only now to learn that love did not stretch as far as they had fantasized during war and captivity. The divorce rate reached new heights after the war. As had been the case after the First World War, the gender order seemed to come apart at the seams amid the chaos and upheavals of Germany's collapse.[41]

And yet again, the myth of comradeship helped the homecoming soldiers to restore the gender order.[42] As historians have observed, the war and postwar years jeopardized and often harmed stable family structures, but in the long run "the family held together." In fact, the family emerged as the "society's last bastion, the ultimate haven of safety," sought after by a society of individuals whose belief systems and material basis of life had been shattered as never before, as the German sociologist Helmut Schelsky noticed in 1953.[43] In its Nazified version, understood as an engine of the racially purified and ideologically united *Volksgemeinschaft*, the concept of comradeship was part of the belief systems that had been rendered moot in 1945. But in its older and more popular meaning it was flexible enough to fit into, and in fact spearhead, a society that longed for privacy instead of politics. Comradeship was, in a way, privatized, i.e. reinvented as a pillar of a gender order that accepted women's empowerment and yet contained it.

Women took part in the veterans' reunions and took over important roles. Yet these roles confirmed male dominance. One such role revolved around the fates of those soldiers who had gone missing in action or into captivity, leaving their loved ones in a state of uncertainty about their whereabouts. In 1953, there were still 1,388,680 Wehrmacht soldiers listed as missing in action.[44] Their families did not know if a husband, father, son, or brother was killed in the war, or whether he had been taken prisoner and would eventually return home. Routinely, missing soldier tracing services worked with the veterans' associations to clarify the fates of these soldiers. Under the aegis of the Red Cross, those attending veterans' reunions were asked to review lists of names of those missing in action and to provide information about them. In the 1950s, such name lists were presented to some 750,000 West German veterans, which resulted in 1,270,000 leads, and 260,000 names struck from the rosters.[45] The veterans' movement in the 1950s and 1960s drew much of its reputation from administering this search operation. Participating in it was understood as a self-evident duty, a proof of comradeship. Primarily for the benefit of female relatives of former soldiers – mothers, wives, fiancées, daughters – the tracing service responded to a pressing practical concern. It also gave the women's longing for their men a prominent platform. It showed the veterans cared for the female victims of the war, not only for the men. Ultimately, then, the focus of the tracing service was not women but men. It was the men who were missed.

And while some wives accompanied their men to veterans' reunions, many of them did not. "Wartime comradeship is worse than marriage!" was the ironic way one of Fritz Farnbacher's comrades addressed the priority of the veterans' reunion over family matters. Farnbacher couldn't agree more. After his return from Soviet captivity, he quickly re-established himself in civilian life as a court clerk and happy husband. When he learned about the "call up" to the first reunion of his old regiment in Bamberg in 1953, he was about to become a father. But it was beyond question that he had to leave his heavily pregnant wife to see his old comrades in Bamberg. After his arrival, rumors spread like wildfire through the pavilions: "Farnbacher's just had a son!" A medic from Farnbacher's regiment immediately approached him and offered to be the child's godfather. Farnbacher had already bestowed this role on his brother, so his comrade was given the honor of being vice-godfather, the duties of which he was expected to fulfill. He even took part in the confirmation of Farnbacher's son. The manner of this appointment as godparent was no more an anomaly than Farnbacher's prioritizing his comrades' reunion over the forthcoming family event. Farnbacher's wife was the sister of a fallen wartime comrade.[46]

This was not particularly exceptional. Family life and men's affairs were not mutually irreconcilable but complementary. Male bonding was not completely eclipsed by family. For the 6,000 participants at the first reunion of the 78th Storm Division, or the 2,000–3,000 at the later ones, there was never sufficient overnight accommodation in Tübingen to house the throngs of veterans. What did one do? One celebrated the whole night through; pub closing times were done away with for this very reason. One did not want women around since brawls were not unlikely in such a highly inebriated atmosphere. More importantly, the heroic stories about the scores of enemy tanks one had knocked out, despite running out of ammunition, were not intended for the opposite sex, especially since the less intoxicated wives might not be as easily impressed as one's comrades.[47]

The concept of comradeship maintained the balance in the relationship between male companionship and family life. It did so without questioning the dominance of the male bond, yet highlighting the familial and "motherly" capacities of all-male societies, which had been in evidence in the army as well as in captivity. Reflecting on their memories, former POWs did not hide but boasted of their household skills in making beds and cooking, acquired "at the most depraved stage of their lives" and "under inhuman hardships," i.e. during internment.[48] Tales such as these served to emphasize not only the past independence of the male bond from real women but also their members' present readiness to use household skills on behalf of civilian society and its women at home. Thus the comrades filled the gaps the fallen had left in their own families, for instance by marrying the wife of the buddy killed in war.

About 2.5 million children grew up in post-1945 Germany as half-orphans, most of them without a father. How could one cure this "fatherless society"?[49] In order to "replace the missing manly and fatherly" element in a child's upbringing and to make sure that, in a "world without fathers," all children would still enjoy the "basic experience of fatherliness," the Heimkehrer League proposed in 1955 that survivors should be encouraged to step in for their fallen comrades and "protect the children, invite them for lunch, wash their laundry for them, take care of the bureaucratic red tape," and not least to teach the youngsters social responsibility and good citizenship – the proper role of a father. Distrust of women who raised children on their own was not openly articulated but not entirely absent either. "The mother is unable to replace the father: otherwise the children will lose not only their father but also their mother," the Heimkehrer League advised its readers. It was imperative that mothers should not cease to be mothers, else the distinction between manliness and femininity would no longer be honored, if the children never had a father figure.[50]

This kind of neighborly help also counted as a demonstration of comradeship. In order to survive in a society of civilians, comradeship had to be disarmed. In the 1950s and 1960s, veteran culture did its utmost to dispel the image of the "cheap club nonsense," "chummy sanctimoniousness," and evenings of beer-filled war nostalgia. "Ladies' circles" had been a part of nationalist and militaristic associational life in the past. In veterans' associations after the Second World War, however, women were no longer segregated into special clubs, but were integrated into male patterns of sociability. Moreover, as wives increasingly took part in reunions and weekend trips, the children also had to be taken into account. Out of veterans' gatherings emerged "family gatherings." For the women there was the "coffee and cake" ritual, for the men a target shooting match, and for the children fun and games such as egg-and-spoon, sack races, *Würstchenschnappen* (bobbing for sausages) were offered. At the *Würstchenschnappen*, comrades both young and old, male and female, eagerly joined in.[51]

When the veterans' meetings opened their doors to women and even children, it was not in an offensive spirit but rather in a defensive one. The Wehrmacht veterans' movement in West Germany never gained the kind of popularity its activists had hoped for. Thanks to the Cold War and the strategic interests of the USA in Germany's rearmament, and in anticipation of the Federal Republic's contribution to NATO, the prohibition of veterans' leagues was suspended in 1949. (In communist East Germany, the GDR, the prohibition remained in place and no veterans' movement ever operated openly.) Yet fear of war in tandem with antimilitarist sentiments among the German civilian population kept an aggressive veterans' culture in check. A survey conducted in 1951 revealed that only a minority, roughly one-third of all former soldiers, could be considered potential recruits by veterans' associations; 31 percent of the West German population welcomed them, while 43 percent opposed them; 25 percent of the former soldiers questioned reported on formal contacts "with numerous comrades," with a majority of the positive responses coming from former officers; a further 25 percent retained connections with only one or two comrades – with friends among comrades, that is; 47 percent of all polled veterans, however, no longer had any contacts with their former comrades.[52]

These surveys also suggested that veterans were not prone to drifting toward political radicalization. Indeed, there was virtually no open support for extreme right-wing movements, let alone paramilitary or Nazi movements, not least because they were rigorously prosecuted by the occupational authorities and considered no longer socially acceptable.[53] Certainly not all veterans fell in love with the democratic constitution and the Allied authorities, but the veterans, especially their leaders, knew that they had to comply with them.

Yet the overall success of the veterans' movement was limited. The Kyffhäuserbund, which had reached a peak membership of 2 to 3 million during the Weimar years, was reconstituted in 1952 but barely attracted 100,000 members. The largest of all veterans' associations was not even a veterans' association, at least not technically. The Verband der Heimkehrer, Kriegsgefangenen und Vermisstenangehörigen Deutschlands (VdH), or Association of Repatriates, Prisoners of War, and Relatives of the Missing, included and represented ex-servicemen only insofar as they had been POWs. In fact, however, the Heimkehrerverband, or Heimkehrer League, as it was usually called, took over the role the Kyffhäuserbund and its local branches, the Kriegervereine, or Soldiers' Clubs, had had in nineteenth- and early twentieth-century Germany. Like the Kyffhäuserbund before 1933, the VdH maintained a widespread local network. By the 1950s and 1960s, roughly 500,000 members stood in its ranks; 150,000 took part in its national reunion in 1955. Attendance reached 250,000 in 1957, and was higher still throughout the 1960s, only to fall back to just under 100,000 by the early 1970s. Like the Kyffhäuserbund, the VdH was the only mass organization of former Wehrmacht soldiers in West Germany that operated countrywide and was centrally led. And just like the old Kyffhäuserbund, the VdH lobbied professionally and launched a subsidiary welfare program on behalf of its members. In contrast to the earlier veterans' leagues, however, it was not a military past, but past suffering in captivity, that was central to the VdH's remembrance activities.[54]

Lobbying on behalf of former professional soldiers was at the top of the agenda of the Verband deutscher Soldaten (VdS), or League of German Soldiers, founded in September 1951. Yet this group was able to mobilize no more than 100,000 members, 200,000 at best. An umbrella organization, it had several larger organizations in its fold, including the Verband Deutsches Afrika-Korps (Association of the German Africa Corps), the Traditionsgemeinschaft "Großdeutschland" (Association of the Panzer Corps Großdeutschland), and the Hilfsgemeinschaft auf Gegenseitigkeit der Soldaten der ehemaligen Waffen-SS (Mutual Aid Association of Former Armored SS Soldiers), or HIAG.[55] The last of these incorporated some 60,000 followers – a fraction of the surviving population of Waffen-SS veterans. With the exception of the HIAG and the VdS, these organizations did not perceive themselves as interest groups, however. Like the numerous smaller regimental associations set up in the early 1950s, they wanted to facilitate the reunion of comrades, commemorate the war dead – typically during the larger gatherings – and keep alive the memory of the soldiers' deeds and sacrifices in war. Identity politics was their goal, rather than lobbying, and certainly not paramilitary action. It was these local associations and their genuinely nostalgic attitude that made up the fabric of the West German veterans' movement. There was frequent discussion of establishing greater, nationwide operating associations such as the Stahlhelm, the Reichsbund, or indeed the Kyffhäuser had been in the interwar period, but these ideas never materialized. Instead the post-1945 veterans' culture remained decentralized, comprising a diverse plethora of local associations that guarded their independence and indulged in self-sufficiency.

Initially, reunions of the veterans of former regiments or divisions attracted thousands of people: 6,000 former members of the 78th Infantry and Storm Division joined the first reunion in 1951. This was nearly everyone whose name and address the committee had been able to identify. The Association of the 114th and 14th regiments in Constance, which resumed its prewar traditions in 1954, brought in about 3,500 people, almost all those invited by its committee.[56] But these figures are deceptive. The initial euphoria did not last. Even during their heydays in the 1950s, second and further reunions typically drew only half of the overall association's membership or even less: the second meeting of the former 78th Storm Division in 1953 gathered only 3,000 veterans; 3,800 in 1956, 3,000 again in 1959, 2,500 in 1963, and in 1973 and 1976 only about 1,000.[57] Afterwards there were even fewer. Those who did not show up, had not turned away entirely but prioritized career and family life, and maintained connection with the associations through financial contributions, and newsletter subscriptions, and they stayed in touch with comrades who lived in the area. They attended the annual reunions only every five or ten years.[58] Very few associations were able to mobilize consistently high numbers of the surviving members of their respective former units. An example is the 4th Mountain Division; it managed to mobilize 3,000 out of 7,000 survivors even in 1970.[59] Veterans' associations' success in mobilizing members nevertheless fell far short of expectations, even if one takes into account that some decrease was a natural consequence of old age and death. Internal and public complaints about "the lack of interest among most of the comrades" were common. In contrast to the initial success of the 78th Division, barely 200 people showed up at the first reunion of the 290th Infantry Division in 1953; 1,400 had been invited. For the second reunion in 1955, the activists lowered their expectations and anticipated the attendance of merely 100; they even debated whether to cancel the whole affair altogether.[60]

Precise and comprehensive membership statistics for the Wehrmacht veterans' movement are unavailable. The VdH placed the figure at around 500,000 in the mid-1950s, which was probably exaggerated. But the high rate of participation evident in some regimental and divisional associations was not representative of the Wehrmacht as a whole. Numerous Wehrmacht units, especially the divisions formed in the later stages of the war, as well as the rear-area and garrison formations, did not establish veterans' associations at all. That was left to the older, long-serving units, those that had already existed before the war or were formed in its early phases, and especially frontline units. Altogether, over 100 divisional associations can be tracked, in addition to an equal number of organizations at regimental, battalion, and company level.[61] Yet even generous estimates suggest that no more than a mere 10 percent of the roughly 10 million former soldiers living in West Germany during the 1950s kept in touch with at least one branch of the veterans' movement.[62]

The desire to exchange wartime memories after 1945, and to keep the memory of one's military service alive, was also defined by a noticeable generational split. The active veteran circles of the former Wehrmacht were almost entirely comprised of the age cohorts drafted before 1943 and born before 1925. These were those who experienced the military victories through 1942. The last age group that the veterans' associations were able to reach out to was born in 1924 and recruited in 1942.[63] The younger ones, by contrast, showed significantly less interest in the veterans' associations. These age cohorts, born from 1925 onward, were sent to the front as replacements for the old units, divisions, and regiments; they were typically poorly trained and equipped, and often regarded their time in the Hitler Youth as a meaningless obligation they had been forced to endure, as oral historians have noted.[64] They subsequently experienced military defeat, unending retreats, and finally, the total collapse. Their wartime memories were not grounded in the kind of comradeship that had been cultivated from the time that soldiers first entered the recruit depot, which the more experienced soldiers such as Helmut Wißmann or Franz Wieschenberg could fall back on.

As we have seen, however, even these soldiers had never entirely managed to overcome their desire to return home to civilian society. Their loyalty seesawed between the all-male society at the front lines or in the rear and their real families at home. Many, probably most, eventually tended to transfigure these contradictory experiences in an individualistic way. Those who were not filled with disgust when looking back on their "lost years" could pride themselves on having proved they were men who somehow managed to survive thanks to their own individual skills, astuteness, slyness, or simply luck. They had survived through a combination of malice and finesse, muddling their way through of their own volition. If they credited the experience of comradeship, they had individual comrades, i.e. friends, in mind, not the cohesion of their units.[65]

Most former soldiers had simply had enough of war; they returned home to a country that had been bitterly defeated and widely devastated, and where public recognition of the soldiers' sacrifices was marginal, doubtful, or indeed missing completely. So the former soldiers dedicated themselves to family and profession. Feelings about former comrades could be rather negative, or overshadowed by memories of deprivation, forlornness, and humiliation, so it was not really the time to glorify military service as a rite of masculine passage. A former Wehrmacht first lieutenant who returned from Yugoslav captivity in 1951, and was fortunate enough to regain his old position as a school deputy headmaster, wanted nothing to do with postwar associations that claimed to recreate the old community of fate and hardship, as he said critically. "Indeed I hardly think that this community of hardship even functioned all that well. Only in retrospect, as our discussions at our *Stammtisch* in Kiel clearly show, do we glorify our composure, abominate our weaknesses, and bask in the feeling that we've withstood a rigorous test. That is also one of the reasons why I don't attend the Heimkehrer reunions," he wrote in 1968 in a letter to the chairman of the POW circle involved, the Werschetz Community. A few of "those comrades, with whom I had really bonded" in war, he continued, he had met coincidentally in Kiel, some also through correspondence. But none was keen to spend time and money on going to reunions. "We all have plenty to do 'today' and rarely broach the topic of 'yesterday' in our conversations," he explained. As this letter shows, this veteran did not completely lose links with his former comrades, indeed went to some lengths to maintain them, yet primarily in the private sphere of the local *Stammtisch*, which in 1968 counted eight members.[66] These unofficial networks of affiliation exemplify the informal periphery of the veterans' movement, which tended to avoid the organized clubs and associations and their reunions. In fact, the pattern of bonding practiced by this veteran followed the concept of friendship, not of comradeship. He socialized with those former comrades he liked, not with the entire group that at some point had been thrown together. He engaged in individualistic sociality and despised the coerced community.

Those former soldiers who kept their war memories to themselves, or relegated them to the private sphere of bars and studies, constituted the overwhelming majority of veterans in West Germany. (In communist East Germany, an organized veterans' culture was suppressed.) According to an Allensbach Institute survey in 1956, 49 percent of enlisted men talked about their time as soldiers only grudgingly, while 13 percent never did at all – roughly two out of three in total. Yet it was precisely through their silence that the vast majority of "anti-veterans" failed to influence the public discourse. They did not establish a narrative of collective memory to counter the offerings of the activists. They did not present an alternative to the veterans' movement and its war stories. Privatizing, individualizing, or simply blocking out their war experiences and memories, the silent majority opted out of the public debate about the meaning of the war, about the lessons that could be drawn from their wartime experiences, and the morality of participation, relinquishing that task to the minority of veteran activists, who ultimately succeeded in shaping the public debate, at least in the 1950s and 1960s, as the following chapters show. Only later on, as a result of the shift of West German society toward leftist agendas and pacifist attitudes, did they lose ground and saw themselves increasingly devalued and eventually even stigmatized.

NOTES

1 Gerhard Förster and Richard Lakowski (eds.), *1945: Das Jahr der endgültigen Niederlage der faschistischen Wehrmacht: Dokumente*, 2nd edn. (Berlin: Militärverlag der DDR, 1985), pp. 361, 363–65.

2   Heinz Nawratil, *Die deutschen Nackriegsverluste unter Vertriebenen, Gefangenen und Verschleppten* (Munich: Herbig, 1986), p. 32; Rüdiger Overmans, *Deutsche militärische Verluste*, p. 316; Pascale R. Bos, "Feminists Interpreting the Politics of Wartime Rape: Berlin, 1945; Yugoslavia, 1992–1993," *Signs*, 31 (2006), 995–1025.

3   Werner Ratza, "Anzahl und Arbeitsleistungen der deutschen Kriegsgefangenen," in Erich Maschke (ed.), *Die deutschen Kriegsgefangenen des Zweiten Weltkrieges: Eine Zusammenfassung* (Bielefeld: Gieseking, 1974), pp. 185–230; Ratza, *Die deutschen Kriegsgefangenen in der Sowjetunion: Der Faktor Arbeit* (Bielefeld: Gieseking, 1973); Overmans, *Deutsche militärische Verluste*, pp. 284–92; Andreas Hilger, *Deutsche Kriegsgefangene in der Sowjetunion, 1941–1956: Kriegsgefangenpolitik, Lageralltag und Erinnerung* (Essen: Klartext, 2000).

4   Diether Cartellieri, *Die deutschen Kriegsgefangenen in der Sowjetunion: Die Lagergesellschaft* (Bielefeld: Gieseking, 1967), p. 167.

5   Ibid., pp. 1, 64, 76–77, 167, 240; Hedwig Fleischhacker, *Die deutschen Kriegsgefangenen in der Sowjetunion: Der Faktor Hunger* (Bielefeld: Gieseking, 1965).

6   Wulf Wunnenberg, "Psychologische Beobachtungen in einem Kriegsgefangenenlager: Ein Beitrag zum Thema 'Stacheldrahtpsychose,'" *Studium Generale*, 3 (1950), 21–31 (at p. 24); Albrecht Lehmann, *Gefangenschaft und Heimkehr: Deutsche Kriegsgefangene in der Sowjetunion* (Munich: Beck, 1986), pp. 42–90, esp. 75–78; Cartellieri, *Die deutschen Kriegsgefangenen in der Sowjetunion*, pp. 90, 95–96; Stefan Karner, *Im Archipel GUPVI: Kriegsgefangenschaft und Internierung in der Sowjetunion 1941–1956* (Vienna: Oldenbourg, 1995), p. 116; Dietmar Sauermann and Renate Brockpähler, *"Eigentlich wollt ich ja alles vergessen . . . ": Erinnerungen an die Kriegsgefangenschaft 1942–1955* (Münster: Coppenrath, 1992).

7   Gert Robel, *Die deutschen Kriegsgefangenen in der Sowjetunion: Antifa* (Bielefeld: Gieseking, 1974).

8   Haffner, *Defying Hitler*, pp. 284–91.

9   Max Ernst Graf Solms, "Soziologische Probleme der Kriegsgefangenschaft in unserer Zeit," *Studium Generale*, 3 (1950), 44–54 (at p. 49).

10 Anton Neufischer, *Von Kurland ins Kohlenbergwerk im Donbass* (Konstanz: [1981]), pp. 183–84. Cf. Sauermann and Brockpähler, *Eigentlich wollt ich ja alles vergessen*, pp. 136–37.

11 Sauermann and Brockpähler, *Eigentlich wollt ich ja alles vergessen*, pp. 139–43; Cartellieri, *Die deutschen Kriegsgefangenen*, pp. 145, 246–47, 267–68.

12 Sauermann and Brockpähler, *Eigentlich wollt ich ja alles vergessen*, p. 142.

13 Neufischer, *Von Kurland ins Kohlenbergwerk im Donbass*, pp. 124–26.

14 Lehmann, *Gefangenschaft und Heimkehr*, pp. 77–78; Sauermann and Brockpähler, *Eigentlich wollt ich ja alles vergessen*, pp. 226–34.

15 Cartellieri, *Die deutschen Kriegsgefangenen*, pp. 167–69, 272.

16 Lehmann, *Gefangenschaft und Heimkehr*, pp. 86–90; Cartellieri, *Die deutschen Kriegsgefangenen*, pp. 269–70; Fritz Arnold, *Freundschaft in den Jahren der Feindschaft* (Munich: Hanser, 1998), pp. 90–93 (US camp).

17 Kurt W. Böhme, *Geist und Kultur der deutschen Kriegsgefangenen im Westen* (Bielefeld: Gieseking, 1968), p. 6.

18 Quoted in Hilger, *Deutsche Kriegsgefangene in der Sowjetunion*, p. 264.

19 Cartellieri, *Die deutschen Kriegsgefangenen*, pp. 167–69.

20 Neufischer, *Von Kurland ins Kohlenbergwerk im Donbass*, pp. 183–84.

21 Author's interview with seven members of the "Kameradenhilfswerk der 78. Sturmdivision," 1995.

22 *Alte Kameraden*, 1977/78–79, pp. 24–25: and Frank Bösch, *Das konservative Milieu: Vereinskultur und lokale Sammlungspolitik in ost- und westdeutschen Regionen (1900–1960)* (Göttingen: Wallstein, 2002), pp. 195–96.

23 Wißmann, letter to Edith, Feb. 19, 1941.

24 *Frankfurter Hefte*, 1956, No. 11, "Zustimmung und Kritik."

25 Klaus F. Geiger, *Kriegsromanhefte in der BRD: Inhalte und Funktionen* (Tübinger Vereinigung für Volkskunde, 1974).

26 English translations: Hans Hellmut Kirst, *The Revolt of Gunner Asch* (Boston: Little, Brown, 1955), *Forward, Gunner Asch!* (Boston: Little, Brown, 1956), *The Return of Gunner Asch* (Boston: Little, Brown, 1957). Cf. *Handbuch Innere Führung* (Bonn: Bundesverteidigungsministerium, 1957), pp. 40, 107, 113; Walter Nutz, "Der Krieg als Abenteuer und Idylle: Landser-Hefte und triviale Kriegsromane," in Hermann Wagener (ed.), *Gegenwartsliteratur und Drittes Reich: Deutsche Autoren in der Auseinandersetzung mit der Vergangenheit* (Stuttgart: Reclam, 1977), pp. 265–83; Michael Kumpfmüller, "Ein Krieg für alle und keinen: Hans Hellmut Kirst: *08/15* (1954/55)," in Hermann Wagener (ed.), *Von Böll bis Buchheim: Deutsche Kriegsprosa nach 1945* (Amsterdam: Rodopi, 1997), pp. 249–64.

27 Jürgen Ritsert, "Zur Gestalt der Ideologie in der Popularliteratur über den Zweiten Weltkrieg," *Soziale Welt*, 15 (1964), 244–53; Hermann Wagener, *Von Böll bis Buchheim: Peter Bamm, Die unsichtbare Flagge: Ein Bericht* (Munich: Kösel, 1952).

28 Heinrich Böll, "Entfernung von der Truppe" (1964), in *Werke: Romane und Erzählungen*, vol. IV, pp. 287, 319.

29 Ulrich Bröckling, *Disziplin: Soziologie und Geschichte militärischer Gehorsamsproduktion* (Munich: Fink, 1997), p. 280; Erhart Schütz, "Fluchtbewegung, militant: Zu Alfred Anderschs Krieg," in Wagener (ed.), *Von Böll bis Buchheim*, pp. 183–98.

30 Thomas Kraft, *Fahnenflucht und Kriegsneurose: Gegenbilder zur Ideologie des Kampfes in der deutsch-sprachigen Literatur nach dem Zweiten Weltkrieg* (Würzburg: Koenigshausen & Neumann, 1994).

31 Michael Schornstheimer, *Die leuchtenden Augen der Frontsoldaten: Nationalsozialismus und Krieg in den Illustriertenromanen der Nachkriegszeit* (Berlin: Metropol, 1995).

32 In Memoriam. Gefallenen-Gedenkrede, gehalten von Dr. Tim Gebhardt . . . , *Alte Kameraden*, Sonderdruck für die 260. ID, Stadtarchiv Ludwigsburg, Depositum 260.I.D., Papers of Tim Gebhardt.

33 Ibid.

34 So said the retired Colonel General Student at the first postwar reunion of the "Green Devils" (a parachutist unit) in 1951, *Die Zeit*, Aug. 2, 1951.

35 *Alte Kameraden*, 1963, No. 2, p. 19.

36 *Der Heimkehrer*, 1954, No. 5, p. 2; ibid., March 25, 1956, p. 1.

37 Keynote of the chairman of the Werschetz "camp community" association, Erhard Vogel, at a meeting on Sept. 18, 1976, Bundesarchiv-Militärarchiv Freiburg, MP 23; *Der Heimkehrer*, April 15, 1977, p. 1.

38 *Der Heimkehrer*, Aug. 25, 1960, p. 9; ibid., Jan 10, 1963, p. 3; ibid., Aug 10, 1966, p. 9.

39 Ibid., Dec. 20, 1957, p. 5, request for a woman minister in the new federal government.

40 Ibid., March 10, 1959, p. 7; cf. ibid., Feb. 15, 1972, p. 3.

41 Elizabeth D. Heineman, "The Hour of the Woman: Memories of Germany's Crisis Years and the West German National Identity," *American Historical Review*, 101 (1996), 354–95; Frevert, *Women in German History*, pp. 255–76.

42 For other aspects of this process of "remasculinization," see Frank Biess, *Homecomings: Returning POWs and the Legacies of Defeat in Postwar Germany* (Princeton University Press, 2006); Robert G. Moeller, "The 'Remasculinazation' of Germany in the 1950s: Introduction," *Signs*, 24 (1998), 101–06; Moeller, *War Stories: The Search for a Usable Past in the Federal Republic of Germany* (Berkeley: University of California Press, 2001).

43 Helmut Schelsky, *Wandlungen der deutschen Familie* (Stuttgart: Enke, 1953), pp. 63, 87–92.

44 Kurt W. Böhme, *Gesucht wird . . . Die dramatische Geschichte des Suchdienstes* (Munich: Süddeutscher Verlag, 1965), p. 111; cf. Klaus Mittermaier, *Vermisst wird . . . Die Arbeit des deutschen Suchdienstes* (Berlin: Ch. Links, 2002), pp. 15–38, 48.

45 *Alte Kameraden*, 1959, no. 5, pp. 3–7.

46 Letter of Fritz Farnbacher to author, Sept. 26, 1994.

47 Author's interview with veterans of the 78th Division, 1995.

48 *Der Heimkehrer*, Jan. 15, 1956, pp. 12–13.

49 Lu Seegers, *"Vati blieb im Krieg": Vaterlosigkeit als generationelle Erfahrung im 20. Jahrhundert – Deutschland und Polen* (Göttingen: Wallstein, 2013), p. 10.

50 *Der Heimkehrer*, May 18, 1955, p. 3; see also the poem "My Father" in *Alte Kameraden*, June 1956, p. 1.

51 *13er Post*, 1955, No. 2, pp. 10–15, photo p. 15; ibid., 1956, No. 2, p. 22; ibid., 1958, No. 2, p. 19; ibid., 1959, No. 3, pp. 8–10; ibid., 1960, No. 3, no page number; ibid., 1961, No. 3, pp. 6–7; *Alte Kameraden*, 1955, No. 10, p. 18; *Vorwärts*, Sept. 11, 1959; *Der Heimkehrer*, July 20, 1955, p. 4.

52 Office of the US High Commissioner for Germany, Press Release issued by No. 838, Jan. 8, 1952, Archiv der Sozialen Demokratie Bonn, OS, Abt. VdS #177 (polls of summer 1951); summary in Anna J. Merritt and Richard L. Merritt (eds.), *Public Opinion in Semisovereign Germany: The HICOP Surveys 1949–1955* (Urbana: University of Illinois Press, 1980), pp. 145–46. See also Institut für Demoskopie Allensbach, *Die Stimmung im Bundesgebiet, November 1951*, No. 23: *Soldatenvereinigungen*, copy in Bundesarchiv Koblenz, B 145/4221 (poll of November 1951).

53 Alaric Searle, "Veterans' Associations and Political Radicalism in West Germany, 1951–1954," *Canadian Journal of History*, 8 (1999), 221–48; Peter Dudek and Hans-Gerd Jaschke, *Entstehung und Entwicklung des Rechtsextremismus in der Bundesrepublik: Zur Tradition einer besonderen politischen Kultur*

(Opladen: Westdeutscher Verlag, 1984), pp. 79–124; Krafft Freiherr Schenck zu Schweinsberg, "Die Soldatenverbände in der Bundesrepublik," in Georg Picht (ed.), *Studien zur politischen und gesellschaftlichen Situation der Bundeswehr: Erste Folge* (Witten: Eckart, 1965), pp. 96–177.

54 Birgit Schwelling, *Heimkehr – Erinnerung – Integration: Der Verband der Heimkehrer, die ehemaligen Kriegsgefangenen und die westdeutsche Nachkriegsgesellschaft* (Paderborn: Schöningh, 2010); Wolfdietrich Kopelke, *Freiheit ohne Furcht: Zehn Jahre Heimkehrerverband* (Bad Godesberg: VdH, 1960). On the figures, see *Der Heimkehrer*, May 1955, p. 8; ibid., June 25, 1955, pp. 1–2; ibid., March 5, 1956, pp. 5–6; ibid., June 25, 1957; ibid., Aug. 10, 1961, pp. 1–2 (120,000 at the 1961 reunion); ibid., July 15, 1971, pp. 1–2; ibid., June 30, 1975, pp. 1–2 (about 80,000 in 1971 and 1975, the last nationwide meeting).

55 Jay Lockenour, *Soldiers as Citizens: Former Wehrmacht Officers in the Federal Republic of Germany, 1945–1955* (Lincoln: University of Nebraska Press, 2001); James M. Diehl, *The Thanks of the Fatherland: German Veterans After the Second World War* (Chapel Hill: University of North Carolina Press, 1993); Hans Körber (ed.), *Soldat im Volk: Eine Chronik des Verbandes Deutscher Soldaten (VdS)* (Wiesbaden: Wirtschaftsverlag, 1989); Karsten Wilke, *Die "Hilfsgemeinschaft auf Gegenseitigkeit" (HIAG) 1950–1990: Veteranen der Waffen-SS in der Bundesrepublik* (Paderborn: Schöningh, 2011).

56 *Der Seehase*, 1965, No. 65.

57 *Festschrift der "78. Infanterie- und Sturmdivision" zum "13. Treffen" 1989* (Tübingen: private print, 1989), copy owned by author.

58 Interview with veterans of the 78th Infantry and Storm Division, 1995; Interview with Dr. Hans Mehrle, 1995.

59 *13er Post*, 1970–71; *Schwäbische Zeitung* (Ulm), April 20, 1970.

60 Letter of the 290th I.D. veterans' association tracing service chair E. B. to one member F., June 28, 1955, and detailed report on its activities thus far, Bundesarchiv-Militärarchiv, MP 28/13.

61 This calculation is based on the lists of such associations as *Deutscher Soldatenkalender*, 1953–1962, and *Deutsches Soldatenjahrbuch*, 1963ff., as well as *Alte Kameraden*.

62 Schenck zu Schweinsberg, "Die Soldatenverbände in der Bundesrepublik," pp. 105–06.

63 This is an extrapolation from membership data (all privately owned) from the following regimental and divisional veterans' associations: 78th Storm and Infantry Division (1996); 215th Infantry Division (1994); 4th Battalion of 260th Infantry Division (1995); Infantry Regiment 10 (1985, plus undated lists, about 1995); Infantry Regiment 18 (1997). (The associations recorded the birthdays of their members in order to send out congratulations and suchlike.) Interestingly, only the Heimkehrer League managed to reach out to former servicemen, i.e. POWs, across all age groups; my calculation is based on membership data of the regional branch Baden-Württemberg in 1999: Out of 4,640 male members (plus 5 with no birth year data), between 80 and 234 were born in a year between 1910 and 1919, while the birth years of 1920 to 1926 "provided" consistently more than 300 members each, and

the one of 1927 still 258 (1928 only 99, but the Wehrmacht no longer drafted this birth year).

64 Matthias von Hellfeld and Arno Klönne, *Die betrogene Generation: Jugend in Deutschland unter dem Faschismus* (Cologne: Pahl-Rugenstein, 1985); and esp. Rudolf Schörken, *Jugend 1945: Politisches Denken und Lebensgeschichte* (Frankfurt: Fischer Taschenbuch Verlag, 1994).

65 Various oral history studies have analyzed this type of war memory (sometimes by conflating postwar memories, which the interviews indeed document, and experiences during the war, which the interviews cover only sporadically), most of them already conducted by the 1970s and 1980s. See Lutz Niethammer, "Heimat und Front: Versuch, zehn Kriegserinnerungen aus der Arbeiterklasse des Ruhrgebietes zu verstehen," in Niethammer (ed.), *"Die Jahre weiß man nicht, wo man die heute hinsetzen soll": Faschismus-Erfahrungen im Ruhrgebiet* (Berlin: Dietz, 1983), pp. 163–232; Hans Joachim Schröder, *Die gestohlenen Jahre: Erzählgeschichten und Geschichtserzählung: Der Zweite Weltkrieg aus der Sicht ehemaliger Mannschaftssoldaten* (Tübingen: Niemeyer, 1992), pp. 882–921; Ludger Tekampe, *Kriegserzählungen: Eine Studie zur erzählerischen Vergegenwärtigung des Zweiten Weltkrieges* (Mainz: Gesellschaft für Volkskunde in Rheinland-Pfalz, 1989), pp. 151–218; Barbara Keller, *Rekonstruktion von Vergangenheit: Vom Umgang der "Kriegsgeneration" mit Lebenserinnerungen* (Opladen: Westdeutscher Verlag, 1996); Vera Neumann, *Nicht der Rede wert: Die Privatisierung der Kriegsfolgen in der frühen Bundesrepublik: Lebensgeschichtliche Erinnerungen* (Münster: Westfälisches Dampfboot, 1999); Klara Löffler, *Zurechtgerückt: Der Zweite Weltkrieg als biographischer Stoff* (Berlin: Reimer, 1999). See also Fritz, *Frontsoldaten*, pp. 219–32.

66 Letter of Günther D. to Erhart Sch., June 16, 1968, Bundesarchiv-Militärarchiv Freiburg, MP 23.

8 Integration

"Nearly the entire world brings charges against Germany and against the Germans," moaned the German philosopher Karl Jaspers in 1946, responding to the belief in the "collective guilt" of the Germans that had become widespread in Anglophone countries during the war. While most Germans met this generalization with denial or incomprehension, Jaspers sought to make distinctions rather than entirely dismiss the "guilt question." He distinguished between criminal guilt, which involved prosecutable crimes; political guilt, which arose from supporting a criminal regime; moral guilt, which involved those who had acted under orders; and metaphysical guilt, which arose out of the solidarity between people as people and made everyone responsible for all the injustices which they had not resisted. Jaspers tried to breathe new life into a moral code that the wartime community discourse had rendered obsolete. He strove to counteract Germans' defensive reactions against the accusations of guilt that began immediately after the war. These reactions were largely rooted in notions of honor and shame; the Nuremberg Tribunal was interpreted as a "national dishonor" – not because of the crimes that had brought it into existence, but because it was others, not Germans, who were judging Germans. And so Jaspers too was caught up in the mire of shame culture, a sense of squirming under the gaze of others rather than answering to one's individual conscience. "Soldierly honor" was sacred to Jaspers, even though he had never been a soldier. And what was more honorable in war than showing comradeship? "Those who have been loyal in their comradeship, unflinching amid danger, and have proven themselves through bravery and practicality," Jaspers said, "they have retained something inviolable in their sense of self. This pure soldierly, yet simultaneously human, aspect is common to all nationalities. Probation is not merely the absence of responsibility, but where it remains untarnished by bad deeds or in execution of obviously evil orders, it is a cornerstone of life's meaning." Inspired by the comradeship myth, the epitome of *communitas*, Jaspers absolved the "good comrade." Comradeship outshone the "evil acts," Jaspers enunciated, ignoring or obfuscating the morality of complicity that had been nourished by comradeship as well.[1]

Jaspers was not alone. Even before the Nuremberg Trials had started, another German, Ernst Friedländer, a veteran of the First World War who left Germany in 1931 because of his Jewish heritage, sang a eulogy to comradeship, which, in his view, was the one thing the Nazis could not taint. Comradeship, he said, was "completely independent from National Socialism." It was the one "decent" thing that soldiers brought with them out of the war, something that could be put to good use in the "peacetime world." In fact, he said, a "different comradeship," freer than in war, could be found everywhere, in schools and universities, in businesses and in offices, trade organizations and private clubs. In Friedländer's view, the renewal of comradeship subsequently led to a seamless renewal of another soldierly ideal that had escaped being tarnished by National Socialism: Germany.[2]

Jaspers and Friedländer took up the pre-Nazi tradition of German war memory. The eternal morality of the comradeship myth, supposedly unsullied by Nazi evil, was to help the former Wehrmacht soldiers expunge their complicity in criminal warfare, to integrate them into a new democratic era, and to make them re-emerge as proponents of a new and peaceful European order. Thanks to its polyvalence, the concept of comradeship was indeed fit for the task of purifying Hitler's soldiers from the "stigma of violence"[3] that tainted the genocidal Nazi war. The concept of comradeship had always lived off the diversity of its meanings, of the modes of behaviour it depicted, and of the emotional conditions it allowed. As a comrade, one could simultaneously qualify as a good family father and a scurrilous drinking buddy, someone who selflessly looked after his battlefield companion, but then murdered innocent civilians and boasted about the crime afterwards. Charged with exonerating German soldiers from their complicity in the Nazi genocidal project, the integrative appeal of the comradeship myth was stretched to its limits. It meant turning a blind eye to the crimes of the Germans and emphasizing their suffering from the crimes, actual or supposed, of the enemies.

"A question of guilt? – That will not be discussed here," confirmed Gebhard Müller, the Minister-President of the state of Baden-Württemberg, in his keynote to the 78th Storm Division reunion in Tübingen in 1956. Remembering the "euphoria of the advance and the victories" was not possible, Müller suggested, without thinking of the "abyss of despair and defeat, the onslaught of misery and death" that followed the heroic deeds. "After courageously enduring years of war and hardship, after unspeakable sacrifices, filled with devoted love to the fatherland, the division went down fighting with its shield pure and untarnished," echoed the city's mayor at the same event. Only 1,500 out of 20,000 newly recruited soldiers were left after the breakdown of the Central Front in July 1944. Thousands had been lost in the previous battles. In total, the division lost 20,000 men. And the sacrifices did not end with the war, the speakers unanimously confirmed. The soldiers' real ordeal began with the "march into captivity," and 5,000 were still missing in the 1950s.[4]

Their suffering and their sacrifices cleansed the soldiers from their guilt of being complicit in genocide. It was not by coincidence that the Heimkehrer League became the prevailing mass organization of former Wehrmacht soldiers in Germany after 1945. No other type of veterans' association would have been able, as it was, to shift the focus of German war memory from the agency of the soldier to the suffering of the POW. More than any other league could have done, the Heimkehrer League was able to secure a privileged place for the Wehrmacht soldiers in the great community of victims (*Opfergemeinschaft*), the concept to which the Germans resorted in order to counter accusations of guilt by the outside world. In early 1950, the Federal Chancellor Konrad Adenauer declared that the suffering endured in Soviet captivity by German POWs was tantamount to that inflicted by the crimes of the Third Reich.[5] In the same fashion, the Heimkehrer League expended considerable energy in proving scientifically that the "extreme living conditions" in Russian POW camps were equal to those in the Nazi concentration camps, notwithstanding the fact that some of the latter were specifically designed as death camps.[6]

A focus of veterans' war memory was the concept of comradeship as the epitome of the "human," i.e. altruistic, and affectionate side of the community of suffering. Veteran reunions in post-Nazi Germany were typically labeled *Kameradschaftstreffen*, or "comradeship meetings," not "veterans' meetings," even less "front soldiers' meeting," as they had been called in the interwar period. In fact, the language of the veterans' culture generally avoided the term veteran and replaced it with comrade, or *Kamerad*. It was the humane, communal heritage of the war more than anything else that they claimed to keep alive. As Gebhard Müller said in his 1956 speech, the reunions were of the "greatest humanitarian significance" as they did not cultivate "old animosities" but helped preserve a precious "bond, forged at a time . . . when comradeship had grown into the embodiment of virtue per se." These were "years of human probation! Years of barbarity and evil in which – this may sound odd – man, more than ever, had to demonstrate the goodness in him."[7]

The invocation of the humanity of comradeship prepared the way for veterans to integrate themselves into the new democratic society – in other words, to overcome the Nazi socialization most of them had absorbed before becoming soldiers. Winning the "Hitler Youth generation" for West German democracy was a top priority for all major political parties, whether conservative, liberal, or social democratic.[8] Statements of solidarity by leading politicians made it clear that the new state did not intend to shut the old soldiers out. The rearmament plans were only one of many incentives, although an important one. Without rehabilitating the "eternally prevailing soldierly ideals," and the Wehrmacht itself, that rearmament was unlikely to attract a broad consensus of support.[9] Hence West German politicians such as Adenauer and Kurt Schumacher launched official exonerations of Wehrmacht and Waffen-SS soldiers, after General Eisenhower, now NATO Supreme Commander, had led the way by confirming in January 1951 that "the German soldier" had "fought bravely and honorably for their homeland." Echoing Eisenhower, Adenauer recognized in 1952 in parliament "all those of our countrymen who in the framework of high soldierly traditions fought honorably." He confirmed that the "great achievement of the German soldier, despite all aspersions of past years . . . will remain alive in our people." Both Adenauer and Eisenhower restricted their exonerations to individual soldiers who had fought "honorably," implicitly excluding those who had not, and so avoided exonerating the Wehrmacht as an institution. Former soldiers could however draw moral comfort from public recognition and contribute to Adenauer's aim of blending "the moral virtues of the soldier with democracy."[10]

Organizations of the extreme right did re-emerge occasionally onto the political scene.[11] However, fears about whether these groups had the potential to unleash a new paramilitary or anti-democratic mass political movement proved to be unfounded. In the 1950s, for instance, the newly reconstituted Stahlhelm attracted some suspicious attention and could be found in many local branches of the HIAG. But the Stahlhelm remained irrelevant.[12] The leaders of the veterans' movement deliberately distanced themselves from extremist platforms. Far rightist ideas and activists occasionally found fertile ground in certain sections of the veterans' associations but usually only on a local level, not among the leaders. This was true even for the HIAG, the veterans' organization of the Waffen-SS soldiers, the fighting SS soldiers as opposed to those serving in the camps or with the Einsatzgruppen or in the Himmler administration. Yet a significant number of their members gravitated to extremely rightist positions and never abandoned crucial parts of the Nazi ideology. By and large, however, any impulse toward extremism and positions that might be categorized as anti-constitutional was quickly suppressed by the federal and regional leadership.[13]

Communities cannot exist without "others," those who do not belong. The Other is less rigidly determined in democracies and pluralistic societies than in dictatorships but is never completely absent. In West German society, as in other Western democracies in the 1950s, the theory of totalitarianism helped to identify the Other. Directed against communist as well as fascist dictatorships, this antagonistic theory facilitated the accommodation of Hitler's former soldiers in the new democratic state. They had demonstrated their anti-communist, i.e. anti-totalitarian credentials during the Eastern campaign, and in the 1950s, they needed only to distance themselves from the other type of totalitarianism, Nazism.[14]

The versatility of comradeship could accommodate such divergence, although it meant walking a tightrope. Comradeship was based on reciprocity; it was an obligation. It had more to offer than trading war stories and playing the "remember-when" game. It thrived on regeneration. It meant staying in touch with old comrades, attending the annual reunions, or at least subscribing to the membership journal of the veterans' associations in order to indicate that one was "interested in what became of one's old comrades." And it meant standing by those comrades who had not been as fortunate as the others after coming home from war or captivity. Severely war-wounded or unemployed comrades were to be helped out of the lurch with donations or a temporary job. One returning Swabian soldier, in a show of "true comradeship," offered his home to a destitute comrade and his asthma-afflicted son from the industrial (and war-destroyed) city Aachen, helping to reduce the boy's suffering through the clean mountain air.[15] Most regimental associations established *Kameradenhilfswerke*, or comrades' relief organizations, funded through members' donations. In the early 1960s, about ten individuals benefited from the "Comrades' Relief Organization of the former 78th Storm Division"; on average, each received 100 to 150 marks per year – it was symbolic in terms of financial aid, but it was still a demonstration of lifelong comradeship in the eyes of the veterans. The social service system of the Heimkehrer League was more substantial; it included a medical service, a "rest and recovery organization" boasting "thousands" of affiliated recreational homes, and a housing construction program.[16]

In the early 1950s, hardly anything reminded Germans of their own suffering from the war as vividly as the missing soldiers tracing service. The tracing service also embodied the meaning of comradeship. With more than a million Wehrmacht soldiers still listed as missing in action in the early 1950s, the tracing service operated at almost every larger veterans' reunion, trying to find former comrades of the missing soldiers and to determine their whereabouts. It was understood as a self-evident duty that you would take part in this – an act of comradeship that defined the great community of German victims of the war, a victims' community that did not sink into passivity but retained a manly attitude and remained active and never gave up. Nobody would be left behind; nobody would be forgotten. This law of comradeship extended especially to those German POWs who had been accused of being "war criminals" by the Soviet Union, and been subjected to public show trials in 1949–50. Their release topped West Germany's political agenda in the 1950s. On the fifth anniversary of the German capitulation, it was not the end of the war or of the Nazi dictatorship or even the millions of war deaths that the Federal Republic officially remembered; rather, a "Day of Allegiance" was held, dedicated to the alleged 500,000 unaccounted prisoners-of-war. In reality there were only 50,000, but Germans did not know (and were not really interested in) the actual number. They bought into hugely inflated figures, which confirmed Germans' self-perception as victims rather than perpetrators of the Nazi war.[17]

In October 1950, the first official "Prisoners-of-War Day" was observed, complete with nationwide ringing of church bells and a minute's silence, all of which was preceded by a parliamentary vote. In October 1952, this "comradely commemoration" evolved into a "German pilgrimage of allegiance." A two-minute traffic pause was observed, and a minute's silence, so it could involve all West Germans.[18] The Heimkehrer League collected "loyalty lists" with the signatures of 7 million Germans who supported their comrades in captivity.[19] The fact that the presumed number of POWs had gradually dropped did not temper the integrative power drawn by post-National Socialist Germany from its anxiety over the mistreated, imprisoned soldiers.[20] The "politics of the allegiance" reached a high point with Chancellor Adenauer's triumphal return from his trip to Moscow in September 1955.[21] West Germany and the Soviet Union resumed full diplomatic relations and trade negotiations, and the Soviet Union promised to release the last German prisoners of war, about 10,000 in number, still in Soviet captivity. According to a representative poll, 37 percent of the West German population in 1956 considered the return of the POWs as the most important event of the year. No other topic attracted as much public attention – 4 percent thought rearmament the most important; even fewer mentioned the prospect of German reunification, or economic issues like wages, inflation, or pensions.[22]

Post-Nazi Germany's self-perception as a nation of victims of the war facilitated the integration of Hitler's soldiers into democracy and civilian society. The concept of comradeship established continuity from war to peace. As comrades, the soldiers had fought the war; as comrades, they had withstood the challenges of captivity; as comrades, they provided the new democracy with a model of solidarity. The larger associations established contacts with all democratic parties in federal, state, and local parliaments, and avoided partisan affiliations to only one of them. Conversely, the parties were committed to integrating the war veterans into the young democracy, if for no other reason than to win them as voters. While the veterans' associations may have attracted fewer former soldiers than expected, the political parties, especially the catch-all parties including the SPD, could not afford to ignore a group of roughly one-third of the West German population that sympathized with the veterans or identified themselves as such.[23] Instead, these parties worked feverishly on entertaining good relationships with them, and the veterans' associations learned quickly to lobby effectively, which enabled them to stake out their position in the new parliamentary democracy. Members of the Heimkehrer League could be found in all Bundestag parties. From 1953 their number fluctuated between 40 and 70, with a peak in 1965 of 81 (of 496) Bundestag deputies; 37 of them belonged to the CDU/CSU, 30 to the SPD, and 14 to the FDP.[24]

The veterans' movement was a core element of the social-political landscape in the Federal Republic of the 1950s and 1960s. When politicians strove to be addressed as "comrades" by the Heimkehrer League, they did so not merely for political gain. Many of them had served with the Wehrmacht themselves, and comradeship was deeply embedded in their own war experience and moral values. Helmut Schmidt, the SPD leader and federal chancellor in the late 1970s, was representative of this attitude. He traced his political engagement in the Social Democratic Party to his experience of comradeship during the war. His striving to be "democratic" arose from his need and desire for freedom that developed during the Nazi years, and to be "social" from the comradeship, solidarity, and brotherhood he had experienced as a soldier. "For me these were synonyms, merely different names for the same principle," he said. Out of the experience of comradeship, Schmidt crafted a definition of solidarity uninhibited by traditional connotations of class struggle.[25] Comradeship and solidarity merged into a harmonious model of a society that was gradually finding its way toward liberal democracy.

In the veterans' culture, and more broadly in West Germany's war memory, comradeship was imagined as an engine of democracy. Indeed, the semantics of the concept had always called for egalitarian social relationships even when it was used to uphold authority and hierarchy. Comradeship was the egalitarian oil in the power machine that could not function without inequality. "We behaved democratically," claimed a U-boat officer in hindsight, although he and his comrades, as he said, had not known much about democracy and although the "last word" had always been with the commander. This type of democracy was goal-oriented, it demanded cooperation, and it meant "sticking together – wherever or whatever the objective may be." For this veteran, the word "democratic" was reduced to a cooperative, egalitarian leadership style, as opposed to an elitist and arrogant one. The commander had regularly sought the advice of his subordinates. This had made the social climate in his ship "democratic."[26] In the same fashion, the veterans' social culture could be considered democratic. In fact, the leaders of the divisional and regimental associations were typically drawn from the lower officer ranks or even from the non-commissioned officers who were not given to trumpeting their status but prided themselves on their comradely attitude as superiors, following the model of Ernst Wurche. And it paid off. For the "simple *Landser*," remembered one of them decades later, the "moment of glory" in his life came when, at one of the first veterans' reunions in the 1950s, his former company commander slapped him on the shoulder, and invited him to sit at the officers' table and to talk using first name only. Then even the simple *Landser* knew that "comradeship was not a hollow phrase."[27]

This kind of symbolic promotion extended wartime comradeship into postwar comradeship; it established continuity between martial dictatorship and a civilian society based on a democratic constitution. In the same fashion, the speakers at veterans' reunions appealed to their audiences to use the experience of wartime comradeship, the leveler of "class, confession, and professional distinction," as lubricant in the new democratic society.[28] The concept of democracy came to symbolize a community, a form of government driven by unity and based on acclamation, not one that embraced conflict or disputes between competing parties, classes, or interests. Comradeship as the oil of such a democracy ensured political calm, social harmony, and economic resurgence. By embedding their self-concept firmly in wartime comradeship, politicians like Helmut Schmidt were able to pursue a consensus-oriented democratic path, a strategy that distanced the Federal Republic from the political fragmentation of the Weimar years and overcame "divisive" party politics.[29] "Comradeship – mutual care, mutual commitment," according to Gebhard Müller's 1956 keynote speech, was "part of the foundation upon which the new state was built. For the spiritual elements of a democratic form of government were, in the final analysis, respect for others, and working together and for each other, for the benefit of the whole."[30]

And comradeship suggested not only domestic but also international political harmony, the veterans believed. They presented themselves as advocates of international reconciliation, distancing themselves from the

revanchist traditions of their predecessors in the Weimar Republic. The
semantic polyvalence of the concept of comradeship made it possible.
"Spassiba" is the Russian word for "thank you." It was also the title of
a story told by a veteran to the journal *Alte Kameraden*, or *Old Comrades*, in December 1955, in which he related his experience as an officer
on Christmas Eve 1942 on the Eastern Front. The barracks in which
his company was quartered, although situated in a hostile area, exuded
warmth and conviviality that evening. "The *Spieß* (first sergeant) thought
of himself as the mother of a family, and was busily going back and
forth with a large sack, and helping the Santa Claus glue on his beard
(made out of flax from the armoury)." The mail, which had been put
on hold for two weeks, was distributed, and the "connection to home"
became "heartfelt" and the sense of togetherness stronger. "The room
had become an island" in an ocean of war, "a magical ark filled with
the essence of home." It radiated comradeship. For a conscientious officer such as the narrator, this kind of atmosphere could not last forever.
The lieutenant soon stepped out into the night. He knew his duty – you
had to know when to stop and not become absorbed by the moment.
He needed to tend to the other units of his company and check up on
the remote and isolated sentries. And it was not only his own men he
cared for. He was committed to a universal concept of comradeship,
one that included the defeated enemy, and his welfare duties extended
also to include "our prisoner company" of Russian POWs, "who built
roads and felled trees for us." In comparison to the Germans' barracks,
their accommodations seemed "dark and cramped . . . the contrast to our
lighthearted merry-making could not have been greater," he noticed.
But this impression was misleading. Behind the cold and darkness, there
was warmth and brightness – comradeship. There was a buzz of activity
among the prisoners. Someone from the group approached the officer
with an object in his hand and said in broken German: "Lieutenant, we
wish to do you a favour." The speechless German was handed a lamp
"made out of a bicycle tire, adorned with carved wooden animal figures,
and hand-forged chains for hanging. They had spent many nights working on this after returning from their hard days . . . The faces of the group
remained expressionless, but in their eyes was an unimaginable sense of
bliss." The lieutenant's own longing for home receded into the background; in its place arose "a very different feeling, one of togetherness,"
and one that was not limited to his own Aryan race but included the
Slavs as well. He humbly said "spassiba" to them over and over, eventually climbing back into his sled and driving away, "happily into the white
and endless landscape, the long night that stretched through the Russian
lands."[31]

The Wehrmacht veteran who told this story in 1955 participated in Operation Barbarossa from the very beginning. At an early stage in summer 1941, he came to know all too well its un-chivalrous side, not least the implementation of the Criminal Orders. At one point his unit captured a Russian man wearing a leather jacket, shortly after 200 of their comrades had been taken prisoner by the Red Army, stabbed, mutilated, and blown to pieces with hand grenades, allegedly on the orders of this same man, who was suspected of being a commissar. "After that," this veteran recalled in the 1990s, it was impossible to deal with this prisoner "from the standpoint of comradeship." He was shot.[32]

Of course, stories like this were seldom relayed in public after 1945. In their place, others were told, ones that "proved" that veterans, as soldiers, had acted according to the highest traditions of chivalry against unarmed enemies, according to a concept of comradeship that was embedded in the traditions of Christian mercy and pity. There was the German *Landser* who first carried his own lieutenant under fire from the battlefield in the East and then was killed in action while performing another, even more altruistic act of comradeship: he "tried to rescue a toddler from a burning shed" in Russia.[33] There were the German soldiers who carried a seriously injured, helpless Russian soldier to their emergency station after realizing that his own comrades had abandoned him. Later on, this story went, some Russian women demonstrated their gratitude by taking care of one of those German soldiers, now himself injured.[34] The message of these stories was always the same. They were to prove the Germans' commitment to a concept of comradeship that had, supposedly, neutralized racist and nationalist hatred even in the East. It was "the comradeship from one people to another."[35]

There is no reason to doubt the veracity of these stories. Their mythical character resulted from their context and their messages. Mythical war memory retained useful memories and expelled bad ones, according to the needs of the storytellers who coped with the past in order to manage the present and build the future. The storytellers had choices. They could tell stories that would lead to a new war, or that promoted working for a peaceful future. They could tell stories that disclosed or hid the cruelties of their own troops. The West German veterans of the Nazi war chose to tell stories that presented them as bearers of humanity in the midst of an utterly brutal and inhuman war. These stories allowed them both to establish a sense of continuity in their own lives and yet to welcome the political and social change of the postwar era. If they had told different stories, they might have been relegated to the fringes of social and political life.

Old soldiers' memories of "fighting, killing, destroying" still flared up at private gatherings at the local *Stammtisch* and sometimes in public.

But these depictions assumed a defensive tone. They had "looked death in the eyes too often," the soldiers claimed, "for them to wish for another war."[36] In this way they advocated a fundamental, yet by no means a total, change from the interwar period. In the Cold War era of the 1950s and 1960s, few people imagined a world without any kind of war or soldiers. But more and greater efforts than previously were made to avoid another war. Veterans adapted and conformed to these new developments. They wanted to be integrated into a world order that advocated peace. Hence they presented themselves as "the first, oldest, and true peace movement." They did not mean the movement of the radical pacifists but rather the one dedicated to military deterrence and rearmament that received widespread approval all over Europe and in Germany from the mid-1950s onwards. It complied easily with the West German concept of a new army of "soldiers for peace," as the military planner (and former Wehrmacht officer) Wolf Graf Baudissin phrased it.[37]

The Cold War and the build-up of the Western military alliance, which included Germany, provided a framework that allowed German veterans selectively to integrate their wartime memories into the larger goal of preserving peace. The military alliance demanded the supranational exchange of military know-how; led by General Franz Halder, numerous German officers in POW camps had already placed themselves at the disposal of the Americans immediately after the war.[38] Although the flow of information generally ran only in one direction, these exchanges paved the way for "comradely cooperation between victors and vanquished," and breathed new life into the vision of international soldiery.[39] No later than 1950, Wehrmacht veterans started establishing contacts with former enemies, well aware that these contacts secured respectability for both old and new German soldiers, domestically and internationally. The contacts went far beyond knowledge transfer between higher military echelons and included encounters between regimental Wehrmacht veterans' associations and their former adversaries on the various battlefields; the incorporation of the Heimkehrer League into international ex-servicemen's and POW organizations; and the efforts of the Volksbund deutsche Kriegsgräberfürsorge (VdK), the German War Graves Commission, to care for and maintain German soldiers' cemeteries, both at home and abroad.

The Heimkehrer League forged partnerships between local branches and parallel French organizations, and represented German soldiers' leagues in international organizations of POWs and frontline veterans (Frontkämpfer).[40] Great meaning was attached to the international reunions of old military units that had opposed each other during the war. As early as the 1950s, representatives from leagues of British veterans, who had once waged war against the Germans, regularly attended the reunions of the Association of the German Africa Corps. In addition, the VdK and other veterans' associations began organizing tourist trips to military cemeteries in western-, southern-, and northern Europe, as well as to North Africa. Embedded in a kind of touristic conviviality, these trips to the former battlefields and the graves of fallen comrades engendered pride in the Wehrmacht's fighting morale and yet allowed the veterans to include themselves in a grand community of mourning and suffering survivors.[41] No one focused on memories that might have stirred up resentments. "How the times have changed since 1940," noted the joyful conclusion from a "Memorial Trip of the II./A.R. 215 to its old positions" on May 19 and 20, 1962. "Wherever we went, our former adversaries from the war, Alsatians and Frenchmen, welcomed us with friendliness and courtesy."[42]

In the 1950s and 1960s Hitler's soldiers made their peace with the democratic and parliamentary constitution, and they adapted to the politics of international reconciliation, at least within the Western hemisphere and military alliance. Well into the 1960s, comradeship was also seen as a model for social harmony at the workplace, in a way that echoed the discourse of the interwar period. At the death of Hermann Reusch – chairman of the Gutehoffnungshütte, board member of the Federation of German Industry, and notorious anti-unionist – his obituaries praised his "work comradeship," emphasizing how he had been "an understanding friend and a good comrade" to his employees.[43] In other corporate sectors as well, and especially in uniformed institutions such as the police or fire departments, in youth organizations and sports teams, and occasionally in gender relations, comradeship remained a core virtue.[44]

War veterans, keepers of the grail of comradeship, did anticipate during the economic upswing of the Adenauer era that things might change. As early as 1958, and increasingly as time passed, the old comrades suggested that the "satiety" of West German society and its "addiction to entertainment, tourism, and recreation" might not leave much space for honoring comradeship.[45] Where everything revolved around personal careers and private consumption, it might seem anachronistic for the notion of a forced "community of fate" to attract enthusiasm. Its fate was far from sealed by the 1960s, however. The Bundeswehr, based on conscription, was firmly anchored in the social fabric of West German society in the 1960s – even amongst the younger generation. Young Germans who did not wish to be disadvantaged in their professional careers accepted the draft and went into the "Bund," as the new army was popularly known. As a result of the abuse of conscription by the Third Reich, the West German constitution offered a relatively far-reaching right to refuse the draft. But through the 1970s, the conscientious objector was confronted with the asocial stigma of the shirker, even though he was obliged to serve with a social or medical institution and for a longer time than his drafted peers. This service was called a "substitute (service)" in order to emphasize the primacy of military service in the public consciousness. It was not a blemish, but an advantage to have "served" as soldier. This did not mean that the stern tone of the barracks yard lived on in firms and businesses. It was not soldierly spirit in the sense of an inherited militarism that thrived, nor even veneration for the old uniform, but more an appreciation of an individual's evident willingness to endure the indignities and the pressure to conform that came with military initiation, the entry ticket into the male community. Doors that would usually have remained closed were opened for "comrades," among whose numbers the veterans of the Bundeswehr were also counted, not least because former Wehrmacht soldiers often held the senior positions in private companies and civil administration and so decided who would be offered a job or given a promotion.[46]

For the conscripts of the Bundeswehr, military service was overwhelmingly a positive experience. Public opinion polls regularly inquired about their attitudes before and after they had served. Key motivations for taking up the challenge of the draft included hopes for career advancement – personal motives, not the desire for experiencing comradeship – or just the attraction of going with the crowd; 24 percent of young men questioned in 1956 expected to receive "specialist technical training" that they would be able to put to good use for later "professional advancement." The majority, however, 39 percent, regarded military service as a must, something that they had to get behind them, so that they would not be drafted and pulled out of their careers later on "when it is most inconvenient." Other considerations played a secondary role at this point – before they actually entered the military. A full 6 percent expressed the desire to learn "the business of real men."[47] But after the period of military service was completed, things looked rather different. In another poll in 1964, 35 percent still claimed they had learned something through military service; 38 percent, however, looked back with pride on this rite of passage; and an overwhelming majority of 73 percent waxed nostalgic about the comradeship they had experienced in the Bund.[48]

And so the veterans of the previous army had good reason to envision a rosy future for the concept of comradeship, even if civilian society drifted toward individualization, consumerism, and materialism. In the mid-1960s the old comrades, the Wehrmacht veterans, were still pleased with themselves. Their goal, to integrate their "experience from yesterday" – the blessings and the magnitude of comradeship in war – with those of the "adolescent generation of tomorrow," as Tim Gebhardt put it in his commemoration address in 1955, was nearly achieved, thanks to the renewal of military conscription.[49] And the hopes of some veterans went even further. In early 1962, the myth of comradeship experienced a veritable resurgence, when the Bundeswehr, through its rescue operations in the wake of a mining accident in the Saarland and a flooding disaster in Hamburg, demonstrated how much the civilian society had to gain from military comradeship. Comradeship means "protection and rescue of defenseless civilians, security for a peaceful future for our Volk," exulted the veterans' movement. The vision of the great "comradeship that would encompass the entire Volk" was promulgated in March 1962, a few months after the construction of the Berlin Wall in August 1961, i.e. at a time when the division of Germany into East and West was (literally) cemented and not likely to be overcome soon. And yet the euphoria of some advocates of comradeship included the communist part of Germany. For even there, thanks to the conscription that was introduced in East Germany as well, comrades were to be found. Like the Bundeswehr, the East German National People's Army placed comradeship at the top of its list of cardinal virtues. Comradeship, firmly anchored in both East and West, would, according to one Wehrmacht veteran, be a budding seed of national unity that would transform the NVA into a "boomerang for the SED rulers," the leaders of the East German Sozialistische Einheitspartei, or Socialist Unity Party.[50]

NOTES

1 Karl Jaspers, *The Question of German Guilt* (New York: Dial Press, 1947; German orig. 1946). See Anson Rabinbach, *In the Shadow of the Catastrophe: German Intellectuals Between Apocalypse and Enlightenment* (Berkeley: University of California Press, 1997), pp. 129–65; Aleida Assmann and Ute Frevert, *Geschichtsvergessenheit – Geschichtsversessenheit: Vom Umgang mit deutschen Vergangenheiten nach 1945* (Stuttgart: DVA, 1999), pp. 80–96, 112–39.

2 Ernst Ferger (i.e. Ernst Friedländer), *Deutsche Jugend: Fünf Reden* (Zurich: Niehans, 1945), pp. 12, 40–44. See "Ernst Friedländer 75," *Frankfurter Allgemeine Zeitung*, Feb. 4, 1970.

3 Michael Geyer, "The Stigma of Violence, Nationalism, and War in Twentieth-Century Germany," *German Studies Review*, 15 (1992), 75–110, Special Issue, *German Identity*.

4 *Furchtlos und treu: Wiedersehen der 78. Sturmdivision am 24./25. Mai 1952 in Tübingen* (Tübingen: private print, 1952).

5 Moeller, *War Stories*, esp. pp. 21–31; Biess, *Homecomings*, pp. 179–202.

6 Thus, explicitly, *Der Heimkehrer*, Nov. 10, 1962, pp. 1–2; see E. G. Schenck and Wolf v. Nathusius (eds.), *Extreme Lebensverhältnisse und ihre Folgen,*

6 vols. (Bad Godesberg: Verband der Heimkehrer, 1958–64); Svenja Golter-mann, *Die Gesellschaft der Überlebenden: Deutsche Kriegsheimkehrer und ihre Gewalterfahrungen im Zweiten Weltkrieg* (Munich: Deutsche Verlags-Anstalt, 2009).

7 Manuscript of the speech, Sept. 9, 1956, Archive of the Kameradenhilfswerk 78, copy owned by author.

8 Friedhelm Boll, "Hitler-Jugend und 'skeptische Generation': Sozialdemokratie und Jugend nach 1945," in Dieter Dowe (ed.), *Partei und soziale Bewegung: Kritische Beiträge zur Entwicklung der SPD seit 1945* (Bonn: Dietz, 1993), pp. 33–58.

9 An important role in the Social Democratic Party (SPD) was played by the World War I and Wehrmacht veteran Carlo Schmid; see minutes of a meeting of leading politicians including Schmid, Kurt Schumacher (SPD chairman), and various former Wehrmacht officers in Bad Godesberg, March 23, 1951, Archiv der Sozialen Demokratie, Bonn, Fritz Erler papers, No. 143. More largely on these discussions, see Lockenour, *Soldiers as Citizens*, pp. 93–124.

10 The quotations are in Frevert, *A Nation in Barracks*, pp. 260–61. See David Clay Large, *Germans to the Front: West German Rearmament in the Adenauer Era* (Chapel Hill: University of North Carolina Press, 1996), pp. 114–15; Bert-Oliver Manig, *Die Politik der Ehre: Die Rehabilitierung der Berufssoldaten in der frühen Bundesrepublik* (Göttingen: Wallstein, 2004).

11 Kurt Tauber, *Beyond Eagle and Swastika: German Nationalism Since 1945*, 2 vols. (Middletown, CT: Wesleyan University Press, 1967).

12 Dudek and Jaschke, *Entstehung und Entwicklung des Rechtsextremismus*, pp. 115–23.

13 Wilke, *Die "Hilfsgemeinschaft auf Gegenseitigkeit."* My assessment is also based on a perusal of the extensive internal files of the federal and some regional committees of the HIAG, Bundesarchiv-Militärarchiv, Freiburg, MP 4, which Wilke did not use.

14 Dominik Geppert, *Die Ära Adenauer* (Darmstadt: Wissenschaftliche Buchge-sellschaft, 2002), p. 90.

15 *Der Heimkehrer*, Dec. 20, 1962, p. 6.

16 *Der Heimkehrer*, Sept. 15, 1960, p. 8; ibid., July 10, 1960, p. 6; ibid., July 10, 1961, p. 14; Kopelke, *Freiheit ohne Furcht*, pp. 97–134.

17 Biess, *Homecomings*, pp. 179–80.

18 *Der Heimkehrer*, Nov. 1952, p. 2.

19 Ibid., Aug. 25, 1961, p. 1.

20 *Alte Kameraden*, Aug. 25, 1961, p. 1.

21 Moeller, *War Stories*, pp. 88–122.

22 *Der Heimkehrer*, Jan. 25, 1961, p. 1.

23 See above, p. 229.

24 Diehl, *The Thanks of the Fatherland*, pp. 109–226; and Jörg Echternkamp, *Soldaten im Nachkrieg: Historische Deutungskonflikte und westdeutsche Demokratisierung 1945–1955* (Munich: De Gruyter Oldenbourg, 2014). Heimkehrer data: *Der Heimkehrer*, Oct. 25, 1966, pp. 1–3; see also ibid., Feb. 25, 1964, p. 5; ibid., April 25, 1962, p. 1; ibid., May 25, 1961, p. 8.

25 Schmidt, "Politischer Rückblick auf eine unpolitische Jugend," p. 234; and Schmidt, *Pflicht zur Menschlichkeit: Beiträge zu Politik, Wirtschaft und*

Kultur (Düsseldorf: Econ, 1981), p. 258. Cf. Martin Rupps, *Helmut Schmidt: Politikverständnis und geistige Grundlagen* (Bonn: Dietz, 1997).

26 Hess, *Die Männer von U 995*, pp. 42, 44–45, 51.

27 Letter of Heinrich St. to author, May 28, 1996, on a regimental reunion in 1955.

28 *Tübinger Chronik*, May 26, 1952, report on meeting of the 78th Storm Division; cf. *Der Heimkehrer*, July 10, 1965.

29 In the same fashion as Schmidt, see Karl Carstens, *Erinnerungen und Erfahrungen* (Boppard: Boldt, 1993), p. 631. (Unlike the Social Democrat Schmidt, Karstens was a leading politician of the conservative Christian Democratic Union; he was President of the FRG from 1979 to 1984.) See also Romano Guardini, *Das Ende der Neuzeit: Ein Versuch der Orientierung* (Basel: Werkbund, 1950), p. 80.

30 Report in the local newspaper, *Schwäbisches Tagblatt*, Sept. 10, 1956; see also *Stuttgarter Nachrichten*, Sept. 10, 1956.

31 *Alte Kameraden*, Dec. 1955, pp. 1–2.

32 Author's interview with Hanns-Karl Vorster (pseudonym), 1994.

33 *Alte Kameraden*, 1964, Nos. 7–8, pp. 21–22.

34 Ibid., 1957, No. 7, p. 12.

35 Ibid., 1957, No. 10, p. 8. Cf. ibid., 1960, No. 1, p. 4; and *Der Heimkehrer*, 1952, No. 4, p. 1.

36 *Alte Kameraden*, 1960, No. 1, p. 10.

37 Detlef Bald, *Militär und Gesellschaft 1945–1990: Die Bundeswehr in der Bonner Republik* (Baden-Baden: Nomos, 1994), pp. 56–57.

38 Charles B. Burdick, "Vom Schwert zur Feder: Deutsche Kriegsgefangene im Dienst der Vorbereitung der amerikanischen Kriegsgeschichtsschreibung über den zweiten Weltkrieg: Die organisatorische Entwicklung der Operational History (German) Section," *Militärgeschichtliche Mitteilungen*, 10/2 (1971), 69–80; Bernd Wegner, "Erschriebene Siege: Franz Halder, die "Historical Division" und die Rekonstruktion des Zweiten Weltkrieges im Geiste des deutschen Generalstabes,"in Ernst Willi Hansen, Gerhard Schreiber, and Bernd Wegner (eds.), *Politischer Wandel, organisierte Gewalt und nationale Sicherheit* (Munich: Oldenbourg, 1995), pp. 287–302. On the susceptibility of the American public to the image of an honorable German war in the East, see Ronal Smelser and Edward J. Davies II, *The Myth of the Eastern Front: The Nazi–Soviet War in American Popular Culture* (New York: Cambridge University Press, 2008).

39 Georg Meyer, "Zur Situation der deutschen militärischen Führungsschicht im Vorfeld des westdeutschen Verteidigungsbeitrages 1945–1950/51," in Militärgeschichtliches Forschungsamt (ed.), *Anfänge westdeutscher Sicherheitspolitik 1945–1956*, vol. I: *Von der Kapitulation bis Pleven-Plan* (Munich: Oldenbourg, 1982), pp. 577–726 (at 678).

40 Retrospective account in *Der Heimkehrer*, Jan. 15, 1982, p. 3; see also ibid., 1952, No. 9, p. 5; ibid., 1953, No. 12, pp. 1–2; ibid., Dec 5, 1954, p. 1; ibid., June 5, 1955, p. 3, and so on. On local partnerships, see, e.g., ibid., Aug. 25, 1959, p. 9; ibid., June 10, 1961, p. 13.

41 Georg Willmann, *Kriegsgräber in Europa: Ein Gedenkbuch* (Munich: Bertelsmann, 1980); Manfred Wittig, "'Der Tod hat alle Unterschiede ausgelöscht':

Anmerkungen zur Geschichte und Ideologie des Volksbundes Deutsche Kriegsgräberfürsorge nach 1945," in Michael Hütt et al. (eds.), *Unglücklich das Land, das Helden nötig hat: Leiden und Sterben in den Kriegsdenkmälern des Ersten und Zweiten Weltkrieges* (Marburg: Jonas, 1990), pp. 91–98; *Alte Kameraden*, 1957, No. 7, pp. 18–19; ibid., 1957, No. 11, pp. 2–3. Advertisements of the VdK for such trips and reports of related trips organized by veterans' associations appeared often in *Alte Kameraden* and *Der Heimkehrer*, e.g. *Alte Kameraden*, 1959, No. 4, pp. 16–17.

42 *Alte Kameraden*, 1963, No. 7, pp. 31–32.

43 *Frankfurter Allgemeine Zeitung*, Dec. 27, 1971, obituaries for Reusch.

44 Wolfgang Schulenburg, "Über die Kameradschaft," *Westermanns Pädagogische Beiträge*, 10 (1958), 269–77. Günther Grigoleit, *Kameradschaft – Freundschaft* (Breitsohl: Kreuzverlag, 1980).

45 *Der Heimkehrer*, July 10, 1958, p. 1; ibid., Sept. 25, 1978; *Alte Kameraden*, 1967, No. 7, p. 11.

46 Frevert, *A Nation in Barracks*, pp. 259–72; Wolfgang Zapf, *Beiträge zur Analyse der deutschen Oberschicht*, 2nd edn. (Munich: Piper, 1965), pp. 136–49; Manfred Lesch, *Die Rolle der Offiziere in der deutschen Wirtschaft nach dem Ende des Zweiten Weltkrieges* (Berlin: Duncker & Humblot, 1970); Cornelia Rauh-Kühne, "Hans Constantin Paulssen: Sozialpartnerschaft aus dem Geiste der Kriegskameradschaft," in Paul Erker and Toni Pierenkämper (eds.), *Deutsche Unternehmer zwischen Kriegswirtschaft und Wiederaufbau: Studien zur Erfahrungsbildung von Industrie-Eliten* (Munich: Oldenbourg, 1999), pp. 109–92; author's interview with Gerd Frühe (former navy officer, in the 1980s human resources director at Lufthansa).

47 *Jahrbuch für öffentliche Meinung*, 1957, p. 155; *Freiwillig zur Bundeswehr?* (Allensbach: Institut für Demoskopie, 1956).

48 Friedrich Weltz, *Wie steht es um die Bundeswehr? Eine Dokumentation des "Stern" durch Infratest* (Hamburg: Nannen, 1964), p. 67.

49 In Memoriam. Gefallenen-Gedenkrede, gehalten von Dr. Tim Gebhardt . . . , *Alte Kameraden*, Sonderdruck für die 260. ID, Stadtarchiv Ludwigsburg, Depositum 260.I.D., Papers of Tim Gebhardt; *Der Heimkehrer*, Sept. 8, 1955, p. 1, "Kameraden zwischen gestern und morgen."

50 *Alte Kameraden*, March 1962, pp. 1, 3–4 (quotations); *Der Heimkehrer*, March 10, 1962, p. 8; ibid., March 25, 1962, p. 7. Ullrich Rühmland, *NVA: Nationale Volksarmee der DDR in Stichworten*, 7th edn. (Bonn: Bonner Druck-und Verlagsgesellschaft, 1985), pp. 112–13.

9   Demonization

These hopes, however, were built on deceptions. Over the next few decades, the images of the new and the old German armies, the Bundeswehr and the Wehrmacht, were drawn into a process in which military values eroded and the myth of comradeship was turned upside down. Comradeship would eventually cease to stand for the best of humanity in the face of the inhumanity of war. Instead it would be perceived as its evil motor. The comradeship of soldiers, since the dawn of modernity glorified as the epitome of selfless dedication to the fatherland and as the nucleus of civilian society, moved to the dark, immoral margins of society, representing its evil Other. A series of scandals targeting both Bundeswehr and former Wehrmacht soldiers reflected and accelerated the erosion of military values in the West German democracy. At the root of this process lay the taming of the East–West confrontation and secular societal changes. In 1962, at the climax of the Cold War, 63 percent of West Germans expressed fear of a Soviet attack; in the early 1980s only 50 to 40 percent; and in 1988, even before the Cold War ended, a mere 25 percent did so.[1] The less Germans feared another war in Europe, the less they were willing to pay for arms and armies, to spend precious months of their lives on military service, and to buy into military ideologies. This cultural demilitarization was paralleled by the fundamental transition from industrial to post-industrial society, and the subsequent individualization and diversification of lifestyles and moral values. Crucially for the German development, this Silent Revolution, as the American political scientist Ronald Inglehart named it in 1971, coincided with an increasingly critical examination of the Nazi past and of the guilt and responsibility of Germans at that time.[2]

But the dynamic of these processes could not be anticipated in the early 1960s. The optimism of German veterans was by no means delusional, as even a brief look at war memory beyond Germany after 1945 shows. In other parts of the world, most prominently in the United States, the mythical concept of comradeship indeed saw a formidable revival in the late twentieth century. It was already part of American soldiers' remembrance of the war from 1945 on, however. During and after the war, American civilian society was not free of animosities toward the returning soldiers who, it was suspected, might form "a lawless band of trained killers running rampant across America." But these fears did not prove true. Most soldiers easily reintegrated into civilian society, thanks to the generous GI Bill, and thus allowed for a romanticization of the Second World War as an "ennobling experience of collective effort," as the historian Andrew Huebner has said.[4] J. Glenn Gray, who entered the war in 1941 as a private and was discharged in 1945 as a second lieutenant, in his 1959 *The Warriors: Reflections on Men in Battle* praised comradeship, born out of the "presence of danger" and "the consciousness of an obstacle to be overcome through common effort," as a special "appeal of war," at its height "not unlike an aesthetic ecstasy."[3] Gray, of course, wrote as a trained philosopher embedding his personal experiences in mythical Western thinking about the communal power of war. Nonetheless, his voice is representative of both individual recollections and the media of collective war memory, especially novels and movies. Comradeship was a leitmotif of American World War II memories as well, although it was understood in a more individualized and rational fashion than in Germany. In American World War II memory and popular culture, the concept of comradeship equaled buddy relations and friendships among soldiers, radiating sympathy instead of destiny, and often it was replaced by concepts such as teamwork or solidarity in order to indicate what its meaning was: not so much an exceptional communal experience but a vehicle to mutually survive the service and to control the damage to their lives and minds the service might cause.

Autobiographical memoirs, academic discourses – based not least on empirical studies such as Stouffer's *The American Soldier* – and a plethora of war novels and Hollywood movies promulgated the image of the army as a melting pot, in which the experience of comradeship in battle – the buddy system – neutralized conflicting civilian identities and animosities between different immigrant groups, and welded "reluctant" and "rather cynical" recruits into committed team players – into better citizens, that is.[5] This is not to say that the novels or movies that filled American popular war memory from the mid-1940s to the early 1960s simply fabricated a rosy picture of the soldiers' experiences. Instead, frustration, degradation, and disillusionment of individual soldiers through arbitrary military hierarchies, selfish officers, and battlefield horrors constituted a powerful theme of fictional as well as autobiographical accounts.[6] But then it was the "appeal to the team spirit" that protruded from all the chagrin, anger, and annoyance as "perhaps the only positive motivation" of the soldiers, as the literary scholar Peter Aichinger has stated.[7] Hollywood movies such as *Battleground, Sands of Iwo Jima* (both 1949), *The Young Lion,* and *The Naked and the Dead* (both 1958) glorified or execrated army life, and yet they agreed on the sanctity of the solidarity of the combat group. Even one of the more critical Hollywood products, the film adaptation of Norman Mailer's 1948 novel, ends with a homage to comradeship when the wounded Lieutenant Hearns lectures his superior, General Cummings, on what the yield of the war experience was: "Two men carried me eighteen miles through the jungle," not out of fear but "out of love . . . There is a spirit in men that will survive all the reigns of terror and all the hardship . . . The spirit in men is godlike. Eternal. Indestructible."[8]

America's Bad War, the one in Vietnam, interrupted this tale about the Good War and its socially regenerating and morally improving effects only for a while. More than anything else before, the My Lai massacre revealed the criminal potential and the cruel dynamic of male solidarity in war. Neither academic analyses nor mass media nor the fictional representation of the Vietnam War hid this dark side of teamwork and comradeship. But in excusing this dark side, they followed the German way of coping with the stigma of military violence after the Holocaust. Just like the German *Landser,* the Vietnam soldier appeared not as perpetrator who had choices and took the wrong ones but instead as victim of the war – as victim of "the difficult terrain, a shadowy enemy, and an increasingly brutal and stalemated war," and most of all, of corrupt politicians at home and of a military machine that had trained him to destroy life and to abandon the civilian morale he had grown up with.[9]

This early victimizing depiction of the soldier and the decay of the reputation of the military in the 1970s allowed for a little praise of the bright side of comradeship. Much more was allowed in the new genre of anti-war movies that emerged at the end of this decade. It resurrected the concept of male comradeship in war as the epitome of humanity and as an altruistic and communal "anti-structure" (Victor Turner) to a selfish, corrupt, and deceptive civilian "structure" at home.[10] As the literary scholar Susan Jeffords has shown, this resurrection of the male bond was the core piece of what she calls the "remasculinization of America" – the revival of patriarchal values and images of men and masculinity which the Vietnam crisis had undermined and weakened. Jeffords identifies this strategy – which reaffirmed not only a male-dominated gender order but also the public adoration of military values – in a broad range of fictional and nonfictional works by authors representing different political opinions and pursuing different political agendas; the list ranges from books such as Michael Herr's *Dispatches* (1977), Richard Nixon's *No More*

Victims (1985), and William Broyles's *Brothers in Arms* (1986) to war movies such as *The Deerhunter* (1978), *First Blood* (1982), *Rambo* (1985), and *Full Metal Jacket* (1987). These representations portray Vietnam soldiers as victims of American society, and especially of a government that is characterized as weak, false, and treacherous. It is in opposition to these feminized characters and institutions that the soldiers and veterans renew their manly status by retreating into, relying on, and regaining strength from "the masculine bond – commitments between men that are seen to cross barriers of racial, ethnic, class, age, geographic, religious or social differences" and surpass "legal, bureaucratic, familial, or other social connections." While "women must be effectively and finally eliminated from the masculine realm," the soldiers and veterans are shown as able to take over reproductive features usually performed by women and establish the "self-sufficient community of the masculine bond" that can "survive and thrive without women." As such, it embodies the nucleus of society per se, in fact a "new world" that serves as model for reorganizing and renewing the entire American society.[11]

The parallels between the myth of comradeship built in post-Vietnam America and the one in Germany after the *First* World War are obvious. In both cases, the myth helped society cope with the emotional, moral, and political damage caused by war traumas and humiliating defeats. In both cases, the myth insisted on the soldiers' commitment to, and their ability to preserve, a kind of communal humanity that civilian society had abandoned or betrayed although its political values and identity essentially depended on it. "Comradeship," Broyles explained in his account of his return to Vietnam in 1984, "makes war intelligible for the citizen soldier." Comradeship, "writ large, is patriotism." The comrade is the one you "trust with anything" including "your life." And this way, comradeship transcends differences of "race, personality, education," whatever separates people in civilian society, or in "peace."[12] It is the soldiers in war who make America – the melting-pot conception of America – real through their comradeship. And the veterans continue doing so at home, as the three friends and comrades Mike, Steven, and Nick demonstrate in *The Deer Hunter*, most spectacularly when they manage to use their Vietcong oppressors' sadism for a dramatic escape action; it's only their ultimate solidarity that overcomes physical and mental destruction, not leading to a happy end at home but yet enabling them, and America, to move on. And so comradeship is the fuel that allows the social machinery to keep going in other stories, especially, and not by accident, in crime drama TV series, such as *Magnum, P.I.* (1980–88) and *Miami Vice* (1984–89); in all these stories, the bonds of men, hammered in war, appear as a social tool to bring wrongdoers to justice – to fight evil, to do good; it is their comradeship that promotes the Vietnam veterans to guides and teachers of their nation.[13]

The revival of comradeship in 1980s America did not remain an episode but continued in the 1990s and beyond, both in popular culture and in state politics. In the most popular TV crime series such as *NCIS* (premiered in 2003), former marines, having served in the Gulf, the Iraq, or the Afghanistan wars, insist that "there is no such thing as a former marine," embody the principle of "no one is left behind," and re-enact the morals of comradeship, proving its benefits for civilian society on an almost daily basis.[14] Even presidential foreign politics takes up, or is judged on the basis of, the "no one left behind ethos."[15] Since the end of the twentieth century, however, the American public no longer looks only at the most recent or ongoing wars in Iraq or Afghanistan in order to learn about the vibrant workings of the brotherhood of combat; instead, more than ever before it is the Second World War, the undoubted model of a Good War, that serves to celebrate its eternal truth. While World War II novels and movies in the long 1950s barely avoided critical undercurrents when detailing the military culture, the new epic war dramas, such as Steven Spielberg's *Saving Private Ryan* (1998) or the TV miniseries *Band of Brothers* (2001), display the brotherhood of combat no less gloriously than the most deliberate voices in post-1918 and post-1945 Germany did.[16] Remarkably, the revival of World War II comradeship in popular culture went along with, or was even preceded by, a new local culture of war memorials. They too "were centered completely on the idea of the 'buddy system' or the story of returning men" who "survived the war not only through courage but also through an extensive effort of mutual assistance in the prison camps," as John Bodnar has explained with regard to monuments honoring the disaster, sacrifice, and endurance of American soldiers at Bataan in the Philippines in 1942.[17]

In the 1990s such a memorial culture was no longer thinkable in Germany, even less so later. While the United States faced a tendency toward devaluation of the military in the 1970s, it was reversed only shortly after the end of the Vietnam War. The opposite happened in Germany at the same time. Here, too, the late 1960s and early 1970s saw a hitherto unknown questioning of military values. But there was no counterweight to contain it. Instead, the gap between civilian society and armed forces widened. It did so in other parts of Europe as well, but it was Germany where the cultural demilitarization and the Silent Revolution, the individualization of lifestyles, coincided with an ever more critical view of the Nazi past, especially among younger Germans who, naturally, gained weight and power the more the older generations passed away.[18]

In 1968, the student rebellion climaxed, and so did the challenge to authoritarian structures, and the denunciation of former Nazis' continuing or resurrected influence; the Federal Chancellor of Germany, Kurt Georg Kiesinger, had been a member of the NSDAP. In the shadow of this uproar, a young journalist, Günther Wallraff, published the personal diary of his service with the Bundeswehr. It became a bestseller – a widely read eyewitness account of the "inhuman absurdity of military drill" and the "pathology of military morality." The consoling effect of comradeship was not among Wallraff's experiences. On the contrary, the time he served with the Bundeswehr against his will – his request to be acknowledged as a conscientious objector had been declined – drove him to seek psychiatric counseling.[19] Of course, experiences like Wallraff's were not new in the history of the German or any other drafted army; Wallraff was not the first to accuse the army of destroying the individual's personality. Remarque had done so after the First World War, and after the Second World War Hans Hellmut Kirst's *08/15* (1954–55), a no less popular trilogy of novels and subsequent movies, satirized "pig-like NCOs and hopelessly sappy, ingenuous officers" in the former Wehrmacht and presented them as the Wehrmacht's social "normality." It scathingly indicted the underhand methods of military discipline, and issued a warning against their revival in the new German armed forces. In *08/15*, a Wehrmacht drill sergeant, Kirst's bully Platzeck, appeared as the successor to Remarque's Himmelstoß.[20] Popular magazines too confronted readers with stories about Wehrmacht officers who had not missed an opportunity to torment "silly, mischievous, but in general kindhearted comrades." Some of their victims broke down; others, just as Remarque's Paul Bäumer had done before, sought protection in "comradeship, against which a martinet like this Pauli did not stand a chance."[21] And this again was the point of these World War II novels. Just as Remarque's classic anti-war novel had done, they elevated the alleged reality of comradeship as the one social force able to save the soldiers' integrity.

The change around 1970 was obvious. Wallraff's denunciation of the Bundeswehr was not an isolated document. A few years before Wallraff's *J'accuse* appeared, a huge scandal shook the reputation of the Bundeswehr much more than this report of a man who could easily be classified as a wimp or a griper who just didn't meet the bar. In the Nagold barracks, close to the idyllic Black Forest, a recruit died as result of brutal training methods – as it turned out, the same as had been used by Nazi elite troops such Hermann Göring's paratroopers. Nothing had been learned, so it seemed. In the liberal democracy of the 1960s, the Bundeswehr seemed to be an anachronistic relic of the totalitarian past, not a foundation of liberal democracy.[22] Around 1970, it was not only antimilitarist activists like Wallraff who denounced the inhumanity of military service; scientists too analyzed it more critically than ever before, and not only in Germany. Erving Goffman's theory of the "total institution," paralleling monasteries, prisons, and barracks, was the most influential one, and it had many successors in Germany.[23] They did not offer many new insights; the mechanisms of tearing down the civilian self and of the build-up of the soldierly group identity had been described before. But there was a new assessment: The recruit's initiation through humiliating rituals was no longer celebrated as a prerequisite of a masculine rite of passage, but denounced as both pointless and inhumane. The pressure to conform and sacrifice one's individuality, once a noble objective of military initiation, now became the focus of severe criticism. Comradeship was no longer the social oil of ennoblement, but rather incitement to brutalization.

By the end of the 1970s, reports of alcohol abuse and of "terror" inflicted by soldiers on new recruits triggered consternation in the general public. It appeared that the "Holy Ghost" – the German term for the torturing of an outsider by his comrades – celebrated its resurrection in the Bundeswehr, manifesting itself in brutal pecking orders, alcohol-induced hazing, sadistic and violent excesses, compulsory freezing showers, verbal abasement, and the "red ass" culture that defined the military routine. In civilian society, the perception grew that the "school of the nation" had in fact become the "drinking school of the nation." Even when comradeship was not the only cause, its praise was increasingly seen as a mere cover for the "degrading" social culture in the army.[24]

Remarkably, popular World War II memory supported the slow degradation of comradeship, perhaps unwittingly, as was shown by *Little Quast*, the hero of a 1978 German World War II novel by Heinz G. Stachow. Quast, a simple Wehrmacht *Landser*, fought till the bitter end, not out of "loyalty to the Führer" but out of comradeship. "Leaving my comrades in the lurch, who were every bit as dedicated to me as I was to them – that would have been unthinkable," the *Landser* Quast explains. Rooted in a long tradition of popular war memory, *Little Quast* sought to rescue the old masculine social paradigm: men dedicated to "overcoming the great shit together." Even in 1978, this undertaking was not entirely hopeless. Major parts of German society still adhered to past and new soldierly ideals. Yet the novel, published at the end of a decade of increasing unease about the Nazi past and about the present armed forces, felt obliged to admit that such justifications could be perceived as "over-inflated," "suspicious," or "old-fashioned." And there was even more doubt about comradeship. "The men slowly allow themselves to get tanked and then enjoy sharing stories about their exploits with women," observed Quast.

"They all see themselves as heroes, whom no woman can resist." Some of them drink themselves into a "mess" and exemplify the philosophy of life, or more accurately, the philosophy of death, of the wartime *Landser*: "Take what you can today. For tomorrow you'll be dead or mutilated." Excesses and "messes" of any type were easily justified by this motto.[25]

Barely any of the post-1945 war novels or films refrained from depicting great drinking bouts, where comrades connected with each other. The further removed the reworking of wartime comradeship became from the reality of the war, the more good, clean, and caring comradeship faded into the background, replaced by bad, dirty, and scurrilous comradeship – and all this in order to cater to the needs of the entertainment industry. The veterans, of course, were appalled when soldiers were "portrayed in war novels as egoists, criminals, cowards, drunks, in other words, exclusively people who resembled the lowest egoist."[26] It especially enraged the veterans' movement (and the general staff of the Bundeswehr) that the entertainment industry portrayed officers and non-commissioned officers as the ringleaders of this sordid comradeship. If the expectation among prospective Bundeswehr recruits was to find buddies with whom they could "go out drinking" or "every now and then raise hell," it was a concept of comradeship they derived from the popular war literature genre, one that had little in common with the ideals promoted by the veterans themselves.

The German army (and not only the German) had been known before this for group terror, initiation rituals, and group drinking excesses. What was new around 1980 was the sensibility of civilian society. The social culture of male brutality no longer fitted into the way this society consti-tuted itself or its "citizens in uniform."[27] In the late 1960s, the number of conscientious objectors grew substantially; in 1968 their numbers passed 10,000 for the first time; by 1980, this figure climbed to 60,000, and by 1990 it reached 100,000. The legal hurdles that had obstructed objec-tion to military service were dropped in 1980. This act reflected a secular shift in ideologies, a fundamental cultural demilitarization of Germany (and other European countries). While conscientious objectors had pre-viously had to pass an arbitrary examination of their conscience in front of Bundeswehr soldiers if they wanted to avoid being imprisoned for their position, they could from 1980 on simply choose between military ser-vice and the civilian equivalent. By the end of the 1990s, there were equal numbers of military conscripts and conscientious objectors.[28] Increasing numbers of the younger generation no longer saw military socialization as a requirement for becoming a man. Instead, civilian service in hos-pitals or homes for old people allowed young German men to establish an alternative masculine ideal, one that spurned the chauvinistic, hyper-masculine male community, its pecking orders, and glorification of the iron discipline of men. Cooperation between female nurses and young men (no matter how conflict-laden this atmosphere could be) governed the transition from boyhood to manhood. In the reunited Germany of the 1990s at the latest, military service relinquished its hegemonic significance.[29]

Those who still opted for the "Bund" hoped to acquire specialist technical skills, and to experience comradeship. They were not disappointed. At the beginning of the 1990s, 77 percent of all conscripts still saw comradeship as the most important experience in their term of service.[30] But what kind of comradeship was this? According to critical insiders, the Bundeswehr was a cold, "impersonal army."[31] It was impossible for real comradeship to establish itself, because nearly everyone went home at the end of the day, bemoaned even insiders. Civilian values, based on personal interests and ambitions, infiltrated the armed forces and perforated the practice of comradeship. Internal assessments complained that "comradeship" for recruits meant not much more than organizing the commute home together or, even worse, was used "against or not on behalf of the Bundeswehr."[32] Comradeship meant borrowing a buddy's car in order to visit a girlfriend, helping each other cheat with the legal car inspection, and raising funds needed for the next boozing session. What critical observers articulated here was not new, of course, when it came to detecting the darker aspects of comradeship. Violating norms or even laws together had always been a crucial feature of comradeship, just one that wasn't necessarily exposed to the public or one's superiors. What was new was the increased sensibility of both the military leadership and civilian society vis-à-vis those darker aspects of comradeship. Especially in public perception, it seemed that solidarity among soldiers, the comradeship once so glorified, was just a means to do harm to others and to undermine the law.

This shift in values occurred against the backdrop of a social reordering: The contrast between civilian and military society mirrored the one between the educated and the lower classes. The armed forces were subject to a process of proletarianization. Most *Gymnasium* graduates turned down military service, while men with elementary and middle school degrees went into the Bund. And the same change affected the officer corps. Nearly 75 percent of the officers commissioned after 1973 had a lower-class background. Before World War II, they would have not have been able to run through the military ranks beyond NCO. In the Third Reich the officer corps was still recruited from the upper and educated classes, who – more than the lower classes – idolized a soldier, and especially an officer, as the epitome of a real man.[33] Change began at the end of the Second World War, but only in the late twentieth century were these historical foundations of the armed forces turned upside down. Educated Germans despised the draft and any professional military career. And with the loss of the educated middle classes, the army also lost its intellectual mouthpiece, the force that had traditionally emulated and praised soldierly virtues in civilian society. Increasingly, it was the conscientious objectors and the unenthusiastic draftees who dominated the public debate and the image of military culture.

But the devaluation of comradeship in German society was a result not only of ideological shifts in the younger generations. From the late 1970s, civilian society worried more than before about the inner workings of the army and the dark, dirty, even criminal side of comradeship; the multifaceted depictions of morally good comradeship fell by the wayside. The origin of this process, however, reached back to the immediate postwar period. It was rooted in the public debate on the morality of the Wehrmacht, and of the Waffen-SS; the scandals about the Bundeswehr added further to the increasing stigmatization and demonization of the army at large. Thanks to the blemishing of the SS at the Nuremberg Trials and the exoneration of the Wehrmacht by German politicians and prominent Americans and British, the war veterans enjoyed some protection from the stigma of the Nazi war. The trials against Nazi perpetrators in West Germany in the 1950s and 1960s still almost exclusively targeted members of the Einsatzgruppen and concentration camp guards, not soldiers of the Wehrmacht, and only rarely Waffen-SS soldiers. Instead, former ordinary soldiers were included in Germany's self-perception as a grand community of war victims. The imagery of Germans as victims of war and dictatorship provided the cultural roof of the postwar democracy. Pointing to their sacrifices in war and in captivity, the veterans managed to take a lead in public debates on the past throughout the 1950s. Thanks to its polyvalence, the concept of comradeship supported the veterans' integration into the new civilian and democratic society and yet allowed them to maintain their own identity as soldiers of a past war carried out by a criminal regime. The ambiguous relationship of both the veterans and the concept of comradeship to the crimes of the Third Reich, and leftist Germans' search for the truth about the complicity of the soldiers, together changed the way Germans perceived both – the veterans and the concept of comradeship.

Comradeship, as we have seen, was based on reciprocity; it was an obligation. In the 1950s it meant watching out for those former comrades who were still in captivity, especially in the Soviet Union. Demonstrating solidarity with them was a requirement of comradeship. Each and every one of the late-returning POWs exemplified the vitality and efficacy of comradeship. Once home, former POWs were not expected simply to lose themselves in their private lives. Instead, they had to keep the promise they had allegedly given their comrades left behind in Soviet camps – that they would not be forgotten. Those who "broke their word" committed a capital crime against the holy laws of comradeship and excluded themselves from the postwar community of comrades.[34]

Even prominent veterans and former Wehrmacht leaders, such as General Geyr von Schweppenburg, were bound by this code of loyalty. In 1953, the former tank corps commander was scheduled to testify at a court in France as a key witness for the defense of Waffen-SS General Bittrich, whose troops had executed members of the French resistance while under his command. Afraid that the French would charge him too with war crimes, Geyr stayed clear of the trial and consequently faced accusations that he "abandoned his comrade between the lines." Geyr justified his refusal to attend the trial by arguing that, for him, "more was on the line than for Bittrich." Indeed, Geyr played an important role as advisor in the rearmament of West Germany. He therefore wanted to avoid being seen as bedfellow – comrade – of a war criminal. It was exactly this – allowing his own personal welfare to dictate his actions – that a good comrade would never do.[35]

Geyr demeaned himself in the eyes of the veterans almost in the same fashion as the *Kameradenschinder* (comrade flayers, torturers of their comrades) and *Kameradenverräter* (comrade snitchers) in the Soviet internment camps. These were German POWs who cooperated with the Soviet anti-fascist committees (Antifa) or spied on and denounced their comrades for personal gain, often delivering them to Soviet tribunals.[36] The Antifa organized the informant system in Soviet camps, designed to gauge National Socialist sentiments and uncover involvement in war crimes. During Soviet captivity, and even more afterwards in West Germany, the Antifa symbolized the destruction of comradeship.[37] The same was true for those who supported the "National Committee for a Free Germany" and the "League of German Officers." These men had "excluded themselves once and forever from the ranks of decent comrades," as one veteran put it in 1962, expressing the general mood of the postwar period.[38] These traditions went back to the Nazi era. "Treason is comrade murder" was printed in bold red letters on a leaflet that every soldier had to carry in his pay book, warning him not to cooperate with the Soviets in the event of capture.[39] The code of loyalty and comradeship was thus tied into the continuities of anti-communism from Nazi Germany to Cold War Germany.

The *Kameradenverräter* and *Kameradenschinder* in Soviet prison camps committed sacrilege. Back home in the 1950s, they had to contend with vengeance from those they had betrayed. The Heimkehrer League circulated blacklists and launched an outright hunt for *Kameradenverräter* and *Kameradenschinder*, supported by the judicial system.[40] Between 1948 and 1950, nearly one hundred former POWs were given prison sentences ranging from five to fifteen years in West Germany, because as members of a camp administration they had mistreated or denounced other prisoners, and had been party to physical abuse, manslaughter, or deprivation of liberty. The last charge was applied to those "traitors" whose denunciations led to the conviction of German POWs as "war criminals" in the Soviet Union or Yugoslavia.[41] And it was not only veterans' associations and the criminal justice system that pursued these "noncomrades": the new West German army, the Bundeswehr, did so as well. Its selection committee (Personalgutachterausschuss), when reviewing the backgrounds of former Wehrmacht and Waffen-SS professional soldiers who applied to the ranks of the Bundeswehr, paid much attention to possible "infringements against ethical principles." Former soldiers who had disregarded their obligation to care for comrades, or had denounced or bullied them, were not acceptable. However, it was only the period of captivity that was scrutinized. What the applicants had done during the war, specifically whether or not they had violated international law and committed war crimes or crimes against humanity, played no role.[42]

The hunt for the "criminals" who had violated the ethical principles of comradeship in Soviet captivity deflected attention from debates on and investigations into crimes committed by German soldiers during the war. Until 1958, Nazi perpetrators were rarely brought to justice in West Germany. It was only then that the Einsatzgruppen Trial in Ulm drew the attention of the public, of prosecutors, and of police to the "murderers among us," those Germans who were complicit in the Holocaust and other mass crimes during the war and yet went on with their lives, unchallenged and unpunished.[43] But these murderers – typically members of the SS and the Gestapo or other sectors of Himmler's troops, and in the 1960s also camp guards – were not thought of as ordinary soldiers. The Wehrmacht veterans, although never entirely safe from suspicions, managed to take their troops out of the firing line in public debates about the Nazi past and to whitewash the reputation of Hitler's army, as opposed to the SS. The anti-totalitarian consensus of the Western democracies made it possible for them to put the blame for Nazi crimes on the elite of the Third Reich. Questions about the possible complicity of ordinary Germans – including soldiers – could be deflected, not least by focusing on the crimes committed by communists in POW camps and happening under Stalin's and his successors' communism.

Popular war memory, war novels, and movies, as we have seen, widely affirmed this consensus and helped whitewash the Wehrmacht soldiers. Stories inquiring into crimes committed by ordinary soldiers against unarmed adversaries, Jews, prisoners, women, or children, found only small audiences in West Germany, if any; yet these stories were available. An early example was Wolfgang Staudte's movie *The Murderers Are Among Us*, produced immediately after the war and first shown in 1946. It portrays the former military surgeon Dr. Mertens returning home from war in 1945, a broken man, traumatized and escaping into alcoholism. By accident, he meets his former captain Ferdinand Brückner. Brückner, who ordered the shooting of a hundred civilians in a Polish village on Christmas Eve 1942, was a cold-blooded murderer with no regrets. Now, very soon after the war, he is a successful businessman, and jovial, cooperative, and open-minded, or so the audience is made to think. The epitome of a good comrade. And yet he is the "murderer among us." Mertens, not the perpetrator, is haunted by that shooting action; he had witnessed it but not intervened. Now he wants to kill the murderer. It is only his friend, Susanne, with whom he falls in love, a concentration camp survivor, who prevents him from doing so; instead they bring Brückner to trial and re-establish justice.[44]

Comradeship was not a theme of this movie; it was about German bystanders, who had not wanted mass murder but had not prevented it either. They are traumatized, victimized, the movie shows, thus confirming the basic consensus of postwar Germany about the fatherland's suffering through war. And yet, it is not by accident that this movie was produced in East Germany. Here, the critique of the Wehrmacht's complicity in the Nazi crimes against humanity was deliberately articulated under the communist regime, not least in order to denounce West Germany's supposed (and in part actual) covering up of Nazi crimes. So it was that an East rather than a West German writer would be the one to expose the criminal dynamic of comradeship. Franz Fühmann, a former Wehrmacht soldier who after Antifa schooling in Soviet imprisonment returned to East Germany, published in 1955 the novella *Kameraden*, or *Comrades*, a parable on the preparation, implementation, and cover-up of the Wehrmacht's crimes in the Soviet Union, not least the involvement of allegedly innocent bystanders in these crimes. The story focuses on three soldier-friends who are stationed in East Prussia on the eve of the attack against the Soviet Union. One night they go out looking for girls, or at the very least a pub, in the neighboring village. But the excursion into impure comradeship derails into crime. On the way, the three spot a heron, which ignites their hunting fever. Although it is strictly prohibited "to fire a shot along the border without orders," the lure of the forbidden proves too strong. Two of the soldiers, Josef and Karl, squeeze their triggers at the same time, hitting not just the bird, but also a little girl who happens to be passing by. As it turns out, she is the daughter of the major of their unit. What now? For the two perpetrators there is no debate: Keep mum and cover it up. Thomas, the sole witness who has not participated, is "in shock, defenseless and unwillingly implicated in the murder," and wants to run away. Yet he immediately remembers his Hitler Youth camp, where it had been drummed into his head: "Our honor means loyalty! Woe to him who betrays his comrades! He will be excommunicated from his Volk! To be German means standing together for good or for evil! That is why we are the chosen people, we the guardians of the Nibelungen loyalty!" And Karl explains, "if you have never whacked anybody, you are not a real fella." Thomas takes a bullet out of his cartridge belt and discards it, so that each is now missing one bullet and the real perpetrator cannot be determined. The criminal deed is now vested in the "conspiratorial community." An oath threatens the "Judas" with death. "Whoever even thinks about betraying one of the others, no one can protect him."

The story continues. During field exercises, the battalion discovers the corpse of the murdered girl. The unexpected saviour is Josef's father, an "old fighter" and high-ranking SS officer, who is accompanying the division general. Josef discloses everything to his father. He has a "National Socialistic solution" to hand. He explains to his son that Germans are not murderers. Only Bolsheviks are. So it was they who were responsible for the murdered child. The body is found only after it has been – it is suggested to the reader – mutilated by the SS, its face "cut up" until "it was unrecognisable," in order to shift blame for the shameful act onto the "Russian sub-humans," and stoke the soldiers' desire for vengeance: "But the hour has come for the murderers! Comrades, you will avenge your commander!" And this they do. They encounter little resistance to their advance into the East. In a small village, all of the inhabitants, men, women, and children, are herded into the square, where two randomly selected girls are hanged on the major's orders, "in revenge for the death of his daughter."[45]

One may doubt the aesthetic quality of Fühmann's novella. Its message is ponderous and overdone. Yet within the larger realm of collective memory of the National Socialist war, the story takes a remarkable position. Uniquely and appropriately, it interprets comradeship as the social cement and symbolic infrastructure of the mass murder that Germans committed against the subjugated populations, in the name of racial and ideological warfare, and under cover of an anti-partisan campaign. And it exposes what comradeship always had been about: a cover-up tool. In the 1950s, the West German audience, however, was not interested in this kind of enlightenment, despite – or maybe because of – the uncertainty and unease that percolated through the convulsive confirmation of the former soldiers' innocence. Whatever they had done in war, the former soldiers, not to mention former SS and police men, did not know when the past would boil up. And they did not want to be reminded of it. Instead, they sought once and for all to wipe the slate clean of the past. A "general amnesty" should allow the West German democracy to move on. This idea could claim a long tradition in the history of warfare.[46] "Throughout history," the initiators of a 1952 campaign for "general amnesty" declared, "war and political upheaval have precipitated actions that violated established international laws and national rights, and which therefore could have been punished." The conviction that "general satisfaction was a greater commodity than the application of broken laws" was embedded in a tradition of "political reason," which had prevailed since the Edict of Nantes and the Peace of Westphalia. Only an amnesty, "oblivio perpetua et amnestia" as it was formulated in 1648, could transcend feelings of revenge and resentment among the former adversaries, the former soldiers said.[47]

The invocation of the tradition of forgetting, and its partial realization through the amnesty law (*Straffreiheitsgesetz*) of 1954 not only obfuscated individual misdeeds, but also the fundamental break with the traditions of European warfare that Hitler's war effected. Whether the amnesty would also extend to killings outside of actual military operations remained controversial even within the veterans' movement. Not everyone would be pardoned, and not everyone was able to take advantage of the loyalty that comradeship required. A Hauptsturmführer of the SD, the SS intelligence service, who "along with his men had shot several tens of thousands of Jews and mentally ill people outside of Minsk," would willingly be sacrificed by the veterans' community.[48] He was not one of them – the army – but one of the other side, the NSDAP and the SS. Veterans' organizations rallied behind the consensus view of the West German public, which drew a line beyond handing over the few managers of the Holocaust from the SS, SD, and Einsatzgruppen, in order to save the bystanders and accomplices, the masses of soldiers, including their generals, regardless of what they had done.

"Where crime starts, comradeship ends," claimed a popular dictum, invented by an HIAG leader and adopted throughout the veterans' movement.[49] Who, then, was a criminal, and what constituted a crime? According to age-old military moralities, comradeship represented the humane element of the army, the humane counter to the inhumanity of war, as the Wehrmacht veterans never tired of repeating, and also the counter to the evil of National Socialism, as the Jewish-German Ernst Friedländer had confirmed in 1945. In other words, not necessarily spoken by Friedländer but often invoked by veterans in West Germany, comradeship per se stood above crime. This semantic jumble could be used to excuse almost any kind of brutality against enemy civilians in war when it came to deciding who was to be protected by comradeship and who was not, only to be abandoned as a criminal. A crime was not defined by the deed itself, but rather by its purpose, according to the morality of comradeship. What mattered was whether or not the perpetrator had acted in the interests of his comrades. He who stuck to this ethical code of the community was a good comrade, not a criminal.

There were of course exceptions. Field Marshal Ferdinand Schörner was tried before a German court upon his return from Soviet captivity in 1955 for the legendary "thousand nooses" he unleashed against German soldiers in the Kurland Pocket in the final phases of the war, and this was met with widespread approval among veterans, from the Heimkehrer League down to the VdS. Yet when they broke off their comradeship with him, it was not because of his brutal treatment of "deserters" and "cowards," for whom no veteran's heart would beat, but because just before the capitulation Schörner used his Fiseler Storch (a small aircraft) to defect to the American lines, and "abandoned" his troops.[50]

Overall, however, it was the crimes of others – those who did not count as soldiers, whether with the Wehrmacht or the Waffen-SS – that were questioned. Even a man such as Sepp Dietrich did not qualify as criminal. One of the most famous, most energetic, and most successful Waffen-SS leaders, he was not only a close personal friend of Hitler but was also the epitome of a comradely leader. He was put on trial and sentenced to prison in 1946 because units under his command, without his knowledge, had committed atrocities against American prisoners in Malmedy during the Ardennes Offensive, but this certainly did not diminish his popularity. And neither did his role in the shootings of SA leaders during the so-called "Night of the Long Knives," the cold-blooded murder of SA and Wehrmacht leaders in 1934, for which he was indicted in 1957, shortly after having served his first ten-year prison sentence for the Malmedy massacre. The 1934 murders were an entirely different matter, which no longer left his criminal character in doubt. Yet the HIAG did not refuse comradeship to him or to any other of its own troop leaders, no matter what crimes they had committed, as long as they had stood by their men; when he was finally released from prison in 1958 and denied a pension by the West German government, his former comrades raised enough for him to live comfortably. When he died in 1966, 5,000 war comrades attended his funeral.[51]

The HIAG's solidarity with Sepp Dietrich was an exceptional case but the Wehrmacht veterans' associations observed the same policy. To them, the decency of their army commanders could not be questioned merely because they were brought to trial as war criminals for having carried out or passed on criminal orders, or because war crimes occurred in areas under their jurisdiction. A popular excuse for war crimes stood always ready to justify such deeds – the *Befehlsnotstand*, the alleged lack of choice of the subordinate who would have jeopardized his own life had he refused even orders to murder civilians.[52] Two prominent examples were the former Waffen-SS officers Walter Reder and Herbert Kappler, responsible for the massacres of Italian civilians in Marzabotto and the Fosse Ardeatini respectively. Each was given a life sentence in Italy. And yet they enjoyed unrestricted solidarity from all parts of the West German veterans' movement. They committed the massacres, which were reprisals for partisan attacks, on the orders of superiors, and this was sufficient for the German veterans' associations – the HIAG and Wehrmacht associations – to absolve the two officers from their responsibility.[53] It was nothing less than "comradely duty" to devote oneself wholeheartedly to securing their release.[54] A petition in 1958 for the benefit of Major Reder, who was imprisoned in Gaeta in Italy, garnered 290,000 signatures, including 20,000 from soldiers of Germany's former enemy nations. Each signature bore witness to the vitality of the "still vibrant sense of chivalry and comradeship among the soldiers."[55]

Yet to claim that these signatures made Walter Reder's fate the focus of the entire wartime generation, as veterans' newspapers exulted, was a far too optimistic view.[56] Such a unity had never existed. The wartime generation itself was divided. The myth of the "clean Wehrmacht" was hardly grounded in a broad societal consensus in postwar Germany. A minority of Germans kept, and articulated, their doubts from early on. In 1953, 55 percent of the West German population believed that accusations against behavior of German soldiers in the occupied territories were not legitimate, but 21 percent held the opposite view, and nearly as many (18 percent) were undecided.[57] All efforts by the veterans to assert their support of the democratic state and of international reconciliation, all invocations of altruistic comradeship, and all affirmations that they had fought the war as had other soldiers, could not dispel the fog of complicity that hung over them. Two out of five West Germans did not really trust the old soldiers and their tales. Their suspicions were backed not so much by the Social Democratic Party – who did not want to lose the veterans as voters or potential voters – but by the trade unions and other leftist political organizations, especially those of the victims of the Nazi regime, and the left-wing press, none of them dependent on votes in political elections.

In 1954, the DGB (Deutscher Gewerkschaftsbund), the West German umbrella organization of all branch trade unions, denounced the "732 leagues of ex-soldiers" and regimental associations as "enemies of democracy" in a popular pamphlet.[58] More suggestive than analytical, it painted the handful of extreme right-wing organizations and the many politically neutral organizations with the same "brown" brush. The DGB did not exactly know, or didn't say, what these associations actually did or what the motives of their leaders and members were. Yet the suspicions sufficed. Under the guidance of the DGB, West Germany's political left continuously accused the ex-soldiers' leagues, with their social service programs and commitment to democracy, of merely "camouflaging" their "real purpose," which was to resurrect the spirit of militarism and nationalism.[59] And so leftist mass media warned time and again of the veterans' alleged "war romanticism" that portrayed the war as a "great jaunt into the wide world."[60]

The trade unions certainly exaggerated the threat to democracy by the veterans' movement. Like other conspiracy theories and enemy stereotypes, the distrust of the unions served to establish unity within. So it did on other occasions. Often, the Nazi or Fascist charge went hand in hand with the charge of militarism, both serving as rhetorical weapons of the political Left in its battle against the Right. Under the motto, "Democracy is in danger," the Hessian workers' youth mobilized 2,000 members in the summer of 1960 to demonstrate against a planned gathering of the Kyffhäuserbund that was endorsed by the local branch of Young Union, the youth organization of the CDU, the major conservative party of West Germany. The Kyffhäuser cancelled its gathering, yet the counter-rally went ahead as planned. Erich Kuby, now an icon of West German leftist journalism, gave the keynote speech, hailing the victory the Left had achieved by this counter-rally over the "militarists" before it even came down to a "battle."[61]

In the 1960s, marches and protest actions like this rarely targeted the politically inconspicuous regimental and divisional veterans' associations. It was only when the student rebellion of 1968 propelled the search for remnants of the Nazi past in the West German present that these associations, too, were drawn into the fight against "right-wing extremism."[62] In the university town of Tübingen, where former members of the 78th

Storm Division had long been embedded in local society, students in 1968 welcomed the sixth national reunion of the 78th with fliers campaigning "Against Fascism and Militarism," and then staged a "teach in" on the market square, just as the veterans started gathering there. At that time the overall political climate still ensured that the local press stood behind the veterans. The *Schwäbisches Tagblatt* sarcastically reported that the students received a palpable hands-on "lecture on the psychology of the old front-soldiers" physically inflicted by these very ex-soldiers.[63]

In the 1950s and 1960s, critique and protest against the veterans' associations were articulated by the trade unions and various smaller leftist associations, but not by the major political parties. Things changed fundamentally in the 1970s. In the aftermath of the 1968 student rebellion and a general shift toward the political left in West German society – in 1969, the SPD took over the federal government and ran the country together with the small liberal party until 1982 – the Social Democrats joined the fray. Occasionally even the conservative Christian Democrats followed suit. In the late 1970s, after the TV miniseries *Holocaust* succeeded in dramatically increasing public awareness of the murder of the Jews (and of the Nazi society that allowed it), there was no going back. The big political parties such as the SPD took a much more explicit stance than ever before against the HIAG, and subsequently also against less exposed sections of the veterans' movement. The SPD had previously shied away from alienating the World War II veterans, instead honoring them as a valuable asset in political elections, but voices of SPD members now grew louder in demanding the expulsion of all HIAG members from the party, and in 1981 the SPD issued a formal incompatibility resolution; a member of the SPD could no longer be an HIAG member.[64] At the same time, the SPD-controlled federal administration used the official Report on the Protection of the Constitution to brand the HIAG as an extreme right, anti-constitutional organization, a symbolically loaded slap in the face for the HIAG. When the SPD lost control over the federal administration in 1982, the new CDU-led government dropped this stigmatization – and the SPD protested vehemently. From then on, the liberal and leftist mass media outlets honed in on the HIAG, and the SPD and other leftist organizations incited spectacular public protests against HIAG gatherings. After this, the HIAG was no longer able to hold its reunions or even smaller meetings publicly without facing protest marches or resolutions and thus attracting a scandal. City councils caved in under public pressure, cancelling previously scheduled HIAG gatherings.[65]

The efforts of former Waffen-SS soldiers to be recognized as "soldiers just like all others," as the SPD leader Kurt Schumacher once said in an address to them, largely failed. This became obvious in the 1980s, in spite of their never-ending attempts to distance themselves from the so-called Allgemeine SS, from the SD (the intelligence service) of the SS, and from the Totenkopf (death's-head) units, which provided the concentration camp guards. The Waffen-SS had been branded by the Nuremberg Trials verdict together with the rest of the SS, so, by association, the HIAG never shook off suspicions of trivializing or denying the Holocaust, of allowing their secret circles to trade war stories about infamous massacres such as the one at Oradour, of raising silent toasts to Hitler, and of singing old Nazi songs.

Time and again, however, the Wehrmacht came under fire from the Left as well. As early as 1966, the writer Rudolf Krämer-Badoni unleashed a scandal when, in a commemorative speech at a joint cere-mony of the Heimkehrer League and the VdK, he urged Germans to over-come their reluctance to deal with the Nazi past. "*We* were the barbarians in the last war," Krämer-Badoni declared, pointing out the complicity of ordinary Germans long before it became popular to do so.[66] During the 1970s, this critical approach to West Germans' coming to terms with the past (*Vergangenheitsbewältigung*) attracted several influential proponents, and increasingly put the former soldiers into a defensive position. For the first time in 1979, for instance, the local media in Tübingen, while still serving as a forum for the self-presentation of the veterans of the 78th division, yet allowed a critical debate on their euphemistic view of the past.[67] It was less and less the former soldiers, but others who determined what was said, and how, about the wartime past.

The famous speech of President Richard von Weizsäcker on May 8, 1985 was a milestone in these developments. Weizsäcker, a CDU politi-cian, on the fortieth anniversary of the end of the Second World War articulated German responsibility for the crimes of Third Reich, asked Germans to face up to the past, and disavowed one of the most cherished defenses of older Germans when he said: "When the unspeakable truth of the Holocaust then became known at the end of the war, all too many of us claimed they had not known anything about it or even suspected anything."[68] Not surprisingly, the veterans' associations felt provoked and were embarrassed; at least the CDU would not let them down, they had assumed. Yet the tune changed. It was no longer only the Left but also prominent representatives of the CDU who were demanding a crit-ical assessment of the complicity of ordinary Germans during the war. From 1985 on, the veterans' long-lasting rule over the collective memory of the Nazi past and the war was challenged by a growing choir of critical voices in the media and in politics.

The more the war veterans drifted to the margins of society, the more the semantics of comradeship darkened. Comradeship had supposedly been a force for good, but this humane depiction of comradeship came under scrutiny until the opposite was widely accepted. Comradeship was demonized. It no longer seemed an antitoxin against Nazism but appeared to have been the poison. Some representatives of the veterans' movement had early on made it easy for their critics, of course. After his release from captivity, the highly decorated paratroop general, Hermann Ramcke, demanded at a veterans' gathering in 1951 the "immediate release" from Soviet and Western captivity not only of Wehrmacht and Waffen-SS POWs, but also of "our brave comrades from the SD," the SS security service, one of the core groups of the Holocaust perpetrators.[69] Time and again, throughout the fifties and sixties, scandals emerged as Nazi generals appeared at veterans' gatherings. In the sixties, as we have seen, the HIAG moved yet further to the margins of the mainstream veterans' movement by demonstratively promoting the former SS commander Sepp Dietrich as its figurehead. The Social Democrat and former Wehrmacht officer Helmut Schmidt reminded the HIAG of its guiding principle: "When crimes are committed, all old comradeship must end."[70] It was this very principle that the HIAG disowned when it applauded Dietrich, in the opinion of Schmidt and most of the German public. But in the HIAG's view, Dietrich was a comrade, not a criminal.[71]

Grand Admiral Erich Raeder, sentenced to life for war crimes in Nuremberg but released in 1955, had always "warmheartedly" stood by his men, so to treat an "old chief" like him as a "comrade among comrades" was an obligation for veterans, one anchored in their code of honor.[72] This was the sticking point for the veterans, and they would not surrender it simply in order to adjust to pluralistic democracy. Eventually, comradeship, the solidarity of former soldiers, trumped integration into civilian society. The latter, however, did not accept this priority. "Comradeship is a good thing," the SPD commented in a press release on the veterans' embracing of Raeder in 1956, "but is comradeship a value in itself? Raeder was a minion of Hitler... Hitler was a criminal, and this fact cannot be concealed by a deeply felt sense of comradeship, lest one invite accusations of moral callousness. Do the former members of the Navy not understand that comradeship must end when a member of their organization was responsible for supporting the policies of a criminal? The rules of comradeship are only valid insofar as they remain in harmony with the moral principles of a free society."[73] This statement highlighted the gap between the veterans' depiction of comradeship and the morals of the democracy. For the veterans, individual choices and responsibilities could not overrule the dogma of sticking together. At least this was how Hitler's former soldiers interpreted the concept of comradeship.

The military reformers in the Bundeswehr under Colonel Wolf Graf von Baudissin tried to implant a different notion of comradeship, one that demanded "ethical commitments" that complied with "one's knowledge and conscience." Without "personal responsibility" there can be "no sustainable comradeship," only "camaraderie," Baudissin stated in 1956, referring to the common juxtaposition of good comradeship and evil camaraderie, allowed by the the German language. And so the Bundeswehr soldiers who celebrated the release of Grand Admiral Dönitz from Spandau prison in 1966 were accused of "misplaced comradeship."[74] The Baudissin reforms attempted to integrate comradeship into a military morality suited to a pluralistic democracy, but the Dönitz affair revealed that this goal found not only adherents in the Bundeswehr but also opponents. And the opponents were by no means willing to give in; they repeatedly demonstrated their notion of comradeship in spectacular avowals of sympathy for prominent, often pro-Nazi Wehrmacht officers.[75]

From the early 1980s, West Germany's peace movement gained enormous popular support, not least in response to the NATO Double-Track Decision. Conscientious objectors won respectability; the soldiers lost it. Germans distanced themselves from the armed forces more deliberately than ever. Time and again, when younger Germans were debating how to remember World War II, they chose the Wehrmacht deserters as their new heroes and dethroned those soldiers who had risked their lives and limbs for the German fatherland – and been good comrades.[76] For both old soldiers and new, the winds of change were becoming ever stronger. They reacted by withdrawing from the public and then from the civilian world altogether – not at once, but gradually between the early 1980s and the mid-1990s when the Wehrmacht exhibition of the Hamburg Institute for Social Research attracted millions of Germans and revealed to the entire country (and beyond) that an unknown number of ordinary Germans, including the fathers and grandfathers of visitors to the exhibition, participated in the terror against Jews, enemy civilians, and POWs in the East, and even enjoyed it. At this point, the Wehrmacht veterans entered the stage of the public memory of the war again – and they lost their last battle.

In the early 1980s, numerous veterans' associations, including the HIAG and the "Comradeship League Fallschirmpanzerkorps Hermann Göring," chose no longer to announce their reunions publicly but to gather in hiding. Anticipating public protests, they tried to conceal their reunions as recreational events, or rendered them "closed events."[77] This cult of secrecy, however, only aroused further doubts and seemed to confirm older suspicions about the veterans' political reliability: Had they really accepted democracy and overcome the old Nazi ideas? Critical observers felt that all the "ado about comradeship" merely contributed to the cultivation of Nazi attitudes, and helped to hide war criminals. In the case of radical fringe groups such as the "Silent Help for POWs and Internees," or the so-called "Naumann Circle" that had been uncovered by British intelligence in 1953, this was certainly true.[78] And the Fallschirmpanzerkorps Hermann Göring was indeed deeply involved in war crimes, especially at the end of war, and so were units of the Waffen-SS, although the details were not known in the 1980s. But groups such as "Silent Help" did not so much protect former Wehrmacht soldiers as members of the Gestapo and the (General) SS, even though they maintained loose ties to the HIAG. Crucially, however, it was the HIAG that always came under suspicion for collaborating with these criminal networks. The situation was further aggravated by contacts between some HIAG members and right-wing extremist parties.[79]

And all this was done in the name of comradeship. An SPD politician who wanted to expose such contacts in 1982 had to endure accusations from his "old comrades" that he was an "idiot" and "did not understand anything about comradeship," and yet he had served five years as a soldier and another five years as a POW.[80] In return, the left-liberal public agreed in the 1980s that comradeship was by no means a social tool to prevent war crimes and murder, rather the contrary. "Which comradeship is being cultivated here? The comradeship of the murderous executioners of Klissura and Distomo?" asked another SPD politician, Uwe Lambinus, scrutinizing a gathering in 1984 of the 4th SS Police-Tankgunner Division in idyllic Marktheidenfeld. In 1944, one of the division's companies murdered 200 men, women, and children in Greece in retaliation for a partisan attack. Lambinus, born 1941, protested on behalf of the post-Nazi generations against the SS-men and denounced their "false cultivation of tradition and comradeship."[81]

Lambinus also railed against attempts by the "gentlemen of the 4th SS Division" to portray themselves as "part of the regular former Wehrmacht," and thereby equate the SS to "all *Landsers*." This differentiation was characteristic of the politics of memory still current in the 1980s.[82] At that time, criticism was leveled against the HIAG and the Waffen-SS but barely targeted the regimental associations of the Wehrmacht. Yet this reprieve was not to last. The crimes that were being discussed became increasingly intertwined in the civil-social discourse about both old and new soldiers. The veterans saw themselves accused of being "murderers" or "Rambos" – the American blockbuster *First Blood* was released in 1982 – and not just because of the atrocities and crimes against humanity not long since tried before German and Allied courts.[83] Left-wing defamations accused former soldiers in general of being murderers, taking up a radical pacifistic tradition as it had been articulated since the early twentieth century. They depicted every war as a criminal act; the deadly actions of soldiers as murder; the soldiers themselves, therefore, as murderers. The words of the famous pacifist Kurt Tucholsky, "Soldiers are murderers," resounded through the land; in 1982, a district court handed down a judgment that made it allowable to call any soldier a "professionally trained murderer."[84] The war of annihilation that Germany unleashed seemed to justify this verdict, rendering any distinctions between regular and criminal warfare, as defined by international law, a farce.

Comradeship had been the virtue that made war bearable, even a stigmatized, genocidal war. Amid the pacifistic climate of the 1980s, however, comradeship lost its power as the humane counterweight to the destructiveness of war.[85] Comradeship itself was suspect: It might not counter but in fact enable this destructiveness, and especially its criminal dimension. The younger generations of Germans, who had not experienced the war, developed a disgust for all the "fuss over comradeship" and the "detestable comradeship rituals of the veterans."[86] And these sentiments intensified and spread the more veterans retreated out of public view and into private, i.e. seemingly subversive, conspiratorial settings.

In fact, this isolation was at least partially also the result of a demographic shift and generational change. The war generation was leaving the public stage. In so far as they had not already passed away, they retired from active professional life, from influential positions as judges, journalists, teachers, politicians, employers, and recruiters. By 1980, the generation born in 1910 had reached retirement age, and over the following decade so did the age cohorts born up to 1924, the last cohort of former soldiers that the veterans' organizations had had some success in recruiting. More and more veterans were becoming frail or dying. Up until 1979, the former 78th Storm Division, which can be taken as representative, was still at the pinnacle of its prestige. Its "ceremony for the commemoration of the war dead" at the market square in Tübingen was again, as it had been so many times before, an impressive display that still attracted some 1,500 people. But when they were planning the next reunion, slated for 1982, the conveners feared a considerable decline of attendance and worried about what that would mean for their public appearance. Since the "anticipated, significantly reduced number of participants . . . would not form a visual impression" befitting such a ceremony, they abstained from holding the event in the market square, moving the ceremony to the division's memorial on Neckar Island – a picturesque place, but one that was outside the town centre. The number of participants remained at about 500 throughout the 1980s.[87] Prominent political figures no longer graced these gatherings with their presence. All that remained of any official recognition was the sponsorship of Fallschirmjägerbattalion (Paratroop Battalion) 251 of the Bundeswehr, an elite unit, but a small one.[88]

The participation rate fell even more throughout the 1990s. By this time, veterans had bid their farewell to the general public completely. They withdrew into a military subculture cultivated by the Bundeswehr, which suffered itself from dwindling prestige in civilian society. From 1992 on, the old comrades of 78th Division held their reunions in the barracks of the Fallschirmjägerbattalion 251 in Calw, a small town 25 miles away from Tübingen. This retreat was of great symbolic significance. The old veterans no longer dominated German collective war memory as they had done for decades. It was no longer they, but younger Germans who had the say. And what younger Germans said was a radical departure from the past, not only in Tübingen but more widely in the entire, now reunified country. In 1991, Tübingen's local gazette issued a series of scathing remarks on a meeting of the 78th veterans' association. "In short military-style commands," the paper mocked, the "ex-fighters" were ordered around before they were allowed to gather in front of a "raised German flag."[89]

These currish comments, however, were merely a prelude to a much more offensive campaign that climaxed in 1995, with the opening of the Wehrmacht Exhibition of the Hamburg Institute for Social Research. The exhibition not only documented the crimes of the Wehrmacht against civilians and POWs during its war of annihilation in the East; what made the exhibition so provocative – the veteran activists went to the barricades to protest against, as they saw, a defamation campaign, and eventually the German Bundestag debated the exhibition most controversially and emotionally – were the hundreds of amateur photos it showed taken by Wehrmacht soldiers. They exposed the pleasure ordinary soldiers, not the Wehrmacht leadership, took in torturing Jews and other civilians, and the initiative taken by regular troops – not the SS Einsatzgruppen or the Gestapo – to carry out genocide and mass murder.[90]

The events in Tübingen reflected the uproar all over the country. Whereas the chairman of the 78th Division's association had still insisted in 1991 that German soldiers had been incapable of committing atrocities, testimony from a former corporal given in Soviet captivity, now used in the exhibition's accompanying publications, described the destruction of Russian villages by the division, the "scorched earth tactics" during the winter retreat of 1941–42. In May 1995, the Tübingen newspaper drew attention to these events and upset the veterans; they felt betrayed by both their former "comrade" who, still alive and now interviewed by the media, actually confirmed his older postwar testimony, and by the local journalists who now more deliberately than ever changed sides. The decades-long mutual cooperation between Tübingen town society and the old soldiers collapsed. A few months later, on Memorial Day (*Volkstrauertag*) in autumn 1995, fliers and handouts were distributed that decried the "crimes of the 78th Division." In January 1996 unknown vandals sprayed red paint (the color of the Nazi banner) on the commemorative plaque on the division's war memorial on the Neckar Island. In September 1996, in a spectacular undertaking that was supported by the DGB, the German Trade Unions Confederation, the memorial was covered in a shroud; a short time later the commemorative plaque was stolen. The veterans' group thereafter decided to commemorate their war dead unannounced, and in silence.[91] Later, even the Fallschirmjägerbattalion 251 yielded to public pressure and terminated its sponsorship of the 78th veterans' association. The Bundeswehr could no longer afford to protect the former German army that seemed to have indulged in evil just as Himmler's murder troops had done.[92]

But the withdrawal of the Bundeswehr from the veterans' association was by no means the result of any actual conflict between young and old soldiers; instead the Bundeswehr only yielded to the pressure of civilian society and its politicians and media who became increasingly sensitive to real or suspected tendencies of neo-Nazism and xenophobia.[93] In truth, the armed forces were that one institution of the German state that still harbored understanding for the morality of the veterans, and especially for the concept of comradeship, including its conspiratorial aspects. Thinking about the crimes of the Wehrmacht as displayed by the Hamburg exhibition in 1995, a Bundeswehr officer explained (in an anonymous interview), "with comrades, you know...you just stick together," even if one of them does a "stupid thing...I don't know... like these shootings [of civilians in World War II]. You would seek to cover that up. That's just how it goes. This exactly is it what defines comradeship among soldiers."[94] This particular soldier had been raised and trained in former communist East Germany, and together with other officers of the East German army he had been brought into the Bundeswehr after German reunification. His comment indicates a fundamental shift in Central European society. The ideological gap between communism and democracy no longer mattered. Instead, a new curtain – not an iron one but still a tight one – separated all kinds of soldiers from civilian society. While comradeship remained a virtue for soldiers, civilian society looked at it as synonym of evil per se.

Crucially, this demonization of comradeship applied to old soldiers and young soldiers equally. As civilian society saw it, comradeship among young soldiers too seemed to nourish only evil and cruelty. In the summer of 1997, for instance, the German public stumbled upon an event that had happened more than a year before but had been covered up – thanks to comradeship or camaraderie. A non-commissioned officer and six enlisted men from the Bundeswehr made a film including "scenes of extreme brutality: rapes, crucifixions, executions, and the torture of civilians, namely by Bundeswehr soldiers," reported the papers. The producers of this film were themselves soldiers on active duty, members of the Jägerbattalion (infantry battalion) 571. Apparently they were also the first audience of the film, which, as it turned out, was shown repeatedly within the "circle of comrades" to great approval, and "even to their superiors, who knew about the affair and had covered it up," according to a TV commentator. The outrage was unanimous. The producers of this video seemed to embody the "stereotype of soldiers as murderers," and to pervert "the mission of the legitimate state-sponsored use of force to provide cover for marauding, murderous bands, driven by basic instincts." This abomination seemed to have arisen out of a somber social culture in which solidarity – comradeship – trumped everything else and where the destruction of established ethics was prized as the ultimate bond between criminals.[95]

A commentator at the *Frankfurter Allgemeine Zeitung* reminded readers of the "strict moral economy" that soldiers, as the representatives of state-sanctioned violence, had to exercise.[96] And indeed, the official language of the Bundeswehr still offered a comforting interpretation of comradeship. "Comradeship serves the universal implementation of soldierly vows, and is based on tolerance and nobleness of heart," explained a Bundeswehr general in a newspaper interview in 1998 when once again some Bundeswehr soldiers had boasted of neo-Nazi attitudes. Referring to the Bundeswehr concept of civilians in uniform, he further stated: "The tolerance inherent to comradeship prevents extreme political expressions. Those who condone or conceal extremism, are not able to plead misunderstood comradeship, but are guilty through complicity. No, these neo-Nazi episodes have nothing to do with comradeship," he exclaimed. This had been the very question posed by the civilian interviewer. "What is comradeship? Is it the key to explaining the neo-Nazi episodes in the Bundeswehr?" The general was unable to charm away the misgivings. The military insider and the civilian observer were talking at cross-purposes. Their ideas about comradeship couldn't be further apart. The journalist insisted on a dark concept of comradeship as a hotbed of evil.[97] This was the notion of comradeship German civilian society in the 1990s had adopted, and not without reason. Comradeship had become symbolic of a subculture that represented the opposite of everything that civilian society held in high regard. The general insisted on the innocent meaning of comradeship as the epitome of humanity, just as soldiers had done throughout the twentieth century when they felt impelled to protect the "evil" depths of the military world from the doubts of civilian society. But by the end of the century, civilian society was no longer willing to accept the soldiers' plea.

NOTES

1 Bald, *Militär und Gesellschaft*, pp. 129–31.
2 Ronald Inglehart, "The Silent Revolution of Europe: Intergenerational Change in Post-Industrial Societies," *American Political Science Review*, 65/4 (1971), 991–1017; Ulrich Beck, *Risk Society: Towards a New Modernity* (London: Sage, 1992), pp. 91–153; Dagmar Barnouw, *The War in the Empty Air: Victims, Perpetrators, and Postwar Germans* (Bloomington: Indiana University Press, 2005); Assmann and Frevert, *Geschichtsvergessenheit, Geschichtsversessenheit*, pp. 258–71; Thomas Kühne (ed.), *Von der Kriegskultur zur Friedenskultur? Zum Mentalitätswandel in Deutschland seit 1945* (Münster: Lit, 2000).
3 Gray, *The Warriors*, pp. 39, 43, 45.
4 Huebner, *Warrior Image*, pp. 52 (lawless band), 277 (collective effort).
5 Peter Aichinger, *The American Soldier in Fiction, 1880–1963: A History of Attitudes Toward Warfare and the Military Establishment* (Ames: Iowa State University Press, 1975), p. 42. Sebastian Haak, *The Making of The Good War: Hollywood, das Pentagon und die amerikanische Deutung des Zweiten Weltkriegs 1945–1962* (Paderborn: Schöningh, 2013), pp. 18–20.
6 The latter is meanwhile represented prominently by Fussell, *Wartime*; and Fussell, *The Boys' Crusade: The American Infantry in Northwestern Europe, 1944–1945* (New York: Modern Library, 2003). On the immediate postwar decades, see Huebner, *Warrior Image*, esp. pp. 97–167; John Bodnar, *The "Good War" In American Memory* (Baltimore, MD: Johns Hopkins University Press, 2010); Jeanine Bassinger, *The World War II Combat Film: Anatomy of a Genre* (Middletown, CT: Wesleyan University Press, 2003).
7 Aichinger, *The American Soldier in Fiction*, p. 41.
8 Quoted in Haak, *The Making of The Good War*, p. 193. The message of the 1948 novel was more ambiguous; see Norman Mailer, *The Naked and the Dead* (New York: Rinehart, 1948).
9 Huebner, *Warrior Image*, pp. 277–78; Eric T. Dean, "The Myth of the Troubled and Scorned Vietnam Veteran," *Journal of American Studies*, 26 (1992), 59–74; Jonathan Shay, *Achilles in Vietnam: Combat Trauma and the Undoing of Character* (New York: Athenaeum, 1994); Patrick Hagopian, *The Vietnam War in American Memory: Veterans, Memorials, and the Politics of Healing* (Amherst: University of Massachusetts Press, 2009).
10 Turner, *The Ritual Process*, pp. 95–96.
11 Jeffords, *The Remasculinization of America*, pp. xii–xiv (quotations), 40–41, 54–86.

12 William Broyles, Jr., *Brothers in Arms: A Journey From War to Peace* (New York: Knopf, 1986), pp. 76–78, 199–200; cf. Jeffords, *The Remasculinization of America*, p. 57.

13 Jeffords, *The Remasculinization of America*, p. 136. See also Michael Anderegg (ed.), *Inventing Vietnam: The War in Film and Television* (Philadelphia, PA: Temple University Press, 1991).

14 Brian Stelter, "Quiet Series Celebrates a Milestone Few Others Reach," *New York Times*, Feb. 6, 2012, www.nytimes.com/2012/02/07/arts/television/in-an-ncis-milestone-mark-harmons-agent-gibbs-looks-back.html?_r=0 (accessed April 6, 2015).

15 Christopher Harris, "'No One Left Behind' Ethos Up For Debate After Bowe Bergdahl Deserter Allegations," *International Business Times*, June 3, 2014, www.ibtimes.com/no-one-left-behind-ethos-debate-after-bowe-bergdahl-deserter-allegations-1594035; Penny Starr, "Rep. Salmon: Obama 'Hasn't Lifted a Finger' to Help U.S. Marine in Mexico Jail," *cnsnews*, June 11, 2014, http://cnsnews.com/news/article/penny-starr/rep-salmon-obama-hasnt-lifted-finger-help-us-marine-mexico-jail (both accessed April 6, 2015).

16 John Bodnar, "Saving Private Ryan and Postwar Memory in America," *American Historical Review*, 106 (2001), 805–17.

17 Bodnar, *The "Good War" in American Memory*, p. 126, on a 1991 memorial in Deming, NM; see the illustrations following p. 84, Bataan Memorial, Las Cruces, New Mexico, 2002.

18 James J. Sheehan, *Where Have All the Soldiers Gone? The Transformation of Modern Europe* (Boston: Houghton Mifflin, 2008).

19 Günther Wallraff, *Mein Tagebuch aus der Bundeswehr* (Cologne: Kiepenheuer & Witsch, 1992; 1st edn. 1970), quotations from the blurb of the 1992 edition.

20 Kirst, *The Revolt of Gunner Asch*, and *The Return of Gunner Asch*.

21 Schornstheimer, *Die leuchtenden Augen der Frontsoldaten*, pp. 173–74, also for the quotations (from contemporary journals). Cf. Rolf Düsterberg, *Soldat und Kriegserlebnis: Deutsche militärische Erinnerungsliteratur (1945–1961) zum Zweiten Weltkrieg: Motive, Begriffe, Wertungen* (Tübingen: Niemeyer, 2000).

22 *Der Spiegel*, Nov. 13, 1963, pp. 52–56, "Tiefste Gangart"; ibid., Dec. 18, 1963, p. 25, "Solche Bengels."

23 Erving Goffman, *Asylums: Essays on the Social Situation of Mental Patients and Other Inmates* (Garden City, NY: Anchor, 1961), pp. 1–124; Hubert Treiber, *Wie man Soldaten macht: Sozialisation in "kasernierter Vergesellschaftung"* (Düsseldorf: Bertelsmann, 1973); *Stories in Oliv: Ein Kasernenreport* (Dortmund: Weltkreis Verlag, 1978); Gerhard Armanski (ed.), *Junge, komm bald wieder: Von der Bundeswehr* (Reinbek: Rowohlt, 1983).

24 Press release of Federal Ministry of Defense, "Bundeswehr und Alkohol," July 26, 1979, copy in Fachinformationszentrum der Bundeswehr, Bonn, Document U 6292; Helmut W. Ganser (ed.), *Technokraten in Uniform: Die innere Krise der Bundeswehr* (Reinbek: Rowohlt, 1980); *Süddeutsche Zeitung*, June 6, 1980, "Subkultur in der Bundeswehr." *Westdeutsche Zeitung*, March 5, 1981, "Schlaglicht. Kameraden."

25 Heinz G. Stachow, *Der kleine Quast* (Munich: Droemer Knaur, 1979), pp. 116–17, 119, 142, 150, 158, 168, 208. On the positive reception by the veterans' movement, see *Der Heimkehrer*, July 15, 1978, p. 7; and ibid., Jan. 15, 1980, p. 1. Another example of this type of war literature is the bestseller Lothar-Günther Buchheim, *Das Boot* (Munich: Piper, 1973), engl. edn. *The Boat* (New York: Knopf, 1975); cf. Michael Salewski, *Von der Wirklichkeit des Krieges: Analysen und Kontroversen zu Buchheims "Boot,"* 2nd edn. (Munich: Deutscher Taschenbuch-Verlag, 1985).

26 Rolf Elble, *Vom künftigen deutschen Offizier: Aktuelle Gedanken zum Offizierberuf* (Bonn: Offene Worte, 1955), p. 83. Cf. Salewski, *Von der Wirklichkeit des Krieges*, pp. 43–50.

27 Bald, *Militär und Gesellschaft*, pp. 53–88.

28 Ibid., pp. 118–23; Frevert, *A Nation in Barracks*, pp. 272–74.

29 Heinz Bartjes, "Der Zivildienst als die modernere 'Schule der Nation,'" in Kühne (ed.), *Von der Kriegskultur zur Friedenskultur*, pp. 130–45.

30 Hanne-Margret Birckenbach, *Mit schlechtem Gewissen – Wehrdienstbereitschaft von Jugendlichen* (Baden-Baden: Nomos, 1985).

31 Raimund Grafe and Matthias Zimmer, "Der Rekrut, der aus der Kälte kam," in Wolfram Wette (ed.), *Der Krieg des kleinen Mannes: Eine Militärgeschichte von unten* (Munich: Piper, 1992), pp. 416–39.

32 *Wehrdienst im Urteil von Mannschaftsdienstgraden des Heeres, Gutachten 8/89 des Sozialwiss. Instituts der Bundeswehr* (1989), p. 9, Fachinformationszentrum der Bundeswehr Bonn, Document SA 7271.

33 Bald, *Militär und Gesellschaft*, pp. 89–99; cf. Detlef Bald, "Kriegskult und Friedensmentalität der militärischen Elite in den neunziger Jahren," in Kühne (ed.), *Von der Kriegskultur zur Friedenskultur*, pp. 110–27.

34 *Der Heimkehrer*, Oct. 10, 1961, p. 9 (quotation); *Alte Kameraden*, 1961, No. 9, pp. 15–16; ibid., 1957, No. 7, p. 15.

35 *Der Heimkehrer*, July 1953, p. 1; ibid., Aug. 1953, p. 2.

36 Biess, *Homecomings*, pp. 154–67.

37 Robel, *Die deutschen Kriegsgefangenen*, pp. 93–312.

38 Letter of H. G. to Erich Heimeshoff, President of the Heimkehrer League, Nov. 5, 1962, Archive of the Verband der Heimkehrer, Bonn, unnumbered. Cf. *Der Heimkehrer*, Nov. 1955, p. 2; ibid., Feb 10, 1961, pp. 1, 4.

39 *Kriegsgefangene – Voennoplennye: Sowjetische Kriegsgefangene in Deutschland: Deutsche Kriegsgefangene in der Sowjetunion* (Düsseldorf: Droste, 1995), p. 50 (facsimile).

40 Detailed correspondence in Archive of the Verband der Heimkehrer, Bonn, from 1950 on, unnumbered.

41 Frank Biess, "'Russenknechte' und 'Westagenten': Kriegsheimkehrer und (De)legitimierung von Kriegsgefangenschaftserfahrungen in Ost- und Westdeutschland nach 1945," in Klaus Naumann (ed.), *Nachkrieg in Deutschland* (Hamburger Edition, 2001), pp. 59–89 (at 62–68); *Der Heimkehrer*, March 1953, p. 3; ibid., Aug. 1953, p. 8; ibid., June 10, 1956, p. 7.

42 "Directives for the selection of professional soldiers" etc., Ministry of Defense, May 24, 1956, copy in Archiv der sozialen Demokratie, Bonn, Fritz Erler papers, No. 140.

43 Kerstin Freudiger, *Die juristische Aufarbeitung von NS-Verbrechen* (Tübingen: Mohr Siebeck, 2002); Jörg Osterloh and Clemens Vollhals (eds.), *NS-Prozesse und deutsche Öffentlichkeit: Besatzungszeit, frühe Bundesrepublik und DDR* (Göttingen: Vandenhoeck & Ruprecht, 2011).

44 Ulrike Weckel, "The Mitläufer in Two German Postwar Films: Representation and Critical Reception," *History and Memory*, 15/2 (2003), 64–93; Anke Pinkert, *Film and Memory in East Germany* (Bloomington: Indiana University Press, 2008), pp. 27–42.

45 Franz Fühmann, "Kameraden," in Fühmann, *Erzählungen 1955–1975* (Rostock: Hinstorf, 1977), pp. 9–11, 13–14, 18–28, 32–34, 42–43, 45–48; Stephan Braese, "Unmittelbar zum Krieg – Alfred Andersch und Franz Fühmann," in Naumann (ed.), *Nachkrieg in Deutschland*, pp. 472–97.

46 *Der Heimkehrer*, May 1952, p. 1; *Alte Kameraden*, 1953, No. 3, p. 12.

47 *Der Heimkehrer*, March 1952, p. 5; ibid., Jan. 15, 1957, p. 7; Norbert Frei, *Adenauer's Germany and the Nazi Past: The Politics of Amnesty and Integration* (New York: Columbia, 2002), pp. 1–92.

48 *Alte Kameraden*, 1962, No. 11, p. 2.

49 *Neue Rheinzeitung*, July 17, 1958, statement of HIAG leader Kurt Meyer on the allegation the HIAG protected former concentration camp guards; Wilke, *Die "Hilfsgemeinschaft auf Gegenseitigkeit,"* pp. 246–54.

50 Bernd Kasten, "Pensionen für NS-Verbrecher in der Bundesrepublik 1949–1963," *Historische Mitteilungen der Ranke-Gesellschaft*, 7 (1994), 262–82 (at p. 271); cf. Schornstheimer, *Die leuchtenden Augen der Frontsoldaten*, pp. 163–64.

51 *Stuttgarter Nachrichten*, Sept. 21, 2012.

52 Herbert Jäger, *Verbrechen unter totalitärer Herrschaft: Studien zur nationalsozialistischen Gewaltkriminalität* (Frankfurt: Suhrkamp, 1982); Frei, *Adenauer's Germany and the Nazi Past*, pp. 203–33; *Der Heimkehrer*, April 25, 1959, p. 6.

53 Joachim Staron, *Fosse Ardeatine und Marzabotto: Deutsche Kriegsverbrechen und Resistenza: Geschichte und nationale Mythenbildung in Deutschland und Italien (1944–1999)* (Paderborn: Schöningh, 2002).

54 *Alte Kameraden*, 1958, No. 2, p. 4, article titled "Gaeta Action Became a Spontaneous Demonstration of Comradeship." On Reder's responsibility, see *Der Heimkehrer*, June 25, 1967, p. 2.

55 *Alte Kameraden*, 1958, No. 2, p. 4, reprint of an article from *Der Freiwillige*, the newspaper of the HIAG.

56 Ibid.

57 *Jahrbuch für öffentliche Meinung*, 1947, p. 137.

58 *Feinde der Demokratie* (Bonn: DGB, 1954), copy in Archiv der Sozialen Demokratie, Bonn, Organisationssammlung des Parteivorstandes der SPD, VdS, Box 176. On the expanded reprint of 1956, which denounced even the Heimkehrer League as one of the "enemies of democracy," see the embarrassed statement in *Der Heimkehrer*, Feb. 10, 1957, pp. 1–12.

59 Resolution of the Youth Council of the city of Mannheim, *Mannheimer Morgen*, Nov. 10, 1951. Cf. *Deutsche Soldaten-Zeitung*, 1953, No. 3 ("Gewerkschaften gegen Demokratie"), and *Der Heimkehrer*, April 10, 1956, p. 5, "Die kalte Schulter des DGB." On similar accusations against the veterans'

comradeship cult by a West German TV documentary, titled "The Best Years of my Life," in 1960, see *Alte Kameraden*, 1960, No. 2, p. 2.

60 *Ruhr-Wort* (Essen), Oct. 7, 1961 (quotation). See also *Die Zeit*, June 19, 1959; and *Der Heimkehrer*, July 10, 1959, p. 7.

61 Reports in *Frankfurter Rundschau*, July 26, 1960; *Deutsche Zeitung*, July 23, 28, 1960; *National-Zeitung*, July 26, 1960; *Neues Deutschland* (GDR), July 26, 1960.

62 *Alte Kameraden*, 1962, No. 6, p. 2, and letters of R. K. to the veterans' association of the 291st Infantry Division, Aug. 15, 1954, May 12, 1955 (quotation), Bundesarchiv-Militärarchiv Freiburg, MP 28, v. 3.

63 *Schwäbisches Tagblatt*, Sept. 9, 1968, and minutes of the proceedings of the assembly of the Comrades' Support Task (*Kameradenhilfswerk*) 78, Sept. 7, 1968, copy owned by author.

64 Wilke, *Die "Hilfsgemeinschaft auf Gegenseitigkeit,"* pp. 344–49.

65 *Frankfurter Rundschau*, May 26, 1983 (Hersfeld); ibid., March 8, 1984 (Bad Harzburg); *Der Stern*, March 29, 1984, p. 220 (Oberaula); *Süddeutsche Zeitung*, April 5, 29, 1985; *Die Zeit*, April 26, 1985 (Nesselwang, protest march of 5,000 people); *Süddeutsche Zeitung*, April 10, 1986 (Nesselwang city council prohibits further HIAG meetings). Wilke, *Die "Hilfsgemeinschaft auf Gegenseitigkeit,"* pp. 364–77.

66 *Der Heimkehrer*, Dec. 10, 1966, pp. 1–2 ("Fast ein Skandal"), and related letters to the editor, ibid., Jan. 10, 1967, p. 9.

67 *Schwäbisches Tagblatt*, Aug. 28–29, 1979.

68 James M. Markham, "'All of Us Must Accept the Past,' the German President Tells M.P.s," *New York Times*, June 9, 1985, www.nytimes.com/1985/05/09/world/all-of-us-must-accept-the-past-the-german-president-tell-s-mp-s.html; see also Markham, "Facing up to Germany's Past," *New York Times*, June 23, 1985, http://www.nytimes.com/1985/06/23/magazine/facing-up-to-germany-s-past.html (both accessed Jan. 20, 2015).

69 *Münchner Illustrierte*, Aug. 11, 1951 ("Ramcke fordert: 'rehabilitiert SD'").

70 *Die Zeit*, Nov. 12, 1965, letter to the editor, on a related report, ibid., Oct 29, 1965, "Sepp Dietrich saß auf der Empore."

71 *Die Welt*, Oct. 26, 1965, "Es war nicht nur Sepp Dietrich da . . . "

72 *Frankfurter Rundschau*, July 4, 1956.

73 *SPD-Pressedienst*, June 5, 1956, Archiv der Sozialen Demokratie, Bonn, ZASS, HQ 99.

74 *Der Heimkehrer*, July 25, 1956, p. 8. B. C. Hesslein, *Die unbewältigte Vergangenheit der Bundeswehr: Fünf Offiziere zur Krise der Inneren Führung* (Reinbek: Rowohlt, 1977), p. 18. Cf. Bald, *Militär und Gesellschaft*, p. 59.

75 *Frankfurter Allgemeine Zeitung*, Aug. 6, 1966, "Blaue Kameraderie."

76 Wolfram Wette (ed.), *Deserteure der Wehrmacht: Feiglinge – Opfer – Hoffnungsträger? Dokumentation eines Meinungswandels* (Essen: Klartext, 1995).

77 *Frankfurter Rundschau*, Nov. 8, 1984.

78 Oliver Schröm and Andrea Röpke, *Stille Hilfe für braune Kameraden: Das geheime Netzwerk der Alt- und Neonazis*, 2nd edn. (Berlin: Links, 2002); Ulrich Herbert, *Best: Biographische Studien über Radikalismus, Weltanschauung und Vernunft, 1903–1989* (Bonn: Dietz, 1996), pp. 461–76; Frei, *Adenauer's Germany and the Nazi Past*, pp. 277–302.

79 Wilke, *Die "Hilfsgemeinschaft auf Gegenseitigkeit,"* pp. 289–418.

80 *taz*, Sept. 16, 1982, "NS-Kameradschaft ist gemeinnützig."

81 *Sozialdemokratischer Pressedienst*, Oct. 15, 1984, Archiv der Sozialen Demokratie, Bonn, OS, HIAG.

82 Ibid.

83 "Rambos von gestern," *Der Stern*, Oct. 21, 1993, pp. 245–46.

84 *Der Heimkehrer*, Sept. 15, 1982, p. 1; Michael Hepp and Viktor Otto (eds.), *"Soldaten sind Mörder": Dokumentation einer Debatte 1931–1996* (Berlin: Links, 1996).

85 Martin Schröter, *Held oder Mörder? Bilanz eines Soldaten Adolf Hitlers* (Wuppertal: Hammer, 1991), pp. 39–48.

86 *Süddeutsche Zeitung*, April 18, 1984, p. 1, on a reunion of Waffen-SS veterans.

87 Typed report of "Kameradenhilfswerk 78" on its 10th reunion, Sept. 17–18, 1982, and *Festschrift der "78. Infanterie- und Sturmdivision" zum "13. Treffen" 1989*, copies owned by author.

88 Letter of Staatsministerium Baden-Württemberg to Kameradenhilfswerk 78, July 20, 1989, copy owned by author. The Heimkehrer League, a much bigger association, had similar experiences since the 1970s – *Der Heimkehrer*, April 30, 1973, p. 1.

89 *Schwäbisches Tagblatt*, Sept. 21, 23, 1991; letters of secretary of Kameradenhilfswerk 78 to the publisher of this paper, Sept. 22, 23 1991, copies owned by author.

90 Hannes Heer et al. (eds.), *The Discursive Construction of History: Remembering the Wehrmacht's War of Annihilation* (Basingstoke: Palgrave Macmillan, 2008); Hamburger Institut für Sozialforschung (ed.), *Besucher einer Ausstellung*; Klaus Latzel, "Soldatenverbände gegen die Ausstellung 'Vernichtungskrieg. Verbrechen der Wehrmacht 1941–1944' – der lange Schatten des letzten Wehrmachtsberichts," in Michael Th. Greven and Oliver von Wrochem (eds.), *Der Krieg in der Nachkriegszeit: Der Zweite Weltkrieg in Politik und Gesellschaft der Bundesrepublik* (Opladen: Leske + Budrich, 2000), pp. 325–36.

91 Hannes Heer (ed.), *"Stets zu erschießen sind Frauen, die in der Roten Armee dienen": Geständnisse deutscher Kriegsgefangener über ihren Einsatz an der Ostfront* (Hamburger Edition, 1995), p. 47; *Schwäbisches Tagblatt*, May 6, 1995; ibid., Nov. 20, 21, 1995; ibid. Sept. 2, 1999; Jens Rüggeberg, "Streit um ein Denkmal – Streit um das Gedenken," *Geschichtswerkstatt*, 29 (1997), 158–64; author's interview with members of Kameradenhilfswerk 78, 1995.

92 Tobias Pflüger, "Bundeswehr und 'alte Kameraden,'" *Wissenschaft & Frieden*, 1999, No. 3, p. 71.

93 Paul Schäfer, "Bundeswehr und Rechtsextremismus," Dossier no. 28, *Wissenschaft & Frieden*, 1998, No. 2, www.wissenschaft-und-frieden.de/seite .php?dossierID=054 (accessed Jan. 23, 2015). Lorenz Knorr, *Rechtsextremismus in der Bundeswehr* (Bad Homburg: VAS, 1998).

94 Quoted in Klaus Naumann, "Kameraden oder Komplizen? Der Zwiespalt ganz normaler Berufssoldaten," in Hamburger Institut für Sozialforschung (ed.), *Besucher einer Ausstellung*, p. 34.

95 *Frankfurter Allgemeine Zeitung*, July 9, 1997, "Sieben Mann"; ibid., July 21, 1997, letters to the editor; *Rhein-Zeitung*, July 7, 1997, "Folterspiele in der Bundeswehr", http://archiv.rhein-zeitung.de/on/97/07/07/topnews/bw.html (accessed March 15, 2015). Cf. *Spiegel online*, Oct. 25, 1996, http://www.spiegel.de/politik/deutschland/bundeswehrskandale-scheinerschiessungen-und-kreuzigung-a-444655.html (accessed March 15, 2015).

96 *Frankfurter Allgemeine Zeitung*, July 9, 1997, "Sieben Mann."

97 *Frankfurter Allgemeine Magazin*, Oct. 1, 1998, pp. 58–59.

Conclusion
Protean Masculinity and Germany's Twentieth Century

"There is something to be said for using risk to forge social bonds," a young American anthropologist pointed out in 2015 to Sebastian Junger, a popular writer probing into the dramatic increase of PTSD syndromes among American war veterans since World War II. Scrutinizing a broad range of scholarly inquiries into war experiences of contemporary as well as past societies, Junger blamed the "enormous chasm between military and civilian society in this country" – the USA – for the homecoming soldiers' readjustment problems. Soldiers in war, and especially in battle, experienced an extraordinary "closeness and cooperation" that "danger and loss" – the death of comrades – is able to engender, Junger explained. Returning home, American soldiers "miss the war because it was, finally, an experience of human closeness that they can't find back home. Not the closeness of family, which is rare enough, but the closeness of community and tribe. The kind of closeness that gets endlessly venerated in Hollywood movies but only actually shows up in contemporary society when something goes wrong – when tornadoes obliterate towns or planes are flown into skyscrapers." Only then do communal bonds re-emerge that post-industrial societies otherwise have abandoned and replaced by "solipsism and alienation." PTSD of former soldiers, then, is not only the result of the loss of the intense connectivity they experienced in war. It is also the response to a civilian society that doesn't know what the soldiers "went through" and, even worse, doesn't in fact really care.[1]

Junger's observations were not as new as they may have seemed when the popular American magazine *Vanity Fair* published them in June 2015. As this book has shown, the fascination with "human closeness" in battle – the social cohesion and solidarity of soldiers, typically described as camaraderie or comradeship in the English language, *Kameradschaft* in German – as well as grievance against modern civilian society's lack of such bonds, is more than a hundred years old. In Germany both this fascination and the grievance became popular after the defeat of 1918; the Nazis rose to power not least by promising to close the gap between the soldiers' experience and civilian society. After 1945, it was this conjunction – the Nazis' employment of the concept of soldierly solidarity for their genocidal project – that deepened the gulf between the military and civilian society in Germany even more than in other modern and post-industrial societies such as the United States. To be sure, even German civilian society has kept a few spots, such as team sports, where "comradeship" can be praised without instigating concerns about its dark side, and active soldiers remain even more attached to it. But the army in Germany leads a marginal existence. The evil side of comradeship dominates the public discourse; if one Googles the German word *Kameradschaft*, one is led to neo-Nazi pages or reports on neo-Nazi activities more than to anything else. This is the difference between a widely pacifist country such as Germany and a country such as America that remains heavily engaged in war. In America, praising the bonds of battle publicly and to a civilian audience is still common and popular, even, or only, in a romanticized fashion. Not so in Germany.

In search of an explanation for this change over the course of the twentieth century in Germany, this book has zeroed in on the complexity and paradoxes of comradeship. In its core meaning, comradeship, as distinguished from the concept of friendship, denotes the close emotional ties of a small group of people, such as soldiers who need to cooperate in order to avert danger or cope with hardships. While friendship caters to the individual self, is rooted in mutual sympathy of individuals, and may be abandoned at any time, comradeship denotes the relationship of people who cooperate, work, and live together not by choice but by coercion, by accident, or by fate. They have to stick together until the vital task is done or the lethal danger averted. It is this ominous aura of fate and destiny – comradeship as the solidarity of a community of fate – that originated its popularity in Germany's age of total wars as well as in other parts of the world and in other periods including the present. Comradeship in war, the "band of brothers" forged in blood (Shakespeare), is beyond individual agency, individual pleasure, individual benefits. Ultimately, it commands the sacrifice of the self on behalf of the outfit, the army, the nation. And it relieves one of individual responsibility and guilt feelings; the group takes over responsibility. In post-industrial societies that adore and burden the self, such a concept of solidarity is no longer understood; at best, it is romanticized.

In Germany's twentieth century, under the influence of two total wars that forced the bulk of the adult male population and an unforeseen number of women and children to face mass death, comradeship drew its attraction from its inclusive, pacifying, and even therapeutic power. This power was more than just a fabrication, as a diverse range of scholarly studies as well as an even broader range of first-hand testimonies shows. War propaganda, war memory, and war fantasies may have exaggerated it, yet there is no doubt that insiders – soldiers – actually experienced it.

Comradeship meant reconciling, even harmonizing different personalities, different positions, different identities, different emotions, and different capabilities. Defined by its separation from civilian society, the group of comrades lived together, shared food, space, time, duties, skills, emotions, joys, sorrows, and dangers, and established their own rules. Comradeship meant a diverse group of men – the typical social condition of drafted mass armies in twentieth-century European wars – putting aside conflicting civilian identities, their ties to social classes, racial identities, religious affiliations, ideological belief systems. These men were to adopt a new sense of belonging as soldiers. A nuanced set of masculine standards made soldiers replace civilian life-saving morality by the martial morality of death – of killing and getting killed.

Influential scholars have argued that military masculinity, especially in Germany in the era of total war, was defined by the repudiation of femininity – of whatever was attributed to females and female behavior, such as domesticity, tenderness, and compassion. This book begs to differ. To be sure, comradeship was the army's moral machine to spur aggression, to guarantee fighting morale, and to instill conformity, before and during battle. The comrade was the one who stormed into the battle, instead of staying behind. Consequently, heroic and "hard" concepts of manhood, including decisiveness, aggression, brutality, control over others and oneself always ranked high in the hierarchy of manliness. But in the social practice of male interaction, diversity and flexibility were needed. The soldiers' daily routine of social interaction as well as the exceptional experience of the battlefield allowed for, or even demanded, the display of femininely coded affection: tenderness, empathy, caring, tolerance toward emotional breakdowns, moments or periods of weakness. Soldiering provided men with a male identity that eventually was not defined by repudiation but by integration of femininity, and thus allowed men to experience themselves as *whole* human beings in a way that seemed, at least to many of them, not possible in civilian lives. What eventually counted when it came to assessing manliness was the ability to enliven the social dynamic and social cohesion of the group – of an exclusively male society. It could be done in various ways – by demonstrating heroism on the battlefield, by rescuing wounded comrades from it, or by organizing sentimental Christmas parties afterwards. An inclusive concept of soldierly masculinity allowed rather different types of soldier to establish male identities. And its protean fabric allowed them to switch between different emotional and moral states without losing their male identity. In this way, the concept of comradeship built bridges over diverging experiences, united disrupted identities, and eventually even showed how femininity and masculinity, tenderness and toughness, could be on good terms within one person, one *man*.

It was this protean concept of manliness and the notion of comradeship as the social practice of male interaction that governed the emotional and moral roller-coaster of German soldiers in the Second World War even more than in the first one, and it did so not despite but because of the genocidal dimensions of the Second World War. The moral grammar of comradeship always obeyed the same rule: Anything was allowed that enriched and intensified social life. Defined simultaneously by its separation from, by re-enacting and yet mocking at, civilian society, comradeship created a new society from scratch. The male bond staged itself as autonomous. By showing feminine qualities and staging family-like settings, exclusively male societies did not simply remind themselves of their ties to the civilian world at home; instead, they demonstrated the male bond's independence from real women and real families – from civilian society and civilian morality. The message was: Being on our own, we men are able to generate a warm sense of family, even if we fight cold-bloodedly a few seconds later. We may miss the world at home, but now we create it ourselves.

Demonstrating the independence of male society from the world at home went far beyond performing family-like sociability and solidarity in the face of lethal danger. An entire set of "manly" rituals, all of them violating or transgressing domestic and civilian norms, served to confirm the claim for autarchy. Excessive drinking, tales of sexual adventures, misogynistic rhetoric, rowdyism, even collective rape – all this gained its social momentum from being "celebrated" – practiced, reported, or applauded – *together*. Whether fueled by misogyny or motherliness, by heroism or charity, toughness or tenderness, the "anti-structure" of comradeship relied on challenging the "structure" of the civilian world outside.

These social mechanisms apply to small groups – face-to-face units, or primary groups – in many armies in war, not only in the twentieth century and certainly not only the German ones. Whether the social dynamic of comradeship propels fighting morale, serves to cover up delinquency, or excites mutinies, is contingent upon the ideological dispositions of the members, decisions of the formal or informal group leaders, and institutional or situational contexts.

From the time of the First World War, the German discourse on war experience and the morality of soldiering, inspired by the Christian imagery of brotherly love and sacrifice, enthused about comradeship's redemptive power. The good comrade was beyond the evil of mass death and destruction, and the practice of comradeship in the frontline platoons was hailed as a model to deliver the German fatherland from the evil of inner disruption and disunity – to establish a true *Volksgemeinschaft*. The Nazis capitalized on this popular fascination with comradeship in order to promote their own, racially exclusive and militarized vision of *Volksgemeinschaft*. Although always embedded in the interdependence of inclusion and exclusion, the pre-Nazi discourse on comradeship was open to the idea of international, interracial, and interethnic brotherhood. In the First World War and after, frontline comradeship brought Jewish and gentile soldiers together, and the peaceful encounter of soldiers on both sides of the front lines, though rare in historical reality, still informed the public discourse on comradeship under the Nazi regime.

The racist foundation of Operation Barbarossa no longer allowed for such reconciliatory liberalism. The Nazis pushed for a racially exclusive redefinition of comradeship as a vehicle of the purely Aryan *Volksgemeinschaft* under the unconditional command of Hitler. Not all individual Wehrmacht soldiers agreed on this concept of comradeship or on the Nazi genocidal project, Nazi racism, and antisemitism. But the ethics and the social dynamic of comradeship silenced the dissenters. Comradeship was the virtue of the bystander. It demanded that one conform, do what everyone else did, or look the other way. In the early years of the war in the East, German soldiers could do so easily because the initial grand victories suffocated pangs of conscience about their own entanglement in genocidal warfare. In the later period of the war, ubiquitous fears of revenge of the enemies may have actuated guilt feelings but only to put the soldiers even more deliberately into a state of fatalism, a couldn't-care-less attitude, in which the fight till the bitter end seemed to be the only option left.

Fatalism took possession also of those younger soldiers who found themselves thrown into the war without sufficient training and at a time when the Third Reich's utopian megalomania had been replaced by dystopian desperation. But enough veteran soldiers were still left to spread the spirit of comradeship. It was no longer a euphoric comradeship but a sinister one, the virtue of sticking it out, together. Although protean masculinity allowed men to switch back and forth between manlier and more feminine practices and attitudes, they could switch back and forth only so long. You were not supposed to stay permanently in femininely coded states but to overcome them, sooner or later. Hard masculinity and its correlates, toughness, aggressiveness, stoicism, endurance, self-control, remained the vanishing point of all protean masculinity. Tender manliness became respectable in the presence of death. The sphere of death ensured that the symbolic hierarchies were operative. For it was not the soft side of man that defined him, but his ability to overcome it, not just once and for all, but again and again. The link between the two poles was the experience of suffering and the stoicism that was required to cope with it. The soldier-man accepted states of weakness, defeat, and suffering, but he also knew how to get up again, and to eventually keep functioning and fighting. This concept of stoic, resilient, indestructible manliness made the German soldiers keep fighting till the end of the Second World War, at a time when they could no longer believe in the Final Victory the regime never tired of conjuring up.

In post-Nazi Germany, the remembrance of their suffering in war, and their stoicism in enduring all the pain, allowed the former soldiers to blank out their knowledge of the criminal dynamic of the war and yet to celebrate the manliness they had demonstrated on the fields of death. It was no longer an aggressive manliness, however, but a defensive one, entrenched in the experience of suffering, sacrifice, and defeat that had always spurred the construction of military masculinity. Accepting this uncertainty, knowing about the risk of falling and yet knowing how to get up again, was precisely what made a man and paradoxically granted some certainty amidst the uncertainty. The cement of the male community was the shared knowledge of this uncertainty. You were not the only one. You knew that your comrades were with you.

Just as it had done after 1918, the myth of comradeship after 1945 again helped former soldiers to cope with the evil of war, and the trauma of mass death, by emphasizing the good of war, the ultimate experience of "closeness and cooperation" in the midst of disruption and destruction. Although only a minority of these former soldiers accepted this kind of assistance, it was they who dominated the public discourse on war and masculinity through the 1970s, supported by the Cold War climate that protected both old and new soldiers and thus the construction of military masculinity. When the Cold War ended in the late 1980s, younger generations of Germans had already made up their minds about the conjunction of male bonding and criminal warfare that was only obfuscated by complex, protean concepts of masculinity. Only then did the pact between old and new soldiers and civilian society fall apart, not necessarily leaving the latter in a state of "solipsism and alienation" but rather urging it to seek out new ways of achieving "closeness and cooperation."

NOTE

1 Sebastian Junger, "The Bonds of Battle," *Vanity Fair*, June 2015, pp. 106–11, 142–45. Cf. Junger, *War* (New York: Twelve, 2010).

Index